رشتهٔ سیستم آواشناسی

واکه‌های کشیده

نماد	مثال	آواشناسی
iː	sheep	/ʃiːp/
ɑː	farm	/£ fɑːm, $ fɑːrm/
ɔː	horse	/£ hɔːs, $ hɔːrs/
uː	shoe	/ʃuː/
ɜː	bird	/£ bɜːd, $ bɜːrd/

واکه‌های کوتاه

نماد	مثال	آواشناسی
ɪ	ship	/ʃɪp/
e	head	/hed/
æ	hat	/hæt/
ʌ	cup	/kʌp/
ɒ (Br)	sock	/£ sɒk/
ʊ	foot	/fʊt/
ə	above	/əˈbʌv/
ɚ (Am)	mother	/$ ˈmʌð.ɚ/

دو آوایی‌ها

نماد	مثال	آواشناسی
eɪ	day	/deɪ/
aɪ	eye	/aɪ/
ɔɪ	boy	/bɔɪ/
aʊ	mouth	/maʊθ/
əʊ (Br)	nose	/£ nəʊz/
oʊ (Am)	nose	/$ noʊz/
ɪə (Br)	ear	/£ ɪəʳ/
ea (Br)	hair	/£ heaʳ/
ʊɜ (Br)	pure	/£ pjʊəʳ/

همخوان‌های بی‌واک

نماد	مثال	آواشناسی
p	pen	/pen/
t	town	/taʊn/
k	cat	/kæt/
f	fish	/fɪʃ/
θ	think	/θɪŋk/
s	say	/seɪ/
ʃ	she	/ʃiː/
tʃ	cheese	/tʃiːz/

همخوان‌های واک‌دار

نماد	مثال	آواشناسی
b	book	/bʊk/
d	day	/deɪ/
g	give	/gɪv/
v	very	/'ver.ɪ/
ð	the	/ðə/
z	zoo	/zu:/
ʒ	vision	/vɪʒn/
dʒ	jump	/dʒʌmp/
l	look	/lʊk/
r	run	/rʌn/
j	yes	/jes/
w	we	/wi:/
m	moon	/mu:n/
n	name	/neɪm/
ŋ	sing	/sɪŋ/
h	hand	/hænd/

نمادها و علایم دیگر

نماد	معنی	مثال
£	تلفظ بریتانیایی	rock /£ rɒk/
$	تلفظ امریکایی	rock /$ rɑ:k/
ˈ	تکیهٔ اصلی	expectation /ˌek.spekˈteɪ.ʃᵊn/
ˌ	تکیهٔ ثانویه	
.	تقطیع هجا	system /ˈsɪs.təm/
ʳ	r فقط زمانی در انگلیسی بریتانیایی تلفظ می‌شود که قبل از واکه بیاید.	four /£ fɔːʳ/ → four apples /fɔːr æp.l̩z/
علایم آواشناختی ایتالیک (= مورب نوشته شده) و علایم ð، ä، ŋ، ü	این علایم و علایم آمده در بخش آواشناسی را می‌توان حذف کرد و آنها را تلفظ نکرد.	lunch /lʌntʃ/
̩	نشان دهندهٔ واجی بودن علامت آواشناختی	little /ˈlɪt.l̩/
ᵊl، ᵊm، ᵊn	به صورت əl و یا l̩ تلفظ می‌شود.	label /ˈleɪ.bᵊl/ → /ˈleɪ.bəl/ یا /ˈleɪ.bl̩/
i		happy /ˈhæp.i/
t̬ (Am)		butter /$ ˈbʌt̬.ɚ/
ɔ̃:		restaurant /£ ˈres.tᵊr.ɔ̃:/

IELTS Dictionary
English - Persian

For
postgraduate students and
those preparing for
IELTS, GRE, TOEFL

By

Dr. Esmail Zare-Behtash

Lecturer in
Sistan and Balouchestan University
and Substitute Teacher at
University of Cambridge

Editor
Ali Bahrami

2003

زارع بهتاش، اسماعیل، ۱۳۳۴
فرهنگ انگلیسی ـ فارسی IELTS ویژه دوره‌های تحصیلات تکمیلی و
داوطلبان.../ اسماعیل زارع بهتاش، ویراستار: علی بهرامی. ـ تهران: رهنما،
۱۳۸۲.
۵۴۱ ص.، ۲۱×۱۲ س م.

ISBN 964-367-079-1

فهرستنویسی براساس اطلاعات فیپا
ص. ع. به انگلیسی:
Zare-Behtash Esmail
IELTS Dictionary English - Persian.
۱. زبان انگلیسی -- واژه‌نامه‌ها -- فارسی. الف. بهرامی، علی، ۱۳۳۸ -
1.1. English Language - Dictionaries - Persian.
مترجم. ب. عنوان.

فا ۴۲۳   PE ۱۶۴۵/ف۲از۱۳

                          کتابخانه ملی ایران
م۸۱-۴۷۵۲۹

Dr. Esmail Zare-Behtash
IELTS Dictionary English-Persian for postgrduate students and
thos preparing for IELTS, GRE, TOEFL
ISBN 964-367-079-1
All rights reserved. No part of this book may be reproduced in
any form or by any means without the prior permission, in
writing, from the Publisher.
RAHNAMA PUBLICATIONS
Copyright © 2003
Enghelab Ave., Shohadaye Zhandarmerie St. (Moshtagh St.),
Between Fravardin & Fakhre Razi, No. 220 Tehran, Iran.
P. O. Box: 13145/1845 Tel: (021)6416604 & 6400927
http://WWW.RAHNAMAPRESS.COM
Email: RAHNAMAPRESS@HOTMAIL.COM

فرهنگ انگلیسی ـ فارسی
IELTS

ویژه دوره‌های تحصیلات تکمیلی

و داوطلبان شرکت در امتحانات

IELTS , TOEFL , GRE

ـ حاوی ۳۵۰۰ مدخل و واژه به‌همراه تلفظ بریتانیایی و امریکایی، تعریف انگلیسی، معادل‌های دقیق فارسی و ...

ـ متداول‌ترین واژه‌ها برای داوطلبان شرکت در امتحانات IELTS ، GRE ، و TOEFL ؛ مدرسین و دانشجویان و ...

دکتر اسماعیل زارع بهتاش

عضو هیأت علمی دانشگاه سیستان و بلوچستان

و

استاد جانشین در دانشگاه کمبریج

ویراستار
علی بهرامی

زارع بهتاش، اسماعیل، ۱۳۳۴

فـرهنگ انگلیسی ـ فارسی IELTS ویژه دوره‌های تحصیلات تکمیلی و داوطلبان.../ اسماعیل زارع بهتاش، ویراستار: علی بهرامی. ـ تهران: رهنما، ۱۳۸۲.

۵۴۱ ص.، ۱۲×۲۱ س‌م.

ISBN 964-367-079-1

فهرستنویسی براساس اطلاعات فیپا

ص.ع. به انگلیسی:

Zare-Behtash Esmail
IELTS Dictionary English - Persian.

۱. زبان انگلیسی -- واژه‌نامه‌ها -- فارسی. الف. بهرامی، علی، ۱۳۳۸ - مترجم. ب. عنوان.

1.1. English Language - Dictionaries - Persian.

۱۳ز۲ف/ ۱۶۴۵ PE

۴۲۳/فا

کتابخانه ملی ایران

۸۱-۴۷۵۲۹م

فرهنگ انگلیسی - فارسی IELTS ، دکتر اسماعیل زارع بهتاش، ویراستار: علی بهرامی، حروفچینی: دبیر، تیراژ: ۳۰۰۰، لیتوگرافی: سلطانی، چاپخانه: دانش چاپ اول: بهار ۱۳۸۲ ، ناشر: انتشارات رهنما، مقابل دانشگاه تهران خیابان فروردین، نبش خیابان شهدای ژاندارمری، پلاک ۲۲۰ تلفن: ۶۴۰۰۹۲۷ - ۶۴۱۶۶۰۴، فاکس: ۶۴۶۸۱۹۴، فروشگاه رهنما، سعادت‌آباد خیابان علامه طباطبایی پلاک ۸ ، تلفن : ۲۰۹۴۱۰۲، نمایشگاه کتاب رهنما مقابل دانشگاه تهران، پاساژ فروزنده تلفن : ۶۹۵۰۹۵۷
شابک: ۱-۰۷۹-۳۶۷-۹۶۴

حق چاپ برای ناشر محفوظ است

قیمت ۲۹۵۰۰ریال

Preface

This dictionary is designed to serve as a reference to the spelling, pronunciation, part of speech, and meaning of over 3,500 carefully selected words that appear most frequently on standardized English tests (such as IELTS, GRE, TOEFL) throughout the world. It contains a strong working vocabulary of college-level words.

It is intended for use by writers, translators, teachers, students and those who are interested in building up their English vocabulary.

This reference book is prepared in dictionary format. Each entry contains its pronunciation (British and American), part of speech, its most frequent Persian meaning(s), and a sentence or sentences illustrating its use.

با نام و یاد حضرت دوست

سخنی با خوانندگان

فرهنگی که در پیش رو دارید براساس کتاب واژگان (۱۹۹۰) انتشارات بارون تدوین شده است. با توجه به سابقهٔ تدریس در کلاس‌های اعزام و تافل، و تدریس در کلاس‌های آماده‌سازی همکاران هیأت علمی برای امتحانات اعزام به خارج در کنار تدریس در کلاس‌های دوره‌های مترجمی، همواره مترصد آن بودم که این کتاب را ترجمه کنم و در اختیار علاقمندان قرار دهم. ولی متأسفانه کار اجرایی و تدریس در دوره‌های روزانه و شبانه این فرصت را مهیا نکرد، تا اینکه با محبت ریاست محترم پژوهشی وزارت علوم، تحقیقات و فناوری این مجال دست داد تا برای فرصت مطالعاتی عازم دانشگاه کمبریج بشوم. در کنار کارهای تحقیقاتی مربوط به ادبیات قرن نوزدهم انگلستان؛ و مطالعهٔ فرهنگ‌های انگلیسی و متون ترجمه شده برای تهیهٔ فیش جهت تألیف فرهنگ دانشگاهی فارسی - انگلیسی، فرصتی دست داد تا با استفاده از فرهنگ انگلیسی بین‌المللی کمبریج (۱۹۹۶)، به تدوین این فرهنگ بپردازم.

این فرهنگ حاوی متداول‌ترین واژه‌هایی است که به نظر مؤلفین آن، دانشجویان دانشگاه‌ها، نویسندگان، منشی‌ها، و نمونه‌خوان‌ها به‌طور روزمره با آن‌ها مواجه می‌شوند. طبیعی است که همین لغات اساسی، واژگان رسانه‌های گروهی را تشکیل می‌دهد و به همین دلیل است که این لغات در سؤالات امتحانی زبان انگلیسی ورود به دوره‌های عالی دانشگاه‌ها در تمامی رشته‌ها مطرح می‌شوند تا بدینوسیله توان دانشجو را در درک مطالب خواندنی و شنیداری و ایجاد ارتباط با یکدیگر محک بزند.

لازم به ذکر است که تلفظ لغات به‌صورت کامل به دو شکل بریتانیایی و امریکایی با استفاده از فرهنگ انگلیسی بین‌المللی کمبریج و با استفاده از علایم معیار آواشناسی نوشته شده است. مهم‌ترین مسئله در یادگیری تلفظ، تمرین است. برای نیل به این هدف لازم است قبل از مراجعه به معنی واژه، تلفظ آن واژه را براساس تکیهٔ اصلی که با علامت /'/ مشخص شده، تمرین کرد. برای مثال، اگر کلمهٔ فارسی "فرخنده" را در نظر بگیریم، متوجه می‌شویم که برای تلفظ این کلمه، هجای /خز/ با فشار بیشتری (در مقایسه با هجاهای دیگر) ادا می‌شود. همین موضوع در مورد زبان انگلیسی نیز صدق می‌کند. برای تمرین می‌توانیم هجای تکیه‌دار را چند بار به تنهایی تلفظ کنیم و سپس هجا(های) دیگر

را به آن اضافه کنیم. برای مثال، جهت تلفظ واژهٔ deflect /dɪˈflekt/، می‌توان چند بار هجای دوم یعنی /flekt/ را تلفظ و تمرین کرد تا تسلط بیشتری روی این هجا داشت و سپس هجای اول یعنی /dɪ/ را به آن افزود تا به صورت dɪˈflekt تلفظ شود.

همچنین هویت دستوری (جزء کلام) هر واژه بلافاصله پس از تلفظ آن واژه آورده شده و معادل(های) داده شده، به انگلیسی و فارسی، براساس همین نقش دستوری ارائه گردیده است، و با توجه به همین هویت دستوری، واژهٔ مربوط در جمله (جملات) به‌کار رفته تا خوانندگان بتوانند همان معنی (معانی) را از جمله استنباط کنند. شایان ذکر است در صورت تعدد معنی، آن واژه در دو جملهٔ متفاوت به‌کار برده شده تا معانی مختلف را بتوان در کاربردهای متفاوت نشان داد. البته در کتاب واژگان بارون، جملهٔ دوم ارائه نشده، ولی اینجانب با توجه به تجربهٔ شخصی و با استفاده از فرهنگ انگلیسی بین‌المللی کمبریج این کار را انجام داده‌ام. در ضمن در مواردی در جملات کتاب واژگان را تغییر داده‌ام و به جای آنها جملاتی آورده‌ایم که بتوانند علاوه بر کاربرد، نکات دستوری مخصوصاً کاربرد حروف اضافه و یا عبارت‌های اسمی/ فعلی را نشان دهند. این امر در فرهنگ و در بخش جملات به‌صورت مورب (= ایتالیک) نشان داده شده است. برای مثال، واژهٔ homage، در ترکیب با فعل "pay" می‌آید، بنابراین "pay" ایتالیک تایپ شده است، و یا واژهٔ dregs در متون مطبوعاتی به‌صورت ترکیب *dregs of society* می‌آید که آن نیز به‌صورت ایتالیک آمده است.

بعضی از واژه‌ها در هویت دستوری خاصی کاربرد بیشتری دارند و مؤلفین کتاب واژگان ترجیح داده‌اند که مدخل اصلی دارای همین هویت دستوری باشد. به همین دلیل مؤلفین تلاش کرده‌اند در مواردی پس از کاربرد آن واژه در جملهٔ مثال حالت صفتی یا فعلی همان واژه را ذکر کنند. بنده سعی کرده‌ام این کار را در سطح گسترده‌ای در طول فرهنگ انجام دهم تا خوانندگان آشنایی بیشتری با کلمات مشتق یک واژه پیدا کنند.

جهت اینکه خوانندگان در خواندن جملات و معنی آنها نیازی به فرهنگ دیگری نداشته باشند، در پایان هر بخش الفبایی، فهرستی از لغات مهم درج شده است. البته معانی داده شده در این فهرست فقط مربوط به جملاتی است که در داخل همان بخش به‌کار رفته، چه بسا که واژه می‌تواند معانی متعددی داشته باشد، ولی معنی مد نظر ما در جمله همانی است که در فهرست ذکر شده است.

دو مطلب برای یادگیری واژگان و افزایش معلومات لغوی حائز اهمیت است: اول

اینکه سعی کنیم هر روز تعدادی از واژه‌ها را برگزینیم و در متن کتاب و یا روی برگه‌هایی بنویسیم و آنها را یاد بگیریم. مطلب دوم و مهمتر این است که بتوانیم واژه‌هایی را که یاد می‌گیریم. در صحبت‌های خود و در بافت‌های دیگر به کار ببریم و در صورت امکان آنها را جایگزین واژه‌های هم معنی بکنیم که قبلاً بلد بودیم. به‌نظر می‌رسد که سعی نکرده‌ایم (و یا کمتر سعی کرده‌ایم) واژه‌هایی را که یاد می‌گیریم، جایگزین واژه‌های قبلی بکنیم. این امر سبب می‌شود که واژه‌های غیر فعال (passive) در ذهنمان بیشتر از واژه‌های فعال (active) باشد. به‌عنوان مثال شاید اولین واژه و ترکیبی که برای "ترسیدن" یاد گرفته‌ایم همان "be afraid of" باشد و هر موقع به آن بر می‌خوریم، همین معادل در زبان انگلیسی به ذهن می‌رسد. در حالی که بعدها با ترکیب "be scared of" آشنا شده‌ایم، ولی نخواسته‌ایم یا نتوانسته‌ایم از این ترکیب بهره بجوییم. مسلماً اساتید در بدو یادگیری زبان ترجیح داده‌اند که با ترکیب اول آشنا شویم، ولی در سطوح بعدی که با واژه‌ها و ترکیب‌های هم معنی نیز آشنا شده‌ایم، نتوانسته‌ایم واژه و ترکیب‌های جدید را به کار ببریم.

البته با برنامه‌ریزی دقیق و منظم می‌توان هر روز دایرهٔ معلومات لغوی را افزایش داد تا بدینوسیله بتوان بیشتر و راحت‌تر از متون انگلیسی استفاده کرد، چرا که هدف امتحانات زبان نیز همین است.

در پایان از مدیر مسئول انتشارات رهنما، آقای محمد جواد صبائی، ویراستار آقای علی بهرامی، و حروفچین محترم سرکار خانم نجمهٔ ابراهیمی به خاطر تایپ و حروفچینی دقیق تشکر می‌نمایم و از خداوند متعال توفیق تمامی خدمتگزاران نظام مقدس جمهوری اسلامی را مسئلت دارم.

اسماعیل زارع بهتاش
کمبریج
شهریور ماه ۱۳۸۰

For

    my father and

        in memory of my mother

A a

a.ban.don /ə'bæn.dən/ *v.* to give up, to stop doing sth., to leave

ترک کردن، رها کردن، متوقف کردن، دست کشیدن از

1) When the rebel troops arrived, the village had already been *abandoned*.
2) She *abandoned* her husband and children.

a.base /ə'beɪs/ *v.* to lower, to humiliate

کوچک کردن (خود را)، خوار کردن

The President is not willing to *abase* himself before the nation.

a.bash /ə'bæʃ/ *v.* to embarrass

خجالت دادن، شرمنده کردن

He was not at all *abashed by* her open admiration.

    a.bashed: *adj.*   شرمسار، شرمنده، خجل

a.bate /ə'beɪt/ *v.* to subside, to decrease, to lessen

فروکش کردن، کاهش یافتن، برطرف کردن

They waited for the storm to *abate*.

    a.bate.ment: *n.*   فروکش، کاهش

ab.bre.vi.ate /ə'briː.vi.eɪt/ *v.* to shorten, to contract, to abridge

ab.di.cate

خلاصه کردن، به اختصار نوشتن، مختصر کردن

The lecturer had to *abbreviate* her speech.

ab.bre.vi.a.tion: *n*   اختصار، علامت اختصاری، کوته‌نوشت

ab.di.cate /ˈæb.dɪ.keɪt/ *v.* to give up formally, to renounce

کناره‌گیری کردن (از سلطنت)، استعفا دادن، صرف‌نظر کردن

King Edward VIII *abdicated* (the British throne) in 1936.

ab.di.ca.tion: *n.*   سلب مسئولیت، کناره‌گیری (از سلطنت)

ab.duct /æb.ˈdʌkt/ *v.* to take away by force, to kidnap

دزدیدن، ربودن (آدم)

The director was *abducted* from his car by terrorists.

ab.duc.tion: *n.*   آدم‌دزدی، آدم‌ربایی

ab.er.ra.tion /ˌæb.əˈreɪ.ʃən/ *n.* wandering away, deviation, failure of rays to focus

انحراف، نابهنجاری، گیجی، (فیزیک) کج‌نمایی

I had a mental *abberation* and forgot we had a meeting today.

ab.er.rant: *adj., n.*   نابهنجار، غیرعادی

a.bet /əˈbet/ *v.* to help or encourage sb. to do sth. wrong or illegal

هم‌دستی کردن، شریک جرم (کسی) شدن

His accountant aided and *abetted* him in the fraud.

aider and abettor: *n.*   هم‌دست، مشوق در کار بد

a.bey.ance /əˈbeɪ.əns/ *n.* suspended action

مسکوت، معوق، به‌حالت تعلیق

The deal was held in *abeyance* until his arrival.

ab.hor /£ əˈbɔːʳ, $ æbˈhɔːr/ *v.* to hate, to detest

نفرت داشتن از، متنفر بودن از

ab.ject   3   **a.bom.in.ate**

They *abhor* all forms of racism.

  ab.hor.rence: *n.*   انزجار، نفرت، بیزاری

ab.ject /ˈæb.dʒekt/ *adj.* extreme, hopeless, without self-respect

نکبت‌بار، رقت‌انگیز، خفت‌آور

They lived in *abject* poverty.

ab.jure /£ əbˈdʒʊʳ, $ -dʒʊr/ *v.* to give up, to renounce upon oath

برگشتن از (اعتقاد، سوگند، مذهب)، دست کشیدن از، صرف‌نظر کردن از

He *abjured* his belief.

  ab.jura.tion: *n.*   روگردانی، تکذیب

a.blu.tion /əˈbluː.ʃᵊn/ *n.* washing, ceremonial washing

استحمام، شستشو، غسل

His daily *ablutions* were accompanied by loud noises.

ab.ne.ga.tion /ˌæb.nɪˈgeɪ.ʃᵊn/ *n.* self-sacrifice, repudiation

فداکاری، ایثار، از خودگذشتگی

He praised the army's competence and *abnegation*.

  ab.ne.gate: *v.*   دست کشیدن از، بر خود حرام کردن

a.bol.ish /£ əˈbɒl.ɪʃ, $ -ˈbɑː.lɪʃ/ *v.* to cancel, to put an ent to

موقوف کردن، لغو کردن، برچیدن

I think bullfighting should be *abolished*.

  a.bo.li.tion: *n.*   الغا، لغو، برچیدن

a.bom.in.ate /£ əˈbɒm.ɪ.neɪt, $ -ˈbɑː.mɪ-/ *vt.* to hate very much, to loathe

متنفر شدن از، نفرت داشتن از، بد آمدن از

Moses *abominated* the idol worshipping.

  a.bom.in.a.tion: *n.*   انزجار، عمل شنیع

ab.o.ri.gi.nal /ˌæb.əˈrɪdʒ.ɪ.nəl/ *adj., n.* native, primitive

قدیمی، بومی، بومی استرالیا

His studies include *aboriginal* forests.

    Ab.o.ri.gi.ne: *n.*   بومی استرالیایی، بومی استرالیا

a.bort.ive /£ əˈbɔː.tɪv, $ -ˈbɔːr.t̬ɪv/ *adj.* fruitless, unsuccessful

بی ثمر، بی حاصل، نافرجام، ناموفق

We had to abandon our *abortive* attempts.

    a.bor.tion: *n.*   شکست، ناکامی؛ سقط جنین

a.brade /əˈbreɪd/ *v.* to wear away by friction, to erode

سائیدن، خراشیدن

The skin of his leg was *abraded* by the sharp rocks.

    a.bra.sion: *n.*   خراشیدگی، سایش، ساییدگی

a.bridge /əˈbrɪdʒ/ *v.* to shorten, to condense

خلاصه کردن، تلخیص کردن، کوتاه کردن

She's currently *abridging* her book.

    a.bridge.ment: *n.*   خلاصه، تلخیص

ab.ro.gate /£ ˈæb.rəʊgeɪt, $ -rə-/ *v.* to abolish, to end formally

منسوخ کردن، لغو کردن، نسخ کردن

The treaty was *abrogated* in 1929.

    ab.ro.ga.tion: *n.*   لغو، نسخ

ab.scond /£ æbˈskɒnd, $ -ˈskɑːnd/ *v.* to go away suddenly and hide

گریختن و ناپدید شدن، متواری شدن، فرار کردن

They *absconded from* the country *with* the company's money.

    ab.scon.der: *n.*   فراری

ab.solve /£ əbˈzɒlv, $ -ˈzɑːlv/ *v.* to pardon, to acquit

تبرئه کردن، بخشیدن، عفو کردن

The report *absolved* him *from/of* all blame for the accident.

ab.so.lu.tion: *n.*   عفو، بخشش؛ (آیین مسیحیت) آمرزش

ab.stain /æbˈsteɪn/ *v.* to refrain, to restrain, not to do sth.

امتناع کردن، خودداری کردن، پرهیز کردن؛ از دادن رأی خودداری کردن

He took a vow to *abstain from* smoking.

ab.sten.tion: *n.*   امتناع، خودداری: رأی ممتنع

ab.stem.i.ous /æbˈstiː.mi.əs/ *adj.* temperate, esp. in eating, etc.

اعتدال‌گر، مرتاض منش، میانه‌رو

He has led a very *abstemious* life.

ab.stin.ence /ˈæb.stɪ.nənts/ *n.* restraint from eating or drinking

امساک، پرهیز، خویشتن‌داری

The doctor recommended total *abstinance* from salted food.

ab.stin.ent: *adj.*   خویشتن‌دار، پرهیزگار

ab.stract /ˈæb.strækt/ *adj.* theoretical, not concrete

انتزاعی، مجرد، غیرملموس

To him, hunger was an *abstract* concept.

ab.struse /æbˈstruːs/ *adj.* difficult, obscure, profound

پیچیده، مشکل، غامض، مبهم

He read *abstruse* works in philosophy.

a.buse /əˈbjuːz/ *v.* to use or treat wrongly or badly, to maltreat

سوء استفاده کردن از، بدرفتاری کردن با

She is continually *abusing* her position.

a.bus.ive: *adj.* بد دهان، فحش‌آمیز، پر از فحش

a.but /əˈbʌt/ *v.* to be next to, to border upon

مجاور (جایی) بودن، کنار / جنب (جایی) بودن

Their house *abutted* (onto) the police station.

a.bys.mal /əˈbɪz.məl/ *adj.* bottomless; very bad

بسیار عمیق، ژرف؛ فوق‌العاده بد، افتضاح

The film was *abysmal*.

ac.cede /akˈsiːd/ *v.* to agree; to take an important position

رضایت دادن، قبول کردن؛ به‌مقامی دست یافتن

1) He didn't *accede* to their demand for blackmail.

2) Queen Victoria *acceded to the throne* in 1837.

ac.cess.ion: *n.* رضایت؛ جلوس

ac.cel.er.ate /£ əkˈsel.ə.reɪt, $ -ɚ.eɪt/ *v.* to move faster

سرعت بخشیدن، تندتر کردن، سرعت گرفتن

The car *accelerated* to overtake the bus.

ac.cel.er.a.tion: *n.* شتاب

ac.cess.i.ble /əkˈses.ə.bl/ *adj.* easy to reach, easy to obtain; easy to understand

در دسترس، دست یافتنی؛ قابل فهم

1) The park is easily *accessible* on foot.

2) The film was *accessible* to a wider public.

ac.cess.ory /£ əkˈses.ᵊr.i, $ -ɚ-/ *n.* additional object, useful but not essential

لوازم جانبی، وسایل غیرضروری

The *accessories* she bought cost more than the dress.

ac.claim /əˈkleɪm/ *v.* to praise, to applaud

ac.cli.mate   7   ac.cost

هورا کشیدن برای، ابراز احساسات کردن برای

People *acclaimed* every victory and decried every defeat.

ac.clam.a.tion: *n.*   تشویق، تحسین، هورا

ac.cli.mate /əˈklaɪ.meɪt, ˈæk.lɪ-/ *v.* to adjust to climate, to accustom

خو گرفتن، عادت کردن

It takes more time to *acclimate* oneself to new environments.

ac.cli.mat.ize: *v. Br.* and *Aus.*   خو گرفتن (با محیط جدید)

ac.cliv.i.ty /əˈklɪvətɪ/ *n.* an upward slope

سربالایی

The car could not go up the *acclivity* in high gear.

ac.co.lade /ˈæk.ə.leɪd/ *n.* praise and approval

تحسین، تشویق، تمجید

In Hollywood, an "Oscar" is the highest *accolade*.

ac.com.plice /£ əˈkʌm.m.plɪs, $ -ˈkɑːm-/ *n.* partner in crime, accessary

شریک جرم، همدست

He was arrested as an *accomplice* in the murder.

ac.cord /£ əˈkɔːd, $ -ˈkɔːrd/ *n.* agreement, harmony

قرارداد، پیمان؛ توافق؛ هماهنگ

1) They signed a peace *accord*.

2) The project is *in accord with* the government's policy.

ac.cost /£ əˈkɒst, $ -ˈkɑːst/ *v.* to approach and speak first to a person

جلوی (کسی را) گرفتن، سر راه (کسی) سبز شدن؛ سر صحبت را (با کسی) باز کردن

When the two young men *accosted* me, I was frightened.

ac.cou.tre /£ ə'ku:trə, $ ə'ku:.tɚ/ *v.* to equip, to dress

مجهز کردن، تجهیز کردن

The fisherman was *accoutred* with the best goods.

ac.cou.tre.ments: *n.* ساز و برگ، تجهیزات

ac.cre.tion /ə'kri:ʃ°n/ *n.* growth, increase

تجمع، افزایش، تراکم، انباشت

The *accretion* of wealth marked the family's rise in power.

ac.crue /ə'kru:/ *v.* to increase in number or amount

انباشته شدن، جمع شدن؛ تعلق گرفتن

You must pay the interest which has *accrued* on your debt.

ac.cru.al: *n.* سوددهی، افزایش طبیعی

a.cer.bi.ty /£ ə'sɜ:.bə.ti, $ -'sɜ:r.bə.t̬i/ *n.* bitterness, sharpness

تندی، نیشداری، گزندگی، تلخی

The *acerbity* of his book shocked a lot of people.

a.ce.tic /£ ə'si:.tɪk, $ -t̬ɪk-/ *adj.* vinegary

سرکه‌ای، (مربوط به) سرکه

The salad had an exceedingly *acetic* flavor.

ac.id.u.lous /£ ə'sɪdjʊləs, $ -ɪdʒəl-/ *adj.* slightly sour; sharp, caustic

ترش مزه؛ تند، گزنده

He was unpopular because of his *acidulous* remarks.

ac.know.ledge /£ ək'nɒl.ɪdʒ, $ -'nɑ:.lɪdʒ/ *v.* to admit, to recognize

اذعان کردن، تصدیق کردن، اقرار کردن، تأیید کردن

He *acknowledged* the existence of another motive for the crime.

ac.me /'æk.mi/ *n.* top, the highest point

نهایت، اوج، حد اعلا

Politics is *the acme* of mysticim.

a.cous.tic /ə'kuː.stɪk/ *n.* related to the quality of sound

صوتی، (مربوط به) صوت

The microphone converts *acoustic* waves to electrical signals for transmission.

ac.qui.esce /ˌæk.wi'es/ *v.* to accept or agree to sth. unwillingly

با اکراه رضایت دادن، تن در دادن، گردن نهادن به

He reluctantly *acquiesced to/in* the plans.

ac.qui.es.cence: *n.* تسلیم، رضایت با اکراه

ac.qui.es.cent: *adj.* مطیع، تسلیم، فرمانبردار

ac.quit.tal /£ ə'kwɪt.ᵊl, $ -'kwɪt̬-/ *n.* deliverance from a charge

تبرئه، برائت

The first trial ended in a hung jury, the second in *acquittal*.

ac.quit: *v.* تبرئه کردن

ac.rid /'æk.rɪd/ *adj.* sharp, bitter, strong

تند، زننده، غلیظ

The *acrid* oder of burnt gunpowder filled the room.

ac.ri.mo.ni.ous /£ ˌæk.rɪ'məʊ.ni.əs, $ -'moʊ-/ *adj.* bitter and angry

تند، زننده، نیشدار

It was his *acrimonious* remarks which made them

concerned.

ac.ri.mo.ny: *n.*   تندی، اوقات تلخی، خشونت، عصبانیت

ac.tu.a.ri.al /£ ˈæk.tju.ə.ri.əl, $ -er.i-/ *adj.* calculating, relating to insurance statistics

آماری، (مربوط به) آماربیمه

According to recent *actuarial* tables, life expectancy is greater today.

ac.tu.a.ry: *n.*   کارشناس بیمه

ac.tu.ate /ˈæk.tʃu.eɪt, -tju-/ *v.* to motivate; to make sth. work

به کار انداختن؛ سبب شدن، انگیزه دادن به، برانگیختن

What *actuated* you to reply to the letter so hastily?

a.cu.i.ty /£ əˈkjuː.ə.ti, $ -ə.ṭi/ *n.* accuracy, sharpness

(حواس) تیزی، دقت

Tiredness also affects visual *acuity*.

ac.u.men /ˈæk.jʊ.mən/ *n.* mental keenness, shrewdness

شمّ، بینش؛ هوش، ذکاوت

He has considerable financial *acumen*.

ad.age /ˈæd.ɪdʒ/ *n.* wise saying, proverb

مَثَل، ضرب‌المثل

There is much truth in the old *adage* about fools and their money.

ad.a.mant /ˈæd.ə.mənt/ *adj.* hard, inflexible

مُصِرّ؛ انعطاف‌ناپذیر، سرسخت

He's absolutely *adamant in/about* not going there.

a.dapt /əˈdæpt/ *v.* to make fit or suitable, to alter, to modify

تغییر دادن، جرح و تعدیل کردن؛ سازگار کردن

1) The play had been *adapted* for children.

2) Some animals could not *adapt* to a changing environment.

ad.apt.a.tion: *n.*   انطباق، سازگاری: تنظیم، اقتباس

ad.dic.tion /əˈdɪk.ʃⁿn/ *n.* habitual need, compulsive use

عادت شدید، اعتیاد

His *addiction* to drugs caused his friends much grief.

ad.dict.ed: *adj.*   معتاد

ad.dle /ˈæd.l/ *v.* to make one's brain confused, to make crazy

گیج کردن، آشفته کردن

I think my brain's been *addled* by the heat!

ad.dled: *adj.*   آشفته، گیج؛ فاسد، گندیده

ad.duce /£ əˈdjuːs, $ -ˈduːs/ *v.* to present as evidence, to give proof

ارائه دادن، اقامه کردن؛ استناد کردن به

She *adduced* several facts to support her thesis.

a.dept /əˈdept/ *adj.* skilled, expert at

خبره، ماهر، استاد

She's very *adept* at/in making people feel at their ease.

ˈa.dept: *n.*   انسان ماهر

ad.here /£ ədˈhɪəʳ, $ -ˈhɪr/ *v.* to stick fast to

چسبیدن؛ پای‌بند بودن؛ پیروی کردن

(1) These tiles are not properly *adhered to* the wall.

(2) I will *adhere to* his opinion.

ad.he.sion, ad.her.ence: *n.*   حمایت، هواداری، پشتیبانی، وفاداری

ad.her.ent: *adj.*   چسبنده؛ حامی، مرید، طرفدار

ad.i.pose /£ ˈæd.ɪ.pəʊs, £ -pəʊz, $ -ə.poʊs/ *adj.* fatty

چربی، چربی‌دار

Excess *adipose* tissue should be avoided by middle-aged people.

ad.junct /ˈædʒ.ʌŋkt/ *n.* something joined or added

ضمیمه، جزء؛ کمک، دستیار

The computer course was a useful *adjunct* to my other studies.

ad.jure /£ əˈdʒʊəʳ, $ -ˈdʒʊr/ *v.* to ask seriously, to request solemnly

درخواست کردن، تقاضا کردن؛ (دادگاه) سوگند دادن

The judge *adjured* him to answer truthfully.

ad.jur.a.tion: *n.*   تقاضا، درخواست، اصرار

ad.mon.ish /£ ɒdˈmɒn.ɪʃ, $ -ˈmɑː.nɪʃ/ *v.* to warn, to reprove

تذکر دادن، گوشزد کردن؛ هشدار دادن

His mother *admonished* him for eating too quickly.

ad.mon.ish.ment, ad.mon.i.tion: *n.*   تذکر، گوشزد، هشدار

a.dore /£ əˈdɔːʳ, $ -ˈdɔːr/ *v.* to love sb. very much, to like sth. very much

دوست داشتن، پرستیدن

Let us *adore* God for all His works.

a.dorn /£ əˈdɔːn, $ -ˈdɔːrn/ *v.* to decorate, to make sth. beautiful

تزئین کردن، زینت دادن، آراستن

Wall paintings and carved statues *adorned* the temple.

a.dorn.ment: *n.*   تزئین، آرایش

a.droit /əˈdrɔɪt/ *adj.* skillful and quick

زرنگ، زیرک؛ ماهر، زبردست

He became *adroit* at dealing with difficult questions.

ad.u.la.tion /ˌæd.jʊˈleɪ.ʃən/ *n.* admiration, flattery

تملق، چاپلوسی

She loves *adulation*.

a.dul.ter.ate /£ əˈdʌl.tə.reɪt, $ -tɚ.eɪt/ *v.* to make sth. weaker or of worse quality, to debase

مواد تقلبی قاطی چیزی کردن، تقلب کردن

It is a crime to *adulterate* foods without informing the buyer.

a.dul.ter.a.tion: *n.*   تقلب (در مواد غذایی)

ad.um.brate /ˈæd.əm.breɪt/ *v.* to give a general idea, to overshadow

اشاره کردن؛ خبر (از چیزی) دادن، حکایت (از چیزی) کردن

The play opens with a fierce storm which *adumbrates* the violence to follow.

ad.um.bra.tion: *n.*   خبر، اشاره

ad.vent /ˈæd.ˌvent, -vənt/ *n.* arrival

ظهور، پیدایش؛ ورود

They were unaware of the *advent* of the Nuclear Age.

ad.ven.ti.tious /ˌæd.vənˈtɪʃ.əs, -ven-/ *adj.* accidental, casual

اتفاقی، پیش بینی نشده

It was an *adventitious* meeting.

ad.verse /£ ˈæd.vɜːs, £ -ˈ-, $ ædˈvɜːrs/ *adj.* unfavorable, hostile

نامطلوب، نامناسب، بد

The match was cancelled due to *adverse* weather conditions.

ad.vers.i.ty /£ ədˈvɜːˌsə.ti, $ -ˈvɜːr.sə.ti/ *n.* poverty, misfortune

سختی، گرفتاری، ناملایمات؛ بداقبالی

The road to happiness is paved with *adversities*.

ad.vert /£ ˈæd.vɜːt, $ -vɜːrt/ *v.* to refer to

توجه دادن به، اشاره داشتن به

You should not *advert* to this matter so frequently.

    ad.vert.ence: *n.*   توجه، اشاره

ad.vo.cate /ˈæd.və.kət/ *v.* to speak in support of, to plead for

دفاع کردن از، حمایت کردن از

She *advocates* freedom for the slaves.

ae.gis /ˈiːdʒɪs/ *n.* defense, shield, protection

تحت حمایتِ، زیر لوایِ

Under the *aegis* of the Bill of Rights, we enjoy our most treasured freedoms.

ae.on /£ ˈiː.ɒn, $ -ɑːn/ *n.* ages, long period of time

(به‌صورت جمع) سالیان سال، سال‌های متمادی، قرون متمادی

It has taken *aeons* for our civilization to develop.

aes.thet.ic /£ esˈθetɪk, $ -θeṭ-/ *adj.* artistic, showing great beauty

هنرمندانه، هنری؛ هنر شناختی، زیبایی شناختی

The new building has little *aesthetic* value.

    aes.thete: *n.*   هنرشناس، زیبایی شناس

    aes.thet.ics: *n.*   زیبایی شناسی

af.fa.ble /ˈæf.ə.bl̩/ *adj.* friendly, kind, easy to talk, courteous

مهربان، بامحبت؛ خوشرو، خوش برخورد؛ دوستانه

She was quite *affable* at the party.

af.fect.ed /əˈfek.tɪd/ *adj.* not sincere, artificial, pretended

متظاهر؛ ساختگی، تصنعی؛ پرتکلف

I hate that *affected* smiles of hers.

af.fect.a.tion: *n.* رفتار تصنعی، ادا، ژست، تظاهر

af.fi.da.vit /ˌæf.əˈdeɪ.vɪt/ *n.* written statement made under oath

اقرارنامه (پس از ادای سوگند)

He presented his statement in the form of an *affidavit*.

af.fi.li.a.tion /əˌfɪl.iˈeɪ.ʃən/ *n.* joining, associating with

وابستگی؛ عضویت؛ ارتباط

His *affiliation with* the political party was of short duration.

affiliate oneself to   به‌عضویت در آمدن، وابسته کردن
be affiliated with   وابسته بودن

af.fi.ni.ty /£ əˈfɪn.ɪ.ti, $ -ə.t̬i/ *n.* kinship, attraction or sympathy for

قرابت، شباهت؛ پیوستگی، پیوند

He felt an *affinity with/ for* all who suffered.

af.firm.a.tion /£ ˌæf.əˈmeɪʃən, $ -ɚ-/ *n.* a promise to tell the truth without swearing on the Bible

(دادگاه) اظهار قطعی بدون سوگند خوردن

The Constitution provides for oath or *affirmation* by officeholders.

af.flu.ence /ˈæf.lu.ənts/ *n.* abundance, wealth

فراوانی، وفور؛ رفاه؛ ثروت

Walking through the center of the city, I was struck by its air of *affluence*.

af.flu.ent: *adj.* ثروتمند؛ مرفه

af.fray /əˈfreɪ/ *n.* a fight in a public place, public brawl

نزاع در ملأ عام؛ کتک‌کاری، دعوا

He was badly mauled by the fighters in the *affray*.

a.gape /əˈgeɪp/ *adj.* openmouthed

با دهان باز، حیرت‌زده

The girls were *agape* with excitement.

a.gen.da /əˈdʒen.də/ *n.* a list of matters to be discussed at a meeting

دستور جلسه

There were several important items on the *agenda*.

ag.glom.er.a.tion /£ əˌglɒm.əˈreɪ.ʃ°n, $ -ˌglɑːmə-/ *n.* collection, heap

مجموعه، توده، کُپه

The country is an *agglomeration* of different ethnic and religious groups.

ag.grand.ize /əˈgræn.dɪz/ *v.* to increase or intensify

افزایش دادن، تقویت کردن، تشدید کردن

He tried to *aggrandize* his power to act aggressively in internationl affairs.

ag.grand.ize.ment *n.*

کسب قدرت، جاه‌طلبی

ag.gre.gate /ˈæg.rɪ.geɪt/ *adj.* sum, total

جمع، حاصل جمع، کل

The *aggregate* wealth of this country is staggering to imagination.

a.ghast /£ əˈgɑːst, $ -ˈgæst/ *adj.* horrified

بهت‌زده، مات و مبهوت؛ وحشت‌زده

She was *aghast* at the extent of the damage to her car.

a.gil.i.ty /£ əˈdʒɪl.ɪ.ti, $ -ə.t̬i/ *n.* nimbleness

چابکی، چالاکی، فرزی

He has got the *agility* of a mountain goat.

ag.ile: *adj.*   فرز، چالاک، چابک

ag.i.tate /ˈædʒ.ɪ.teɪt/ *v.* to striv up, to disturb; to argue

مضطرب کردن، نگران کردن؛ جرّ و بحث کردن

1) The news will only *agitate* her.
2) The unions were *agitating* for higher pay.

ag.i.ta.tion: *n.*   اضطراب؛ ناآرامی؛ مبارزه؛ تبلیغ

ag.nos.tic /£ æɡˈnɒs.tɪk, $ -ˈnɑː.stɪk/ *n.* one who is skeptical of the existence of God

منکر وجود خداوند، لاادری

Although he was born a catholic, he was an *agnostic* for his adult life.

a.grar.i.an /£ əˈɡreə.ri.ən, $ -ˈɡrer.i-/ *adj.* related to the land or to its cultivation

کشاورزی؛ مالکیت ارضی؛ ارضی

Agrarian production in the region has increased.

ag.ro.nom.ist /əˈɡrɒnəmɪst/ *n.* scientist engaged in the managment of land

خاک‌شناس

Because the country did not heed the warnings of its *agronomists*, it was faced with serious famine.

a.gron.o.my: *n.*   زراعت (علم)

a.lac.ri.ty /£əˈlæk.rə.ti, $ -ți/ *n.* eagerness, cheerful readiness

شور و شوق، رغبت، طیب خاطر

She accepted the money with *alacrity*.

al.che.my /ˈæl.kə.mi/ *n.* medieval chemistry, magic

a.li.as   18   al.lege

کیمیاگری؛ قدرت جادویی، معجزه

The changing of baser metals into gold was the goal of the students of *alchemy*.

a.li.as /ˈeɪ.li.əs/ *n.* an assumed name

اسم مستعار؛ معروف به

John Smith's *alias* was Bob Jones.

a.li.en.ate /ˈeɪ.li.ə.neɪt/ *v.* to separate, to make hostile

بیگانه کردن، گریزان کردن، از خود دور کردن، فراری دادن

His attempts to *alienate* the two friends failed because they had complete faith.

  a.li.en.a.tion: *n.*   بیگانگی، جدایی؛ احساس بیگانگی

al.i.ment.a.ry /£ æl.ɪˈmen.tºr.i, $ -tə-/ *adj.* supplying nourishment

غذایی؛ گوارشی

The *alimentary* canal in our bodies is so named because digestion of food occurs there.

al.i.mo.ny /£ ˈæl.ɪ.mə.ni, $ -moʊ-/ *n.* money paid by a husband to his divorced wife

نفقه

She was awarded $ 200 monthly *alimony* by the court.

al.lay /əˈleɪ/ *v.* to calm, to pacify

برطرف کردن، کاستن از (ترس و اضطراب)

The crew tried to *allay* the fears of the passengers.

al.lege /əˈledʒ/ *v.* to state without proof

ادعا کردن، اظهار داشتن

It is *alleged* that he had worked for the enemy.

  al.le.ga.tion: *n.*   ادعا، اظهار؛ اتهام

al.le.go.ry /£ ˈæl.ə.gə.ri, $ -gɔː.r.i/ *n.* story in which characters are used as symbols; fable

تمثیل، حکایت؛ داستان نمادین

Attar's *Conference of Birds* can be read as ***allegory***.

al.le.vi.ate /əˈliː.vi.eɪt/ *v.* to make (pains, problems, etc) less severe, to relieve

تسکین دادن، آرام کردن؛ کاستن از

The drugs did nothing to ***alleviate*** her pain.

al.li.ter.a.tion /£ ə.lɪt.əˈreɪ.ʃᵊn, $ ə.lɪt-/ *v.* repetition of beginning sound in poetry

تجانس آوایی

"The furrow followed free" is an example of ***alliteration***.

al.lo.cate /ˈæl.ə.keɪt/ *v.* to assign

تخصیص دادن، اختصاص دادن

The government ***allocated*** $ 10 million for health education.

al.lo.ca.tion: *n.* تخصیص؛ بودجه، اعتبار؛ سهم، سهمیه

al.loy /ˈæl.ɔɪ/ *n.* a mixture as of metals

آلیاژ

Brass is an ***alloy*** of copper and zinc.

al.loy: *v.* ضایع شدن، بی‌ارزش شدن

al.lude /əˈluːd/ *v.* to refer indirectly

اشاره کردن، تلویحاً گفتن

Try not to ***allude*** *to* this matter in his presence.

al.lu.sion: *n.* اشاره، کنایه، تلمیح

al.lu.vi.al /əˈluː.vi.əl/ *adj.* consisting of earth and sand left by rivers, floods, etc.

آبرفتی

The farmers found the *alluvial* deposits at the mouth of the river very fertile.

a.loft /£ əˈlɒft, $ -ˈlɑːft/ *adv.* upward

بالا، بالای بالا

The sailor climbed *aloft* into the rigging.

a.loof /əˈluːf/ *adj.* apart, not to take part in

دور، کنار؛ گوشه‌گیر

He kept *aloof from* politics.

al.ter.ca.tion /£ ˌɒl.təˈkeɪ.ʃᵊn, $ ˌɑːl.tɚ-/ *n.* wordy quarrel

نزاع، منازعه، کشمکش

The *altercation* between the two men started inside the restaurant.

al.tru.i.sm /ˈæl.tru.ɪ.zᵊm/ *n.* unselfish aid to others, generosity

نوع‌دوستی، ایثار، گذشت

The philanthropist was noted for his *altruism*.

al.tru.ist: *n.*   نوع دوست، ایثارگر
al.tru.ist.ic: *adj.*   نوع‌دوستانه، ایثارگرانه

a.mal.gam.ate /əˈmæl.gə.meɪt/ *v.* to combine, to unite in one body

در هم ادغام کردن، یکی کردن

The unions will attempt to *amalgamate* their groups into one national body.

a.mal.gam.a.tion: *n.*   ادغام، اختلاط

a.mass /əˈmæs/ *v.* to collect, to accumulate

جمع کردن، انباشتن، اندوختن

The miser's aim is to *amass* and hoard as much as gold as possible.

am.a.zon /£ ˈæm.ə.zᵊn, $ -zɑːn/ *n.* female warrior

شیرزن، زن جنگجو

Ever since the days of Greek mythology we refer to strong and aggressive women as *amazons*.

am.bi.dex.trous /ˌæm.bɪˈdek.strəs/ *adj.* able to use both hands with equal ease

دو دست توان، ذوالیمینین؛ بسیار ماهر

A player in baseball should be naturally *ambidextrous*.

am.bi.ence /£ ˈæm.bi.ᵊnts, $ ˌɑːm.biˈɑːnts/ *n.* atmosphere, environment

جو، فضا، حال و هوا، محیط

She went to the restaurant not for the food but for the *ambience*.

am.bi.gu.ous /æmˈbɪɡ.ju.əs/ *adj.* doubtful in meaning

مبهم، گنگ، دو پهلو

We hoped he would clarify his *ambiguous* remarks.

am.bi.gu.ity: *n.*   ابهام: تضاد، ناهمخوانی

am.bi.va.lence /æmˈbɪv.ə.lənts/ *n.* having opposing emotional feelings

تردید، دو دلی، تزلزل

Her *ambivalence about/ towards* marriage confused everybody.

am.bi.va.lent: *adj.*   مردّد، دودل؛ ضد و نقیض

am.ble /ˈæm.bl̩/ *n.* moving at an easy pace

پیاده‌روی، گام‌های آهسته

There's nothing I enjoy more than a leisurely *amble* across the moor.

am.bro.si.a /£ æmˈbrəʊ.zi.ə, £ -ʒə, $ -ˈbroʊ.ʒə/ *n.* food of the gods; a very pleasant food

مائده بهشتی؛ غذای لذیذ

Ambrosia was supposed to give immortality to any human who ate it.

am.bu.la.to.ry /ˈæmbjʊlətəri/ *adj.* able to walk

سرِپا

He was described as an *ambulatory* patient because he was not confined to his bed.

a.me.li.or.ate /əˈmiː.ljə.reɪt/ *v.* to improve, to make better

بهبود بخشیدن، بهتر کردن

Foreign aid is badly needed to *ameliorate* the effects of the drought.

a.men.a.ble /əˈmiː.nə.bḷ/ *adj.* willing to accept, readily managed

حاضر، مایل؛ مطیع؛ حرف شنو

He was *amenable* to any suggestions which came from them.

a.mend /əˈmend/ *v.* to correct, to change

اصلاح کردن، تجدیدنظر کردن، تصحیح کردن

MPs (Members of the Parliament) urged to *amend* the press law.

a.mend.ment: *n.* اصلاح؛ متمم، اصلاحیه
a.mend.a.ble: *adj.* قابل اصلاح، اصلاح‌پذیر

a.me.ni.ti.es /£ əˈmiː.nɪ.tiz, $ əˈmen.ə.t̬iz/ *n.* agreeable manners, courtesies; facility

احترامات، تعارفات؛ وسایل آسایش، امکانات رفاهی

1) She observed the social *amenities*.
2) This town lacks *amenities*.

a.mi.a.ble /'eɪ.mi.ə.bl̩/ *adj.* lovable, agreeable

خوش خلق، خوش‌رو؛ دوستانه

His *amiable* character pleased all who had dealings with him.

am.ic.a.ble /'æm.ɪ.kə.bl̩/ *adj.* friendly

دوستانه، مسالمت‌آمیز

The dispute was settled in an *amicable* manner.

a.miss /ə'mɪs/ *adj.* wrong, faulty

نادرست، اشتباه، غلط

Is there anything *amiss*?

am.i.ty /£ 'æm.ɪ.ti, $ -ə.t̬i/ *n.* friendship

دوستی، مودت، صلح و صفا

The two groups have lived in perfect *amity* for many years.

am.ne.si.a /æm'niː.zi-ə, -ʒə/ *n.* loss of memory

نسیان، فراموشی، یاد زدودگی

In his later life he suffered periods of *amnesia*.

am.ne.sty /'æm.nɪ.sti/ *n.* pardon

عفو، عفو عمومی

The government *granted amnesty* to all in prison.

a.mor.al /£ ˌeɪ'mɒr.əl, $ˌeɪ'mɔːr-/ *adj.* nonmoral, without moral principles

فاقد اصول اخلاقی، بی‌اعتنا به‌اصول اخلاقی، بی‌بند و بار

The society that he depicts is ***amoral*** and purposeless.

a.morph.ous /£ əˈmɔː.fəs, $ -ˈmɔːr-, eɪ-/ *adj.* shapeless

بی‌شکل؛ درهم و برهم

She was frightened by the ***amorphous*** mass of jelly.

am.phi.bi.an /æmˈfɪb.i.ən/ *n.* an animal which lives both on land and in water

جانور دوزیست

Frogs are classified as ***amphibian***.

am.phi.the.a.ter /£ ˈæmp.fɪˌθɪə.təʳ, $ -fəˌθiː.ə.t̬ɚ/ *n.* a circular or oval building with rows of seats for watching sports, plays, etc.

آمفی تئاتر

The spectators in the ***amphitheater*** cheered the gladiators.

am.ple /ˈæm.pl̩/ *adj.* abundant, more than enough

فراوان، زیاد؛ به‌اندازه

You'll have ***ample*** opportunity to ask questions after the talk.

am.pli.fy /ˈæm.plɪ.faɪ/ *v.* to enlarge

تقویت کردن، بزرگتر کردن، شرح و بسط دادن

His attempts to ***amplify*** his remarks were drowned out by the jeers of the audience.

am.pu.tate /ˈæm.pjʊ.teɪt/ *v.* to cut off part of the body, to prune

(عضو) قطع کردن، بریدن

In the end they had to ***amputate*** his foot to free him from the wrecked car.

a.muck /əˈmʌk/ *adv.* in a state of rage

وحشی، دیوانه، از کنترل خارج شده

The police had to be called in to restrain him after he *ran amuck* in the building

run amuck/amok   وحشی شدن، از کنترل خارج شدن، رم کردن

am.u.let /£ ˈæm.jʊ.lət, $ -jə-/ *n.* charm, talisman

تعویذ، طلسم، نظرقربانی

Around his neck he wore the *amulet* which the witch doctor had given him.

a.na.chron.i.sm /əˈnæk.rə.nɪ.zᵊm/ *n.* an error in chronology

اشتباه تاریخی، واپس گرایی

The modern train was an obvious *anachronism* in the film about London in the 1950s.

an.al.ges.ic /ˌæn.əlˈdʒiː.zɪk/ *adj.* causing insensitivity to pain

مسکن، ضد درد

The *analgesic* qualities of this lotion will provide temporary relief.

an.al.ges.ia: *n.*   بی‌دردی، فقدان حس درد

an.al.og.ous /əˈnæl.ə.gəs/ *adj.* comparable

شبیه، همانند

The experience of mystic trance is in a sense *analogous to* sleep or drunkenness.

a.nal.o.gy /əˈnæl.ə.dʒi/ *n.* similarity, parallelism

شباهت، همانندی؛ تشبیه، مقایسه

1) He drew an *analogy between* the brain and a vast computer.

2) It is sometimes easier to illustrate an abstract concept

by analogy with something concrete.

an.ar.chist /£ ˈæn.ə.kɪst, $ -ˈɚ-/ *n.* a person who rebels against the established order

آنارشیست، دولت ستیز، هرج و مرج طلب

Only the total overthrow of all governmental regulations would satisfy the *anarchist*.

an.ar.chy: *n.* بی‌نظمی، آشوب، هرج و مرج، دولت ستیزی

a.nath.e.ma /əˈnæθ.ə.mə/ *n.* strong curse

نفرین، لعنت، تکفیر

He heaped *anathema* upon his foe.

an.chor /£ ˈæŋ.kəʳ, $ -kɚ/ *v.* to secure or fasten firmly, to be fixed in place

محکم کردن، بستن؛ لنگر انداختن

Be careful where you *anchor* the boat.

an.chor.age: *n.* لنگرگاه؛ پناهگاه، تکیه گاه

an.cil.la.ry /£ ænˈsɪl.ᵊr.i, $ ˈænt.sə.ler.i/ *adj.* providing support or help, additional, extra

جنبی، کمکی، فرعی

Campaigning to change government policy is *ancillary to* the charity's direct relief wrok.

a.ne.mi.a /əˈniː.mi.ə/ *n.* condition in which blood lacks red corpuscles

کم‌خونی

The doctor ascribes his tiredness to *anemia*.

a.ne.mic: *adj.* (مربوط به) کم‌خونی؛ رنگ پریده، کم خون

an.es.thet.ic /£ ˌæn.əsˈθet.ɪk, $ -θeṭ-/ *n.* a substance that makes you unable to feel pain

an.gu.lar 27 **annals**

داروی بی‌هوشی / بی‌حسی

His monotonous voice acted like an *anesthetic* ; his audience was soon asleep.

an.es.the.sia: *n.* بی‌هوشی، بی‌حسی

an.gu.lar /£ ˈæŋ.gjʊ.lər, $ -lɚ/ *adj.* sharp - cornered; stiff in manner

زاویه‌دار، نوک‌تیز؛ خشک، نچسب، یُبس

His features, though *angular*, were curiously attractive.

an.i.mad.ver.sion /ˌænɪmədˈvɜːʃən/ *n.* critical remark

ایراد، خرده‌گیری، عیب‌جویی

He resented the *animadversion* of his critics.

an.i.mat.ed /£ ˈæn.ɪ.meɪ.tɪd, $ -t̬ɪd/ *adj.* lively, full of interest and energy

پرشور و حال، با نشاط، سرزنده؛ (نقاشی) متحرک

Her *animated* expression indicated a keenness of intellect.

an.i.mos.i.ty /£ ˌæn.ɪˈmɒs.ɪ.ti, $ -ˈmɑː.sə.t̬i/ *n.* strong dislike or anger; active enmity

خصومت، عداوت، دشمنی

1) The *animosity between* the rival candidates was obvious to the voters.
2) He *bears no animosity toward* his attackers.

an.i.mus /ˈænɪməs/ *n.* hostile feeling or intent

انزجار، خصومت، کینه‌توزی، عناد

The *animus* of the speaker became obvious when he began to indulge in insulting remarks.

annals /ˈæn.əlz/ *n.* yearly or historical records, history

an.neal   28   **an.nul**

گزارش سالیانه، تاریخچه

The *annals* of the British Parliament are recorded in a publication called Hansard.

to go down in the annals of Iranian history

در تاریخ ایران ثبت شدن

an.neal /əˈniːl/ *v.* to make (metal/ glass) soft by heating and then cooling down

تابکاری کردن (فلز و شیشه)

After the glass is *annealed*, it will be less subject to chipping and cracking.

an.ni.hi.late /əˈnaɪ.ɪ.leɪt/ *v.* to destroy completely, to defeat

منهدم ساختن، نابود کردن؛ شکست دادن

1) The enemy in its revenge tried to *annihilate* the entire population.
2) In the tennis finals Jackson *annihilated* his opponent.

an.ni.hi.la.tion: *n.*   انهدام، نابودی؛ شکست

an.not.ate /£ ˌæn.əʊ.teɪt, $ -ˈə-/ *v.* to add a brief explanation or opinion to a text/ drawing

حاشیه نوشتن بر، شرح و توضیح نوشتن بر

The critic *annotated* many of Shakespeare's plays.

an.not.ated: *adj.*   همراه با شرح و تفسیر، مشروح
an.not.a.tion: *n.*   حاشیه‌نویسی، شرح، تفسیر

an.nu.i.ty /£ əˈnjuː.ə.ti, $ -t̬i/ *n.* yearly allowance

مستمری سالیانه، مقرری سالیانه

She receives a small *annuity* .

an.nul /əˈnʌl/ *v.* to make void

لغو کردن، باطل کردن، فسخ کردن

| a.noint | 29 | an.te.cede |

Many laws made by the former regime have been *annulled* since the coup.

an.nul.ment: *n.* فسخ، ابطال، لغو

grant marriage annulment فسخ عقد ازدواج کردن

a.noint /ə'nɔɪnt/ *v.* (in a religious ceremony) to make someone king or queen, to consecrate

پادشاه / ملکه کردن

The prophet Samuel *anointed* David with oil, crowning him king of Isreal.

a.nom.al.ous /£ ə'nɒm.ə.ləs, $ -'nɑː.mə-/ *adj.* abnormal, irregular

غیرعادی، بی‌قاعده، نابهنجار

He was placed in an *anomalous* position.

a.nom.a.ly: *n.* بی‌قاعدگی، چیز / فرد غیرعادی

a.non.y.mous /£ ə'nɒn.ɪ.məs, $ -'nɑː.nə-/ *adj.* having no name

بی‌نام، بی‌امضاء؛ گمنام، ناشناس

The money was donated by an *anonymous* benefactor.

an.o.nym.i.ty: *n.* گمنامی، ناشناسی

an.tag.on.i.sm /æn'tæg.ə.nɪ.zᵊm/ *n.* hate, extreme unfriendliness, active opposition

ضدیت، دشمنی، خصومت

There's a worrying degree of *antagonism* towards neighbouring states.

an.tag.on.ist: *n.* دشمن، رقیب، حریف

an.te.cede /ˌæn.tɪ'siːd/ *v.* to precede, to be/ go before sth/ sb in time and space

مقدم بودن بر، قبل (از کسی / چیزی) قرار گرفتن

The invention of the radiotelegraph *anteceded* the development of T.V. by a quarter of a century.
an.te.ced.ent: *adj., n.* قبلی، پیشین؛ مرجع
an.te.di.lu.vi.an /£ ˌæn.ti.dɪˈluː.vi.ən, $ -t̬i-/ *adj., n.* extremely old-fashioned, ancient

مال عهد دقیانوس، کهنه؛ آدم اُمَّل

The *antediluvian* customs had apparently not changed for thousands of years.
an.thro.poid /£ ˈænt.θrəʊ.pɔɪd, $ -θrə-/ *adj., n.* manlike

انسان‌نما؛ میمون انسان‌نما

The gorilla is the strongest of the *anthropoid* animals.
an.thro.pol.o.gist /£ ˌænt.θrəˈpɒl.ə.dʒɪst, $ -ˈpɑː.lə-/ *n.* a student
of the history and science of mankind

مردم‌شناس، انسان‌شناس

Anthropologists have discovered several relics of prehistoric man in this area.
an.thro.po.morph.ic /£ ˌænt.θrə.pəʊˈmɔː.fɪk, $ -pəˈmɔːr-/ *adj.* having human form or characteristics

انسان‌گونه، انسان مانند؛ انسان انگار

Primitive religions often have deities with *anthropomorphic* characteristics.
an.ti.cli.max /£ ˌæn.tiˈklaɪ.mæks, $ -t̬i-/ *n.* letdown in thought or emotion

سقوط، اُفت؛ حال‌گیری، یأس، ناامیدی

Coming home after a trip is always a bit of an *anticlimax*.
an.ti.cli.mac.tic: *adj.* با پایانی یأس‌آور

an.ti.pa.thy /ænˈtɪp.ə.θi/ *n.* dislike, aversion, opposition

بیزاری، تنفر، انزجار؛ ضدیت، تضاد

Antipathy for the terrorist group usually increases after a bomb attack.

an.ti.pa.thet.ic: *adj.* ضد، مخالف؛ نفرت‌انگیز

an.ti.sep.tic /£ ˌæn.tɪˈsep.tɪk, $ -tɪ-/ *n.* a chemical used for preventing infection.

مادۀ ضد عفونی کننده، مادۀ گندزدا

It is advisable to apply an *antiseptic* to any wound.

an.ti.the.sis /ænˈtɪθ.ə.sɪs/ *n.* the exact opposite, contrast

نقطه مقابل، عکس، ضد؛ تقابل، تضاد

The *antithesis of/ to* warmongering is pacifism.

an.ti.thet.ic: *adj.* متضاد، ناسازگار

ap.a.thy /ˈæp.ə.θi/ *n.* indifference, lack of caring

بی‌تفاوتی، بی‌اعتنایی، دلسردی، بی‌حوصلگی

She could not understand the *apathy* of the people who never bothered to vote.

ap.a.thet.ic: *adj.* بی‌تفاوت، بی‌اعتنا، بی‌احساس، دلمرده

ape /eɪp/ *v.* to imitate, to mimic

تقلید کردن، ادای کسی را در آوردن

He was suspended for a week because he had *aped* the principal in front of the whole school.

ap.er.ture /£ ˈæp.ə.tʃər, $ -ɚ.tʃɚ-/ *n.* opening, hole

روزنه، شکاف؛ (دوربین) دیافراگم

He discovered a small *aperture* in the wall, through which the insects had entered the room.

a.pex /ˈeɪ.peks/ *n.* tip, climax, summit

رأس، نوک؛ اوج، نقطهٔ اوج

He was at the *apex* of his career.

a.phas.ia /əˈfeɪ.ʒə/ *n.* loss of speech due to injury

زبان‌پریشی

After the automobile accident, the victim had periods of *aphasia*.

a.phas.ic: *adj.* زبان‌پریش، بیمار مبتلا به زبان‌پریشی

aph.o.ris.m /£ ˈæf.ə.rɪ.zᵊm, $ -ɚ.ɪ-/ *n.* a short and cleverly phrased saying, maxim

مَثَل، کلمات قصار، پند و اندرز

Oscar Wild was famous for such *aphorisms* as "Experience is the name everyone gives to their mistakes."

a.pi.ar.y /£ ˈeɪ.pi.ə.ri, $ -er.i/ *n.* a place where people keep bees

زنبورداری

Although he spent many hours daily in the *apiary*, he was very seldom stung by a bee.

a.plomb /£ əˈplɒm, $ -ˈplɑːm/ *n.* confidence and style, poise

اعتماد به نفس

He conducted the meeting with characteristic *aplomb*.

a.poc.a.lyp.tic /£ əˈpɒk.əˈlɪp.tɪk, $ -ˌpɑː.kə-/ *adj.* prophetic of disaster

حاکی از فاجعه، فاجعه‌آمیز، مصیبت‌بار

His *apocalyptic* remarks were dismissed by his audience as wild surmise.

a.poc.a.lypse: *n.* انهدام، تباهی؛ فاجعه

A.poc.a.lypse: *n.* آخر زمان؛ کتاب مکاشفه یوحنا

a.poc.ryph.al /£ əˈpɒk.rɪ.fᵊl, $ -ˈpɑː.krɪ-/ *adj.* not genuine, sham

غیرواقعی، دروغین؛ ساختگی، مجعول

His *apocryphal* tears misled no one.

ap.o.gee /ˈæp.ə.dʒiː/ *n.* highest point, the most successful and popular point

(اخترشناسی) اوج؛ بالاترین یا دورترین نقطه، اعلی درجه

When the moon in its orbit is furtherst away from the earth, it is at its *apogee*.

ap.o.ple.xy /ˈæp.ə.plek.si/ *n.* stroke

سکته مغزی

He was crippled by an attack of *apoplexy*.

ap.o.plec.tic: *adj.* سکته‌ای: جوشی، آتشی، عصبی

a.pos.tate /£ əˈpɒs.teɪt, $ -ˈpɑː.steɪt/ *n.* a person who has given up his religion or political beliefs

مرتد، از دین برگشته

Because he switched from one party to another, his friends shunned him as an *apostate*.

a.poth.e.ca.ry /£ əˈpɒθ.ə.kri, $ -ˈpɑː.θə-/ *n.* druggist

عطار، دواساز، دوافروش

In the *apothecaries'* weight, twelve ounces equal one pound.

ap.o.thegm /ˈæp.ə.θem/ *n.* a pithy and compact saying

گفتهٔ کوتاه و پرمغز

Proverbs are *apothegm* that have become familiar sayings.

a.poth.e.o.sis /£ əˌpɒθ.iˈəʊ.sɪs, $ -ˌpɑː.θiˈoʊ-/ *n.* the best example of sth, glorification, deification

نمونهٔ بارز، مظهر، تجسم؛ تصعید به مقام خدایی

The ***apotheosis*** of a Roman emperor was designed to insure his eternal greatness.

ap.pal /£əˈpɔːl, $ -ˈpɑːl/ *n.* to shock, to dismay

به‌وحشت انداختن، متوحش کردن، شوکه کردن

I was ***appalled by/ at*** the lack of staff in the hospital.

    ap.palled/ ap.pal.ling: *adj.*   متوحش، وحشت‌زده؛ وحشتناک

ap.pa.ri.tion /ˌæp.əˈrɪʃ.ᵊn/ *n.* ghost, phantom, spirit

شبح، روح

He claimed to have seen strange ***apparitions*** at night.

ap.pease /əˈpiːz/ *v.* to pacify, to soothe

راضی کردن؛ آرام کردن، تسلی دادن

She claimed that the government had only changed the law in order to ***appease*** their critics.

ap.pel.la.tion /ˌæp.əˈleɪ.ʃᵊn/ *n.* name, title

نام، عنوان

He was amazed when the witches hailed him with his correct ***appellation***.

ap.pend /əˈpend/ *v.* to attach, to add

ضمیمه کردن، اضافه کردن، افزودن

The author ***appended*** a short footnote to the text explaining the point.

    ap.pend.age: *n.*   ضمیمه، پیوست

ap.po.site /ˈæp.ə.zɪt, -zaɪt/ *adj.* suitable and right, appropriate

مناسب، بجا، به‌مورد

ap.praise   35   **ap.pro.pri.ate**

He was always able to find the *apposite* phrase, the correct expression for every occasion.

ap.praise /ə'preɪz/ *v.* to estimate the value of

قیمت گذاشتن (روی)، ارزشیابی کردن، برآورد کردن

It is difficult to *appraise* the value of old paintings.

ap.prais.al: *n.*   برآورد، ارزیابی، ارزشیابی

ap.pre.hend /ˌæp.rɪ'hend/ *v.* to arrest, to catch; to understand

توقیف کردن، دستگیر کردن؛ فهمیدن، درک کردن، دریافتن

The police will *apprehend* the culprit and convict him before long.

ap.pre.hen.sion: *n.*   درک، فهم؛ بازداشت؛ ترس، بیم

ap.pre.hen.sive /ˌæp.rɪ'hent.sɪv/: *adj.* fearful, anxious

حاکی از نگرانی؛ بیمناک، نگران

His *apprehensive* glances at the people revealed his nervousness.

ap.prise /ə'praɪz/ *v.* to tell, to inform

خبر دادن، مطّلع کردن

The President has been *apprised* of the situation.

ap.pro.ba.tion /ˌæp.rəʊ'beɪ.ʃᵊn/ *n.* agreement, approval

تأیید، رضایت، موافقت

She looked for some sign of *approbation* from her parents.

ap.pro.pri.ate /£ ə'prəʊ.pri.ət, $ -'proʊ-/ *v.* to take possession of, to acquire; to keep to use for

تصرف کردن، صاحب شدن؛ تخصیص دادن، کنار گذاشتن

The ranch owners *appropriated* the land that had originally been set aside for the Indians' use.

ap.pur.ten.ance /£ əˈpɜː.tɪ.nənts, $ -ˈpɜːr.tɪ-/ *n.* appendage, accessory

(در جمع) متعلقات، ضمائم

Books and CDs are among the *appurtenances* of student life.

ap.ro.pos /£ ˌæp.rəˈpəʊ, $ -ˈpoʊ/ *prep., adj., adv.* with reference to, properly

درخصوصِ، راجع به؛ ضمناً؛ بجا، مناسب

I find your remarks *apropos* of the present situation.

ap.ti.tude /£ ˈæp.tɪ.tjuːd, $ -tuːd/ *n.* fitness, skill, talent

استعداد؛ توانایی، قابلیت

My son has *no/ little aptitude* for sport.

aq.ui.line /ˈæk.wɪ.laɪn/ *adj.* curved, hooked

(بینی) عقابی

He can be recognized by his *aquiline* nose, curved like the beak of the eagle.

ar.a.ble /£ ˈær.ə.bl̩, $ ˈer-/ *adj.* fit for plowing

زراعی، مزروعی، قابل کشت

The land was no longer *arable*.

ar.bi.ter /£ ɑː.bɪ.təʳ, $ ˈɑːr.bɪ.tɚ/ *n.* a judge, an umpire

قاضی، داور، حَکَم؛ حکمران

The government will be the final *arbiter* in the dispute over the new road.

ar.bi.tra.ry /£ ˈɑː.bɪ.trə.ri, $ ˈɑːr.bə.trer-/ *adj.* based on personal power; decided, despotic

خودسرانه، زوری؛ دلبخواهی

Any *arbitrary* action on your part will be resented by the

members of the board.

ar.cade /£ ɑːˈkeɪd, $ ɑːr-/ *n.* a covered passage usually lined with shops

بازارچه سرپوشیده، پاساژ

The *arcade* was popular with shoppers because it gave them protection from the winter rain.

ar.cane /£ ɑːˈkeɪn, $ ɑːr-/ *adj.* secret, mysterious

ناشناخته، اسرارآمیز، مخفی

What was *arcane to* us was clear to the psychologist.

ar.chae.ol.o.gy /£ ˌɑːkiˈɒl-ə-dʒi, $ ˌɑːr.kiˈɑːlə-/ *n.* study of artifacts and relics of early mankind

باستان‌شناسی

She teaches *archaeology* at the university.

ar.cha.ic /£ ɑːˈkeɪ.ɪk, $ ɑːr-/ *adj.* antiquated, old fashioned

کهنه، مهجور، منسوخ

"Methinks", "thee", and "thou" are *archaic* words which are no longer part of our normal vocabulary.

ar.che.type /£ ˈɑːkɪ.taɪp, $ ˈɑːr-/ *n.* prototype, the original model

الگوی نخستین، نمونه آرمانی، صورت مثالی

The United States is *the archetype of* a federal society.

ar.che.typ.al: *adj.* نمونه، مثالی

ar.chi.pel.a.go /£ ˌɑːkɪˈpel.ə.gəʊ, $ ˌɑːr.kɪˈpel.ə.goʊ/ *n.* a group of small islands

مجمع‌الجزایر

They visited the Hawaiian *archipelago* last summer.

ar.chive /£ ˈɑː.kaɪv, $ ˈɑːr-/ *n.* public records, place where public records are kept

بایگانی، آرشیو؛ اسناد

I've been studying village records in the local *archive*.

ar.chiv.ist: *n.*   بایگان، مسئول بایگانی

ar.dor /£ ˈɑː.dər, $ ˈɑːr.dɚ/ *n.* heat, passion, zeal

شور و شوق، اشتیاق، هیجان

His *ardor for* her cooled after only a few weeks.

ar.du.ous /£ ˈɑː.dju.əs, $ ˈɑːr.dʒu-/ *adj.* hard, difficult, strenuous

سخت، دشوار، طاقت‌فرسا

His *arduous* efforts had sapped his energy.

ar.got /£ ˈɑː.gəʊ, $ ˈɑːr.goʊ/ *n.* slang

زبان خاص یک گروه، زبان لاتی

They were speaking in a strange *argot* of their own.

a.ri.a /£ ˈɑː.ri.ə, $ ˈɑːr.i-/ *n.* operatic solo

تک‌خوانی، آریا

At her Metropolitan Opera audition, Marian Anderson sang an *aria* from Norma.

ar.id /£ ˈær.ɪd, $ ˈer-/ *adj.* dry, barren

خشک، بایر، لم‌یزرع؛ کم باران

The cactus has adapted to survive in an *arid* environment.

ar.ma.da /£ ɑːˈmɑː.də, $ ɑːr-/ *n.* fleet of warships

ناوگان

The Spanish *armada* was sent by the king of Spain to invade England in 1588.

ar.o.mat.ic /£ ˌær.əʊˈmæt.ɪk, $ ˌer.əˈmæt̬-/ *adj.* fragrant

خوشبو، معطر

Properly fried chicken should be golden, *aromatic* and tasty.

ar.raign /əˈreɪn/ *v.* to charge someone in court, to indict

متهم کردن، اعلان جرم کردن؛ به دادگاه احضار کردن

He was *arraigned* on charges of aiding and abetting terrorists.

ar.raign.ment: *n.* اعلان جرم؛ احضار به دادگاه

ar.ray /əˈreɪ/ *v.* to marshal, to place in proper order

مرتب کردن، نظم بخشیدن، چیدن، به‌نمایش گذاردن

A large number of magazines were *arrayed* on the shelf in the shop.

ar.ray /əˈreɪ/ *v., n.* to clothe, to adorn–finery

لباس، آرایش؛ لباس پوشاندن، آراستن

She liked to watch her mother *array* herself in her finest clothes before going out.

ar.rears /əˈrɪəz/ *n.* being in debt

بدهی (عقب افتاده)

He was in *arrears with/ on* his payments on the car.

ar.ro.gance /£ ˈær.ə.gənts, $ ˈer-/ *n.* pride, haughtiness

تکبّر، غرور، نخوت

The *arrogance* of the nobility was resented by the middle class.

ar.ro.gant: *adj.* متکبّر، پرافاده

ar.ro.gate /£ ˈær.əʊ.geɪt, $ ˈer.ə-/ *v.* to claim without reasonable grounds

به ناحق (به خود) اختصاص دادن یا (برای خود) قائل شدن

He accused the group of *arrogating to* itself the power to punish people.

ar.roy.o /əroi.ə/ *n.* gully

آبکنه، کانال، آبراهه

Until the heavy rains of the past spring, this *arroyo* had been a dry bed.

ar.ti.cu.late /£ ɑːˈtɪk.jʊ.lət, $ ɑːr-/ *adj., v.* effective, distinct; to express, to say

فصیح، روشن، واضح، رسا؛ با صراحت اظهار کردن

1) She gave a witty, entertaining and *articulate* speech.
2) They have had no opportunity to *articulate* their opposition.

artifact /£ ˈɑː.tɪ.fækt, $ ˈɑːr.tɪ-/ *n.* product of primitive culture

شیء دست‌ساز، مصنوع

Bowls and other *artifacts* were discovered during the excavations.

ar.ti.fice /£ ˈɑː.tɪ.fɪs, $ ˈɑːr.tɪ-/ *n.* deception, trickery

ترفند، حیله، مکر

His remorse is just an *artifice* to gain sympathy.

ar.ti.san /£ ˈɑː.tɪ.zæn, $ ˈɑːr.tɪ-/ *n.* manually skilled worker

صنعتگر، کارگر فنی

Artists and *artisans* alike are necessary to the development of a culture.

as.cend.an.cy /əˈsen.dəntsi/ *n.* controlling influence

سلطه، تفوق، برتری

They are in danger of losing their political *ascendancy*.

as.cer.tain /£ ˌæs.əˈteɪn, $ -ɚˈ-/ *v.* to find out for certain, to make certain

فهمیدن، پی‌بردن، دریافتن

The police have so far been unable to *ascertain* the cause of explosion.

a.sce.tic /£ əˈset.ɪk, $ -ˈset̬-/ *adj.* practicing self-denial, austere

زاهد، پارسا؛ زاهدانه

The cavalier could not understand the *ascetic* life led by the monks.

a.sce.ti.ci.sm: *n.*   ریاضت، زهد، پارسایی

a.scribe /əˈskraɪb/ *v.* to refer, to attribute, to assign

نسبت دادن به، مربوط دانستن به؛ اطلاق کردن

People like to *ascribe* human feelings to animals.

a.sep.tic /ˌeɪˈsep.tɪk/ *adj.* medically clean or without infection

ضدعفونی شده، (مربوط به) ضد عفونی

Hospitals lowered the mortality rate as soon as they introduced *aseptic* conditions.

ash.en /ˈæʃ.ən/ *adj.* ash-colored

رنگ پریده، سفید، مثل گچ

His face was *ashen* with fear.

as.i.nine /ˈæs.ɪ.naɪn/ *adj.* stupid

احمقانه، ابلهانه؛ احمق

Your *asinine* remarks prove that you have not considered this problem seriously.

a.skance /£ əˈskɑːnts, $ -ˈskænts/ *adv.* with an indirect look

با شک و تردید، چپ چپ

Looking *askance* at her questioner, she displayed her scorn.

a.skew /əˈskjuː/ *adv., adj.* not straight or level, out of balance

کج، کج و کوله، یک وری؛ چپ چپ

The portrait was hanging *askew* on the wall.

a.sper.i.ty /£ əˈsper.ɪ.ti, $ -ə.t̬i/ *n.* sharpness, severity and force

تندی، درشتی، پرخاش؛ سرمای سخت

1) She will be remembered for her *asperity* of speech.
2) They helped Russia through the *asperities* of winter.

as.per.sions /£ əˈspɜː.ʃənz, $ -ˈspɜːr-, -ʃənz/ *n.* slanderous remarks

تهمت، افترا، دروغ

Do not *cast aspersions on* his character.

as.pir.ant /£ ˈæs.pɪ.rənt, £ əˈspaɪ-, $ ˈæs.pɚ.ənt/ *n., adj.* seeker after position or status

خواهان، داوطلب، آرزومند

She was an *aspirant for* public office.

    as.pire: *v.*   سودای چیزی در سر داشتن، طلبیدن، خواستن
    as.pir.a.tion: *n.*   آرزو، امید، آرمان

as.sail /əˈseɪl/ *v.* to attack someone violently, to assault

حمله ور شدن؛ به باد (انتقاد، سؤال و غیره) گرفتن

He was *assailed with* questions after his lecture.

as.say /əˈseɪ, æsˈeɪ/ *v.* to analyze, to evaluate

آزمایش کردن؛ ارزیابی کردن؛ تجزیه کردن؛ محک زدن

When they *assayed* the ore, they found that they had discovered a very rich vein.

    as.say: *n.*   تجزیه، عیارسنجی، ارزیابی

as.sess.ment /əˈses.mənt/ *n.* appraisal, estimation

بررسی، ارزیابی، برآورد، تخمین

I would like to have your *assessment* of the situation in south America.

as.sess: *v.* ارزیابی کردن، برآورد کردن

as.si.du.ous /ə'sɪd.ju.əs/ *adj.* showing serious interest; diligent

پیگیر، جدّی، کوشا

The government has been *assiduous* in the fight against inflation.

as.si.mi.late /ə'sɪm.ɪ.leɪt/ *v.* to take in, to absorb

جذب کردن؛ همگون ساختن

You shouldn't expect immigrants to *assimilate into* an alien culture immediately.

as.si.mi.la.tion: *n.* جذب؛ ادغام؛ همگونی

as.si.mil.a.ble: *adj.* قابل فهم

as.suage /ə'sweɪdʒ/ *v.* to ease, to lessen (pain)

فرو نشاندن، آرام کردن؛ ارضاء کردن

Not even his promotion *assuaged* his desire for power.

as.ter.oid /£ 'æs.tᵊr.ɔɪd, $ -tə.rɔɪd/ *n.* small planet

سیّارک

Asteroids are also known as "minor planets".

a.stig.ma.ti.sm /£ ə'stɪg.mə.tɪ.zᵊm, $ -ṭɪ-/ *n.* eye defect which prevents proper focus

آستیگماتیسم

The boy suffered from *astigmatism*.

as.tral /'æs.trəl/ *adj.* relating to the stars

ستاره‌ای، ستاره مانند؛ سماوی، اختری

He was amazed at the number of *astral* bodies the new

telescope revealed.

a.strin.gent /ə'strɪn.dʒ²nt/ *adj.* severe, harsh; causing contraction

تند، گزنده، خشن؛ منقبض کننده

His *astringent* criticism was resented by the audience.

as.tro.nom.ic.al /£ ˌæs.trə'nɒm.ɪ.k²l, $ -'nɑː.mɪ-/ *adj.* enormously large or extensive

فوق‌العاده زیاد، عظیم، نجومی

The damage caused by the hurricane is *astronomical*.

a.stute /£ ə'stjuːt, $ -'stuːt/ *adj.* clever, wise, shrewd

زرنگ، تیز(هوش)، زبل

Had he been more *astute* he might have stayed in power longer.

at.a.vi.sm /£ 'æt.ə.vɪ.z²m, $ 'æt̬-/ *n.* resemblance to remote ancestors

بازپیدایی ژنتیکی، بازپیدایی وراثتی

The doctors ascribed the child's deformity to an *atavism*.

at.el.ier /£ ə'telier, $ ˌæt'ljeɪ/ *n.* workshop, studio

کارگاه هنری، آتلیه

The book was full of tales of artists' starving or freezing in their *ateliers*.

a.the.ist.ic /ˌeɪ.θi'ɪs.tɪk/ *adj.* denying the existence of God

الحادی، کفرآمیز

His *atheistic* remarks shocked the religious worshippers.

a.the.ist: *n.*   ملحد

a.troc.i.ty /£ ə'trɒs.ɪ.ti, $ -'trɑː.sɪ.t̬i/ *n.* brutal deed

ظلم، ستم؛ (جمع) فجایع

They are on trial for committing hundreds of war - time *atrocities*.

a.tro.cious: *adj.* فجیع، بی‌رحمانه، شرم‌آور

at.ro.phy /'æt.rə.fi/ *n., v.* wasting away; to become weak

آتروفی، پلاسیدگی، تضعیف شدن، پلاسیدن، تحلیل بردن

Polio victims need physiotherapy to prevent the *atrophy* of affected limbs.

at.ten.u.ate /ə'ten.ju.eɪt/ *v.* to weaken, to make thin

از شدت (چیزی) کاستن، ضعیف کردن

By withdrawing their forces, the generals hoped to *attenuate* the enemy lines.

at.ten.u.at.ed: *adj.* لاغر و کشیده، نحیف، ضعیف شده

at.test /ə'test/ *v.* to testify, to bear witness

گواه بر (چیزی) بودن، تصدیق کردن

Thousands of people came out onto streets to *attest* their support for the government.

at.test.a.tion: *n.* تصدیق، تأیید، استشهاد

at.tri.bute /'æt.rɪ.bjuːt/ *n.* essential quality or feature

صفت، ویژگی، خصیصه

His outstanding *attribute* was his kindness.

at.tri.bute: *v.* نسبت دادن به، ناشی دانستن از

at.tri.tion /ə'trɪʃ.ən/ *n.* gradual wearing down

تضعیف، فرسایش

They decided to wage a war of *attrition* rather than to rely on an all-out attack.

a.typ.i.cal /ˌeɪ'tɪp.ɪ.kəl/ *adj.* not normal, different

غیرعادی، غیرمعمول

They are *atypical* of the way most Americans live.
au.da.ci.ty /£ ɔːˈdæs.ɪ.ti, $ ɑːˈdæs.ɪ.ti/ *n.* boldness, bravery

جسارت، شجاعت، تهور

His *audacity* in this critical moment encouraged us.
    au.da.cious: *adj.*   جسور، بی‌باک؛ پررو
au.dit /£ ˈɔː.dɪt, $ ˈɑː-/ *n.* examination of accounts

حسابرسی

The company has an *audit* at the end of each financial year.
    au.di.tor: *n.*   حسابرس؛ مستمع آزاد
aug.ment /£ ɔːgˈment, $ ɑːg-/ *v.* to increase

افزایش دادن، زیاد کردن؛ بهتر کردن، بهبود بخشیدن

How can we hope to *augment* our forces when our allies are deserting us?
    aug.ment.a.tion: *n.*   افزایش، ازدیاد
au.gu.ry /£ ˈɔː.gjʊ.ri, $ ˈɑː.gjɚ.i/ *n.* omen, prophecy

یمن، شگون؛ پیشگویی

He interpreted the departure of the birds as an *augury* of evil.
    au.gur: *v.*   (از چیزی) خبر دادن، نشانهٔ (چیزی) بودن
au.re.ole /£ ˈɔː.ri.əʊl, $ ˈɔː.r.i.oʊi/ *n.* sun's corona; a halo

هاله؛ تاج خورشید

Many medieval paintings depict saintly characters with *aureole* around their heads.
au.ro.ral /ɔˈrɔːrəl/ *adj.* related to aurora borealis

مربوط به شفق شمالی

The *auroral* display was particularly spectacular that

evening.

au.ro.ra: *n.* شفق قطبی

aus.pi.cious /£ ɔːˈspɪʃ.əs, $ ɑː-/ *adj.* favoring success

فرخنده، خجسته؛ خوش یمن

Their first match was an *auspicious* start.

austere /£ ɔːˈstɪəʳ, $ ɑːˈstɪr/ *adj.* strict, stern, severe

سختگیر، جدی، خشک؛ ساده، بی‌آلایش، بی‌پیرایه

His *austere* behaving prevented us from engaging in our usual foolish activities.

au.ster.ity: *n.* سختی، دشواری؛ ریاضت، زهد؛ سادگی

au.then.ti.cate /£ ɔːˈθen.tɪ.keɪt, $ ɑːˈθen.ṭi-/ *v.* to prove genuine

اصالت (چیزی را) به ثبوت رساندن، تأیید کردن

They used carbon dating tests to *authenticate* the claim that the skeleton was 2 million years old.

au.thor.ize /£ ˈɔː.θəʳ.aɪz, $ ˈɑː.θɚ-/ *v.* to give official permission

اختیار دادن به؛ اجازه دادن، تصویب کردن

The invasion was *authorized* by the President.

au.thor.i.ty: *n.* قدرت، اقتدار؛ مجوز، حکم
au.thor.i.ta.tive: *adj.* مقتدر، قدرتمند؛ تحکیم‌آمیز
au.thor.i.za.tion: *n.* اعطای اختیار؛ اجازهٔ کتبی

au.to.crat /£ ˈɔː.tə.kræt, $ ˈɑː.ṭə-/ *n.* monarch with supreme power

فرمانروای مطلق، خودرأی، مستبد

He was condemned for being a right-wing *autocrat* who ruled his country.

au.toc.ra.cy: *n.* نظام استبدادی، فرد سالاری؛ استبداد

au.to.ma.ton /£ ɔːˈtɒm.ə.tᵊn, $ ɑːˈtɑː.mə.tᵊn-/ *n.* mechanism which imitates actions of haman

ماشین خودکار؛ آدم ماشینی

Writers are presenting stories of *automatons* who can outperform men.

au.ton.o.mous /£ ɔːˈtɒn.ə.məs, $ ɑːˈtɑː.nə-/ *adj.* self-governing

خودگردان، خودمختار؛ مستقل، آزاد

The majority of Scots favor an *autonomous* Scotland.

au.ton.o.my: *n.*   خودگردانی، خودمختاری؛ آزادی عمل، استقلال

au.top.sy /£ ˈɔː.tɒp.si, $ ˈɑː.tɑːp-/ *n.* examination of a dead body

کالبدشکافی

The *autopsy* on the prisoner showed that she had been taking drugs.

au.xi.li.a.ry /£ ɔːɡˈzɪl.iᵊr.i, $ ɑːɡˈzɪl.i.er-/ *adj.* helper; additional

کمکی؛ اضافی

The assistants will receive *auxiliary* rates of pay.

av.a.rice /£ ˈæv.ᵊr.ɪs, $ ˈ-ɚ-/ *n.* greed, strong desire

حرص، طمع، آز

King Midas's *avarice* has been famous for centuries.

av.a.ri.cious: *adj.*   حریص، طمع‌کار، مال‌پرست

av.a.tar /ˈævətɑːʳ/ *n.* incarnation

تجسم، مظهر؛ (در اساطیر هندی) تجسد یکی از خدایان

In Hindu mythology, the *avatar* of Vishnu is thoroughly detailed.

a.ver /£ əˈvɜːʳ, $ -ˈvɜːr/ *v.* to state confidently, to assert

تصریح کردن، تأکید کردن بر

The lawyer *averred* her client's innocence.

a.verse /£ əˈvɜːs, $ -ˈvɜːrs/ *adj.* reluctant, strongly disliking

مخالف، بیزار

He was *averse to* revealing the sources of his information.

a.ver.sion: *n.* مخالفت؛ تنفر، بیزاری

a.vert /£ əˈvɜːt, $ -ˈvɜːrt/ *v.* to turn away; to prevent

جلوگیری کردن، مانع وقوع (چیزی) شدن؛ برگرداندن

1) Starvation can only be *averted* with massive food aid from the government.
2) She *averted* her eyes *from* the dead cat on the highway.

av.id /ˈæv.ɪd/ *adj.* greedy, eager for

مشتاق، خواهان، تشنه

She was *avid for* equal rights for immigrants.

a.vid.i.ty: *n.* اشتیاق، ولع

av.o.ca.tion /ævəˈkeɪʃⁿn/ *n.* secondery or minor occupation

شغل جانبی، شغل دوم

He abandoned his regular occupation and concentrated on his *avocation*.

a.vow /əˈvaʊ/ *v.* to declare openly

اذعان داشتن؛ اعتراف کردن

I must *avow* that I am innocent.

a.vun.cu.lar /£ əˈvʌŋ.kjʊ.ləʳ, $ -lɚ/ *adj.* like an uncle; friendly

مهربان، رئوف؛ پدرانه

His *avuncular* image belies his steely determination.

awe /£ ɔː, $ ɑː/ *n.* solemn wonder

بهت، شگفتی؛ ترس، خوف

awry

The sight of Father Christmas filled the childern with *awe*.

awry /əˈraɪ/ *adv., adj.* distorted, crooked

کج و کوله، یک‌وری؛ نامرتب، خراب

1) He held his head *awry*.
2) Everything went *awry* in the town.

ax.i.om /ˈæk.si.əm/ *n.* self-evident truth

اصل متعارف، اصل بدیهی

It is a widely held *axiom* that governments should not negotiate with terrorists.

a.zure /£ ˈæʒ.ər, £ ˈæz.jʊər, $ -ɚ/ *adj.* sky blue

نیلگون، آبی آسمانی

The once *azure* skies of Athens have been ruined by pollution.

لیستی از لغاتی که در جملات بخش A به کار رفته‌اند:

commit: v.	مرتکب شدن	drought: n.	خشکسالی
competence: n.	کفایت، قابلیت	drown out: v.	تحت شعاع قرار دادن
concept: n.	مفهوم		
concerned: adj.	نگران	duration: n.	مدت، زمان
concrete: adj.	عینی، ملموس	engage: v.	به کاری پرداختن
condemn: v.	محکوم کردن	abstract: adj.	ذهنی، انتزاعی
convict: v.	محکوم کردن	accountant: n.	حسابدار
constitution: n.	قانون اساسی	affected: adj.	آسیب‌دیده، مبتلا
cool: v.	فروکش کردن	aggresive: adj.	پرخاشگر، متهاجم
coup: n.	کودتا		
crack: v.	شکستن، شکاف برداشتن	alien: n., adj.	بیگانه
		allies: n.	متحدین
culprit: n.	مجرم	all-out: adj.	تمام عیار
dealings: n.	روابط، معاشرت	ascribe: v.	نسبت دادن
decry: v.	ناچیز شمردن و انتقاد کردن	attempt: n.	تلاش
		award: v.	دادن، پرداختن
deity: n.	خدا، الهه	beak: n.	منقار
depict: v.	توصیف کردن، نشان دادن	bear: v.	داشتن، نشان‌دادن
		before long: adv.	بزودی
deposit: n.	رسوب	belie: v.	پنهان کردن، پوشاندن
desert: v.	تنها گذاشتن	blackmail: n.	اخاذی، باج‌گیری
detail: v.	به تفصیل بیان کردن	body: n.	مجموعه، واحد
dismiss: v.	وارد ندانستن	bother: v.	به خود زحمت دادن
display: n.	نمایش	brass: n.	برنز
dispute: n.	نزاع، درگیری	bullfighting n.	گاوبازی
donate: v.	اهدا کردن	call in: v.	فراخواندن،

		mythology: *n.*	اسطوره
canal: *n.*	احضار کردن	nastily: *adv.*	مغرضانه
career: *n.*	لوله، مجرا، کانال	negotiate: *v.*	مذاکره کردن
carved: *adj.*	زندگی کاری، شغل	observe: *v.*	رعایت کردن
cavalier: *n.*	کنده‌کاری شده	odor: *n.*	بو
cheer: *v.*	سوارکار، اشراف‌زاده	opponent: *n.*	مخالف
chip: *v.*	هورا کشیدن	ore: *n.*	سنگ معدن
clarify: *v.*	خرد شدن	outperform: *v.*	انجام دادن (بهتر)
intellect: *n.*	روشن کردن	outstanding: *adj.*	برجسته، بارز
invade: *v.*	نیروی عقلانی	overtake: *v.*	سبقت گرفتن
invasion: *n.*	حمله کردن	overthrow *n.*	براندازی
jeer: *n.*	تهاجم، حمله	established: *adj.*	جا افتاده، تثبیت شده
jelly: *n.*	تمسخر، طعنه		
keenness: *n.*	ژله	eternal: *adj.*	جاودانه، ابدی
lecturer: *n.*	تیزی، ذکاوت	ethnic: *adj.*	نژادی
leisurely: *adv.*	سخنران، استاد	excavation: *n.*	حفاری
	با تأنی، بدون عجله	exceedingly: *adv.*	بسیار، بی‌اندازه
limb: *n.*	دست و پا، عضو		
lotion: *n.*	کِرِم	expectancy: *n.*	توقع، امید
maul: *v.*	زخمی کردن	expression: *n.*	احساسی؛ حالتِ چهره
mishad: *v.*	گمراه کردن		
monotonous: *adj.*	یکنواخت، خسته کننده	face: *v.*	مواجه شدن
		fail: *v.*	به نتیجه نرسیدن
moor: *n.*	بوته‌زار	famine: *n.*	قحطی، گرسنگی
MP: *n.*	نمایندهٔ مجلس	favor: *v.*	طرفداری کردن
mystic: *adj.*	عرفانی	fertile: *adj.*	حاصلخیز
mysticism: *n.*	عرفان	financial: *adj.*	مالی

fraud: *n.* کلاهبرداری	wild: *adj.* احساساتی، بدون تفکر
frog: *n.* قورباغه	witch doctor: *n.* جادو پزشک
furrow: *n.* خط، شیار	wrecked: *adj.* تصادف کرده (وسیله)
glance: *n.* نگاه	
grant: *v.* اعطا کردن، دادن	pave: *v.* هموار کردن
hail: *v.* خوش‌آمد گفتن، صدا زدن	philanthropist: *n.* بشردوست
heap: *v.* انباشتن، بار کردن	polio: *n.* فلج اطفال
heed: *v.* توجه کردن	primitive: *adj.* نخستین، بدوی
hung: *adj.* بدون صدور رأی	ranch: *n.* مزرعه (دامداری)
hurricane: *n.* توفان، تندباد	recommend: *v.* توصیه کردن
idol worshipping: *n.* بت‌پرستی	record: *n.* سند، مدرک
immigrant: *n.* مهاجر	relics: *n.* بقایا
immortality فنا‌ناپذیری	relief: *n.* تسکین
indicate: *v.* نشان از ... بودن	remorse: *n.* ندامت، توبه
indulge: *v.* زیاده‌روی کردن	resent: *v.* آزردن، مخالفت کردن
take a vow: *v.* قول دادن، قسم خوردن	restrain: *v.* کنترل کردن
	rigging: *n.* طناب‌های بادبان و دکل
temple: *n.* معبد	
temporary: *adj.* موقتی	rival: *n.* رقیب، حریف
tissue: *n.* بافت	saintly: *adj.* روحانی، ملکوتی
trance: *n.* جذبه، خلسه	sap: *v.* از توان انداختن
treasured: *adj.* ارزنده	settle: *v.* حل و فصل کردن
union: *n.* اتحادیه	scorn: *n.* تمسخر، طعنه
victim: *n.* قربانی حادثه	shun: *v.* دوری جستن، اجتناب کردن
vein: *n.* رگه، رگ	
wage: *v.* دست زدن به (حمله)	spectacular: *adj.* جالب، دیدنی
warmongering: *n.* جنگ‌طلبی	spectator: *n.* تماشاچی

staff: *n.*	کارمند	surmise: *n.*	حدس، گمان
stagger: *v.*	مبهوت کردن	suspend: *v.*	معلق کردن
sting: *v.*	نیش زدن	switch: *v.*	تغییر (موضع) دادن
subject: *n.*	معرِض		

B b

bab.ble /ˈbæb.l̩/ *v.* to chatter idly

جویده جویده گفتن، بلغور کردن

Don't *babble*—I can't understand what you're saying.

bac.cha.na.li.an /ˌbæk.əˈneɪ.li.ən/ *adj.* drunken

(مربوط به) عیاشی یا لهو و لعب

Emperor Nero attended the *bacchanalian* orgy.

    bac.cha.nal: *n.*   میگساری، لهو و لعب

bad.ger /£ ˈbædʒ.əʳ, $ -ɚ/ *v.* to annoy, to pester

اذیت کردن، کلافه کردن؛ نق زدن

She had to change her telephone number because she was *badgered* by obscene phone calls.

bad.i.nage /ˌbæd.ɪ.nɑːʒ/ *n.* teasing conversation

مزاح، شوخی، بذله گویی

But enough of this *badinage*! What are you really here for?

    exchange badinage: *v.*   شوخی کردن، مزاح کردن

baf.fle /ˈbæf.l̩/ *v.* to frustrate; to perplex

گیج کردن؛ مات و مبهوت کردن

She was completely *baffled* by his strange behaviour.

    baf.fle.ment: *n.*   سردرگمی، تحیّر

bag.a.telle /ˌbæg.əˈtel/ *n.* small amount, trifle

چیز جزئی، هیچ، کار بی‌اهمیت

A thousand pounds is a mere *bagatelle* to him.

bait /beɪt/ *v.* to tease, to harass, to make angry

زجر دادن، عذاب دادن، زخم زبان زدن

The soldiers *baited* the prisoners, terrorizing them.

bear-baiting   انداختن خرس‌ها به جان همدیگر (جهت سرگرمی)

bale.ful /ˈbeɪl.fᵊl/ *adj.* full of evil intentions

شوم، نحس، شیطانی

The drought was a *baleful* omen.

bale.ful.ly: *adj.*   به حالت خصمانه، تهدیدآمیز

balk /£ bɔːk, $ bɑːlk/ *v.* to be unwilling; to foil

اکراه داشتن، پا پس کشیدن، سرباز زدن؛ خنثی کردن

When she learned they were planning to escape, she *balked* their attempt.

balk: *n.*   مانع، سد؛ تیر چوبی

bal.last /ˈbæl.əst/ *n.* heavy substance used to add stability or weight

وزنهٔ تعادل

The ship was listing badly to one side; it was necessary to shift the *ballast*.

balm /bɑːm/ *n.* something that relieves pain

مرهم، مایهٔ تسلی، آرامش

Friendship is certainly the finest *balm* for the pangs of disappointed love.

balm.y /ˈbɑː.mi/ *adj.* mild, fragrant

(هوا) ملایم، مطبوع؛ خوشبو، معطر

It was a *balmy* night and we sat on the grass talking until after midnight.

ba.nal /bə'nɑːl/ *adj.* boring, hackneyed

خسته‌کننده، سطح پایین، پیش پا افتاده، تکراری

His frequent use of clichés made his essay seem *banal*.

ba.nal.i.ty: *n.* حرف بی‌مزه، بی‌مزگی

band.y /'bæn.di/ *v.* to speak, to exchange blows or words

دهان به دهان شدن، یکی به دو کردن

The President refused to *bandy* words with the reporters.

bane /beɪn/ *n.* cause of ruin, poison

بلای جان، مایهٔ گرفتاری

That cat is the *bane* of my life.

bane.ful /'beɪn.fəl/ *adj.* ruinous, poisonous

مخرب، زیانبار

His *baneful* influence was feared by all.

ban.ter /£ 'bæn.tər, $ -t̬ɚ/ *n.* good-natured ridiculing, badinage

متلک، شوخی، خوشمزگی

He considered himself a master of witty *banter*.

ban.ter: *v.* متلک گفتن، شوخی کردن

barb /£ bɑːb, $ bɑːrb/ *n.* sharp projection from fishhook

نوک، سر؛ زخم زبان، نیش

1) The *barb* from the fishhook caught in his finger as he grabbed the fish.
2) Nobody was left in any doubt that the *barb* was aimed at the President.

ba.roque /£ bə'rɒk, $ -'rɑːk/ *adj.* highly ornate

باروک؛ پر نقش و نگار

They found the *baroque* architecture amusing.

bar.rage /£ ˈbær.ɑːʒ, $ bəˈrɑːʒ/ *n.* continuous firing, attack

سد آتش؛ رگبار / سیلی از (انتقادات و غیره)

The company was forced to retreat through the *barrage* of heavy cannons.

bar.rist.er /£ ˈbær.ɪ.stəʳ, $ -stɚ/ *n.* counsellor-at-law, lawyer

وکیل مدافع، وکیل دعاوی

He started as a *barrister*, but when he found the practice of law boring, turned to writing.

bar.ter.er /£ ˈbɑː.tərəʳ, $ ˈbɑːr.t̬ɚr/ *n.* trader

تاجر، بازرگان

The *barterer* exchanged trinkets for the natives' furs.

bar.ter: *v.*   معاوضه کردن، مبادله کردن، پایاپای معامله کردن

bask /£ bɑːsk, $ bæsk/ *v.* to lie or sit enjoying the warmth esp. of the sun

دراز کشیدن، آرمیدن، لمیدن

We sat out on the balcony, *basking* in the sun.

bas.soon /bəˈsuːn/ *n.* reed instrument of the woodwind group

باسون (= نوعی ساز بادی)

In the orchestra, the *bassoon* is related to the oboe and the clarinet.

bas.ti.on /ˈbæs.tɪ.ən/ *n.* fortress; defense

پناه، دژ، برج، حفاظ؛ (مجازی) پایگاه

Once a *bastion* of democracy, under its new government the island became a dictatorship.

bate /ˈbeɪt/ *v.* to let down, to restrain

Until it was time to open the presents, the children had to *bate* their curiosity.

with bated breath   در نهایت نگرانی

bat.ten /£ ˈbætᵊn, $ ˈbæt̬-/ *v.* to grow fat, to thrive upon others

(از کسی) چریدن، رشد کردن

We cannot accept a system where a favored few can *batten* in extreme comfort while others toil.

bau.ble /£ ˈbɔːbl̩, $ ˈbɑː-/ *n.* trinket, trifle

زیورآلات بدلی؛ زرق و برق

The child was delighted with the *bauble* she had won in the grab bag.

bawd.y /£ ˈbɔːdi, $ ˈbɑː-/ *adj.* indecent, obscene

رکیک، مستهجن

She took offense at his *bawdy* remarks.

be.a.ti.fic /ˌbiːəˈtɪf.ɪk/ *adj.* giving bliss, blissful

مسرت‌بخش، شادی‌بخش، شیرین

The angels in the painting have *beatific* smiles.

be.at.i.tude /£ biˈæt.ɪ.tjuːd, $ -ˈæt̬.ɪ.tuːd/ *n.* blessedness, state of bliss

شادیِ معنوی، احساس معنوی

Growing closer to God each day, the mystic achieved a state of indescribable *beatitude*.

the Beatitudes   کلمات قصار حضرت مسیح (ع)

be.di.zen /bɪˈdaɪzᵊn/ *v.* to dress with vulgar finery

لباس رنگ وارنگ و زننده پوشیدن

The witch doctors were *bedizened* in all their gaudiest costumes.

be.drag.gle /bɪˈdrægl/ *v.* to wet thoroughly

گل‌آلود کردن، خیس و کثیف کردن

We were so *bedraggled* by the severe storm that we had to change into dry clothing.

    be.drag.gled: *adj.*   کثیف، ژولیده، گِلی

be.guile /bɪˈgaɪl/ *v.* to delude, to cheat, to amuse

سرگرم کردن؛ (وقت) گذراندن؛ گول زدن

He *beguiled* himself during the long hours by playing solitaire.

be.he.moth /bɪˈhiːmɒθ/ *n.* huge creature, something of monstrous size or power

موجود یا انسان غول پیکر، غول

Sportscasters nicknamed the linebacker "The *Behemoth*."

be.hold.en /£ bɪˈhəʊl.dən, $ -ˈhoʊl-/ *adj.* obligated, indebted

مدیون، بدهکار

Since I don't wish to be *beholden* to anyone, I cannot accept this favor.

be.hoove /**be.hove** *Br.* /£ bɪˈhəʊv, $ -ˈhoʊv/ *v.* to be suited to; to incumbent upon

(برای کسی) ضرورت داشتن، اولیٰ بودن

In this time of crisis, it *behooves* all of us to remain calm.

be.la.bor /£ bɪˈleɪ.bər, $ -bɚ/ *v.* to beat soundly, to assail verbally

مضروب کردن، (به کسی) تاختن

He was *belaboring* his opponent.

be.lat.ed /£ bɪˈleɪ.tɪd, $ -t̬ɪd/ *adj.* delayed

به تعویق افتاده، خیلی دیر، دیرتر از موعد

He apologized for his ***belated*** note of condolence.

be.lea.guer /£ bɪˈliː.gəʳ, $ -gɚ/ *v.* to besiege, to surround

محاصره کردن، به تصرف درآوردن

As soon as the city was ***beleaguered***, life became more subdued.

be.lea.guered: *adj.* در محاصره، محاصره شده؛ به ستوه آمده، عاجز

be.lie /bɪˈlaɪ/ *v.* to contradict, to give a false impression

تصور غلط (از چیزی) به‌دست دادن؛ رد کردن، تأیید نکردن

Television pictures of starving children ***belie*** official reports.

be.lit.tle /£ bɪˈlɪt.l̩, $ -ˈlɪt̬-/ *v.* to disparage, to deprecate

دست کم گرفتن؛ بی‌اهمیت جلوه دادن

Stop ***belittling*** yourself — your work is highly valued.

bel.li.cose /£ ˈbel.ɪ.kəʊs, $ -koʊs/ *adj.* warlike, wishing to fight

جنگ‌طلب، ستیزه‌جو

His ***bellicose*** disposition alienated his friends.

bel.li.ger.ent /£ bəˈlɪdʒ.ºr.ənt, $ -ˈɚ-/ *adj.* quarrelsome

متخاصم، ستیزه‌جو، پرخاشگر

I don't know why she always seems so ***belligerent*** towards me.

ben.e.dict.ion /ˌben.ɪˈdɪk.ʃºn/ *n.* blessing

رحمت الهی، برکت، لطف خدا

The appearance of the sun after the many rainy days was like a ***benediction***.

ben.e.fac.tor /£ ˈben.ɪ.fæk.təʳ, $ -t̬ɚ/ *n.* donor patron

Scrooge later became Tiny Tim's ***benefactor***. آدم نیکوکار، خیّر؛ ولی نعمت

ben.e.fac.tress: *n.* زن نیکوکار و خیّر

ben.e.fi.cia.ry /£ ˌben.ɪˈfɪʃ.ªr.i, $ -i.er.i/ *n.* one who receives a gift or advantage

وارث؛ ذی‌نفع

Her husband was the chief ***beneficiary*** of her will.

be.nev.o.lent /bɪˈnev.ªl.ªnt/ *adj.* generous, charitable

خیرخواهانه؛ مهربان؛ نیکوکار، خیرخواه

His ***benevolent*** nature prevented him from refusing any beggar who accosted him.

be.nev.o.lence: *n.* نیکوکاری، احسان؛ نیکی؛ خیرخواهی

be.night.ed /£ bɪˈnaɪ.tɪd, $ -t̬ɪd/ *adj.* overcome by darkness, without knowledge or moral

جاهل، ناآگاه، در جهل فرو رفته

In the ***benighted*** Middle Ages, intellectual curiosity was discouraged by the authorities.

be.nign /bɪˈnaɪn/ *adj.* kindly, favorable, not malignant

مهربان، رئوف؛ ملایم، معتدل؛ (بیماری) بی‌خطر

Martha is a ***benign*** old lady who wouldn't hurt a fly.

be.nign.i.ty: *n.* عطوفت، مهربانی

ben.i.son /ˈbenɪzªn/ *n.* blessing

برکت، لطف الهی، سعادت

Let us pray that the ***benison*** of peace once more shall prevail among the nations.

be.rate /bɪˈreɪt/ *v.* to scold strongly

سرزنش کردن، پرخاش کردن

His mother *berated* him for making a mess.

be.reave.ment /bɪˈriːv.mənt/ *n.* state of loss by death of a friend or a relative

مصیبت، داغ، داغدیدگی

Parents who have lost a child often never get over their *bereavement*.

suffer a bereavement: *v.*   عزادار بودن
be.reaved: *adj.*   عزادار، داغدار

be.reft /bɪˈreft/ *adj.* feeling great loss, lacking

فاقدِ، محروم (از)، عاری، بی‌بهره

The foolish gambler soon found himself *bereft* of funds.

ber.serk /£ bəˈzɜːk, $ -ˈzɜːrk/ *adj.* frenzied

عصبانی، کفری، از کوره در رفته

Angered, he went *berserk* and began to wreck the room.

be.smirch /£ bɪˈsmɜːtʃ, $ -ˈsmɜːrtʃ/ *v.* to soil, to defile

هتک حرمت کردن، آبروی کسی را بردن، بدنام کردن

His jealous brother *besmirched* him in front of a large group of his colleagues.

bes.ti.al /ˈbes.ti.əl/ *adj.* beastlike, brutal

جانوری، حیوانی؛ غیرانسانی، سبعانه، وحشیانه

We must suppress our *bestial* desires and work for peaceful ends.

be.stow /£ bɪˈstəʊ, $ -ˈstoʊ/ *v.* to confer, to give sth as an honor or gift

اعطا کردن، ارزانی داشتن

The chancellorship of the University was *bestowed upon* him in 1995.

be.stow.al: *n.* اعطا، بخشش

be.troth /£ bɪˈtrəʊð, $ -ˈtroʊð/ *v.* to become engaged to marry

نامزد کردن

She was ***betrothed*** to her cousin at an early age.

be.troth.al: *n.* نامزدی

bev.y /ˈbev.i/ *n.* large group

گروه، دسته، فوج

The movie actor was surrounded by a ***bevy*** of starlets.

bib.u.lous /ˈbɪbjʊləs/ *adj.* inclined to drink, affected by alcohol

الکلی، دائم‌الخمر، توأم با مستی

We could not help laughing at his ***bibulous*** farewells.

bi.cam.e.ral /£ ˌbaɪˈkæm.ər.əl, $ -ɚ.əl/ *adj.* two-chambered

دارای دو مجلس، دو مجلسی

The United States Congress is a ***bicameral*** body.

bick.er /£ ˈbɪk.ər, $ -ɚ/ *v.* to quarrel

دعوا مرافعه کردن، یکی به دو کردن

Will you stop ***bickering***!

bick.er.ing: *n.* کلنجار، دعوا مرافعه

bi.en.ni.al /baɪˈen.i.əl/ *adj., n.* every two years; a plant that lives for two years

دو ساله، هر دو سال یکبار؛ گیاه دو ساله

The plant bore ***biennial*** flowers.

bi.fur.cate /£ ˈbaɪ.fə.keɪt. $ -fɚ-/ *v.* to divide into 2 parts

(جاده، رودخانه) دوشاخه شدن؛ (مسئولیت) تقسیم شدن

1) The sample of water was taken from the point where the river ***bifurcates***.

2) The responsibility was ***bifurcated*** between two ministries.

big.ot.ry /ˈbɪg.ə.tri/ *n.* stubborn intolerance

تعصّب، تحجّر، خشک مغزی

Commentators believe there's no other reason for the killings than a wave of ***bigotry*** and hatred.

bi.got.ed: *adj.* متعصب، متحجر

bi.li.ous /ˈbɪl.i.əs/ *adj.* affected by bile, irritable

دچار صفرا، مبتلا به صفرا؛ کج خلق، بداخلاق؛ مهوع

His ***bilious*** mood was apparent to all who heard him rant about his difficulties.

bile: *n.* صفرا؛ کج خلقی

bilk /bɪlk/ *v.* to swindle, to cheat

کلاه (سر کسی) گذاشتن، (پول کسی را) بالاکشیدن

The man specialized in ***bilking*** insurance companies.

bi.vou.ac /ˈbɪv.u.æk/ *n.* temporary shelter

اردوگاه، پناهگاه

The climbers made a ***bivouac*** and settled down for the night.

bi.zarre /£ bɪˈzɑː^r, $ -ˈzɑːr/ *adj.* strange and unusual

عجیب و غریب، باور نکردنی

The plot of the novel was too ***bizarre*** to be believed.

blanch /£ blɑːn*tʃ*, $ blæn*tʃ*/ *v.* to whiten, to bleach

سفید کردن/ شدن؛ رنگ پریدن، رنگ باختن

Although age had ***blanched*** his hair, he was still vigorous and energetic.

bland /blænd/ *adj.* soothing, mild; without taste

(دارو) ملایم؛ (غذا) بی‌مزه؛ بی‌روح، خسته کننده
1) She used a *bland* ointment for her sunburn.
2) I find chicken a little *bland* unless it's cooked in a really spicy sauce.

blan.dish.ments /ˈblæn.dɪʃ.mənts/ *n.* flattery, pleasant words

زبان‌بازی، چرب زبانی

The couple resisted the media's *blandishments* to reveal their wedding date.

blasé /ˌblɑːˈzeɪ/ *adj.* bored or not excited

سیر، دلزده، زده؛ بی‌تفاوت، بی‌اعتنا

He flies first class so often he's become *blasé* about it.

blas.phem.ous /ˈblæs.fɪ.məs/ *adj.* profane, impious

کفرآمیز

The people in the room were shocked by his *blasphemous* language.

blas.phe.my: *n.* کفر؛ توهین به مقدسات

bla.tant /£ ˈbleɪ.tənt, $ -tənt/ *adj.* loudly offensive

بی‌شرمانه، وقیحانه، دریده

I regard your remarks as *blatant* and ill-mannered.

bla.tan.cy: *n.* وقاحت، گستاخی

bla.zon /ˈbleɪ.zən/ *v.* to decorate with a coat of arms

نقش انداختن، نگاشتن

Blazoned on his shield were the two lambs and the lion.

bla.zon.ed: *adj.* نقش بسته، نگاشته

bleak /bliːk/ *adj.* cold, cheerless

سرد؛ تیره و تار، یأس‌آور؛ افسرده؛ لخت، بی‌حفاظ

The house stands on a *bleak*, windswept moor.

blight.ed /blaɪtəd/ *adj.* suffering from a disease

آفت‌زده، صدمه دیده، آسیب دیده

The extent of the ***blighted*** areas could be seen only when viewed from the air.

blight: *v.* آفت زدن، صدمه زدن، آسیب رساندن

cast a blight on sth ضایع کردن، خراب کردن

His arrival *cast a blight on* the wedding day.

blithe /ˈblaɪð/ *adj.* gay, joyous, without worry

شاد، خوش، بی‌غم، بی‌خیال، آسوده خاطر

Shelley called the skylark a "***blithe*** spirit" because of his happy song.

bloat.ed /£ ˈbləʊ.tɪd, $ ˈbloʊ.t̬ɪd/ *adj.* swollen or puffed as with water or air

باد کرده، پف کرده، ورم کرده

The ***bloated*** corpse was taken from the river.

bloat: *v.* باد کردن، پف کردن

blud.geon /ˈblʌdʒ.ən/ *n.* club, heavy-headed weapon

چماق

His walking stick served him as a ***bludgeon*** on many occasions.

blud.geon: *v.* با چماق زدن، کتک زدن

The two boys had been mercilessly ***bludgeoned*** to death.

blun.der /£ ˈblʌn.dəʳ, $ -dɚ/ *n.* error

اشتباه فاحش، گاف

The criminal's fatal ***blunder*** led to his capture.

blun.der: *v.* دسته گل به آب دادن، گاف کردن

blurt /£ blɜːt, $ blɜːrt/ *v.* to say sth. impulsively

بند را آب دادن، از دهان (کسی) پریدن

Before she could stop him, he ***blurted out*** the news.

bode /£ bəʊd, $ boʊd/ *v.* to foreshadow, to portend

نشان (چیزی) بودن، خبر دادن از

It's not clear what these changes will ***bode*** for people.

bo.gus /£ ˈbəʊ.ɡəs, $ ˈboʊ-/ *adj.* not authentic, counterfeit

جعلی، قلابی؛ کاذب

The police found the distributors of the ***bogus*** twenty-dollar bills.

boi.ster.ous /£ ˈbɔɪ.stᵊr.əs, $ -stɚ-/ *adj.* violent, rough, noisy

شلوغ، متلاطم، ناآرام

The crowd became more ***boisterous*** when he tried to quiet them.

bol.ster /£ ˈbəʊl.stəʳ, $ ˈboʊl.stɚ/ *v.* to support, to prop up; to make stronger

پشت گرمی دادن؛ تقویت کردن

1) Everyone needs to be ***bolstered*** up once in a while.
2) They had to ***bolster*** the roof.

bol.ster: *n.*   پشت گرمی، حمایت؛ متکّا

bom.bast.ic /£ bɒmˈbæs.tɪk, $ bɑːm-/ *adj.* pompous, using inflated language

پرآب و تاب، پرطمطراق

The orator spoke in a ***bombastic*** manner.

bom.bast: *n.*   لاف و گزاف، گنده‌گویی، لاف‌زنی

boor.ish /£ ˈbʊəʳ.ɪʃ, $ ˈbɔː.rɪʃ/ *adj.* rude, clownish

بی‌شعور، بی‌نزاکت، دلقک مآبانه

I found him rather ***boorish*** and aggressive.

boor: *n.* آدم بی‌نزاکت

boun.ti.ful /£ ˈbaʊn.tɪ.fᵊl, $ -tɪ-/ *adj.* generous, showing bounty

سخاوتمندانه، بخشنده؛ سرشار، فراوان

She distributed gifts in a ***bountiful*** and gracious manner.

boun.ty: *n.* بخشش، سخاوت، کرم

bourge.ois /£ ˈbɔː.ʒ.wɑː, $ ˈbʊrʒ-/ *n., adj.* middle class

بورژوا، سرمایه‌دار

The French Revolution was inspired by the ***bourgeois***.

bowd.ler.ize /ˈbaʊd.lə.raɪz/ *v.* to expurgate

(کتاب، نمایش‌نامه و غیره) سانسور کردن، هرزه‌زدایی کردن

The film editors had to ***bowlderize*** the language in the script.

brack.ish /ˈbræk.ɪʃ/ *adj.* slightly salty, somewhat saline

(آب) شور، شور مزه

All they had to drink was ***brackish*** water.

brag.ga.do.ci.o /ˈbræɡədʌʃuː/ *n.* boasting

لاف‌زنی، رجزخوانی

He was disliked because his manner was always full of ***braggadocio***.

bra.va.do /£ brəˈvɑː.dəʊ, $ -doʊ/ *n.* swagger

تظاهر به شجاعت؛ کله‌خری، بی‌پروایی

It was an act of ***bravado*** that made him ask his boss to resign.

bra.zen /ˈbreɪ.zᵊn/ *adj.* clear and obvious, insolent

بی‌شرمانه، وقیحانه؛ وقیح، بی‌حیا

Her ***brazen*** contempt for authority angered the officials.

bra.zen: *v.* پررویی کردن

breach /ˈbriːtʃ/ *n.* breaking of contract or duty; gap

نقض؛ اختلاف؛ شکاف، رخنه

His refusal to work on a Sunday was a ***breach*** of contract.

breach of promise   نقض عهد، پیمان شکنی، خلف وعده

breadth /bredθ, bretθ/ *n.* width; extent

گستره، پهنه؛ وسعت، دامنه

We were impressed by the ***breadth*** of her knowledge.

bre.vi.ar.y /ˈbriː.vɪərɪ/ *n.* book containing the daily prayers

کتاب دعا

The religious sect demanded daily recitals of the ***braviary***.

brev.i.ty /£ ˈbrev.ɪ.tɪ, $ -ə.t̬i/ *n.* conciseness, shortness

اختصار، ایجاز، کوتاهی

The later essays were written with admirable clarity and ***brevity***.

brin.dled /ˈbrɪndᵊld/ *adj.* tawny with spots or streaks

قهوه‌ای خال دار، قهوه‌ای راه راه

He was disappointed in the litter because the puppies were ***brindled*** ; he had hoped for animals of a uniform color.

bris.tl.ing /ˈbrɪs.lɪŋ/ *adj.* rising like bristles; showing irritation

دارای موهای سیخ سیخی؛ عصبانی

The dog stood there, ***bristling with*** anger.

brist.le: *n., v.*   موی زبر؛ (مو) سیخ شدن

broach /£ brəʊtʃ, $ broʊtʃ/ *v.* to open up

مطرح کردن، عنوان کردن

He did not even try to *broach* the subject of poetry.

bro.cade /brəˈkeɪd/ *n.* rich and figured fabric

پارچهٔ گلدوزی شده، زربفت

The sofa was covered with expensive *brocade*.

bro.chure /£ ˈbrəʊ.ʃeʳ, $ broʊˈʃʊr/ *n.* pamphlet

دفترچهٔ راهنما، بروشور

This *brochure* on farming was issued by the Department of Agriculture.

brooch /£ brəʊʃ, $ broʊtʃ/ *n.* ornamental clasp

گل سینه، سنجاق سینه

She treasured the *brooch* because it was an heirloom.

brusque /£ bruːsk, $ brʌsk/ *adj.* blunt, abrupt

عجولانه، سرسری، شتاب‌زده

He was offended by her *brusque* reply.

bu.col.ic /£ bjuːˈkɒl.ɪk, $ -ˈkɑːlɪk/ *adj.* rustic, pastoral

روستایی، محلی؛ چوپانی، شبانی

The painting shows a typically *bucolic* scene with peasants harvesting.

buf.foon.e.ry /£ bəˈfuːnᵊr.i, $ -nɚ-/ *n.* clowning

مسخره‌بازی، مسخرگی، دلقک‌بازی

Enough of *buffoonery* — everybody back to work!

bug.a.boo /ˈbʌgˈəbuː/ *n.* bugbear

مترسک، لولو

If we become frightened by such *bugaboo*, we are no wiser than the birds who fear scarecrows.

bul.li.on /ˈbʊl.i.ən/ *n.* gold or silver in the form of bars

شمش

Much ***bullion*** is stored in the vaults at Fort Knox.

bul.wark /£ ˈbʊl.wək, $ -wɚk/ *n.* fortification, any means of defence or security

حفاظ، حصار؛ محافظ

The navy is our principal ***bulwark*** against invasion.

bump.tious /ˈbʌmp.ʃəs/ *adj.* self-assertive

خودخواه، متکبّر، از خود راضی

His classmates called him a show-off because of his ***bumptious*** airs.

bun.gle /ˈbʌŋ.gl/ *v.* to do sth badly or unsuccessfully

ضایع کردن، خراب کاری کردن، سرهم‌بندی کردن

The attempted robbery was badly ***bungled*** and a guard was shot.

bu.reau.cra.cy /£ bjʊəˈrɒk.rə.si, $ bjʊˈrɑː.krə-/ *n.* government by bureaus

دیوان سالاری، کاغذبازی؛ تشریفات اداری

It is difficult for outsiders to understand the ***bureaucracy*** of the country.

bur.geon /£ ˈbɜː.dʒən, $ ˈbɜːr-/ *v.* to grow forth

روییدن، شکفتن، شکوفا شدن

In the spring, the plants that ***burgeon*** are a promise of the beauty that is to come.

bur.lesque /£ ˈbɜːˈlesk, $ bɜːr-/ *v.* to give an imitation that rediculously

ادای (کسی با چیزی را) در آوردن، مسخره کردن

In his caricature, he ***burlesqued*** the mannerisms of his adversary.

bur.lesque: *n.* نمایش مسخره، واریته

burl.y /£ ˈbɜː.li, $ ˈbɜːr-/ *adj.* husky, muscular

(هیکل) درشت، قوی هیکل، تنومند

He looked up and saw a ***burly*** policeman approaching him.

burn.ish /£ ˈbɜː.nɪʃ, $ ˈbɜːr-/ *v.*, *n.* to polish

صیقل دادن، جلا دادن، برق انداختن؛ جلا، برق، درخشندگی

The ***burnished*** metal reflected the lamplight.

but.tress /ˈbʌt.rəs/ *n.* support or prop

پشتبند، شمع

The huge cathedral walls were supported by flying ***buttress***.

but.tress: *v.* شمع زدن، تقویت کردن، مستحکم کردن

bux.om /ˈbʌk.səm/ *adj.* plump, vigorous, jolly

تپل، خپل

He fell in love with a ***buxom*** hairdresser.

لیستی از لغاتی که در جملات بخش B به کار رفته‌اند:

accost: *v.*	سر راه کسی سبز شدن	gaudy: *adj.*	رنگ وارنگ
adversary: *n.*	رقیب، حریف	get over: *v.*	فائق آمدن
airs: *n.*	افاده، پُز	grab bag: *n.*	کیسهٔ شانس
alienate: *v.*	از خود فراری دادن	gracious: *adj.*	بزرگوارانه، از سر لطف
attempt: *n.*	تلاش		
attempted: *adj.*	نافرجام	hatred: *n.*	تنفر، نفرت
authorities: *n.*	مسئولین	heirloom: *n.*	ارثیهٔ خانوادگی
bill: *n.*	اسکناس	ill-mannered: *adj.*	بی‌ادب، بی‌نزاکت
cannon: *n.*	توپ		
cathedral: *n.*	کلیسای جامع	impulsively: *adv.*	بی‌اختیار
clarinet: *n.*	قره‌نی	indescribable: *adj.*	وصف‌ناپذیر
cliché: *n.*	کلیشه، تکرار مکررات	inspire: *v.*	الهام بخشیدن
coat of arms	نشان، آرم	lamplight: *n.*	نور چراغ
colleague: *n.*	همکار	lead (to): *v.*	منجر شدن (به)
company	(ارتش) گروهان	list: *v.*	کج شدن کشتی
condolence: *n.*	تسلیت	litter: *n.*	توله (حیوانات)
contempt: *n.*	بی‌حرمتی، توهین	make a mess: *v.*	به‌هم زدن
disposition: *n.*	خلق و خوی	mannerism: *n.*	اخلاق، ادا و اصول
drought: *n.*	خشکسالی، قحطی		
farewell: *n.*	خداحافظی	media: *n.*	رسانه‌های گروهی
favored: *adj.*	نور چشمی	moor: *n.*	بوته‌زار
fly: *n.*	مگس	mystic: *n.*	عارف، صوفی
fly: *v.*	سوار (هواپیما) شدن	nickname: *v.*	لقب دادن
flying: *adj.*	(معماری) معلق، شمشیری	oboe: *n.*	اُبوا (ساز بادی)
		obscene: *adj.*	زننده، مبتذل
fur: *n.*	پوست، خز	offend: *v.*	آزردن

officials: *n.*	مسئولین	scarecrow: *n.*	مترسک
ointment: *n.*	پماد، مرهم	script: *n.*	متن
omen: *n.*	شگون، یمن	shield: *n.*	سپر
trinkets: *n.*	زیورآلات ارزان / بدلی	shift: *v.*	جابجا کردن
vault: *n.*	گاو صندوق	show-off: *n.*	آدم چاخان، خودنما
vigorous: *adj.*	پرشور، پرحرارت		
windswept: *adj.*	بادخور	solitaire: *n.*	بازی یک نفره
witch doctor: *n.*	جادو پزشک، جادوگر شفابخش	spicy: *adj.*	تند، ادویه‌دار
		sportscaster: *n.*	گزارشگر ورزشی
witty: *adj.*	بامزه، شوخ	stability: *n.*	ثبات
wreck: *v.*	برهم زدن، خراب کردن	starlet: *n.*	نوستاره
opponent: *n.*	مخالف، رقیب	starving: *adj.*	گرسنه
orgy: *n.*	میگساری	state: *n.*	وضع، حالت
outsider: *n.*	خارجی، بیگانه	store: *v.*	انبار کردن
peasant: *n.*	روستایی	streak: *n.*	خط، رگه
promise: *n.*	نوید	subdued: *adj.*	آرام، ملایم
puppy: *n.*	توله سگ	suppress: *v.*	سرکوب کردن، فرو نشاندن
quiet: *v.*	آرام کردن		
rant: *v.*	با احساس بیان کردن	toil: *v.*	زحمت کشیدن، جان کندن
recital: *n.*	از برخوانی	treasure: *v.*	عزیز داشتن
resign: *v.*	استعفا دادن		

C c

ca.bal /£ kəˈbæl, -ˈbɑːl/ *n.* a small group of conspirators

گروه توطئه‌گر

He was assassinated by a *cabal* of aides within his own regime.

ca.bal: *v.* توطئه کردن

cache /kæʃ/ *n.* hiding place

مخفی‌گاه، انبار موقت (اسلحه و غیره)

The detectives followed the suspect until he led them to the *cache* of explosives.

cache: *v.* انبار کردن، مخفی کردن

ca.coph.on.y /£ kəˈkɒf.ə.ni, $ -ˈkɑː.fə-/ *n.* discord, harsh noise

تنافر آوایی؛ سر و صدا، هیاهو

As we entered the farmyard we were met with a *cacophony* of animal sounds.

ca.dav.er /£ kəˈdæv.əʳ, $ -ɚ/ *n.* corpse, dead body

جسد

In some states, it is illegal to dissect *cadavers*.

ca.dav.er.ous: *adj.* رنگ پریده، رنجور، نزار

cadaverous appearance ظاهری رنجور

ca.jole /£ kəˈdʒəʊl, $ -ˈdʒoʊl/ *v.* to persuade, to coax, to wheedle

با چرب‌زبانی (کسی را) به کاری واداشتن

He realy knows how to *cajole* people into doing what he wants.

ca.jole.ry: *n.*   چرب‌زبانی، زبان‌بازی، تملق‌گویی

ca.lam.i.ty /£ kə'læm.ɪ.ti, $ -ə.t̬i/ *n.* disaster

مصیبت، بلا، فاجعه

A series of *calamities* ruined them.

ca.lam.i.tous: *adj.*   مصیبت‌بار، فجیع

cal.i.ber /£ 'kæl.ɪ.bəʳ, $ -bɚ/ *n.* ability, capacity

استعداد، توانایی، قابلیت

A man of such *caliber* should not be assigned such menial tasks.

cal.li.graph.y /kə'lɪg.rə.fi/ *n.* beautiful writing

خوشنویسی، خطاطی

There is some wonderful *calligraphy* in these old manuscripts.

cal.lous /'kæl.əs/ *adj.* unfeeling, unkind, hardened

بی‌عاطفه، سنگدل، بی‌رحم

He was *callous* to the suffering of the patients.

cal.low /£ 'kæl.əʊ, $ -oʊ/ *adj.* inexperienced, youthful

چشم و گوش بسته، خام، بی‌تجربه

Mark was just a *callow* youth of 16 when he arrived in Paris.

cal.or.if.ic /ˌkæl.ə'rɪf.ɪk/ *adj.* heat producing

گرمازا، حرارت‌زا، انرژی‌زا

Fatty foods have a high *calorific* value.

cal.um.ni.ate /kəˈlʌmnɪeɪt/ *v.* to slander

افترا زدن، تهمت زدن

Shakespeare wrote that love and friendship were subject to envious and *calumniating* time.

cal.um.ny /ˈkæl.əm.ni/ *n.* false and malicious charge

افترا، بهتان، تهمت

He could bear the failure, but he could not bear the *calumny*.

cam.e.o /£ ˈkæm.i.əʊ, $ -oʊ/ *n.* shell or jewel carved in relief

نگین نقش برجسته

Tourists are advised not to purchase *cameos* from the street peddlers of Rome.

ca.nard /£ ˈkæn.ɑːd, $ kəˈnɑːrd/ *n.* false report, rumor

شایعه، افسانه، تصور باطل

It is almost impossible to protect oneself from such a base *canard*.

can.dor /£ ˈkæn.dəʳ, $ -dɚ/ *n.* frankness

صراحت، رک‌گویی

The *candor* and simplicity of his speech impressed all.

can.did: *adj.* رک و راست، صاف و پوست کنده

ca.nine /ˈkeɪ.naɪn/ *adj.* related to dogs, doglike

(مربوط به) سگ

She is a specialist in *canine* psychology and behavior.

can.ker /£ ˈkæŋ.kəʳ, $ -kɚ/ *n.* mouth and ears ulcer; evil

(دهان و گوش) زخم؛ آفت، بلای عمومی

Poverty is a *canker* eating away at the heart of society.

can.ny /ˈkæn.i/ *adj.* shrewd, thrifty

زبل، زیرک؛ حسابگر، مقتصد

These salesmen are a *canny* lot.

cant /kænt/ *n.* jargon of thieves; pious phraseology

زبان حرفه‌ای، زبان خاص؛ زهد فروشی، تزویر، ریا

Many listeners were fooled by the *cant* and hypocrisy of his speech.

cant: *v.* ریاکارانه صحبت کردن

can.tan.ker.ous /£ ˌkæn'tæŋ.kᵊr.əs, $ -kɚ-/ *adj.* ill humored, hard to deal with

تندخو، بدخلق، پرخاشگر

He never stopped complaining; he was a *cantankerous* patient.

can.ta.ta /£ kæn'tɑː.tə, $ kən'tɑː.t̬ə/ *n.* choral work, a short musical work

کانتات (= قطعه‌ای موسیقی آوازی)

The choral society sang the new *cantata* composed by its leader.

can.ter /£ 'kæn.təʳ, $ -tɚ/ *n.* slow gallop

(اسب) چهار نعل کوتاه

I went for a *canter* across the fields.

can.ter: *v.* تاختن، تاخت رفتن

can.to /'kæntəʊ/ *n.* major division of a long poem

(شعر) بند

He was upset when he read one of Sir Walter Scott's *cantos*.

can.vass /'kæn.vəs/ *v., n.* to obtain support, to ask

تبلیغ کردن، نظرخواهی کردن؛ تبلیغ انتخاباتی

I've been out *canvassing* for the Labour Party every evening this week.

ca.pa.cious /kəˈpeɪ.ʃəs/ *adj.* spacious, roomy

جادار، بزرگ

In the *capacious* areas of the terminal, people lingered while waiting for the train.

ca.par.i.son /kəˈpærɪsən/ *n.* showy harness or ornamentation

شنل اسب، دهنهٔ پر زرق و برق

The audience admired the *caparison* of the horse as they made their entrance into the circus ring.

ca.pil.la.ry /£ kəˈpɪl.ər.i, $ ˈ-ə-/ *adj.* having a very fine bore

مویی، موئین

The changes in surface tension of liquids in *capillary* vessels is of special interest to physicists.

ca.pil.la.ry: *n.*

مویرگ

ca.pi.tu.late /kəˈpɪt.jʊ.leɪt/ *v.* to surrender, to accept defeat

تسلیم شدن

The enemy was warned to *capitulate* or face annihilation.

ca.price /kəˈpriːs/ *n.* whim

بوالهوسی؛ هوس

Do not act on *caprice*. Study your problem.

ca.pri.cious /kəˈprɪʃ.əs/ *adj.* fickle, incalculable

متغیّر، ناپایدار، دمدمی، متلون

The storm was *capricious* and changed course constantly.

cap.tion /ˈkæp.ʃən/ *n.* title; text under illustration

عنوان، سرفصل؛ شرح، زیرنویس

I find the *caption* which accompany these cartoons very humorous.

cap.tion: *v.* (زیرعکس و غیره) شرح نوشتن

cap.tious /ˈkæp.ʃəs/ *adj.* faultfinding

عیبجویانه، ایرادگیری

His criticisms were always *captious*, never offering constructive suggestions.

ca.rafe /ˈkær.əf, kəˈræf/ *n.* glass water bottle, decanter

تُنگ، صراحی

Shall we order another *carafe* of red wine?

car.at /£ ˈkær.ət, $ ˈker-/ *n.* unit of weight for precious stones

قیراط (= ۲/۰ گرم)؛ عیار

He gave her a three-*carat* diamond mounted in an 18 *carat* gold band.

car.cin.o.gen.ic /£ ˌkɑː.sᵊn.əʊˈdʒen.ɪk, $ ˌkɑːr.sᵊn.oʊ-/ *adj.* causing cancer

سرطان‌زا

Many supposedly harmless substances have been revealed to be *carcinogenic*.

car.di.nal /£ ˈkɑː.dɪ.nəl, $ ˈkɑːr-/ *adj.* chief, main

اصلی، عمده، اساسی، مهم

The *cardinal* rule of vocabulary-building is to read.

ca.reen /kəˈriːn/ *v.* to sway from side to side, to lurch

(وسیله نقلیه) کج شدن، یک وری شدن

The taxicab *careened* wildly as it rounded the corner.

car.i.ca.ture /£ ˈkær.ɪ.kə.tʃʊəʳ, $ ˈker.ɪ.kə.tʃʊr/ *n.* distortion, burlesque

There was a wonderful *caricature* of the prime minister in the newspaper.

   car.i.ca.ture: *v.*   کاریکاتور کشیدن از

car.mine /£ ˈkɑː.maɪn, $ ˈkɑːr-/ *n.* rich red

قرمز تند، قرمز جگری

He found himself in a room full of *carmine*-nailed women.

car.nage /£ ˈkɑː.nɪdʒ, $ ˈkɑːr-/ *n.* slaughter, violent killing

قتل عام، کشت و کشتار

The battle was a scene of dreadful *carnage*.

car.nal /£ ˈkɑː.nəl, $ ˈkɑːr-/ *adj.* fleshly, sexual

نفسانی، دنیوی، شهوانی، جسمانی، جنسی

The public was more interested in spiritual matters than in *carnal* pleasures.

car.ni.vo.rous /£ kɑːˈnɪv.ᵊr.əs, $ kɑːrˈnɪv.ɚ-/ *adj.* meat-eating

گوشت‌خوار

The lion is a *carnivorous* animal.

   car.ni.vore: *n.*   حیوان گوشت‌خوار

ca.rous.al /£ ˌkær.ʊˈsel, $ ˌker.ə-/ *n.* drunken revel

میگساری

The party degenerated into an ugly *carousal*.

   ca.rouse: *v.*   میگساری کردن، مست کردن

carp.ing /£ kɑːpɪŋ, $ kɑːrpɪŋ/ *adj.* finding fault

عیبجو، ایرادگیر

A *carping* critic disturbs sensitive people.

   carp (about): *v.*   ایراد گرفتن، نق زدن

car.ri.on /£ ˈkær.i.ən, $ ˈker-/ *n.* dead or decaying flesh

لاشه، مردار

On the road ahead a crow tugs on some *carrion* and flies up slowly as we approach.

carte blanche /£ ˌkɑːt ˈblɑːʃ, $ ˌkɑːrt ˈblɑːnʃ/ *n.* unlimited authority or freedom

اختیار تام، آزادی کامل

Use your own discretion in this matter; I give you *carte blanche*.

car.to.graph.er /£ kɑːˈtɒg.rə.fəʳ, $ kɑːrˈtɑːgrə.fɚ/ *n.* maker of maps or charts

نقشه‌کش

Cartographers are unable to provide accurate maps of legal boundries in the Near East.

car.y.at.id /kærɪˈætɪd/ *n.* sculptured column of a female figure

(معماری) ستون زنْ پیکر

The *caryatid* supporting the entablature reminded the onlookers of the columns in Acropolis at Athens.

cas.cade /kæsˈkeɪd/ *n.* a small waterfall

آبشار کوچک، آبشاره

A series of *cascades* had been caused by large boulders which had fallen into the stream.

caste /£ kɑːst, $ kæst/ *n.* social class or rank

کاست (طبقه اجتماعی موروثی در هند)، طبقهٔ اجتماعی

He was born into the lowest *caste*.

cas.ti.gate /ˈkæs.tɪ.geɪt/ *v.* to punish, to chastise severely

تنبیه کردن، سرزنش کردن، به باد انتقاد گرفتن

He decided to *castigate* the culprit personally.

cas.ual.ty /'kæʒ.ju.əɪ.ti/ *n.* serious or fatal accident

تصادف، حادثه، سانحه؛ (بهصورت جمع) تلفات، مجروحان و کشته شدگان

1) The number of *casualties* on the holiday weekend was high.

2) The train was derailed but there were no *casualties*.

cas.u.ist.ry /'kæz:ju.ɪ.stri/ *n.* use of clever arguments to trick people

سفسطه، مغلطه

You are using *casuistry* to justify your obvious violation of decent behavior.

cat.a.cly.sm /£ 'kæt.ə.klɪ.zᵊm, $ 'kæt̬-/ *n.* violent change, upheaval, deluge

فاجعه، مصیبت، بلا؛ انقلاب

A *cataclysm* such as the French Revolution affects all countries.

cat.a.clysm.ic: *adj.*   فاجعهآمیز، مصیبتبار

ca.ta.lyst /£ 'kæt.ᵊl.ɪst, $ 'kæt̬-/ *n.* substance which brings about a chemical change

کاتالیزور، عامل شتاب دهنده

Many chemical reactions cannot take place without the presence of a *catalyst*.

cat.a.pult /£ 'kæt.ə.pʌlt, $ 'kæt̬-/ *n.* slingshot, a launching machine

تیرکمان؛ منجنیق؛ (ناو هواپیمابر) پرتاب کننده

On that type of aircraft carrier, a *catapult* was used to

help launch aircraft.

cat.a.pult: *v.* پرتاب کردن؛ با تیر کمان زدن

cat.a.ract /£ ˈkæt.ə.rækt, $ ˈkæt̬-/ *n.* great waterfall; eye abnormality

آبشار بزرگ؛ آب مروارید

She gazed with awe at the mighty *cataract* known as Niagara Falls.

ca.tas.tro.phe /kəˈtæs.trə.fi/ *n.* calamity, great disaster

فاجعه، مصیبت، بلا، سانحه

1) The Johnstown flood was a *catastrophe*.
2) The emigration of scientists is a *catastrophe* for the country.

cat.e.chi.sm /£ ˈkæt.ə.kɪ.zᵊm, $ ˈkæt̬-/ *n.* teaching in form of question and answer

آموزش از طریق پرسش و پاسخ؛ (مسیحیت) اصول دین

He taught by engaging his students in a *catechism* until they gave him the correct answer.

ca.thar.sis /£ kəˈθɑː.sɪs, $ -ˈθɑːr-/ *n.* purging, cleansing

پالایش، تخلیهٔ هیجانی

Aristotle maintained that tragedy created a *catharsis* by purging the soul of base concepts.

ca.thar.tic: *adj.* پالایشی، مربوط به تخلیهٔ هیجانی

ca.thar.tic /£ kəˈθɑː.tɪk, $ -ˈθɑːr.t̬ɪk/ *n.* purgative

مسهل

Some drugs act as *cathartic* when taken in much larger doses.

cath.o.lic /ˈkæθ.ᵊl.ɪk/ *adj.* broadly sympothetic; liberal

متنوع، گوناگون؛ آزادمنش؛ جامع، همگانی

As a young person he had more *catholic* tastes than he does now.

cau.cus /£ ˈkɔː.kəs, $ ˈkɑː-/ *n.* political meeting

جلسه سیاسی (سران حزب با سازمان)

They held a *caucus* to decide which candidate they will support.

cau.stic /£ ˈkɔː.stɪk, $ ˈkɑː-/ *adj.* sharp or biting, corrosive

نیشدار، گزنده؛ سوزان، سوزآور

She is famous in the office for her *caustic* humour.

cau.ter.ize /£ ˈkɔːtᵊr.aɪz, $ ˈkɑː.t̬ɚ-/ *v.* to burn (an injury) to stop bleeding

سوزاندن (محل زخم را)

In order to prevent infection, the doctor *cauterized* the wound.

cav.al.cade /ˌkæv.ᵊlˈkeɪd/ *n.* parade; procession

صف سواران؛ مراسم؛ وقایع مهم

As described by Chaucer, the *cavalcade* by Canterbury pilgrims was a motley group.

cav.il /ˈkæv.ᵊl/ *v.* to make trivial objections

غرولند کردن؛ ایراد گرفتن، خرده گرفتن، عیب‌جویی کردن

They *cavilled* at the price.

cav.il.er: *n.*   خرده‌گیر، ایرادگیر، عیب‌جو

cav.il: *n.*   ایراد، عیب‌جویی، عیب‌جویی

cede /siːd/ *v.* to transfer, to yield title to

واگذار کردن

I intend to *cede* this property to the city.

ce.ler.i.ty /£ səˈler.ɪ.ti, $ -t̬i-/ *n.* speed, rapidity

عجله، شتاب

Hamlet resented his mother's *celerity* in remarrying within a month after his father's death.

ce.les.ti.al /£ sɪˈles.ti.ᵊl, $ -tʃᵊl/ *adj.* heavenly

آسمانی، سماوی؛ ملکوتی

He wrote about the music of " *celestial* spheres".

cel.i.bate /ˈsel.ɪ.bət/ *adj.* unmarried

مجرد، بی‌همسر

He vowed to remain *celibate*.

cel.i.ba.cy: *n.*   تجرد، بی‌همسری

cen.sor /£ ˈsent.sər, $ -sɚ/ *n.* a person whose job is to read books, films, etc. in order to remove anything offensive from them

مأمور سانسور، سانسورچی

The film will never get past the *censor*.

cen.sor.ious /senˈsɔː.rɪəs/ *adj.* critical

عیب‌جو، خرده‌گیر

Censorious people delight in casting blame.

cen.sure /£ ˈsen.ʃər, $ -ʃɚ/ *v., n.* to blame, to criticize

سرزنش کردن، نکوهش کردن؛ نکوهش، بازخواست؛ سرزنش

The directors were *censured* for their lack of decisiveness during the crisis.

cen.taur /£ ˈsen.tɔːr, $ -tɔːr/ *n.* mythical figure, half man and half horse

قنطورس (موجود اساطیری: نیمه مرد و نیمه اسب)

I was particularly impressed by the statue of the *centaur*

in the Roman Hall.

cen.tri.fu.gal /ˌsen.trɪˈfjuːgᵊl/ *adj.* departing from the center

گریز از مرکز، مرکز گریز (مربوط به)

Many automatic drying machines remove moisture from clothing by *centrifugal* force.

cen.tri.pe.tal /£ ˌsen.trɪˈpiːtᵊl, $ -tᵊl/ *adj.* tending toward the center

مرکزگرا؛ مرکز گرایانه

Does *centripetal* force or the force of gravity bring orbiting bodies to the earth's surface?

cen.tu.ri.on /£ senˈtjʊə.ri.ən, $ -ˈtʊ.i-/ *n.* Roman army officer

فرمانده یک دسته صد نفری در ارتش روم باستان

He was called a *centurion* because he was in command of a company of 100 soldiers.

cer.eb.ral /ˈser.ɪ.brᵊl/ *adj.* relating to the brain or intellect

مغزی، فکری؛ (مربوط به) مخ؛ متفکرانه

The content of philosophical works is *cerebral* in nature and requires much thought.

cer.e.bra.tion /ˌser.ɪˈbreɪ.ʃᵊn/ *n.* thought

تفکر، تعقل

Mathematic problems sometimes require much *cerebration*.

cer.e.brate: *v.*   تفکر کردن

ces.sa.tion /sesˈeɪ.ʃᵊn/ *n.* ending or stopping

قطع، توقف؛ آتش بس

The workers threatened a *cessation* of all activities if their demands were not met.

cease: *v.* خاتمه دادن، متوقف کردن

ces.sion /seˈseɪʃᵊn/ *n.* yielding to another, ceding

واگذاری، انتقال

The *cession* of Alaska to the United States is discussed in this chapter.

chafe /tʃeɪf/ *v.* to make sore by rubbing; to lose patience

ساییدن، زخم کردن؛ خسته شدن، بی‌تاب شدن

1) The bracelet was so tight that it *chafed* my wrist.
2) Passengers are starting to *chafe* at the delay in their flight.

chafe: *n.* زخم، ساییدگی، رفتگی پوست

chaff /£ tʃɑːf, $ tʃæf/ *n.* something worthless, debris

آشغال؛ کاه، سبوس

Be sure you throw out the *chaff* after threshing the wheat.

chaff.ing /£ tʃɑːfɪŋ, $ tʃæfɪŋ/ *adj.* joking, bantering

شوخی‌آمیز، توأم با مزاح

Sometimes his *chaffing* remarks annoy us.

chag.rin /ˈʃæɡ.rɪn/ *n.* vexation, disappointment

آزردگی، رنجش؛ تأثر، تأسف، یأس

His refusal to go with us filled us with *chagrin*.

chag.rin مأیوس کردن، ناراحت کردن

chal.ice /ˈtʃæl.ɪs/ *n.* goblet, consecrated cup

پیاله، جام شراب مقدس

The most famous goldsmiths made many ornately decorated *chalices*.

cha.me.le.on /kəˈmiː.li.ən/ *n.* lizard that changes color in different situations

آفتاب‌پرست؛ آدم بوقلمون صفت

Like the *chameleon*, he assumed the political thinking of every group he met.

champ /tʃæmp/ *v.* to chew noisily

با ملچ ملوچ خوردن، لُف لُف خوردن

There she sat, happily *champing* her breakfast.

cham.pi.on /ˈtʃæm.pi.ən/ *v.* to support

حمایت کردن، دفاع کردن

Martin Luther King, Jr. *championed* the oppressed in their struggle for equality.

cha.ot.ic /£ keɪˈɒt.ɪk, $ -ˈɑː.t̬ɪk/ *adj.* in utter disorder

آشفته، درهم برهم، بی‌نظم

He tried to bring order into the *chaotic* state of affairs.

cha.os: *n.* آشوب، هرج و مرج، آشفتگی

cha.ri.sma /kəˈrɪz.mə/ *n.* divine gift, special power or charm

جذبهٔ جادویی، قدرت افسونی، جاذبه

He had this great *charisma* so that you couldn't take your eyes off him.

cha.ri.sma.tic: *adj.* دارای جذبهٔ جادویی، جاذبه‌دار

char.la.tan /£ ˈʃɑː.lə.tən, $ ˈʃɑːr.lə.tən/ *n.* imposter, quack

شیّاد، شارلاتان

He was called a *charlatan* by his colleagues.

cha.ry /£ ˈtʃeə.ri, $ ˈtʃer.i/ *adj.* doubtful and uncertain

محتاط؛ مراقب، مواظب

She was *chary about / of* using a travel agency that hasn't got official registration.

cha.sm /ˈkæz.ᵊm/ *n.* abyss, gorge

پرتگاه، دره، مهلکه

They could not see the bottom of the ***chasm***.

chas.sis /ˈʃæs.i/ *n.* supporting structural frame

شاسی (اتومبیل)

The body of the car had been ruined but the ***chassis*** was unharmed.

chaste /tʃeɪst/ *adj.* pure, simple; modest, decent

ساده، بی‌پیرایه؛ عفیف، پاکدامن

1) He likes the simple, ***chaste*** lines of the town's architecture.
2) The author instructs married women to be humble, ***chaste*** and obedient.

chast.i.ty: *n.*   سادگی، عفت، پاکدامنی

chas.tise /tʃæsˈtaɪz/ *v.* to punish; to criticize strongly

تنبیه کردن، کتک زدن؛ سرزنش کردن

I must ***chastise*** you for this offense.

chat.tel /£ ˈtʃæt.ᵊl, $ ˈtʃæt̬-/ *n.* personal property

(در جمع) اموال شخصی، لوازم شخصی؛ اموال منقول

The flood caused famine, the spread of disease and the loss of ***chattels***.

chau.vi.nist /£ ˈʃəʊ.vɪ.nɪst, $ ˈʃoʊ-/ *n.* blindy devoted patriot

میهن‌پرست متعصب، جنسیت‌پرست متعصب

1) She called him a male ***chauvinist*** because of his insistence on calling all women "girls".
2) A ***chauvinist*** cannot recognize any faults in his country.

chau.vi.ni.sm: *n.* ميهن‌پرستى افراطى، (جنسيت، نژاد) تعصب

check.er /£ ˈtʃek.ər, $ -ɚ/ *v.* to mark by changes in fortune

قطع كردن، اثر گذاشتن

His long career was *checkered* by prosperity and failure.

check.er: *n.* فراز و نشيب؛ مأمور كنترل

cher.ub.ic /tʃəˈruː.bɪk/ *adj.* angelic, innocent-looking

فرشته‌سان، فرشته مانند؛ معصومانه

The choirboys' *cherubic* pink faces smiled across the church as they sang.

cher.ub: *n.* فرشته؛ كودك معصوم

chi.can.er.y /£ ʃɪˈkeɪ.nᵊr.i, $ -nɚ-/ *n.* trickery

فريب‌كارى، شيادى

The investigation has revealed political *chicanery* and corruption at the highest level.

chide /tʃaɪd/ *v.* to scold, to speak (to sb) severely

سرزنش كردن، ملامت كردن

She *chided* him for his bad manners.

chi.mer.ic.al /kaɪˈmer.ɪ.kᵊl/ *adj.* fantastic, imaginary

خيالى، دور از واقع، موهوم، واهى

Poe's *chimerical* stories are sometimes too morbid for reading in bed.

chi.me.ra: *n.* خيال خام، آرزوى واهى

chi.ro.man.cy /ˈkaɪrəmænsi/ *n.* palmistry

كف بينى

She claimed to predict the future by means of handwriting analysis and *chiromancy*.

chi.rop.od.ist /£ kɪˈrɒp.ə.dɪst, ʃɪ-, $ -ˈrɑː.pə-/ *n.* one who treats disorders of the feet

متخصص پا

He goes to *chiropodist* to have his ingrown nail treated.

chol.er.ic /£ kɒlˈer.ɪk, $ kəˈler-/ *adj.* hot-tempered, very angry

عصبانی، تندخو، برافروخته، عصبی

His flushed, angry face indicated a *choleric* nature.

cho.re.og.ra.phy /£ ˌkɒr.iˈɒg.rə.fi, $ ˌkɔːr.iˈɑː.grə-/ *n.* art of dancing

هنر رقص، طراحی رقص

His style of *choreography* is flamboyant.

chron.ic /£ ˈkrɒn.ɪk, $ ˈkrɑː.nɪk/ *adj.* continuing for a long time

مزمن، کهنه؛ وخیم؛ جدی؛ سابقه‌دار، کهنه‌کار

She suffers from *chronic* headaches.

churl.ish /£ ˈtʃɜː.lɪʃ, $ ˈtʃɜːr-/ *adj.* rude, boorish

دور از نزاکت، بی‌ادبانه، گستاخانه

I thought it would be *churlish* to refuse their invitation.

cil.i.a.ted /ˈsɪliətəd/ *adj.* having minute hairs

(جانورشناسی) مژه‌دار

The paramecium is a *ciliated*, one-celled animal.

cir.clet /ˈsɪɜːklɪt/ *n.* small ring, band

نیم تاج

This tiny *circlet* is very costly because it is set with precious stones.

cir.cu.it.ous /£ sɜːˈkjuː.ɪ.təs, $ sɜːrˈkjuː.ɪ.təs/ *adj.* roundabout, indirect

پیچ در پیچ، پیچاپیچ

Because of the traffic congestion on the main road, he

took a *circuitous* route.

cir.cum.lo.cu.tion /£ ˌsɜː.kəm.ləˈkjuː.ʃᵊn, $ ˌsɜːr-/ *n.* indirect expression

درازگویی، اِطناب

Politicians are expert in *circumlocution*.

cir.cum.scribe /£ ˈsɜː.kəm.skraɪb, ˌ--ˈ-, $ ˈsɜːr-/ *v.* to limit, to confine

محدود کردن

She didn't wish to *circumscribe* their activities.

cir.cum.spect /£ ˈsɜː.kəm.spekt, $ ˈsɜːr-/ *adj.* cautious, prudent

محتاط، محافظه‌کار

Investigating before acting, he tried always to be *circumspect*.

cir.cum.vent /£ ˌsɜː.kəmˈvent, ˈ---, $ ˌsɜːr-/ *v.* to outwit, to baffle

غلبه کردن بر، کلک زدن به، عاجز کردن

In order to *circumvent* the enemy, we will make two preliminary attacks before starting our major campaign.

ci.ta.del /£ ˈsɪt.ə.del, $ ˈsɪt̬-/ *n.* fortress

دژ، قلعه

The *citadel* overlooked the city like a protecting angel.

cite /saɪt/ *v.* to quote, to commend

نقل کردن، ذکر کردن

He *cited* a passage from the Holy Koran to support his argument.

clair.voy.ant /£ ˌkleəˈvɔɪ.ənt, $ ˌkler-/ *adj.* having foresight

غیب‌گو، غیب‌دان

clam.ber   **95**   **cleave**

She claimed she was ***clairvoyant*** and could communicate with the dead.

clair.voy.ance: *n.*   غیب‌دانی، غیب‌گویی

clam.ber /£ ˈklæm.bəʳ, $ -bɚ/ *v.* to climb by crawling

چهار دست و پا بالا رفتن، خود را بالا کشیدن

They ***clambered*** *over/ up* the rocks.

clan.des.tine /klænˈdes.tɪn/ *adj.* secret

سرّی، مخفی، زیرزمینی، مخفیانه

The group held weekly ***clandestine*** meetings in a church.

clar.i.on /£ ˈklær.i.ən, $ ˈkler-/ *adj.* loud and clear

(صدای) شیپور مانند، بلند و واضح

Has the country responded to the Prime Minister's ***clarion** call* for a return to old values?

clarion call: *n.*   بانگ، ندا، نفیر

clau.stro.pho.bi.a /£ ˌklɒs.trəˈfəʊ.bi.ə, $ ˌklɑː.strəˈfoʊ-/ *n.* fear of being locked in

هراس از مکان‌های بسته

She suffers from ***claustrophobia*** so she never travels on underground trains.

clav.i.cle /ˈklæv.ɪ.kl̩/ *n.* collarbone

استخوان ترقوه

The football player broke his ***clavicle*** during a practice scrimmage.

cleave /kliːv/ *v.* to split, to divide

شکافتن، شکاف برداشتن

With one blow of the knight's axe, the rock ***clove*** in twain.

cleav.age: *n.*

شکاف

cleft /kelft/ *n.* split

شکاف، درز

Eagles often nest in a *cleft* in the rocks.

clem.en.cy /ˈklem.ənt.si/ *n.* kindess, lenience; mildness

ملایمت، بخشندگی؛ (هوا) اعتدال

Judge Smith was noted for his *clemency* toward first offenders.

cli.ché /£ ˈkli:.ʃeɪ. $ -ˈ-/ *n.* trite phrase

کلیشه، تکرار مکرّرات

His speeches tend to be boring and *cliché*-ridden.

cliché-ridden   پر از کلیشه/ تکرار مکرّرات

cli.mac.tic /klaɪˈmæk.tɪk/ *adj.* relating to the highest point

اوج، به اوج رسیده، در اوج

When I reached the *climactic* portions of the book, I could not stop reading.

cli.max: *n.*

اوج، نقطۀ اوج

clime /klaɪm/ *n.* region, climate

آب و هوا، اقلیم

His doctor advised him to move to a milder *clime*.

clique /£ kli:k, $ klɪk/ *n.* small group

دار و دسته، باند

Our golf club is run by a very unfriendly *clique* (of people).

cloist.er /£ ˈklɔ.stər, $ -stɚ/ *n.* monastery or convent

دیر، صومعه

The nuns lived in the *cloister*.

cloist.er.ed: *adj.* گوشه‌نشین، معتکف

clov.en /£ ˈkləʊ.vᵊn, $ ˈkloʊ-/ *adj.* split, divided

شکافته

Cows and sheep have *cloven* hooves.

co.ad.ju.tor /kəʊˈædʒʊtərˌ/ *n.* assistant, colleague

دستیار، همکار

He was assigned as *coadjutor* of the bishop.

co.a.lesce /£ kəʊ.əˈles, $ koʊ-/ *v.* to combine, to fuse

در هم ادغام شدن، یکی شدن، یکپارچه شدن

The brooks *coalesce* into one large river.

cock.ade /£ kɒkˈeɪd, $ kɑːˈkeɪd/ *n.* decoration worn on hat

کاکل کلاه، نشان کلاه

Members of that brigade can be recognized by the green and white *cockade* in their helmets.

cod.dle /£ ˈkɒd.l̩, $ ˈkɑː.dl̩/ *v.* to treat gently, to pamper

لوس کردن، بیش از اندازه محبت کردن، نوازش کردن

Don't *coddle* the children so much; they need a taste of discipline.

cod.i.cil /£ ˈkəʊ.dɪ.sɪl, $ ˈkɑː-/ *n.* supplement to a will

متمّم وصیت‌نامه

This *codicil* was drawn up five years after the writing of the original will.

co.erce /£ kəʊˈɜːs, $ koʊˈɜːrs/ *v.* to force, to repress

تحت فشار قرار دادن، مجبور کردن، به زور وادار کردن

Do not *coerce* me *into* doing this; I hate force.

co.er.cion: *n.* اِعمال فشار، زورگویی

co.e.val /£ kəʊˈiː.vᵊl, $ koʊ-/ *adj.* contemporary

معاصر، هم عصر، هم زمان

Their research shows that the dinosaur was *coeval* with the pterodactyl.

cog /£ kɒg, $ kɑ:g/ *n.* tooth projecting from a wheel

دندانه، دنده؛ چرخ‌دنده

On steep slopes, *cog* railways are frequently used to prevent slipping.

co.gent /£ ˈkəʊ.dʒᵊnt, $ ˈkoʊ-/ *adj.* convincing, persuasive

قانع کننده، محکم، مستدل

He presented *cogent* arguments to the jury.

cog.i.tate /£ ˈkɒdʒ.ɪ.teɪt, $ ˈkɑ:.dʒɪ-/ *v.* to think over

تأمل کردن، تفکر کردن، به تأمل پرداختن

I was just *cogitating about/ on/ upon* the meaning of life.

cog.nate /£ ˈkɒg.neɪt, $ ˈkɑ:g-/ *adj.* having the same origin

هم ریشه، هم خانواده

French and Italian are *cognate* languages.

cog.ni.zance /£ ˈkɒg.nɪ.zᵊnts, $ ˈkɑ:g-/ *n.* knowledge

آگاهی، اطلاع، شناخت

The two candidates were kept in full *cognizance* of the international situation.

    cog.ni.zant: *adj.*   آگاه، مطّلع

    take cognizance of: *v.*   مد نظر قرار دادن، توجه کردن

cog.no.men /kɒgˈnəʊmen/ *n.* family name

نام خانوادگی؛ لقب

He asked the court to change his *cognomen* to a more American-sounding name.

co.here /£ kəʊˈhɪəʳ, $ koʊˈhɪr/ *v.* to stick together, to connect, to unite

به هم چسبیدن، به هم ربط داشتن، منسجم بودن

If your argument *coheres*, it forms a persuasive whole.

co.her.ence/ co.he.sion: *n.* انسجام، یکپارچگی، چسبندگی

co.hort /£ ˈkəʊ.hɔːt, $ ˈkoʊ.hɔːrt/ *n.* group of soldiers, companion

گروه، (در جمع) هم قطاران، دار و دسته

Caesar and his Roman *cohorts* conquered almost all of the known world.

co.in.cid.ent /£ kəʊˌɪn.sɪˈdent, $ koʊˌɪn.sɪˈdent/ *adj.* occurring at the same time

همزمان، مقارن، مصادف

Some people find the *coincident* events in Hardy's novels annoying.

co.in.cid.ence: *n.* اتفاق، انطباق، هماهنگی

col.an.der /£ ˈkʌl.ɪn.dəʳ, $ ˈkɑː.lən.dɚ/ *n.* a bowl with a lot of holes in it

آبکش

Before serving the spaghetti, place it in a *colander* to drain it.

col.lab.o.rate /kəˈlæb.ə.reɪt/ *v.* to work together

همکاری کردن

Two writers *collaborated* in preparing this book.

col.lab.o.ra.tion: *n.* همکاری، مشارکت، تشریک مساعی

col.late /kəˈleɪt/ *v.* to compare carefully; to arrange in order

مقابله کردن؛ منظم کردن، مرتب کردن

They *collated* the newly found manuscripts to determine

their age.

col.lat.er.al /£ kəˈlæt.ᵊr.ᵊl, $ -ˈlæt̬.ɚ-/ *n.* security given for loan

وثیقه، گرویی

The sum you wish to borrow is so large that it must be secured by *collateral*.

col.la.tion /kəˈleɪ.ʃᵊn/ *n.* a light meal

پذیرایی مختصر، غذای مختصر

There will be a cold *collation* in the banquetting room.

col.li.er /£ ˈkɒl.i.əʳ, $ ˈkɑː.ljɚ/ *n.* worker in coal mine; ship carrying coal

معدنچی زغال سنگ؛ کشتی زغال کشی

The extended cold has prevented the *collier* from delivering the coal to the docks as scheduled.

col.lo.qui.al /£ kəˈləʊ.kwi.ᵊl, $ -ˈloʊ-/ *adj.* informal and conversational

محاوره‌ای، گفتاری

Using *colloquial* expressions in a formal essay spoils the effect you hope to achieve.

col.lo.quy /£ ˈkɒl.ə.kwi, $ ˈkɑː.lə-/ *n.* informal discussion

گفتگو، گفت و شنود

I enjoy your *colloquy*, but I wish they could be made more formal and more searching.

col.lu.sion /kəˈluː.ʒᵊn/ *n.* secret cooperation for deceit

تبانی، توطئه، همدستی

They discovered a spy acting in *collusion* with their competitors.

col.lude: *v.* تبانی کردن، همدست شدن

co.los.sal /£ kəˈlɒs.ᵊl, $ -ˈlɑː.sᵊl/ *adj.* huge, very large

عظیم، بزرگ، غول‌آسا

In the center of the hall stood a *colossal* wooden statue.

co.ma.tose /£ ˈkəʊ.mə.təʊs, $ ˈkoʊ.mə.toʊs/ *adj.* in a coma; extremely sleepy

در حالت اغما؛ خواب‌آلود، گیج خواب

The long-winded orator soon had had his audience in a *comatose* state.

com.bust.i.bles /kəmˈbʌs.tɪ.bl̩/ *adj.* easily burned

قابل اشتعال، سوختنی؛ (جمع) مواد سوختنی

Wood and coal are both *combustible* substances.

come.ly /ˈkʌm.li/ *adj.* attractive, aggreeable

جذاب، ملیح

I would rather have a *comely* wife than a rich one.

co.mest.i.bles /kəˈmes.tɪ.bl̩z/ *n.* something fit to be eaten

چیز خوردنی، مأکولات

The roast turkey and other *comestibles* made the party memorable.

com.i.ty /£ ˈkɒm.ɪ.ti, $ ˌkɑː.mə.t̬i/ *n.* courtesy, civility

احترام، ادب، نزاکت

A spirit of *comity* should exist among nations.

com.mand.eer /£ ˌkɒm.ᵊnˈdɪəʳ, $ ˌkɑː.mənˈdɪr/ *v.* to sieze by force

به‌زور گرفتن، تصرف کردن

The policeman *commandeered* the first car that approached and ordered the driver to go to the nearest hospital.

com.men.su.rate /£ kəˈmentsjᵊr.ət, $ -sjɚ-/ *adj.* equal in extent

متناسب؛ برابر، مساوی

Your reward will be *commensurate* with your effort.

com.mis.er.ate /kəˈmɪz.ə.reɪt/ *v.* to sympathize

همدردی کردن، ابراز تأسف کردن

Her friends *commiserated* with the widow.

com.mod.i.ous /£ kəˈməʊ.di.əs, $ -ˈmoʊ-/ *adj.* spacious and comfortable

جادار

After sleeping in small roadside cabins, they found their hotel suite *commodious*.

com.mun.al /£ ˈkɒm.jʊ.nᵊl, £ kəˈmjuː-, $ ˈkɑː.mjə-/ *adj.* held in common; of a group of people

مشترک، اشتراک؛ گروهی، فرقه‌ای

1) When they were divorced, they had trouble dividing their *communal* property.
2) *Communal* riots have once again broken out between the two ethnic groups.

com.pact /£ ˈkɒm.pækt, $ ˈkɑːm-/ *n.* agreement, contract

قرارداد، پیمان، موافقت‌نامه

They made a *compact* not to reveal any details.

    com.pact: *v.*　　　　　فشرده کردن، متراکم کردن

    com.pact: *adj.*　　　　　متراکم، فشرده

com.pat.i.ble /£ kəmˈpæt.ɪ.bl̩, $ -ˈpæt̬-/ *adj.* harmonious

سازگار، جور، هماهنگ

1) They were *compatible* neighbors, never quarreling

over unimportant matters.

2) The computer program is not *compatible with* this operating system.

com.pend.i.um /kəmˈpen.di.əm/ *n.* summary

خلاصه، چکیدۀ مفید

This text can serve as a *compendium* of the tremendous amount of new material being developed in this field.

com.pen.sat.ory /£ ˈkɒm.pən.seɪtəri, $ ˈkɑːm-/ *adj* . making up for, repaying

ترمیمی، کمکی، جبرانی

Can a *compensatory* education program make up for the inadequate schooling he received in earlier years?

com.pi.la.tion /£ ˌkɒm.pɪˈleɪ.ʃən, $ ˌkɑːm-/ *n.* gathering

گردآوری، جمع‌آوری، تدوین

A team of four were involved in the *compilation* of the book.

com.pile: *v.* گردآوری کردن، تهیه کردن، تألیف کردن

com.pla.cent /kəmˈpleɪ.sᵊnt/ *adj.* self-satisfied

مغرور، خودپسند؛ رضایت‌مندانه، مغرورانه

There was a *complacent* look on his face as he examined his paintings.

com.pla.cen.cy: *n.* رضایت خاطر، آسودگی خیال

com.plais.ant /£ kəmˈpleɪ.zᵊnt, $ -sᵊnt/ *adj.* trying to please, obliging

متواضع، فروتن؛ حرف شنو

The courtier obeyed the king's orders in a *complaisant* manner.

com.ple.ment /£ ˈkɒm.plɪ.ment, $ ˈkɑːm-/ *n., v.* something that completes; to complete

متمم، مکمل؛ (دستور زبان) مسند؛ کامل کردن، مکمل چیزی بودن

A predicate *complement* completes the meaning of the subject.

com.pli.ant /kəmˈplaɪ.ənt/ *adj.* yielding

مطیع، فرمانبردار

He was *compliant* and ready to conform to the pattern set by his friends.

comply: *v.*   اطاعت کردن، پیروی کردن

com.pli.ance: *n.*   اطاعت، پیروی، تسلیم

com.pli.ci.ty /£ kəmˈplɪs.ɪ.ti, $ -ə.t̬i/ *n.* involvement in a crime

شرکت، مشارکت در جرم

She is suspected of *complicity* in the robbery.

com.port /£ kəmˈpɔːt, $ -ˈpɔːrt/ *v.* to agree; to behave

رفتار کردن؛ هماهنگ بودن، همخوانی داشتن

She *comported* herself with great dignity at her husband's funeral.

com.po.sure /£ kəmˈpəʊ.ʒəʳ, $ -ˈpoʊ.ʒɚ/ *n.* mental calmness

آرامش، خونسردی، خویشتن‌داری

Even the latest work crisis failed to shake her *composure*.

com.pre.hen.sive /£ ˌkɒm.prɪˈhent.sɪv, $ ˌkɑːm-/ *adj.* thorough, inclusive

جامع، وسیع، گسترده، مبسوط

We offer you a *comprehensive* training in all aspects of the business.

com.press /kəmˈpres/ *v.* to squeeze, to contract

فشردن، فشرده کردن، متراکم کردن

She *compressed* the package under her arm.

com.pres.sion: *n.*   فشردگی، فشار، تراکم

com.pro.mise /£ ˈkɒm.prə.maɪz, $ ˈkɑːm-/ *v., n.* to endanger; to settle differences

به خطر انداختن، لطمه زدن؛ مصالحه کردن، کنار آمدن؛ سازش، توافق

1) If we back down on this issue, our reputation will be *compromised*.
2) Party unity is threatened when members will not *compromise*.

com.punc.tion /kəmˈpʌŋk.ʃ°n/ *n.* remorse

ناراحتی وجدان، احساس گناه، پشیمانی، شرمساری

The criminal had shown no *compunction* for his heinous crime.

com.pute /kəmˈpjuːt/ *v.* to calculate, to reckon

محاسبه کردن، حساب کردن

He failed to *compute* the ratio of the object's height to its weight.

com.pu.ta.tion: *n.*   محاسبه، حساب

con.cat.e.nate /kənˈkætɪneɪt/ *v., adj.* to link as in a chain

زنجیره‌ای به هم پیوستن؛ زنجیره‌ای، زنجیروار

It's difficult to understand how these events could *concatenate* as they did without outside assistance.

con.cave /£ ˈkɒŋ.keɪv, $ ˈkɑːn-/ *adj.* hollow, curved inwards

فرورفته، تورفته، گود؛ مقعر

You've lost so much weight; your stomach is almost

concave.

con.cent.ric /kənˈsen.trɪk/ *adj.* having a common center

هم‌مرکز

The target was made of *concentric* circles.

con.cep.tion /kənˈsep.ʃən/ *n.* beginning, forming of an idea

شروع، شکل‌گیری؛ طرح، برداشت، استنباط

Who was responsible for the *conception* of this plan?

con.ceive: *v.*   طراحی کردن؛ تصور کردن

con.ces.sion /kənˈseʃ.ən/ *n.* an act of yielding

سازش، مصالحه؛ تسلیم، پذیرش

Before they could reach an agreement, both sides had to make certain *concession*.

con.ci.li.ate /kənˈsɪl.i.eɪt/ *v.* to win over, to pacify

آرام کردن، دل (کسی را) به دست آوردن، دلجویی کردن

She tried to *conciliate* me with a gift.

con.ci.li.at.ory: *adj.*   مسالمت‌آمیز، دوستانه، آشتی‌جویانه

con.cise /kənˈsaɪs/ *adj.* brief and compact

مختصر، فشرده؛ موجز

The essay was *concise* and explicit.

con.clave /£ ˈkɒŋ.kleɪv, $ ˈkɑːn-/ *n.* private meeting

جلسهٔ محرمانه

He was present at all their *conclave* as a sort of unofficial observer.

con.coct /£ kənˈkɒkt/ *v.* to prepare by combining; to make up

درست کردن، ساختن، تهیه کردن؛ سرهم کردن، از خود در آوردن

How did you ever *concoct* such a strange dish?

con.coct.ion: *n.*   معجون

con.com.it.ant /£ kənˈkɒm.ɪ.tᵊnt, $ -ˈkɑː.mə.tᵊnt/ *n., adj.* that which accompanies

همراه، توأم، هماینده

Loss of memory is a natural *concomitant* of old age.

con.cord.at /£ kənˈkɔː.dæt, $ -ˈkɔr-/ *n.* agreement

توافق (در امور مذهبی)

Under the *concordat*, the state is obliged to maintain Catholic teaching in schools.

con.cur.rent /£ kənˈkʌr.ᵊnt, $ -ˈkɜːr-/ *adj.* happening at the same time

همزمان، مقارن

Working on two *concurrent* projects can be very exhausting.

con.de.scend /£ ˌkɒn.dɪˈsend, kɑːn-/ *v.* to lower oneself, to act haughtily

لطف کردن، منت گذاشتن بر، (خود را) سبک کردن

The king *condescended* to grant an audience to the friends of the condemned man.

    con.de.scen.sion: *n.*   فخرفروشی، افاده، تبختر

con.dign /kənˈdaɪn/ *adj.* adequate, deserved, suitable

(مجازات) بحق، به سزا

The public approved the *condign* punishment.

con.di.ment /£ ˈkɒn.dɪ.mənt, $ ˈkɑːn-/ *n.* seasoning, spice

چاشنی، ادویه

Spanish food is full of *condiment*.

con.dole /kənˈdəʊl/ *v.* to express sympathetic sorrow

تسلیت گفتن

His friends gathered to *condole with* him *over* his loss.

con.dol.ence: *n.* تسلیت

con.done /£ kənˈdəʊn, $ -ˈdoʊn/ *v.* to overlook, to forgive

نادیده گرفتن، چشم‌پوشی کردن؛ عفو کردن، بخشیدن

If the government is seen to *condone* violence, the bloodshed will never stop.

con.duit /£ ˈkɒn.dju:ɪt, $ ˈkɑ:n.du:-/ *n.* channel, passageway for fluids

مجرا، کانال

Water was brought to the army in the desert by a *conduit* from the adjoining mountain.

con.fi.scate /£ ˈkɒn.fɪ.skeɪt, $ ˈkɑ:n-/ *v.* to seize, to commandeer

ضبط کردن، توقیف کردن، مصادره کردن

His passport was *confiscated* by the police at the airport.

con.fla.gra.tion /£ ˌkɒn.fləˈgreɪ.ʃᵊn, $ ˌkɑ:n-/ *n.* great fire

حریق بزرگ

In the *conflagration* that followed the 1906's earthquake, much of San Francisco was destroyed.

con.form.i.ty /£ kənˈfɔ:.mɪ.ti, $ -ˈfɔ:r.mə.t̬i/ *n.* harmony, agreement

پیروی، دنباله‌روی؛ هماهنگی، همرنگی

In conformity with your request, we have cancelled your club membership.

con.geal /kənˈdʒɪəl/ *v.* to freeze, to coagulate

منجمد شدن، سفت شدن؛ لخته شدن

His blood *congealed* in his veins as he saw the monster

rush toward him.

con.gen.i.tal /£ kənˈdʒen.ɪ.tᵊl, $ -t̬ᵊl/ *adj.* existing at birth

مادرزادی

His *congenital* deformity disturbed his parents.

con.glom.e.ra.tion /£ kən.glɒm.ᵊrˈeɪ.ʃᵊn, $ -ˌglɑː.məˈreɪ-/ *n.* mass of material sticking together

مجموعه؛ توده، کپه

In such a *conglomeration* of statistics, it was impossible to find a single area of analysis.

con.gru.ence /£ ˈkɒŋ.gru.ᵊnts, $ ˈkɑːŋ-/ *n.* correspondence of parts

تشابه، تساوی، انطباق

The student demonstrated the *congruence* of the two triangles.

con.i.fer /£ ˈkɒn.ɪ.fəʳ, $ ˈkɑːnɪ.fɚ/ *n.* pine tree

درخت کاج؛ (در جمع) مخروطیان

According to geologists, the *conifers* were the first plants to bear flowers.

con.jec.ture /£ kənˈdʒek.tʃəʳ, $ -tʃɚ/ *n.,v.* guess; surmise

حدس، گمان؛ حدس زدن، پنداشتن

It's pure *conjecture* ; nobody knows the facts.

con.jug.al /£ ˈkɒn.dʒʊ.gᵊl, $ ˈkɑːn-/ *adj.* relating to marriage

زناشویی، زن و شوهری

Some prisoners are permitted *conjugal* visits.

con.jure /£ ˈkʌn.dʒəʳ, $ -dʒɚ/ *v.* to summon a devil; to practice magic

(روح) احضار کردن؛ چشم‌بندی کردن

She was able to *conjure* up the spirits of the dead.

con.niv.ance /kəˈnaɪ.vᵊnts/ *n.* assistance, pretended ignorance

تبانی، هم‌دستی؛ تجاهل

With the *connivance of* his friends, he plotted to embarrass the teacher.

con.nive: *v.*   هم‌دستی کردن، تبانی کردن؛ تجاهل کردن

con.nois.seur /£ ˌkɒn.əˈsɜːʳ, $ ˌkɑː.nəˈsɜːr/ *n.* an expert judge

خبره، صاحب‌نظر

He had developed into a *connoisseur* of fine china.

con.no.ta.tion /£ ˌkɒn.əˈteɪ.ʃᵊn, $ ˌkɑː.nə-/ *n.* suggested or implied meaning

معنای ضمنی

Foreigners frequently are unaware of the *connotation* of the words they use.

con.nu.bi.al /£ kəˈnjuː.bi.ᵊl, $ -ˈnuː-/ *adj.* relating to marriage

(مربوط به) زناشویی یا ازدواج

In his telegram, he wished the newlyweds a lifetime of *connubial* bliss.

con.san.guin.i.ty /ˌkɒnsæŋˈgwɪnɪti/ *n.* kinship

هم‌خونی، خویشاوندی، نزدیکی، محرمیت

The lawsuit developed into a test of the *consanguinity* of the claimant to the estate.

con.sci.en.tious /£ ˌkɒn.tʃiˈent.ʃəs, $ ˌkɑːn-/ *adj.* careful, scrupulous

وظیفه‌شناس، باوجدان؛ دقیق

She is an excellent student—bright, attentive and *conscientious*.

con.se.crate /£ ˈkɒn*t*.sɪ.kreɪt, $ ˈkɑːnt-/ *v.* to dedicate, to santify

وقف کردن، اختصاص دادن

We shall *consecrate* our lives to this noble purpose.

con.sens.us /kənˈsen*t*.səs/ *n.* general agreement

اتفاق نظر، اجماع، توافق کلی

The *consensus* indicates that we are opposed to entering into this pact.

con.se.quen.tial /£ ˌkɒn*t*.sɪˈkwen.tʃᵊl, $ ˌkɑːnt-/ *adj.* important; self important

مهم؛ خودبزرگ بین

Convinced of his own importance, the actor strutted about the dressing room with a *consequential* air.

con.se.quence: *n.* اهمیت، پیامد؛ (در جمع) عواقب
con.se.quent: *adj.* متعاقب، نتیجهٔ

con.son.ance /kɒnsənəs/ *n.* harmony, agreement

سازگاری، توافق، همخوانی

Her agitation seemed out of *consonance* with her usual calm.

con.sort /£ kənˈsɔːt, $ -ˈsɔːrt/ *v.* to associate with

معاشرت داشتن، نشست و برخاست کردن

We frequently judge people by the company with whom they *consort*.

con.sort: *n.* همسر (پادشاه یا ملکه)

con.spi.cu.ous /kənˈspɪk.ju.əs/ *adj.* noticeable, striking

مشخص، چشمگیر، برجسته، مشهور

Janet was *conspicuous* both for her red hair and for her

height.

con.spir.a.cy /kənˈspɪr.ə.si/ *n.* treacherous plot

توطئه؛ تبانی، همدستی

Brutus and Cassius joined in the *conspiracy to* kill Julius Caesar.

con.sti.tu.ent /kənˈstɪt.ju.ənt/ *n.* supporter

رأی دهنده، موکّل

As a senator, he always talked to his *constituents* and heard their problems.

con.straint /kənˈstreɪnt/ *n.* compulsion, repression of feelings

الزام، فشار، زور، محدودیت، قید و بند

They confessed the truth but only under *constraint*.

    con.strain: *v.*   ملزم کردن، مجبور کردن، تحت فشار قرار دادن، مقید کردن

con.strue /kənˈstruː/ *v.* to explain, to interpret

تعبیر کردن، تفسیر کردن

If I *construe* your remarks correctly, you disagree with the theory already advanced.

con.sum.mate /£ ˈkɒn.sə.mət, $ ˈkɑːn-/ *adj.* complete, perfect

کامل، تمام عیار، عالی

With her he would lead a life of *consummate* happiness.

    con.sum.mate: *v.*   به کمال رساندن

con.tam.in.ate /kənˈtæm.ɪ.neɪt/ *v.* to pollute, to spoil the purity

آلوده کردن؛ فاسد کردن، خراب کردن

Much of the coast has been *contaminated* by nuclear waste.

con.ten.tious /kənˈtent.ʃəs/ *adj.* quarrelsome

جنجالی، بحث‌انگیز، مورد اختلاف

She has some rather *contentious* views on education.

con.text /£ ˈkɒn.tekst, $ ˈkɑːn-/ *n.* text, speech

بافت، متن، عبارت، فحوای کلام

The papers quoted my remarks completely out of *context*.

con.ti.gu.ous /kənˈtɪg.ju.əs/ *adj.* adjacent to, touching upon

همجوار، مجاور، نزدیک

The two states are *contiguous with/ to* each other but the laws are quite different.

con.tin.ence /£ ˈkɒn.tɪ.nənts, $ ˈkɑːn.tᵊn.ənts/ *n.* self-restraint

خویشتن‌داری، پرهیزگاری

He vowed to lead a life of *continence*.

con.ti.nent: *adj.* خویشتن‌دار، پرهیزگار

con.tin.gent /kənˈtɪn.dʒᵊnt/ *adj.* conditional

مشروط به، بسته به، موکول به

The continuation of this contract is *contingent on* the quality of your first output.

con.tin.gen.cy: *n.* وابستگی؛ احتمال

con.tor.tion /£ kənˈtɔː.ʃᵊn, $ -ˈtɔːr-/ *n.* distortion, twisting

پیچ و تاب، کج و کولگی، اعوجاج

You should have seen me at my yoga class—I performed all sorts of *contortions*.

con.tort: *v.* پیچ و تاب دادن، کج و کوله شدن

con.tra.band /£ ˈkɒn.trə.bænd, $ ˈkɑːn-/ *adj., n.* illegal trade, smuggling

قاچاق

The Coast Guard tries to prevent traffic in *contraband* goods.

con.tra.vene /£ ˌkɒn.trəˈviːn, $ ˌkɑːn-/ *v.* to contradict, to infringe on

نقض کردن، زیر پا گذاشتن، نادیده گرفتن

I will not attempt to *contravene* your argument because it does not affect the situation.

con.trite /£ ˈkɒn.traɪt, $ ˈkɑːn-/ *adj.* penitent

نادم، پشیمان؛ توأم با پشیمانی، از روی پشیمانی

Her *contrite* tears did not influence the judge when he imposed sentence.

con.tri.tion: *n.*   پشیمانی، ندامت

con.tro.vert /£ ˈkɒn.trə.vɜːt, £ kənˈtrɒv.ət, $ ˈkɑːn.trə.vɜːrt/ *v.* to oppose with arguments

رد کردن، با دلیل خلاف چیزی را ثابت کردن

To *controvert* your theory will require much time.

con.tu.ma.cious /ˌkɒntjʊˈmeɪʃəs/ *adj.* disobedient, resisting authority

سرکش، نافرمان؛ یاغی، طغیانگر

The *contumacious* mob shouted defiantly at the police.

con.tu.ma.cy: *n.*   نافرمانی، طغیان

con.tu.me.ly /ˈkɒntjuːmlɪ/ *n.* insult, scornful insolence

فحاشی، هتاکی، هتک حرمت

The "proud man's *contumely*" is distasteful to Hamlet.

con.tu.sion /£ kənˈtjuː.ʒ°n, $ -ˈtuː-/ *n.* bruise

کبودی

There was a large *contusion to* the right shoulder.

co.nun.drum /kəˈnʌn.drəm/ *n.* riddle, a trick question

معما، چیستان

During the long car ride, she invented *conundrum* to entertain the children.

con.vene /kənˈviːn/ *v.* to assemble, to gather together

گرد آمدن، جمع شدن، فرا خواندن؛ تشکیل جلسه دادن

The Prime Minister *convened* his ministers to discuss the matter.

con.ven.er: *n.*   نماینده؛ دعوت کننده، برگزار کننده

con.vers.ant /£ kənˈvɜː.sᵊnt, $ -ˈvɜːr-/ *adj.* familiar with

آگاه، مطّلع، آشنا

The lawyer is *conversant with* all the evidence.

con.vey.ance /kənˈveɪ.ᵊnts/ *n.* vehicle; transfer

وسیلهٔ حمل و نقل؛ انتقال

During the transit strike, commuters used various kinds of *conveyances*.

con.vic.tion /kənˈvɪk.ʃᵊn/ *n.* strongly held belief

عقیدهٔ راسخ، ایمان، اعتقاد

Nothing could shake his *conviction* that she was innocent.

con.viv.i.al /kənˈvɪv.i.əl/ *adj.* festive, cheerful, gay

شاد، سرحال؛ دوستانه، صمیمانه؛ صمیمی، با صفا

The *convivial* celebrators of the victory sang their college songs.

con.voke /kənˈvəʊk/ *v.* to call together to a meeting

احضار کردن، فرا خواندن، دعوت کردن؛ تشکیل دادن

Congress was *convoked* at the outbreak of the emergency.

con.vo.ca.tion: *n.* احضار، دعوت؛ مجمع

con.vo.lut.ed /£ ˈkɒn.və.luːtɪd, $ ˈkɑːn.və.ruː.t̬ɪd/ *adj.* coiled around; intricate

پیچ در پیچ، پیچیده؛ دشوار

His argument was so *convoluted* that few of us could follow it.

co.pi.ous /£ ˈkəʊ.pi.əs, $ ˈkoʊ-/ *adj.* plentiful

بسیار، فراوان، زیاد

He had *copious* reasons for rejecting the proposal.

co.quette /£ kɒkˈet, $ koʊˈket/ *n.* flirt

(زن) لوند، عشوه‌گر

Because she refused to marry him, he called her a *coquette*.

cor.di.al /£ ˈkɔː.di.əl, $ ˈkɔːr.dʒəl/ *adj.* heartfelt, gracious

صمیمانه، صمیمی، گرم، دوستانه

Our hosts greeted us at the airport with a *cordial* and a hearty hug.

cor.don /£ ˈkɔː.dᵊn, $ ˈkɔːr-/ *n., v.* encircling line of troops or police

حلقهٔ محاصره، صف پلیس؛ محاصره کردن، قرق کردن

The police *cordon* was so tight that the criminals could not leave the area.

cor.nice /£ ˈkɔː.nɪs, $ ˈkɔːr-/ *n.* projecting molding on building

قرنیز، طرّه، گچ‌بری

The *cornice* stones were loosened by the storms.

co.rol.la.ry /£ kəˈrɒl.ᵊr.i, $ -ˈrɑː.lɚ-/ *n.* consequence, accompaniment

نتیجهٔ منطقی، نتیجهٔ طبیعی، لازمه

Unfortunately, violence is the inveitable *corollary of* such a revolutionary change in society.

cor.po.re.al /£ kɔːˈpɔː.ri.əl, $ kɔːrˈpɔːr.i-/ *adj.* bodily, material

جسمانی، مادی

He was not a churchgoer; he was interested only in *corporeal* matters.

cor.pu.lent /£ ˈkɔː.pjʊ.lənt, $ ˈkɔːr-/ *adj.* very fat

خیلی چاق، فربه

The *corpulent* man resolved to reduce.

cor.pu.lence: *n.* چاقی، فربهی

cor.re.la.tion /£ ˌkɒr.əˈleɪ.ʃᵊn, $ ˌkɔːr-/ *n.* mutual relationship

همبستگی، ارتباط متقابل

There is a *correlation* between his height and weight.

cor.rob.or.ate /£ kəˈrɒb.ə.reɪt, $ -ˈrɑː.bə-/ *v.* to confirm, to support with evidence

اثبات کردن، تأیید کردن

Unless we find a witness to *corroborate* your evidence, it will not stand up in the court.

cor.rob.or.a.tion: *n.* اثبات، تأیید، دلیل (دیگر)، شاهد (دیگر)، گواه (دیگر)

cor.ro.sive /£ kəˈrəʊ.sɪv, -zɪv, $ -ˈroʊ-/ *adj.* eating away

خورنده، فرساینده

Stainless steel is able to withstand the effects of *corrosive* chemicals.

cor.ro.sion: *n.* خوردگی، پوسیدگی، فرسایش
cor.rode: *v.* خوردن، پوساندن، فرسودن

cor.ru.gat.ed /£ ˈkɒr.ə.geɪ.tɪd, $ ˈkɔːr.ə.geɪ.t̬ɪd/ *adj.* wrinkled, ridged

چین‌دار، شیاردار، موج‌دار

She wished she could smooth away the wrinkles from his *corrugated* brow.

cor.ru.gate: *v.* چروک خوردن، چین خوردن

cor.sair /kɔːseəʳ/ *n.* pirate; pirate ship

دزدان دریایی؛ کشتی دزدان دریایی (در سواحل آفریقای شمالی)

The *corsairs* were often inspired by racial and religious hatreds.

cor.tege /£ kɔːˈteʒ, $ kɔːr-/ *n.* procession

(در تشییع جنازه) مشایعین، مشایعت‌کنندگان

The funeral *cortege* proceeded slowly down the avenue.

cor.u.scate /£ ˈkɒr.ə.skeɪt, $ ˈkɔːr-/ *v.* to glitter, to scintillate

درخشیدن، برق زدن

His wit is the kind that *coruscate* and startles all his listeners.

cos.mic /£ ˈkɒz.mɪk, $ ˈkɑːz-/ *adj.* relating to the universe; vast or grand

جهانی، مربوط به عالم؛ بسیار عظیم

Physics is governed by *cosmic* laws.

cos.mos: *n.* جهان، عالم، دنیا

co.te.rie /£ ˈkəʊ.tᵊr.i, $ ˈkoʊ.t̬ɚ-/ *n.* group that meets socially, select circle

همفکران، یاران، محفل، حلقه، جرگه

He was invited to join the literary *coterie* that lunched daily at the hotel.

coun.te.nance /£ ˈkaʊn.tɪ.nənts, $ -t̬ᵊn.ənts/ *v.* to approve, to tolerate

تأیید کردن، پشتیبانی کردن، طرفداری کردن

He refused to *coutenance* such rude behavior on their part.

coun.ter.mand /£ ˌkaʊn.təˈmɑːnd, $ -tɚˈmænd/ *v.* to cancel, to revoke

لغو کردن، فسخ کردن، نقض کردن

The general *countermanded* the orders issued in his absence.

coun.ter.part /£ ˈkaʊn.tə.pɑːt, $ -tɚ.pɑːrt/ *n.* matching, corresponding

همتا؛ قرینه، نظیر؛ مکمل

Night and day are *counterparts*.

coup /kuː/ *n.* highly successful action or sudden attack

عمل موفقیت‌آمیز، اقدام قاطع؛ کودتا

The news of his *coup* spread throughout the town.

coup.le /ˈkʌp.l/ *v.* to join, to unite

به هم بستن، به هم وصل کردن

The dining-car was *coupled* onto the last coach.

cou.ri.er /£ ˈkʊr.i.əʳ, $ ˈkɜːr.i.ɚ/ *n.* messenger

پیک، قاصد، فرستاده

The publisher sent a special *courier* to pick up the manuscript.

cov.e.nant /ˈkʌv.ᵊn.ᵊnt/ *n., v.* agreement; to promise

قرارداد، قول‌نامه؛ تعهد کردن

We must comply with the terms of the *covenant*.

cov.ert /£ ˈkəʊ.vɜːt, $ ˈkoʊ.vɜːrt/ *adj.* secret, hidden, implied

سرّی، پوشیده، مخفی، تلویحی

He could understand the *covert* threat in the letter.

cov.et.ous /£ ˈkʌv.ɪ.təs, $ -t̬əs/ *adj.* avaricious, eagerly desirous of

مشتاق، آرزومند؛ حریص، طمع‌کار

The child was *covetous* by nature and wanted to take the toys belonging to his classmates.

cov.et: *v.*   آرزوی (چیزی را) داشتن، غبطه خوردن به

cow.er /£ ˈkaʊ.ər, $ ˈkaʊ.ɚ/ *v.* to shrink from fear or cold

خود را جمع کردن، کز کردن، قوز کردن

The frightened child *cowered* in the corner of the room.

coy /kɔɪ/ *adj.* shy, modest, coquettish

محجوب، شرم‌آلود؛ پر عشوه، عشوه‌گر

She was *coy* in her answers to his offer.

coz.en /ˈkʌzən/ *v.* to cheat, to hoodwink, to swindle

سر کسی کلاه گذاشتن، کلک زدن

He *cozened* his friends in a cheap card game.

crabbed /kræbd, ˈkræb.ɪd/ *adj.* sour, peevish

بدخلق، بدعنق، بداخلاق

You're *crabbed* today — what's upset you?

crass /kræs/ *adj.* stupid, crude or unfeeling

خشک، بی‌روح؛ احمقانه

He made *crass* comments about her worn-out clothes.

cra.ven /ˈkreɪ.vən/ *adj.* cowardly

ترسو، بی‌شهامت؛ بزدلانه

His *craven* behavior in this critical period was criticized.

cre.dence /ˈkriː.dənts/ *n.* belief

I'm not prepared to give *credence to* his complaints.
باور، وقع، اعتبار

cre.do /ˈkriːdəʊ, ˈkreɪ-/ *n.* creed

You cannot describe her extremist political *credo*.
عقیده، ایمان، مرام

cre.du.li.ty /£ krəˈdjuː.lə.ti, $ -ˈduː.lə.ti/ *n.* belief on slight evidence

The witch doctor took advantage of the *credulity* of the superstitious natives.
خوش‌باوری، زودباوری، ساده لوحی

cred.u.lous: *adj.*
خوش‌باور، ساده‌لوح، زودباور

creed /kriːd/ *n.* a set of beliefs

What's your political *creed*?
معتقدات، نظام اعتقادی؛ کیش، آیین، مذهب

cre.scen.do /£ krɪˈʃendəʊ, $ -doʊ/ *n., adj.* growing louder

There has been a rising *crescendo* of violence which started last year.
افزایش تدریجی صدا؛ رو به افزایش

crest.fal.len /£ ˈkrestˌfɔː.lən, $ -ˌfɑː-/ *adj.* dejected, dispirited, sad

The player returned *crestfallen* a few minutes later, with a score of only two.
غمگین، پکر، دمغ، گرفته، افسرده

crev.ice /ˈkrev.ɪs/ *n.* crack, fissure

The lizard darted into a *crevice* between two stones.
شکاف، درز، ترک

cringe /krɪndʒ/ *v.* to shrink in fear

خود را (از ترس) جمع کردن؛ خود را خوار و خفیف کردن

The dog *cringed*, expecting a blow.

cringe-making: *adj.*   مایهٔ شرمساری

cri.te.ri.on /£ kraɪˈtɪə.ri.ən, $ -ˈtɪr.i-/ *n.* a standard

معیار، ملاک، ضابطه

What's the *criterion* you apply to any problem?

crone /£ krəʊn, $ kroʊn/ *n.* an ugly old woman, hag

عجوزه، عفریته

The toothless *crone* frightened us when she smiled.

rot.che.ty /£ ˈkrɒtʃ.ɪ.ti, $ ˈkrɑː.tʃə.ti/ *adj.* ill-natured, cranky, eccentric

بدعنق، بداخلاق، تندخو

By the time the meal began, children were getting tired and *crotchety*.

crux /krʌks/ *n.* crucial point

اصل قضیه، گره

The *crux* of the country's economic problems is its foreign debt.

crypt /krɪpt/ *n.* underground chamber

سرداب کلیسا

Until recently, only bodies of rulers were interred in this *crypt*.

cryp.tic /£ ˈkrɪp.tɪk, $ -ṭɪk/ *adj.* mysterious and difficult to understand

رمزی، مرموز، اسرارآمیز، سرّی

His *cryptic* remarks could not be interpreted.

cub.ic.le /ˈkjuː.bɪ.kl̩/ *n.* a small room

اتاقک؛ رخت‌کن

Can I try this skirt on, please? Yes, there's a *cubicle* free at the end.

cui.sine /kwɪˈziːn/ *n.* style of cooking

پخت و پز، (مربوط به) آشپزی، دست پخت

French *cuisine* is noted for its use of sauces.

cul.de.sac /ˈkʊl.də.sæk/ *n.* blind alley, trap

بن‌بست؛ تله؛ گوشهٔ دنج

The soldiers were unaware that they were marching into a *culdesac*.

cu.lin.ary /£ ˈkʌl.ɪ.nᵊr.i, $ ˈkʌl.ə.ner-/ *adj.* relating to cooking

(مربوط به) آشپزی

Many chefs attribute *culinary* skill to the wise use of spices.

cull /kʌl/ *v.* to pick out, to select

انتخاب کردن، برگزیدن، دستچین کردن

Every month the farmer *culls* the nonlaying hens from his flock and sells them to the butcher.

cul.mi.na.tion /ˌkʌl.mɪˈneɪ.ʃᵊn/ *n.* attainment of highest point

نقطهٔ اوج، منتها درجه؛ نتیجه نهایی، حاصل

Winning first prize was the *culmination* of years of practice and had work.

culp.a.ble /ˈkʌl.pə.bl̩/ *adj.* deserving blame

مقصر، مجرم، گناهکار

He *was held culpable* for all that had happened.

cul.vert /£ ˈkʌl.vət, $ -vɚt/ *n.* artficial channel for water

کانال زیرزمینی، آبگذر

They built a *culvert* at this point to reduce the possibility of the road's being flooded.

cum.ber.some /£ ˈkʌm.bə.səm, $ -bɚ-/ *adj.* heavy, hard to manage

گنده، سنگین؛ دست و پاگیر

He's got a *cumbersome* old computer — it's slow and complicated to use.

cu.pid.i.ty /£ kjuˈpɪd.ɪ.ti, $ -ə.t̬i/ *n.* greed

حرص، طمع، آز

The defeated people could not satisfy the *cupidity* of the conquerors.

cu.rat.or /£ kjʊˈreɪ.tə^r, $ kjɜːrˈeɪ.t̬ɚ/ *n.* superintendent, manager

متصدی (موزه، کتابخانه و غیره)

Mr. Smith is the *curator* of a London museum.

cur.mud.geon /£ kəˈmʌdʒ.ən, $ kɚ-/ *n.* a bad-tempered old person, churlish

آدم بد خلق، آدم ترشرو

You're turning into a complaining old *curmudgeon*!

cur.ry /£ ˈkʌr.i, $ ˈkɜːr-/ *v.* to treat leather; to seek favor

دباغی کردن، تیمار کردن؛ تملق کسی را گفتن

He's always trying to *curry* favor with the boss.

cur.sive /£ ˈkɜː.sɪv, $ ˈkɜːr-/ *adj.* written with rounded letters that are joined together

(خط) شکسته، سرهم

In normal writing, we run our letters together in *cursive* form.

cur.so.ry /£ ˈkɜːs³r.i, $ ˈkɜːr.sɚ-/ *adj.* casual, hastily done

سرسری، شتاب‌زده، سطحی، گذرا

He put aside the papers after a *cursory* study.

cur.tail /£ kəˈteɪl, $ kɚ-/ *v.* to shorten, to reduce

کاهش دادن، کاستن، تقلیل دادن، کوتاه کردن

Illness has *curtailed* her sporting activities.

cy.nic /ˈsɪn.ɪk/ *n.* one who is skeptical or distrustful of human motives

آدم بدبین، آدم منفی، آدم شکاک

I am too much of a *cynic* to believe that he'll keep his promise.

cy.nic.al: *adj.* بدبینانه، عیب‌جویانه؛ بدبین، بدگمان

cy.no.sure /£ ˈsaɪ.nə.sjʊəʳ, $ -ʃʊr/ *n.* center of attention

مرکز توجه، کانون توجه

She was the *cynosure* of all eyes.

لیستی از لغاتی که در جملات بخش C به کار رفته‌اند:

choral society: *n.*	انجمن کُر	aide: *n.*	آجودان، دستیار
claimant: *n.*	مدعی	air: *n.*	ظاهر، قیافه، پُز
coal: *n.*	زغال سنگ	assign: *v.*	محول کردن، اختصاص دادن
colleague: *n.*	همکار		
condemn: *v.*	محکوم کردن	awe: *n.*	بهت، خوف، ترس
congestion: *n.*	تراکم	axe: *n.*	تبر
conspirator: *n.*	توطئه‌گر	back down: *v.*	صرف‌نظر کردن
command: *n.*	فرماندهی	banquetting: *adj.*	پذیرایی
competitor: *n.*	رقیب	base: *adj.*	پست، بی‌ارزش
comply: *v.*	پیروی کردن	be derailed: *v.*	(قطار) از خط خارج شدن
commuter: *n.*	مسافر بین شهری روزانه، دایم‌السفر		
		be obliged: *v.*	ملزم بودن
courtier: *n.*	دربار	bear: *v.*	تحمل کردن
culprit: *n.*	مجرم	bliss: *n.*	خوشبختی
dart: *v.*	خیز برداشتن	bloodshed: *n.*	خونریزی
decent: *adj.*	مؤدبانه	blow: *n.*	ضربه
decisiveness: *n.*	قاطعیت	bodies: *n.*	اجرام
degenerate: *v.*	تبدیل شدن	boulder: *n.*	قلوه‌سنگ
defiantly: *adv.*	جسورانه	boundry: *n.*	سرحد، مرز
deformity: *n.*	تغییر شکل عضو، نقص عضو	brigade: *n.*	گروه، تیپ
		brook: *n.*	جویبار
delight: *v.*	لذت بردن از	brow: *n.*	پیشانی
detective: *n.*	کارآگاه	call: *n.*	فراخوانی، احضار
dignity: *n.*	متانت، آبرو	campaign: *n.*	حمله، مبارزه
director: *n.*	سرپرست	cast blame: *v.*	ایراد گرفتن
dissect: *v.*	(پزشکی) تشریح کردن	choirboy: *n.*	خواننده پسر کُر

disturb: v.	مزاحم شدن، ناراحت کردن
drain: v.	خشک کردن، آب چیزی را کشیدن
dressing room: n.	رختکن
drying machine: n.	دستگاه خشک‌کن
embarrass: v.	خجالت‌زده کردن
emigration: n.	مهاجرت، برون کوچی
engage: v.	وارد کاری کردن، پرداختن
entablature: n.	ستون
entertain: v.	سرگرم کردن
envious: adj.	حسود
estate: n.	مِلک، ماترک
ethnic: adj.	قومی، نژادی
exhausted: adj.	خسته (شده)
explosives: n.	مواد منفجره
extended: adj.	طولانی، ادامه‌دار
flamboyant: adj.	شاد
flock: n.	گله، دسته
flushed: adj.	برافروخته
fool: v.	گول زدن
free: adj.	خالی
heinous: adj.	فجیع
helmet: n.	کلاه
hoof: n.	سُم
hug: n.	(عمل) بغل کردن
hypocrisy: n.	تزویر
impress: v.	تحت تأثیر قرار دادن
infection: n.	عفونت
ingrown: adj.	(ناخن) فرورفته در گوشت
inter: v.	دفن کردن
investigation: n.	بررسی
launch: v.	پرتاب کردن، به‌آب انداختن
lawsuit: n.	دادخواهی
lot: n.	گروه، جماعت
male: adj.	مذکر، مرد
meet: v.	برآورده کردن
menial: adj.	پست، بی‌اهمیت
minute: adj.	بسیار ریز
mob: n.	جمعیت
moisture: n.	رطوبت
morbid: adj.	ترسناک
mount: v.	نصب کردن، کار گذاشتن
native: n.	بومی
newlywed: n.	زوج تازه ازدواج کرده
nonlaying: adj.	(مرغ) غیرتخمی
nun: n.	راهبه

English	فارسی	English	فارسی
offender: n.	متخلف	smooth away: v.	برطرف کردن
orator: n.	خطیب	spoil: v.	ضایع کردن
ornately: adv.	با زرق و برق	startle: v.	شگفت‌زده کردن
outbreak: n.	بروز	steep: adj.	با شیب تند
overlook: v.	مشرف بودن بر	strike: n.	اعتصاب
pact: n.	پیمان	strut: v.	با غرور و تکبر راه رفتن
peddler: n.	دست فروش	subject: n.	دستخوش
plot: v.	نقشه کشیدن	superstitious: adj.	خرافاتی
predict: v.	پیش‌بینی کردن	suspect: v.	سوءظن بردن
preliminary: adj.	مقدماتی	taxicab: n.	تاکسی
proceed: v.	(جلو) رفتن	tension: n.	کشش، تنش
property: n.	دارایی	thresh: v.	خرمن کوبیدن
prosperity	سعادت، خوشبختی	tight: adj.	تنگ
purge: v.	تصفیه کردن	tiny: adj.	کوچک
reduce: v.	(وزن) کم کردن	traffic: n.	معامله، مبادله
relief: n.	نقش برجسته	treat: v.	معالجه کردن
resent: v.	آزرده شدن	trivial: adj.	پیش پا افتاده
resolve: v.	تصمیم گرفتن	unofficial: adj.	غیررسمی
reveal: v.	نشان دادن، آشکار کردن	vein: n.	رگ
rivalry: n.	هم چشمی، رقابت	vessel: n.	رگ، آوند
route: n.	جاده، مسیر	violation: n.	تخطی
schooling: n.	تحصیلات	vow: v.	عهد کردن
scrimmage n.	زد و خورد	waste: n.	مواد زاید
searching: adj.	کامل و دقیق	wheat: n.	گندم
secure: v.	ضمانت کردن	wrinkle: n.	چین و چروک
sibling: n.	هم شیر، خواهر یا برادر	wrist: n.	مچ (دست)
slope: n.	شیب		

D d

da.is /£ ˈdeɪ.ɪs, £ deɪs, $ ˈdaɪ-/ *n.* raised platform for guests of honor

سکّو؛ شاه‌نشین

When he approached the *dais*, he was greeted by cheers from the people who had come to honor him.

dal.ly /ˈdæli/ *v.* to trifle with, to procrastinate

بازی کردن؛ دست دست کردن؛ جدّی نگرفتن

She merely *dallied with* his affections.

dank /dæŋk/ *adj.* damp

مرطوب، نمناک، نمور

The walls of the dungeon were *dank* and slimy.

dap.pled /ˈdæp.l̩d/ *adj.* spotted

خال خالی، خالدار، لکه‌لکه

The sunlight filtering through the screens created a *dappled* effect on the wall.

das.tard /£ ˈdæs.təd, $ ˈdæs.tɚd/ *n.* coward

آدم رذل و پست

This sneak attack is the work of a *dastard*.

das.tard.ly: *adj.*

رذیلانه، زشت

daub /£ dɔːb, $ dɑːb/ *v.* to smear, to spread liquid on sth

رنگ مالی کردن، مالیدن، کثیف کردن با

It doesn't need to be perfect; just **daub** the paint on as quickly as possible.

daunt /£ dɔːnt, $ dɑːnt/ *v.* to intimidate, to lessen the courage of

ترساندن، توی دل (کسی را) خالی کردن

Your threats cannot **daunt** me.

daunt.less: *adj.*   بی‌باک، نترس، جسور، متهور

daw.dle /£ ˈdɔː.dl̩, $ ˈdɑː-/ *v.* to waste time, to loiter

فس‌فس کردن، دست دست کردن، اتلاف وقت کردن

Inasmuch as we must meet a deadline, do not **dawdle** over this work.

dead.lock /£ ˈded.lɒk, $ -lɑːk/ *n.* standstill, stalemate

بن‌بست، شکست کامل

The negotiations had reached a **deadlock**.

dead.pan /ˈded.pæn/ *adj.* wooden, impassive

خشک، بی‌روح، سرد، بی‌احساس

We wanted to see how long he could maintain his **deadpan** expression.

dearth /£ dɜːθ, $ dɜːrθ/ *n.* scarcity

کمبود، کمیابی

There seems to be a **dearth** of good young players at the moment.

de.ba.cle /deɪˈbɑː.kl̩/ *n.* breaking up, downfall

عدم موفقیت کامل، شکست کامل، ناکامی

This **debacle** in the government can only result in anarchy.

de.base /dɪˈbeɪs/ v. to reduce to lower state, to disparage

کم ارزش کردن، بی‌مقدار کردن، سبک کردن، خوار کردن

You *debase* yourself by telling such lies.

de.bauch /£ dɪˈbɔːtʃ, $ -ˈbɑːtʃ/ v. to corrupt, to make intemperate

به فساد کشاندن، اغوا کردن

A vicious newspaper can *debauch* public ideals.

de.bauch.ee: n.   آدم فریب خورده، فاسد
de.bauched: adj.   بی‌بند و بار، عیاش، هرزه
de.bauch.er.y: n.   هرزگی، فساد، عیاشی

de.bil.i.tate /dɪˈbɪl.ɪ.teɪt/ v. to weaken, to enfeeble

ناتوان کردن، ضعیف کردن؛ بیمار کردن

Huge debts are *debilitating* their economy.

de.bon.air /£ ˌdeb.əˈneər, $ -ˈner/ adj. friendly, aiming to please

شاد و سرحال، آراسته، خوش لباس

The *debonair* youth was liked by all who met him, because of his cheerful and obliging manner.

deb.u.tante /£ ˈdeɪ.bjuː.tɒnt, £ ˈdeb.juː-, $ -tɑːnt/ n. young woman making formal entrance into society

معرفی رسمی دختر جوان از خانواده نجبا به جامعه

As a *debutante*, she was often mentioned in the society columns of the newspapers.

dec.a.dence /£ ˈdek.ə.dᵊnts/ n. decay

انحطاط، زوال، سقوط

The moral *decadence* of the people was reflected in the lewd literature of the period.

de.cant /dɪˈkænt/ *v.* to pour gently

با احتیاط ریختن، از ظرفی به ظرف دیگر ریختن

They *decant* wine from its bottle into more attractive container for serving.

de.cap.i.tate /dɪˈkæp.ɪ.teɪt/ *v.* to behead

گردن زدن، سر از تن (کسی) جدا کردن

They did not hang him; they *decapitated* him.

de.cid.u.ous /dɪˈsɪd.ju.əs/ *adj.* losing leaves

(درخت) برگ‌ریز

The oak is a *deciduous* tree.

dec.i.mate /ˈdes.ɪ.meɪt/ *v.* to kill, usually one out of ten

از بین بردن، نابود کردن، تلفات سنگین وارد کردن

We do more to *decimate* our population in automobile accidents than we do in war.

de.ci.pher /£ dɪˈsaɪ.fəʳ, $ -fɚ/ *v.* to decode

رمزگشایی کردن، خواندن

I could not *decipher* the doctor's handwriting.

de.cliv.i.ty /dɪˈklɪvɪtɪ/ *n.* downward slope

سرازیری، سراشیبی

The children loved to ski down the *declivity*.

dé.coll.eté /£ ˌdeɪ.kɒl.ɪˈtiː, $ -ˌkɑː.ləˈtiː/ *adj.* having a low-necked dress

لباس یقه‌باز؛ (زن) دکلته‌پوش

Evening gowns are *décolleté* this season; bare shoulders are again in vogue.

de.com.pos.i.tion /£ ˌdiː.kɒm.pəˈzɪʃ.ᵊn, $ -kɑːm-/ *n.* decay

گندیدگی، پوسیدگی؛ تجزیه، واپاشی

The corpse was in an advanced stage of *decomposition*.

de.com.pose: *v.* متلاشی شدن، تجزیه شدن

dec.o.rous /£ ˈdek.ə.rəs, $ ˈ-ɚ.əs/ *adj.* proper

مؤدبانه، با نزاکت؛ با وقار، متین، شایسته

Her *decorous* behavior was praised by her teachers.

de.co.rum: *n.* ادب، نزاکت، متانت، وقار، شایستگی

de.coy /ˈdiː.kɔɪ/ *n.* lure, bait

طعمه، پرندۀ دام

The wild ducks were not fooled by the *decoy*.

de.coy: *v.* به دام انداختن، گول زدن

de.cre.pit /dɪˈkrep.ɪt/ *adj.* worn out by age

فرسوده، قراضه، اسقاطی؛ (خانه) کلنگی

The *decrepit* car blocked traffic on the highway.

de.cre.pi.tude: *n.* فرسودگی، سالخوردگی، استهلاک

de.cry /dɪˈkraɪ/ *v.* to disparage

ناچیز شمردن، بی‌مقدار کردن، بی‌ارج کردن

She *decried* his efforts as a waste of time.

de.duc.ib.le /£ dɪˈdjuː.sɪ.bl̩, $ -ˈduː-/ *adj.* derived by reasoning

قابل استدلال، قابل استنباط

If we accept your premise, your conclusions are easily *deducible*.

de.fal.cate /ˈdiːfælkeɪt/ *v.* to misuse money held in trust

سوء استفاده کردن (از سپرده)

Legislation was passed to punish brokers who *defalcate* their client's funds.

de.fam.a.tion /ˌdef.əˈmeɪ.ʃən/ *n.* harming a person's reputation

هتک حرمت، افترا، آبروریزی

Such ***defamation*** of character may result in a slander suit.

de.fault /£ dɪˈfɒlt, $ -ˈfɑːlt/ *n.* failure to do

عدم حضور، غیبت، غیاب؛ عدم پرداخت

Because of his failure to appear in the court, she was granted a divorce ***by default***.

de.feat.ist /£ dɪˈfiː.tɪst, $ -t̬ɪst/ *adj., n.*

ناامیدانه، مأیوس کننده؛ آدم ناامید

If you maintain your ***defeatist*** attitude, you will never succeed.

de.fec.tion /dɪˈfek.ʃ°n/ *n.* desertion

ترک؛ جلای وطن؛ پناهندگی

Discontent in the party will lead to further ***defection***.

def.er.ence /£ ˈdef.ªr.ªnts, $ ˈ-ɚ-/ *n.* respect, submission

تمکین؛ ملاحظه، حرمت، احترام

In deference to his desires, the employers granted him a holiday.

de.file /dɪˈfaɪl/ *v.* to pollute, to profane

هتک حرمت کردن از، توهین کردن، ملوث کردن، آلوده کردن

The hoodlums ***defiled*** the church with their scurrilous writing.

de.fin.i.tive /£ dɪˈfɪn.ɪ.tɪv, $ -ə.t̬ɪv/ *adj.* final, complete

نهایی؛ قطعی، مسلم، بی چون و چرا

Her book is the ***definitive*** work on Milton.

de.flect /dɪˈflekt/ *v.* to turn aside

منحرف کردن، منحرف شدن

His life was saved when his cigarrette case ***deflected*** the bullet.

de.fray /dɪˈfreɪ/ *v.* to pay the costs of

هزینه (چیزی را) پرداختن

Her employer offered to ***defray*** the costs of her education.

deft /deft/ *adj.* neat, skillful

ماهر، ورزیده

The ***deft*** waiter uncorked the champagne without spilling a drop.

de.funct /dɪˈfʌŋkt/ *adj.* dead; no longer in use or existence

مرحوم، متوفی؛ منسوخ، قدیمی

The lawyers sought to examine the books of the ***defunct*** corporation.

de.grad.ed /dɪˈgreɪdəd/ *adj.* debased, lowered in rank

خوار، تحقیرشده

The ***degraded*** wretch spoke only of his past glories and honors.

de.i.fy /ˈdeɪ.ɪ.faɪ/ *v.* to idolize, to turn into a god

بت ساختن از؛ به مقام خدایی رساندن، خدا انگاشتن

Admire the rock star all you want; just don't ***deify*** him.

deign /deɪn/ *v.* to condescend

لطف کردن، محبت کردن

He felt he would debase himself if he ***deigned*** to answer his critics.

de.lec.tab.le /dɪˈlek.tə.bl̩/ *adj.* delicious, delightful

مطبوع، لذیذ

We thanked our host for a most *delectable* meal.

de.lete /dɪˈliːt/ *v.* to erase, to strike out

حذف کردن

If you *delete* this paragraph, the composition will have more appeal.

del.e.te.ri.ous /ˌdel.ɪˈtɪə.ri.əs, $ -ˈtɪr.i-/ *adj.* harmful

مضر، زیان‌بار

Workers in nuclear research must avoid the *deleterious* effects of radioactive substances.

de.li.ne.a.tion /dɪˌlɪn.iˈeɪ.ʃən/ *n.* portrayal

توصیف، ترسیم، تعریف، تعیین

He is a powerful storyteller, but he is weakest in his *delineation* of character.

del.i.quesc.ent /delɪˈkwesent/ *adj.* capable of absorbing moisture

رطوبت‌گیر، نم‌پذیر، نم‌گیر

Since this powder is extremely *deliquescent*, it must be kept in a hermetically sealed container.

de.li.ri.um /dɪˈlɪr.i.əm/ *n.* mental disturbance

هذیان؛ روان آشفتگی

The drunkard in his *delirium* saw strange animals.

de.lude /dɪˈluːd/ *v.* to deceive, to mislead

فریب دادن، گول زدن، گمراه کردن

Do not *delude* yourself into believing that he will relent.

de.lu.sion /dɪˈluːʒən/ *n.* false belief, hallucination

هذیان، وهم، توهم، خیال واهی، تصور باطل

This scheme is a snare and a *delusion*.

de.lu.sive /dɪˈluː.sɪv/ *adj.* deceptive, raising vain hopes

موهوم، خیالی، کاذب؛ گول زننده، گمراه کننده

Do not raise your hopes on the basis of his *delusive* promises.

dem.a.gogue /£ ˈdem.ə.gɒg, $ -gɑːg/ *n.* false leader of people

عوام فریب

He was accused of being a *demagogue*.

de.mean /dɪˈmiːn/ *v.* to degrade, to humiliate

سبک کردن، کوچک کردن، خوار کردن

He felt that he would *demean* himself if he replied to the critics.

de.mean.or /£ dɪˈmiː.nər, $ -nɚ/ *n.* behavior, bearing

رفتار، طرز رفتار

His sober *demeanor* quieted the noisy revelers.

de.men.ted /£ dɪˈmen.tɪd, $ -t̬ɪd/ *adj.* insane

دیوانه، آشفته خیال

She became increasingly *demented* and had to be hospitalized.

de.mise /dɪˈmaɪz/ *n.* death

فوت، درگذشت؛ اضمحلال

Upon the *demise* of the dictator, a bitter dispute about succession to power developed.

dem.o.li.tion /ˌdem.əˈlɪʃ°n/ *n.* destruction

تخریب، انهدام

The major aim was the complete *demolition* of all means of transportation.

de.mo.lish: *v.*   درهم کوبیدن، خراب کردن

de.mon.i.ac /ʃ dɪˈməʊ.ni.æk, $ -ˈmoʊ-/ *adj.* fiendish

شیطانی، خبیث، اهریمنی

They devised many ***demoniac*** means of torture.

    de.mon: *n.*   شیطان، دیو، روح شیطانی

dem.o.tic /£ dɪˈmɒt.ɪk, $ -ˈmɑː.t̬ɪk/ *adj.* related to the people

مردمی، عمومی، متداول، همگانی، معمولی

He believed that a ***demotic*** society would lower the nation's standards.

de.mur /£ dɪˈmɜːʳ, $ -ˈmɜːr/ *v.* to delay, to object

مخالفت کردن با، اعتراض کردن به

To ***demur*** at this time will only worsen the already serious situation.

de.mure /£ dɪˈmjʊəʳ, $ -ˈmjʊr/ *adj.* grave, serious, coy

متین، سنگین، موقر، محجوب

She was ***demure*** and reserved.

den.i.grate /ˈden.ɪ.greɪt/ *v.* to blacken

بدنام کردن، تحقیر کردن، دست کم گرفتن

All attempts to ***denigrate*** the character of the President have failed.

den.i.zen /ˈden.ɪ.zᵊn/ *n.* inhabitant of

ساکن، مقیم

Ghosts are ***denizens*** of the land of the dead who return to earth.

de.no.ta.tion /diːnəʊˈteɪʃᵊn/ *n.* meaning

معنی (صریح)

A dictionary will always give us the ***denotation*** of a word.

de.noue.ment /deɪˈnuː.mɑː/ *n.* final outcome of a play

(داستان و نمایش) **گره‌گشایی**

The play was childish written; the *denouement* was obvious to theatergoers.

de.pict /dɪˈpɪkt/ *v.* to portray

توصیف کردن، نشان دادن، تصویر کردن

The author *depicts* the slave owners as kind and benevolent masters.

de.pi.late /£ dɪ.ˈpɪ.leit, $ dɪˈpilait/ *v.* to remove hair

چیدن موهای زاید، موزدایی کردن

Many women *depilate* their legs.

de.plete /dɪˈpliːt/ *v.* to reduce, to exhaust

کاهش دادن؛ مصرف کردن؛ تمام کردن

We must wait until we *deplete* our present inventory.

de.ploy /dɪˈplɔɪ/ *v.* to spread out for battle, to ready

وارد میدان شدن؛ مستقر شدن، موضع گرفتن

The general ordered the battalion to *deploy*.

de.pose /£ dɪˈpəʊz, $ -ˈpoʊz/ *v.* to remove from office, to dethrone

خلع کردن، معزول کردن، سرنگون کردن

The army attempted to *depose* the king.

de.po.si.tion /ˌdep.əˈzɪʃ.ən/ *n.* testimony under oath

شهادت

He made his *deposition* in the judge's chamber.

de.pra.vi.ty /£ dɪˈpræv.ə.ti, $ -t̬i/ *n.* corruption, wickedness

انحراف، فساد، انحطاط

The *depravity* of his behavior shocked all.

dep.re.cate /ˈdep.rɪ.keɪt/ *v.* to disapprove regretfully

مخالفت کردن، انتقاد کردن؛ ابراز تأسف کردن؛ دست کم گرفتن

I must *deprecate* your attitude and hope that you will change your mind.

dep.re.ca.to.ry /£ ˌdep.rɪˈkeɪ.tᵊr.i, $ -kəˈtɔːr-/ *adj.* disapproving

معترضانه، اعتراض‌آمیز

Your *deprecatory* criticism has offended the author.

de.pre.ci.ate /dɪˈpriː.ʃi.eɪt/ *v.* to lessen in value

از ارزش افتادن، مستهلک شدن، ارزش را کاهش دادن

If you neglect this property, it will *depreciate*.

de.pre.da.tion /ˌdep.rəˈdeɪ.ʃᵊn/ *n.* plundering

چپاول، غارت، تاراج

After the *depredation* of the invaders, the people were penniless.

de.pre.date: *v.* غارت کردن، چپاول کردن، تاراج کردن

de.range /dɪˈreɪndʒ/ *v.* to make insane

دیوانه کردن، آشفته پریشان کردن

He was mentally *deranged*.

de.re.lict /ˈder.ə.lɪkt/ *adj.* abandoned

متروک، متروکه

The *derelict* craft was a menace to navigation.

de.ride /dɪˈraɪd/ *v.* to scoff at

به مسخره گرفتن، استهزاء کردن، ریشخند کردن

The people *derided* his grandiose schemes.

de.ri.sion /dɪˈrɪʒ.ᵊn/ *n.* ridicule

استهزاء، تمسخر، ریشخند

They greeted his proposal with *derision* and refused to consider it seriously.

de.ri.va.tive /£ dɪˈrɪv.ə.tɪv, $ -t̬ɪv/ *adj.* unoriginal, derived from another

مشتق، گرفته شده از، اقتباس شده، تقلیدی

Romanian is a *derivative* of Latin.

der.ma.tol.o.gist /£ ˌdɜː.məˈtɒl.ə.dʒɪst, $ ˌdɜːr.məˈtɑː.lə-/ *n.* one who studies and treats skin diseases

متخصص پوست

I advise you to consult a *dermatologist* about your acne.

de.rog.a.tory /£ dɪˈrɒg.ə.tᵊr.i, £ -tri, $ -ˈrɑː.gə.tɔːr-/ *adj.* expressing a low opinion

موهن، توهین‌آمیز، تحقیرآمیز

He was always making *derogatory* remarks about her.

des.cant /ˈdes.kænt/ *v.* to discuss fully

زیادی حرف زدن، مبسوط سخن گفتن

He was willing to *descant* upon any topic of conversation.

de.scry /dɪˈskraɪ/ *v.* to catch sight of

مشاهده کردن، دیدن

In the distance, we could barely *descry* the enemy vessels.

de.se.crate /ˈdes.ɪ.kreɪt/ *v.* to violate the sanctity of

بی‌حرمتی کردن به

The soldiers *desecrate* the temple.

de.sic.cate /ˈdes.ɪ.keɪt/ *v.* to dry up

خشک کردن

People used to *desiccate* food in order to preserve it.

de.sid.er.a.tum /dɪsɪdəˈreɪtəm/ *n.* that which is desired

احتیاج، کمبود، نیازمندی

Our first *desideratum* must be the establishment of peace.

de.spi.ca.ble /dɪˈspɪk.ə.bl̩/ *adj.* contemptible

نفرت‌انگیز، تحقیرآمیز

Your *despicable* remarks call for no reply.

de.spise /dɪˈspaɪz/ *v.* to scorn, to feel a strong dislike

متنفر بودن از

I hate and *despise* that kind of cruel behavior.

de.spoil /£ dɪˈspɔɪl, $ ˌdiː-/ *v.* to plunder

غارت کردن، تاراج کردن، به یغما بردن؛ ویران کردن

Many of the graves have been *despoiled*.

de.spon.dent /£ dɪˈspɒn.dənt, $ -ˈspɑːn-/ *adj.* depressed, gloomy

افسرده، غمگین، نومید، اندوهگین

He became more and more *despondent* every day.

de.spon.den.cy: *n.*   افسردگی، غم، یأس، نومیدی

des.po.ti.sm /£ ˈdes.pə.tɪ.zəm, $ -tɪ-/ *n.* tyranny

استبداد، خودکامگی

People rebelled against the *despotism* of the king.

des.ti.tute /£ ˈdes.tɪ.tjuːt, $ -tɪ.tuːt/ *adj.* extremely poor

فقیر، تهی‌دست

The illness left the family *destitute*.

des.ul.to.ry /£ ˈdes.əl.tər.i, ˈdez-, $ -tɔːr-/ *adj.* aimless, jumping around

بی‌هدف، پراکنده، نامنظم، بی‌هدف

We played a *desultory* game of cards.

de.ter.gent /£ dɪˈtɜː.dʒənt, $ -ˈtɜːr-/ *n.* cleansing agent

مادهٔ پاک‌کننده

Many new *detergents* have replaced soap.

de.ter.mi.nate /£ dɪˈtɜː.mɪnəɪt, $ -ˈtɜːr-/ *adj.* invariable

ثابت، معین، قطعی؛ مصمّم

At the wedding, the procession of the nobles followed a *determinate* order.

det.o.na.tion /£ ˌdet.ᵊnˈeɪ.ʃᵊn, $ ˌdet̬-/ *n.* explosion

انفجار؛ صدای انفجار

The *detonation* could be heard miles away.

de.trac.tion /dɪˈtrækʃᵊn/ *n.* slandering, aspersions

تحقیر، بی‌اعتباری، کوچک شماری

He is offended by your frequent *detraction* of his ability as a director.

det.ri.ment /ˈdet.rɪ.mənt/ *n.* harm, damage

ضرر، زیان، آسیب

You can follow this diet without *detriment* to your health.

de.vi.ate /ˈdiː.vi.eɪt/ *v.* to turn away from

منحرف شدن، دور شدن، دوری جستن

Do not *deviate* from the truth.

de.vi.ate: *adj.* منحرف

de.vi.ous /ˈdiː.vi.əs/ *adj.* going astray, erratic

پر پیچ و خم، انحرافی؛ خلاف، غیراخلاقی

1) He took a rather *devious* route which avoids the city center.

2) His *devious* behavior puzzled everyone.

de.void /dɪˈvɔɪd/ *adj.* lacking

عاری از، فاقدِ

He seems to be *devoid of* any compassion whatsoever.

de.volve /£ dɪˈvɒlv, $ -ˈvɑːlv/ *v.* to pass to others, deputize

محول کردن، واگذار کردن، منتقل کردن

To be a good manager, you must know how to *devolve* responsibility downwards.

de.vout /dɪˈvaʊt/ *adj.* pious, serious

مؤمن، متدین، بااِیمان؛ صدیق، بااِخلاص

He was a *devout* Muslim.

dex.terous /£ ˈdek.stᵊr.əs, $ -stɚ-/ *adj.* skillful

زِبَردست، ماهر، چالاک

The magician was so *dexterous* that we could not follow him as he performed his tricks.

di.a.bol.i.cal /£ ˌdaɪəˈbɒl.ɪ.kᵊl, $ -ˈbɑː.lɪ.kᵊl/ *adj.* devilish

پلید، شیطانی، زشت؛ مزخرف، گَند

This scheme is so *diabolical* that I must reject it.

di.a.dem /ˈdaɪ.ə.dem/ *n.* crown

تاج شاهی؛ اقتدار

The king's *diadem* was on display at the museum.

di.a.lec.tic /£ ˌdaɪ.əˈlek.tɪk, $ -tɪk/ *n.* art of debate

بحث و جدل، احتجاج، استدلال

I am not skilled in *dialectic* and, therefore, cannot answer your arguments as forcefully as I wish.

di.aph.a.nous /daɪˈæf.ᵊn.əs/ *adj.* sheer, transparent

(پارچه) بدن‌نما، نازک

They admired her *diaphanous* and colorful dress.

di.a.tribe /ˈdaɪ.ə.traɪb/ *n.* bitter scolding, invective

انتقاد شدید، حملهٔ سخت

After lunch he *launched into* a long *diatribe against* the government.

di.cho.to.my /£ daɪˈkɒt.ə.mi, $ -ˈkɑː.t̬ə-/ *n.* branching into two parts

دوگانگی، دو شاخگی؛ انشعاب، تقسیم؛ تضاد، اختلاف

There is often a *dichotomy* between what politicians say and what they do.

dic.tum /ˈdɪk.təm/ *n.* authoritative and weighty statement

مَثَل، ضرب‌المثل، اظهار نظر

He always follows the famous American *dictum*, "don't get mad, get even".

di.dac.tic /daɪˈdæk.tɪk/ *adj.* related to teaching, instructional

آموزنده، آموزشی

The *didactic* qualities of his poetry overshadow its literary qualities.

dif.fi.dence /ˈdɪf.ɪ.dəns/ *n.* shyness

کمرویی، عدم اعتماد به نفس، تزلزل، فقدان اعتماد به نفس

You must overcome your *diffidence* if you intend to become a salesperson.

dif.fu.sion /dɪˈfjuː.ʒən/ *n.* wordiness, spreading in all directions

پخش، پراکندگی، اختلاط

Your composition suffers from a *diffusion* of ideas; try to be more compact.

dif.fuse: *v.* پخش کردن، منتشر کردن، اشاعه دادن

di.gres.sive /daɪˈgresɪv/ *adj.* wandering away from the subject

پرت، خارج از موضوع، انحراف از موضوع

His book was marred by his many *digressive* remarks.

di.lap.i.da.tion /dɪˌlæp.ɪˈdeɪ.ʃᵊn/ *n.* ruin because of neglect

خرابی، ویرانی

The *dilapidation* of the building was corrected by several coats of paint.

di.late /£ daɪˈleɪt, $ ˈ--/ *v.* to expand

گشاد شدن، گشاد کردن

In the dark, the pupils of your eyes *dilate*.

di.la.tory /£ ˈdɪl.ə.tri, $ -tɔːr.i/ *adj.* delaying

کُند، کم تحرک

Your *dilatory* tactics may compel me to cancel the contract.

di.lem.ma /daɪˈlem.ə/ *n.* problem, predicament

وضعیت دشوار؛ دوراهی؛ تنگنا

In this *dilemma*, he knew no one to whom he could turn for advice.

dil.et.tan.te /ˌdɪl.ɪˈtæn.ti/ *n.* amateur, dabbler

غیرحرفه‌ای، آماتور

He was not serious in his painting; he was rather a *dilettante*.

dim.in.u.tion /£ ˌdɪm.ɪˈnjuː.ʃᵊn, $ -əˈnuː-/ *n.* lessening, reduction in size

کاهش، تقلیل

There will be a *diminution* in profits for at least the next two years.

di.min.ish: *v.*   کاستن، کاهش دادن، تقلیل یافتن

dint /dɪnt/ *n.* means, effort, using

به وسیلهٔ، با، به کمکِ

She got what she wanted *by dint of* pleading and threatening.

dip.so.ma.ni.ac /ˌdɪp.səˈmeɪ.ni.æk/ *n.* one who has an uncontrollable need to drink alcohol

شخص مبتلا به عطش الکلی، جنون الکل

He was a *dipsomaniac*.

dire /£ daɪəʳ, $ daɪr/ *adj.* disastrous, extreme

مبرم، شدید، حاد؛ وحشتناک، مخوف، هولناک

These people are *in dire need* of help.

dirge /£ dɜːdʒ, $ dɜːrdʒ/ *n.* lament with music

نوحه، مرثیه

The funeral *dirge* stirred us to tear.

dis.a.buse /ˌdɪs.əˈbjuːz/ *v.* to correct a false impression

(از اشتباه) در آوردن، (بر نادرستی چیزی) واقف کردن

I will try to *disabuse* you *of* your impression of my client's guilt.

dis.ar.ray /ˌdɪs.əˈreɪ/ *n.* disorder

بی‌نظمی، به هم ریختگی، آشفتگی

There is general *disarray* among the organizers of the event.

throw sth into disarry: *v.*   بهم زدن، بهم ریختن

dis.a.vow.al /ˌdɪs.əˈvaʊ.ᵊl/ *n.* denial, disclaiming

تکذیب، انکار

His *disavowal* of his part in the conspiracy was not believed by the jury.

dis.a.vow: *v.* تکذیب کردن، انکار کردن

dis.burse /£ dɪsˈbɜːs, $ -ˈbɜːrs/ *v.* to pay out

هزینه کردن، خرج کردن

When you *disburse* money on the company's behalf, be sure to get a receipt.

dis.cern.ib.le /£ dɪˈsɜːnɪbl̩, $ -ˈsɜːr-/ *adj.* perceivable, distinguishable

قابل تشخیص، قابل تمیز

The ships in the harbor were not *discernible* in the fog.

dis.cern.ing /£ dɪˈsɜːnɪŋ, $ -ˈsɜːr-/ *adj.* having insight, observant

با سلیقه، نکته‌سنج، بصیر، موشکاف

This shop sells clothes for the *discerning* customers, Madam.

dis.claim /dɪˈskleɪm/ *v.* to disown, to renounce claim to

از ادعای (چیزی) صرف‌نظر کردن، ترک دعوی کردن

If I grant you this privilege, will you *disclaim* all other rights?

dis.close /£ dɪˈskləʊz, $ -ˈskloʊz/ *v.* to reveal

آشکار کردن، برملا کردن، پرده برداشتن از، فاش کردن

He refused to *disclose* any information about his company's forthcoming product.

dis.clo.sure: *n.* افشا، افشاگری

dis.com.fit /dɪˈskʌmpfɪt/ *v.* to put to rout, to defeat

شکست دادن، مغلوب کردن

This ruse will *discomfit* the enemy.

dis.com.fit.ed: *adj.* ناراحت، معذب

dis.com.fi.ture: *n.* ناراحتی

dis.con.cert /£ ˌdɪs.kənˈsɜːt, $ -ˈsɜːrt/ *v.* to confuse, to upset, to embarrass

اوقات (کسی را) تلخ کردن، ناراحت کردن

The lawyer was *disconcerted* by the evidence produced by his adversary.

dis.con.cert.ed: *adj.* ناراحت، نگران، معذب

dis.con.so.late /£ dɪˈskɒnt.sᵊl.ət, $ -ˈskɑːnt-/ *adj.* sad

غمگین، افسرده، اندوهگین

The death of his son left him *disconsolate*.

dis.cor.dant /£ dɪˈskɔː.dᵊnt, $ -ˈskɔːr-/ *adj.* inharmonious, conflicting

مغایر، مخالف، متضاد

The two leaders had notably *discordant* messages.

dis.count /dɪˈskaʊnt/ *v.* to reduce the amount; to disregard

تخفیف دادن؛ نادیده گرفتن، اهمیت ندادن به

1) We cannot *discount* our prices.
2) Be prepared to *discount* what he has to say about his ex-wife.

dis.cred.it /dɪˈskred.ɪt/ *v.* to defame, to disbelieve

از اعتبار انداختن، بی‌اعتبار کردن؛ بدنام کردن؛ باور نکردن، نپذیرفتن

Evidence of links with drug dealers has *discredited* the President.

dis.crep.an.cy /dɪˈskrep.ᵊnt.si/ *n.* difference, lack of consistency

مغایرت، تضاد، تفاوت، اختلاف، ناهماهنگی

The police noticed some *discrepancies* in his description

of the crime.

dis.crete /dɪˈskriːt/ *adj.* unconnected, separate

جدا، مجزا، منفصل، گسسته، ناپیوسته

The universe is composed of *discrete* bodies.

dis.cre.tion /dɪˈskreʃ.ᵊn/ *n.* power of decision or choice; prudence

قوهٔ تشخیص، بصیرت، شعور؛ احتیاط

Leave the decision to your *discretion*.

dis.crim.i.nat.ing /£ dɪˈskrɪm.ɪ.net.tɪŋ, $ -t̬ɪŋ/ *adj.* able to see differences

دقیق، ظریف، نکته‌سنج، تیزبین

They are *discriminating* shoppers.

dis.crim.i.nate: *v.*   تمیز دادن، فرق گذاشتن

dis.crim.i.na.tion: *n.*   تمیز، تشخیص؛ تبعیض

dis.cur.sive /£ dɪˈskɜː.sɪv, $ -skɜːr-/ *adj.* digressing, rambling

پراکنده، بی‌ربط

They were annoyed and bored by his *discursive* remarks.

dis.dain /dɪsˈdeɪn, dɪz-/ *v.* to treat with scorn or contempt

با دیدهٔ تحقیر نگریستن به؛ اکراه داشتن، عار داشتن

Our posh neighbors seem to be *disdaining* to speak to us.

dis.grun.tle /£ dɪsˈgrʌn.tl̩, $ -t̬l̩/ *v.* to be annoyed, to make discontented

ناراحت کردن، پکر کردن، ناراضی کردن

The passengers are *disgruntled* by the numerous delays.

dis.grun.tled: *adj.*   پکر، دمغ، دلخور؛ ناراضی، ناخشنود

dis.ha.bille /dɪsəˈbiːl/ *n.* in a state of undress

لخت، برهنه

He lounged around the house in a state of *dishabille*.

dis.heart.en /£ dɪsˈhɑː.tᵊn, $ -ˈhɑːr.tᵊn/ *v.* to discourage

مأیوس کردن، ناامید کردن، دلسرد کردن

His failure to pass the exam *disheartened* him.

di.shev.eled /dɪˈʃev.ᵊld/ *adj.* untidy

ژولیده، آشفته، به هم ریخته، نامرتب

Your *disheveled* appearance will hurt your chances in the interview.

dis.in.gen.u.ous /ˌdɪs.ɪnˈdʒen.ju.əs/ *adj.* slighty dishonest

ریاکار، نادرست

His remarks indicated that he was *disingenuous*.

dis.in.ter.est.ed /dɪˈsɪn.trə.stɪd/ *adj.* unprejudiced

بی‌طرف، بی‌غرض، بی‌تفاوت، بی‌اعتنا

The only *disinterested* person in the room was the judge.

dis.joint.ed /£ dɪsˈdʒɔɪn.tɪd, $ -t̬ɪd/ *adj.* disconnected

پراکنده، آشفته، بدون انسجام، بی‌سر و ته

His remarks were so *disjointed* that we could not follow his reasoning.

dis.mem.ber /£ dɪˈsmem.bəʳ, $ -bɚ/ *v.* to cut into small parts

تکه‌تکه کردن، تکه پاره کردن، مُثله کردن

The police found the *dismembered* body of a young man in the bush.

dis.par.age /£ dɪˈspær.ɪdʒ, $ -ˈsper-/ *v.* to belittle

کوچک شمردن، تحقیر کردن، ارزش قائل نشدن برای

Do not *disparage* anyone's contribution; these little gifts add up to large sums.

dis.par.ate /£ ˈdɪs.pᵊr.ət, $ -pɚ.ət/ *adj.* unrelated, basically different

بسیار متفاوت، متمایز، ناهمخوان، غیرقابل مقایسه

It's difficult to organize these *disparate* elements into a coherent whole.

dis.pa.ri.ty /£ dɪˈspær.ə.ti, $ -ˈper.ə.ţi/ *n.* difference

تفاوت، اختلاف، ناهمخوانی

The *disparity* in their ages made no difference at all.

dis.pas.sion.ate /dɪˈspæʃ.ᵊn.ət/ *adj.* calm, impartial

بی‌طرف، منصف؛ بی‌طرفانه، منصفانه

His comments were clear-sighted and *dispassionate*.

dis.per.sion /£ dɪˈspɜː.ʃᵊn, $ -spɜːr-/ *n.* scattering

پخش، انتشار، پراکندگی؛ توزیع

The *dispersion* of emergency supplies will take another week.

dis.pir.it.ed /£ dɪˈspɪr.ɪ.tɪd, $ -ţɪd/ *adj.* lacking in spirit

افسرده، دلسرد، مأیوس، ناامید

He was always *dispirited* on Sunday night because of the prospect of school the next day.

dis.put.a.tious /£ ˌdɪs.pjʊˈteɪ.ʃəs, $ -pjuː-/ *adj.* argumentative

اهل مشاجره، اهل جرّ و بحث

He is a *disputatious* young man.

dis.qui.si.tion /ˌdɪs.kwɪˈzɪʃ.ᵊn/ *n.* long and detailed explanation

گزارش مبسوط، شرح و بسط

I am not about to enter into a *disquisition* on the evils of eating meat.

dis.sec.tion /£ daɪˈsek.ʃ°n, $ dɪ-/ *n.* analysis; cutting apart

تجزیه و تحلیل، بررسی؛ تشریح، کالبد شکافی

The *dissection* of frogs in the laboratory is unpleasant to some students.

dis.sem.ble /dɪˈsem.bl̩/ *v.* to disguise, to pretend

(احساسات) پنهان کردن، وانمود کردن، ریاکاری کردن

He was trying to *dissemble* his motive in joining the group.

dis.sem.i.nate /dɪˈsem.ɪ.neɪt/ *v.* to scatter, to spread

اشاعه دادن، پخش کردن، انتشار دادن

One of the organization's aims is to *disseminate* information about the spread of the disease.

dis.sent /dɪˈsent/ *v.* to disagree

مخالف بودن، مخالفت کردن

Nine people were in favor of the proposal and three *dissented*.

dis.ser.ta.tion /£ ˌdɪs.əˈteɪ.ʃ°n, $ -ɚˈ-/ *n.* formal essay

رساله، پایان‌نامه، تز

You are required to prepare a *dissertation* on some scholarly subject.

dis.sim.u.late /dɪˈsɪmjʊleɪt/ *v.* to pretend, to hide real intentions

(احساسات) پنهان کردن، ریاکاری کردن

She tried to *dissimulate* her grief by her gay attituds.

dis.si.pate /ˈdɪs.ɪ.peɪt/ *v.* to squander, to waste

هدر دادن، از بین بردن، زایل کردن

The young man quickly *dissipated* his inheritance.

dis.so.lute /ˈdɪs.ə.luːt/ *adj.* loose in morals

بی بند و بار، غیراخلاقی، هرزه

The *dissolute* life led by these people is indeed shocking.

dis.so.nance /£ ˈdɪs.ᵊn.ənts, $ -ə.nənts/ *n.* discord

تنافر، ناهمخوانی، ناسازی

Some musicians use *dissonance* to achieve certain effects.

dis.suade /dɪˈsweɪd/ *v.* to advise against

منصرف کردن؛ متقاعد کردن

He could not *dissuade* his friend *from* joining the conspirators.

dis.su.sion: *n.*   انصراف

dis.tend /dɪˈstend/ *v.* to expand, to swell out

ورم کردن، باد کردن، بزرگ شدن

When he is under stress, the veins *distend* on his forehead.

dis.tor.tion /£ dɪˈstɔː.ʃᵊn, $ -ˈstɔːr-/ *n.* twisting out of shape

تغییر شکل، کجی، تحریف

These accusations are *distortions* of the truth.

dis.tort   تحریف کردن؛ کج و کوله کردن

dis.trait /dɪˈstreɪ/ *adj.* absentminded

پریشان خاطر، حواس پرت، آشفته

The teacher often appeared *distrait*.

dis.traught /£ dɪˈstrɔːt, $ -ˈstrɑːt/ *adj.* upset, distracted, worried

پریشان، آشفته

The *distraught* parents searched the ravine for their lost

child.

di.ur.nal /£ ˌdaɪˈɜː.nəl, $ -ˈɜːr-/ *adj.* daily

روزانه، یومیّه

A farmer cannot neglect his *diurnal* tasks at any time.

di.va /ˈdiː.və/ *n.* operatic singer, prima donna

خوانندهٔ اصلی اپرا، ستارهٔ اپرا

As a *diva* she did not indulge in fits of temperament.

di.verge /£ ˌdaɪˈvɜːdʒ, $ dɪˈvɜːrdʒ/ *v.* to follow a different direction, to vary

از هم جدا شدن، از هم فاصله گرفتن، اختلاف پیدا کردن

Their objectives have been *diverging* recently.

di.vers /£ ˈdaɪ.vəz, $ -vɚz/ *adj.* several, differing

مختلف، متفاوت، گوناگون

We could hear *divers* opinions of his ability.

di.verse /£ daɪˈvɜːs, £ ˈ--, $ dɪˈvɜːrs/ *adj.* various

گوناگون، متفاوت، متنوع، مختلف

He has a *diverse* range of interests and experience.

di.ver.si.ty: *n.* گوناگونی، تنوع؛ اختلاف، تفاوت

di.vest /ˌdaɪˈvest/ *v.* to strip, to deprive

خلع (لباس) کردن، سلب کردن، محروم کردن، پس گرفتن

He was *divested* of his power to act.

div.i.na.tion /ˌdɪvɪˈneɪʃ°n/ *n.* foreseeing the future with aid of magic

غیب‌گویی، پیشگویی

Palm–reading is a type of *divination*.

di.vulge /daɪˈvʌldʒ/ *v.* to reveal

افشا کردن، فاش کردن، پرده برداشتن از، برملا کردن

Journalists do not ***divulge*** their sources.

di.vulg.ence: *n.* افشاگری، افشا

do.cile /£ ˈdəʊ.saɪl, £ ˈdɒs.aɪl, $ ˈdɑː.sᵊl/ *adj.* obedient, quiet

سر به راه، رام، آرام، حرف شنو، مطیع

He is a ***docile*** child.

do.cil.i.ty: *n.* سربه‌راهی، حرف شنوی

dock.et /£ ˈdɒk.ɪt, $ ˈdɑː.kɪt/ *n.* a list of legal cases

فهرست، صورت؛ دفتر ثبت دعاوی؛ رسید، پته

The case of Smith vs. Jones was entered in the ***docket*** for July 15.

doc.u.ment /£ ˈdɒk.jʊ.mənt, -ment, $ ˈdɑː.kjʊ-/ *v.* to provide written evidence

مدرک آوردن برای، سند ارائه دادن برای، مستند کردن

She kept all the receipts in order to ***document*** her expenses for the firm.

dod.der.ing /£ ˈdɒd.ᵊr.ɪŋ, $ ˈdɑː.dɚ-/ *adj.* shaky, infirm from old age

ضعیف، نحیف

He is a rather ***doddering*** old man.

dod.der: *v.* (از فرط پیری) آهسته و لرزان حرکت کردن، لنگان لنگان رفتن

doff /£ dɒf, $ dɑːf/ *v.* to take off

(به نشانه احترام کلاه از سر) ***برداشتن***، (لباس) ***از تن در آوردن***

He ***doffed*** his hat to the lady.

dog.ger.el /£ ˈdɒg.ᵊr.əl, $ ˈdɑː.gɚ-/ *n.* poor verse

شعر ضعیف و بی‌ارزش، شعر بند تنبانی

Most of his writing is mere ***doggerel***.

dog.mat.ic /£ dɒgˈmæt.ɪk, $ dɑːgˈmæt̬-/ *adj.* positive, arbitrary

جزم‌اندیش، متعصب؛ تعصب‌آمیز؛ جزمی

Do not be so ***dogmatic*** about that statement; it can be easily refuted.

dol.drums /£ ˈdɒl.drəmz, $ ˈdoʊl-/ *n.* blues, slack period, listlessness

دلتنگی؛ خمودگی، افسردگی، بی‌دل و دماغی

Her career was in the ***doldrums*** during those years.

dol.or.ous /£ ˈdɒl.ᵊr.əs, $ ˈdoʊ.lɚ-/ *adj.* sorrowful, feeling sad

غم‌انگیز، غمگین، اندوهگین

Her music always has a faintly ***dolorous*** feel.

dolt /£ dəʊlt, $ doʊlt/ *n.* stupid person

احمق، بی‌شعور

Don't be such a ***dolt***!

do.mi.cile /£ ˈdɒm.ɪ.saɪl, $ ˈdɑː.mə-/ *n.* house, the place where a person lives

محل اقامت، محل سکونت

Any change of ***domicile*** should be notified to the proper authorities.

dor.mant /£ ˈdɔː.mənt, $ ˈdɔːr-/ *adj.* sleeping, torpid, lethargic

غیرفعال؛ خاموش، نهفته، خفته

The long-***dormant*** valcano has recently shown sign of life.

dor.sal /£ ˈdɔː.sᵊl, $ ˈdɔːr-/ *adj.* on or near the back of

عقبی، پسین

A shark may be identified by its ***dorsal*** fin.

do.tage /£ ˈdəʊ.tɪdʒ, $ ˈdoʊ.t̬ɪdʒ/ *n.* senility

کهولت، پیری، فرتوتی

In his ***dotage***, the old man bored us with long tales of events in his childhood.

dough.ty /£ ˈdaʊ.ti, $ -ṭi/ *adj.* courageous, brave

دلیر، دلاور، شجاع و قوی

She has been for many years a ***doughty*** campaigner for women's rights.

dour /£ dʊər, £ ˈdaʊər, $ dʊr/ *adj.* sullen, stubborn, unfriendly

عبوس، اخمو؛ گرفته، دلتنگ کننده، غم‌انگیز

The normally ***dour*** Mr. James was photographed smiling and joking with friends.

dous.e /daʊs/ *v.* to plunge into water, to drench

در آب فرو رفتن، خیس کردن، آب پاشیدن به

They ***doused*** each other with hoses and water balloons.

dow.dy /ˈdaʊ.di/ *adj.* untidy, slovenly

(لباس) قدیمی، از مد افتاده؛(آدم) بد لباس

He used to wear a ***dowdy*** brown suit.

dregs /dregz/ *n.* sediment; immoral and worthless

پس‌مانده، تفاله، لجن، لرد، ته‌نشست

People tend to regard drug addicts as the ***dregs*** of society.

droll /£ drəʊl, $ droʊl/ *adj.* queer and amusing

مضحک، خنده‌آور، بامزه، با نمک

He was a popular guest because his ***droll*** anecdotes were always amusing.

drone /£drəʊn, $ droʊn/ *n.* idle person; male bee

(آدم) طفیلی، انگل، آدم عاطل و باطل؛ زنبور عسل نر

The would-be writer was in reality nothing but a ***drone***.

drone /£ drəʊn, $ droʊn/ *v.* to talk dully, to buzz or murmur

یکنواخت صحبت کردن، وز وز کردن

He was *droning on and on* about house prices.

dross /£ drɒs, $ drɑːs/ *n.* waste matter

ریم، کف باره؛ آشغال، پس‌مانده

Many methods have been devised to separate the valuable metal from the *dross*.

drudg.er.y /£ ˈdrʌdʒ.ᵊr.i, $ ˈ-ɚ-/ *n.* hard boring work

کار سخت و خسته‌کننده، بیگاری، خر حمالی

Cinderella's fairy godmother rescued her from a life of *drudgery*.

dub.i.ous /£ ˈdjuː.bi.əs, $ ˈduː-/ *adj.* doubtful

مشکوک؛ نامطمئن، نامشخص

These claims are *dubious* and not scientifically proven.

du.en.na /djuˈenə/ *n.* attendant of young female, chaperon

همراه دختر جوان، ندیمه

Their romance could not flourish because of the presence of her *duenna*.

dul.cet /ˈdʌl.sət/ *adj.* sweet sounding

(صدا) گوش‌نواز، دلنشین، شیرین، گرم

The *dulcet* sounds of the birds at dawn were soon drowned out by the roar of traffic.

dup.li.ci.ty /£ djʊˈplɪs.ɪ.ti, $ duːˈplɪs.ə.ţi/ *n.* lack of honesty, hypocrisy

فریب، نیرنگ، تزویر، حقه‌بازی

They were accused of *duplicity* in their dealing with both sides.

dur.ess /£ djʊˈres, $ duː-/ *n.* forcible restraint, threat

فشار، زور، ارعاب

He claimed that he signed the confession under ***duress***.

dwin.dle /ˈdwɪn.dl̩/ *v.* to reduce, to shrink

به تدریج کاهش یافتن، کم شدن

The community has ***dwindled*** to a tenth of its former size in the last two years.

dyn.am.ic /daɪˈnæm.ɪk/ *adj.* active, efficient

پویا؛ فعال، پر جنب و جوش، کارآمد

A ***dynamic*** government is necessary to meet the demands of a changing society.

dys.pep.tic /£ dɪˈspep.tɪk, $ -t̬ɪk/ *adj.* suffering from indigestion

(بیمار) مبتلا به سوء هاضمه؛ (مربوط به) سوء هاضمه

All the talk about rich food made him feel ***dyspeptic***.

dys.pep.si.a: *n.*

سوء هاضمه

لیستی از لغاتی که در جملات بخش D به کار رفته‌اند:

acne: *n.*	جوش صورت، آکنه	faintly: *adv.*	تاحدی، کمی
anecdote: *n.*	حکایت، اتفاق بامزه	fin: *n.*	(ماهی) باله
		fit: *n.*	حالت، حمله، غش
bar exam: *n.*	امتحان وکالت	gay: *adj.*	بشّاش، شاد
battalion: *n.*	گُروهان	gown: *n.*	لباس، ردا
benevolent: *adj.*	نیکوکار، مهربان	grandiose: *adj.*	عظیم
		hermetically: *adv.*	بدون هوا
cheer: *n.*	فریاد شادی	hoodlum: *n.*	آدم شرّ
clear-sighted: *adj.*	فهمیده، روشن بین	hose: *n.*	شیلنگ
		inasmuch as: *adv.*	تا آن جایی که
coat: *n.*	لایه، روکش	indulge: *v.*	زیاده روی کردن
coherent: *adj.*	منسجم، منطقی	inheritance: *n.*	ارث
compel: *v.*	وادار کردن، ناگزیر کردن	lounge: *v.*	استراحت کردن، وقت گذرانی کردن
confession: *n.*	اعتراف، اظهار	mar: *v.*	ضایع کردن، خراب کردن
conspiracy: *n.*	توطئه، تبانی	meet: *v.*	برآورده کردن
conspirator: *n.*	توطئه گر	menace: *n.*	خطر، تهدید
corporation: *n.*	مؤسسه، شرکت	navigation: *n.*	هدایت، جهت یابی
deadline: *n.*	موعد، مهلت، ضرب‌الاجل	neglect: *v.*	بی توجه بودن به
		obliging: *adj.*	دارای حس همکاری، مهربانی
don: *v.*	پوشیدن		
downwards: *adv.*	به رده‌های پایین	on and on: *adv.*	یک ریز، پشت سر هم
drown out: *v.*	محو کردن	overshadow: *v.*	تحت‌الشعاع قرار دادن
drug addict: *n.*	معتاد (به موادمخدر)		
dungeon: *n.*	سیاه‌چال	plead: *v.*	التماس کردن، خواستن

posh: *adj.*	شیک، اعیانی، باکلاس	scurrilous: *adj.*	پر از فحاشی
privilege: *n.*	مزیت، موهبت	slander: *n.*	افترا
procession: *n.*	صف، مراسم	slimy: *adj.*	پر از لجن
prospect: *n.*	فکر، تصور	sneak: *adj.*	دزدکی، مخفیانه
ravine: *n.*	دره عمیق و باریک	sober: *adj.*	هوشیار، عاقل
reasoning: *n.*	استدلال	stir: *v.*	تحریک کردن، به هیجان آمدن
relent: *v.*	کوتاه آمدن، نرم شدن		
require: *v.*	نیاز داشتن	vs. (versus): *prep.*	در برابرِ، در مقابلِ
route: *n.*	مسیر، خط		
ruse: *n.*	حیله، نیرنگ، حقه	whatsoever: *adv.*	هیچگونه
reveler: *n.*	عربده جو	would - be: *adj.*	آتی
scheme: *n.*	برنامه، نقشه، طرح		

E e

ear.thy /£ ˈɜː.θi, $ ˈɜːr-/ *adj.* unrefined, coarse

بی‌ظرافت، بی‌نزاکت؛ رُک، بی‌پرده

His *earthy* remarks often embarrassed the women in his audience.

e.bul.li.ent /ɪbˈʊl.i.ənt/ *adj.* very energetic

پر شور و شوق، سرخوش

Our *ebullient* host could not stop laughing and talking.

ec.cen.tri.ci.ty /£ ˌek.senˈtrɪs.ɪ.ti, $ -ţi/ *n.* oddity, idiosyncrasy

عادت عجیب، رفتار عجیب؛ غرابت، نامتعارف بودن؛ خصیصه فردی بودن

Her *eccentricities* get stranger by the day.

ec.cen.tric: *adj.* غیرعادی، عجیب و غریب

ec.cle.si.as.tic /ɪˌkliː.ziˈæs.tɪk/ *adj.* related to the church

مربوط به کلیسا، کلیسایی

The minister donned his *ecclesiastic* garb and walked to the pulpit.

é.clat /ˈeɪklɑː/ *n.* brilliance, glory

موفقیت درخشان، پیروزی تحسین برانگیز؛ استقبال، تشویق

He completed his task with *éclat*.

ec.lec.tic /ɪˈklek.tɪk/ *adj.* choosing from various sources, varied

He has an *eclectic* taste in music.

ec.lec.ti.ci.sm: *n.* آیین التقاطی، به گزینی

e.clipse /ɪˈklɪps/ *v., n.* to darken, to surpass; darkness

(خورشید یا ماه) گرفتن؛ سایه انداختن بر؛ تحتالشعاع قرار دادن، سربودن؛ خسوف، ماه گرفتگی؛ کسوف، خورشید گرفتگی

The economy has *eclipsed* all other issues.

ec.sta.sy /ˈek.stə.si/ *n.* joy, rapture

وجد، شور، شعف؛ خلسه، جذبه

She went into *ecstasy* over the news.

ed.i.fy /ˈed.ɪ.faɪ/ *v.* to instruct, to correct morally

تهذیب کردن

His purpose was to *edify* and not to entertain his audience.

ed.i.fi.ca.tion: *n.* تهذیب، تزکیه

e.duce /ɪˈdjuːs/ *v.* to draw forth, to elicit

استنتاج کردن، استنباط کردن

He could not *educe* a principle that would encompass all the data.

ee.rie /£ ˈɪə.ri, $ ˈɪr.i/ *adj.* weird, strange

ترسناک، خوفانگیز

In bed at night she heard the *eerie* noise of the wind.

ef.face /ɪˈfeɪs/ *v.* to remove, to rub out

پاک کردن، محو کردن، از بین بردن

The coin had been handled so many times that its date had been *effaced*.

ef.fec.tu.al /ɪˈfek.tju.əl/ *adj.* efficient

مؤثر، ثمربخش، نتیجه‌بخش
They wish to promote an *effectual* understanding between the two countries.

ef.fem.i.nate /ɪˈfem.ɪ.nət/ *adj.* having womanly traits

زنانه، مثل زنان
His voice was high-pitched and *effiminate*.

ef.fer.vesce /£ ˌef.əˈves, $ -əˈr-/ *v.* to bubble over, to show excitement

(از هیجان) بی‌تاب بودن، در پوست خود نگنجیدن
Some of us cannot stand the way she *effervesces* over trifles.

ef.fete /ɪˈfiːt/ *adj.* worn out, exhausted, barren

رو به انحطاط، رو به زوال؛ ناتوان، ضعیف
The literature of the age reflected the *effete* condition of the writers.

ef.fi.ca.cy /ˈef.ɪ.kə.si/ *n.* effectiveness

اثر، تأثیر، اثربخشی، فایده
The *efficacy* of this drug depends on the regularity of the dosage.

ef.fi.gy /ˈef.ɪ.dʒi/ *n.* dummy

تمثال، آدمک، پیکره
The mob showed its irritation by hanging the judge in *effigy*.

ef.flu.vi.um /eˈfluːvɪəm/ *n.* noxious smell

بوی مضر و سمّی
The *effluvium* and the poisons in the air are hazards to life.

ef.front.er.y /£ ɪˈfrʌn.tᵊr.i, $ -t̬ɚ-/ *n.* shameless boldness

گستاخی، جسارت، وقاحت، پررویی

He had the *effrontery* to insult the guest.

ef.fu.sion /ɪˈfjuː.ʒᵊn/ *n.* pouring forth

ابراز احساسات، فوران احساسات

The critics objected to his literary *effusion* because it was too flowery.

ef.fu.sive: *adj.*   احساساتی؛ افراطی

e.go.i.sm /£ ˈiː.gəʊ.ɪ.zᵊm, $ -goʊ-/ *n.* excessive interest in one's self

خودخواهی، خودپرستی، خودپسندی؛ غرور، تکبر

His *egoism* prevented him from seeing the needs of his colleagues.

e.go.ist: *n.*   خودخواه، خودبین، خودپرست، خودپسند

e.go.ti.sm /£ ˈiː.gəʊ.tɪ.zᵊm, $ -goʊ-/ *n.* conceit, vanity

خودخواهی، خودپرستی، خودبینی، خودپسندی

We found his *egotism* irritating.

e.gre.gi.ous /ɪˈgriː.dʒəs/ *adj.* gross, shocking

فوق‌العاده بد، وحشتناک، غیر قابل بخشش

He was an *egregious* liar.

e.gress /ˈiːgres/ *n.* exit, the way out

خروج؛ راه خروج

The sign "To the *Egress*" was upside down.

e.gress: *v.*   خارج شدن

e.jac.u.la.tion /ɪˌdʒæk.jʊˈleɪ.ʃᵊn/ *n.* exclamation

فریاد، غریو، بانگ

He could not repress an *ejaculation* of surprise when he

heard the news.

e.lab.or.a.tion /ɪˌlæb.əˈreɪ.ʃən/ *n.* addition of details

شرح، بسط؛ طول و تفصیل، حواشی

Tell what happened simply, without any *elaboration*.

e.lab.or.ate: *v.* توضیح دادن، شرح دادن؛ بسط دادن

e.la.tion /ɪˈleɪ.ʃən/ *n.* rise in spirits, exaltation

شعف، شادی، ذوق، وجد

She felt no *elation at* finding the purse.

el.e.gi.ac.al /ˌel.ɪˈdʒaɪ.əkl, $ ɪˈliː.dʒi.ækl/ *adj.* mournful, like an elegy

غم‌انگیز، اندوهبار؛ (مربوط به) مرثیه

The essay on the lost crew was *elegiacal* in mood.

el.e.gy: *n.* مرثیه، نوحه

e.lic.it /ɪˈlɪs.ɪt/ *v.* to draw out by discussion

(پاسخ، اطلاعات) بیرون کشیدن، در آوردن

The detectives tried to *elicit* where he had hidden his loot.

e.lix.ir /£ ɪˈlɪk.sɪər, $ -sjɚ/ *n.* cure-all

اکسیر، داروی هر درد بی‌درمان، آب حیات

It's another health product claiming to be the *elixir* of youth.

el.o.quence /ˈel.ə.kwənts/ *n.* expressiveness, persuasive speech

فصاحت، بلاغت، زبان آوری

The crowds were stirred by the President's *eloquence*.

el.o.quent: *adj.* فصیح، بلیغ، سلیس

e.lu.ci.date /ɪˈluː.sɪ.deɪt/ *v.* to explain, to enlighten

توضیح دادن، شرح دادن، روشن کردن

He was called upon to *elucidate* the disputed points in his article.

e.lu.sive /ɪˈluː.sɪv/ *adj.* hard to grasp, baffling, evasive

گنگ، مبهم؛ غیرقابل بیان؛ فرّار، گریز پا

His *elusive* dreams of wealth were costly to those who supported him financially.

e.lu.so.ry /ɪˈluː.sɔry/ *adj.* elusive, evasive

پیچیده، سخت، اندیشه گریز

He argued that the project was an *elusory* one and would bring disappointment at all.

e.ly.sian /eɪliːʒən/ *adj.* relating to paradise, blissful

بهشتی؛ لذت‌بخش، نشاط آور

An afternoon sail on the bay was for her an *elysian* journey.

e.mac.i.ate /ɪˈmeɪ.si.et/ *v.* to make thin and wasted

لاغر کردن، ضعیف کردن، نحیف کردن

He was wan and *emaciated* after his long period of starvation.

e.man.ate /ˈem.ə.neɪt/ *v.* to issue forth

ساطع شدن، صادر شدن؛ نشأت گرفتن، سرچشمه گرفتن

A strong odor of sulphur *emanated* from the spring.

e.man.ci.pate /ɪˈmænt.sɪ.peɪt/ *v.* to set free

آزاد کردن، رهایی بخشیدن

The attempts to *emancipate* the slaves were unpopular in New England.

em.bark /£ ɪmˈbɑːk, $ -bɑːrk/ *v.* to commence; to go on a boat or airplane

مبادرت کردن به، آغاز کردن؛ سوار شدن

He *embarked on* a new career.

em.bed /ɪmˈbed/ *v.* to fix firmly, to place in something

فرو کردن، نشاندن؛ جایگیر کردن، جایگزین کردن

The thorn was *embeded* in her thumb.

em.bel.lish /ɪmˈbel.ɪʃ/ *v.* to adorn

تزیین کردن، زینت دادن؛ آب و تاب دادن

The ceiling was *embellished* with flowers and leaves.

em.bez.zle.ment /ɪmˈbez.l̩.mənt/ *n.* stealing

اختلاس

The bank teller confessed his *embezzlement* of the funds.

em.blaz.on /ɪmˈbleɪ.zᵊn/ *v.* to decorate, to deck in brilliant colors

تزیین کردن، نقش بستن

A clinched fist was *emblazoned on* the tee-shirt.

em.broil /ɪmˈbrɔɪl/ *v.* to become involved in, to entangle

گرفتار کردن، درگیر کردن، گیر انداختن

He became *embroiled* in the heated discussion.

em.bry.o.nic /£ ˌem.briˈɒn.ɪk, $ -ˈɑː.nɪk/ *adj.* undeveloped, rudimentary

آغازین، ابتدایی، مقدماتی، اولیه

The project is still in its *embryonic* stage at the moment.

e.mend /ɪˈmend/ *v.* to correct, to improve

تصحیح کردن، غلط گیری کردن

The text is currently being *emended*.

e.me.ri.tus /£ ɪˈmer.ɪ.təs, emˈer-, $ -t̬əs/ *adj.* retired but retained in an honorary capacity

(استاد دانشگاه) بازنشسته و عضو افتخاری گروه آموزشی

He became *emeritus* professor of English when he retired.

e.me.tic /£ ɪˈmet.ɪk, $ -ˈmeṱ-/ *n.* substance causing vomiting

داروی استفراغ‌آور، داروی قی‌آور

The use of an *emetic* like mustard is useful in cases of poisoning.

em.i.nent /ˈem.ɪ.nənt/ *adj.* high, lofty

معروف، سرشناس؛ برجسته، چشمگیر

After his appointment to this *eminent* position, he seldom had time for his former friends.

e.mis.sa.ry /£ ˈem.ɪ.sᵊr.i. $ -ser-/ *n.* agent, messenger

فرستاده، پیک، قاصد

He has flown to China for a three-day visit as the personal *emissary* of the President.

e.mol.li.ent /£ ɪˈmɒl.i.ənt, $ -ˈmɑː.li-/ *n.* soothing or softening remedy

کِرِم نرم‌کنندهٔ پوست

He applied an *emollient* to the inflamed area.

em.pi.ri.cal /ɪmˈpɪr.ɪ.kᵊl/ *adj.* based on experience

تجربی

He distrusted hunches and placed his reliance on *empirical* data.

em.u.late /ˈem.jʊ.leɪt/ *v.* to rival; to imitate

سرمشق قرار دادن، پیروی کردن؛ رقابت کردن

Our political leaders *emulate* the virtues of the great

spiritual leader.

en.am.ored /£ ɪˈnæm.əd, $ -ɚd/ *adj.* overwhelmed by love

دلبسته، مجذوب؛ دلباخته

I have to say I'm not exactly *enamored with/ of* this part of the country.

en.clave /£ ˈen.kleɪv, $ ˈɑːn-/ *n.* territory enclosed within an alien land

سرزمین محصور، قلمرو بسته

The Vatican is an independent *enclave* in Italy.

en.co.mi.um /£ ɪŋˈkəʊ.mi.ᵊm/ *n.* praise, eulogy

مدح، ستایش، تحسین

He was sickened by the *encomiums* expressed by the speakers.

en.com.pass /ɪŋˈkʌm.pəs/ *v.* to surround, to include

محاصره کردن، در برگرفتن، احاطه کردن

They had been *encompassed* by enemy forces before their allies joined them.

en.croach.ment /£ ɪŋˈkrəʊtʃ.mənt, $ -ˈkroʊtʃ-/ *n.* gradual intrusion

تجاوز، تعدّی، غصب

The *encroachment* of the factories upon the neighborhood lowered the value of the real estate.

en.cum.ber /£ ɪŋˈkʌn.bəʳ, $ -bɚ/ *v.* to burden

دست و بال (کسی را) بستن، دست و پاگیر بودن برای

Some people *encumber* themselves *with* too much luggage when they take short trips.

en.dear.ment /£ ɪnˈdɪə.mənt, $ -ˈdɪr-/ *n.* fond statement

سخن محبت‌آمیز، حرف عاشقانه

Your gifts and *endearments* cannot make me forget your earlier insolence.

en.de.mic /en'dem.ɪk/ *adj.* regularly found, very common

(بیماری) شایع، رایج، بومی

Malaria is *endemic* in many of the hotter regions of the world.

en.dive /'en.daɪv/ *n.* species of leafy plant used in salad

کاسنی فرنگی، اَندیو

The salad contained *endive* in addition to the ingredients usually used.

en.dorse /£ ɪn'dɔːs, $ -'dɔːrs/ *v.* to approve, to support, to agree with

تأیید کردن، تصدیق کردن؛ حمایت کردن؛ پشت‌نویسی کردن

I fully *endorse* everything the chairperson has said.

en.due /ɪn'djuː/ *v.* to endow

ارزانی داشتن، اعطا کردن، بهره‌مند بودن از

He was *endued* with lion's courage.

en.er.gize /£ 'en.ə.dʒaɪz, $ '-ɚ-/ *v.* to invigorate, to make forceful and active

انرژی دادن، نیرو بخشیدن، شور و شوق ایجاد کردن

We shall have to *re-energize* our activities by getting new members.

en.er.vate /£ 'en.ə.veɪt, $ '-ɚ-/ *v.* to weaken

ضعیف کردن، سست کردن

The hot days of August are *enervating*.

en.gend.er /£ ɪn'dʒen.dəʳ, $ -dɚ/ *v.* to cause, to produce

باعث شدن، موجب شدن، به وجود آوردن
The minister's speech didn't *engender* confidence in his judgment.

en.grossed /£ ɪŋˈgrəʊst, $ -ˈgroʊst/ *adj.* absorbed

مجذوب، غرق(در)
She was so *engrossed by/ in* the book that she forgot the cakes in the oven.

en.hance /£ ɪnˈhɑːnts, $ -ˈhænts/ *v.* to improve, to advance

افزایش دادن، بالا بردن، بهبود بخشیدن، تقویت کردن
What can we do to *enhance* our chances of victory?

en.ig.ma /ɪˈnɪg.mə/ *n.* puzzle

معما، راز
In spite of all the attempts to decipher the code, it remained an *enigma*.

en.join /ɪnˈdʒɔɪn/ *v.* to command, to order; to forbid

دستور دادن، امر کردن؛ منع کردن
The owners of the company asked the court to *enjoin* the union from picketing the plant.

en.mi.ty /£ ˈen.mɪ.ti, $ -t̬i/ *n.* ill will, hatred

دشمنی، خصومت
I don't understand his *enmity towards* his parents.

en.nui /£ ˌɒnˈwiː, $ ˌɑːn-/ *n.* boredom

بی‌حوصلگی، احساس بیهودگی / پوچی
The whole country seems to be affected by the *ennui* of winter.

e.nor.mi.ty /£ ɪˈnɔː.mɪ.ti, $ -ˈnɔːr.mə.t̬i/ *n.* an extremely evil act; hugeness

قباحت، شناعت، قبح؛ بزرگی، عظمت

His paintings depict the *enormity* of war.

en.rap.ture /£ ɪnˈræp.tʃəʳ, $ -tʃɚ/ *v.* to please intensely

به وجد آوردن

The audience was *enraptured* by the young soloist's performance.

en.sconce /£ ɪnˈskɒnts, $ -ˈskɑːnts/ *v.* to settle comfortably

(خود را) مستقر کردن، جا خوش کردن

We have *ensconced ourselves in* the most beautiful villa.

en.sue /£ ɪnˈsjuː, $ -ˈsuː/ *v.* to follow, to happen after something else

پیش آمدن، به دنبال آمدن، ناشی شدن از، سرچشمه گرفتن از

Boredom often *ensues* from inactivity.

en.thrall /£ ɪn.θrɔːl, $ -θrɑːl/ *v.* to capture, to enslave

مسحور کردن، مجذوب کردن، هوش و حواس بردن از

From the moment he saw her picture, he was *enthralled* by her beauty.

en.tice /ɪnˈtaɪs/ *v.* to attract, to lure, to tempt

اغوا کردن، اغفال کردن، وسوسه کردن؛ ترغیب کردن

People are being *enticed away from* the profession by higher salaries elsewhere.

en.ti.ty /£ ˈen.tɪ.ti, $ -t̬ə.t̬i/ *n.* real being

ماهیت، جوهر، ذات؛ موجودیت، هستی؛ شیء، چیز

The museums work closely together, but are separate legal *entities*.

en.to.mol.o.gy /£ ˌen.təˈmɒl.ə.dʒi, $ -t̬əˈmɑː.lə-/ *n.* study of insects

I found **entomology** the least interesting part of my course in biology. حشره‌شناسی

en.trance /£ ɪnˈtrɑːnts, $ -ˈtrænts/ v. to keep the attention of, to put under a spell

The children sat silent on the carpet, **entranced** by the cartoon. مجذوب کردن، مسحور کردن

en.treat /ɪnˈtriːt/ v. to ask earnestly, to plead

She **entreated** him to show mercy. تمنا کردن، خواهش کردن؛ التماس کردن

en.trée /£ ˈɒn.treɪ, $ ˈɑːn-/ n. entrance; main meal

By marrying an aristocrat, he gained **entrée** into/ to higher social circles. امکان ورود، اجازهٔ ورود؛ غذای اصلی

en.tre.pre.neur /£ ˌɒn.trə.prəˈnɜːʳ, ˌɑːn.trə.prəˈnɜːr/ n. businessman, contractor

Present tax program discourages **entrepreneurs** from trying new fields of business activity. بازرگان، تاجر؛ پیمانکار

en.vir.on /£ ɪnˈvaɪən, $ -ˈvaɪr.ən/ v. to enclose, to surround

In medieval days, Paris was **environed** by a wall. حصار کردن، دور چیزی را گرفتن

en.vir.ons: n. حول و حوش، حومه، اطراف

eph.e.me.ral /£ ɪˈfem.ər.əl, $ -ɚ-/ adj. short - lived, fleeting

Fame in the world of rock and pop is largely **ephemeral**. زودگذر، گذرا، ناپایدار

ep.ic /ˈep.ɪk/ *n., adj.* long narrative poem

حماسه، داستان حماسی؛ قهرمانی، حماسی، عظیم

1) I'm reading a real *epic* at the moment.
2) They arranged an *epic* banquet in honour of the president.

ep.i.cure /£ ˈep.ɪ.kjʊəʳ, $ -kjʊr/ *n.* connoisseur of food and drink

آدم خوش خوراک

Epicures frequent this restaurant because it features exotic dishes.

ep.i.cur.e.an /£ ˈep.ɪ.kjʊəʳn, $ -kjʊrən/ *n.* a person who devotes himself to pleasures

آدم خوش گذراندن، آدم لذت پرست، آدم عیّاش

In his youth he was an extravagant *epicurean*.

ep.i.gram /ˈep.ɪ.græm/ *n.* witty thought or saying

لطیفه، طنز

The playwright Oscar Wilde was noted for his *epigrams*.

e.pi.logue /£ ˈep.ɪ.lɒg, $ -lɑːg/ *n.* concluding speech

خاتمه، مؤخره، سخن آخر، ختم مقال

The audience was so disappointed that many did not remain to hear the *epilogue*.

ep.i.taph /£ ˈep.ɪ.tɑːf, $ -tæf/ *n.* inscription in memory of a dead person

کتیبهٔ روی مزار، سنگ نوشتهٔ مزار

In his will, he dictated the *epitaph* he wanted placed on his tombstone.

ep.i.thet /ˈep.ɪ.θet/ *n.* descriptive word or phrase

عنوان، لقب، صفت

Few people would apply the *epithet* "dynamic" to the new project leader.

e.pi.to.me /£ ɪˈpɪt.ə.mi, $ -ˈpɪt̬-/ *n.* summary, concise abstract

خلاصه، چکیده

This final book is the *epitome* of all his previous books.

e.pi.tom.ize: *v.* خلاصهٔ (چیزی) بودن، تجسم کامل (چیزی) بودن

e.poch /£ ˈiː.pɒk, $ -pɑːk/ *n.* period of time

دوران، دوره، عصر؛ (زمین‌شناسی) دور

The glacial *epoch* lasted for thousands of years.

eq.uab.le /ˈek.wə.bl̩/ *adj.* uniform, steady, tranquil

یکسان، ثابت، آرام؛ (آب و هوا) معتدل

The south of the country enjoys an *equable* climate where it is rarely too hot and never too cold.

e.qua.ni.mi.ty /£ ˌek.wəˈnɪm.ɪ.ti, $ -t̬i/ *n.* calmness of temperament

آرامش، خونسردی؛ شکیبایی، بردباری

He received the news of defeat with remarkable *equanimity*.

e.ques.tri.an /ɪˈkwes.tri.ən/ *n., adj.* rider on horseback

سوارکار؛ مربوط به اسب سواری یا سوارکاری

They plan to hold the Olympics' *equestrian* events in another part of the city.

e.qui.lib.ri.um /ˌiː.kwɪˈlɪb.ri.əm, ˌek.wɪ-/ *n.* a state of balance

تعادل، توازن، موازنه؛ آرامش

After the divorce, he needed some time to regain his *equilibrium*.

e.qui.nox /£ ˈek.wɪ.nɒks, $ -nɑːks/ *n.* period of equal days and nights

اعتدال (اخترشناسی)

The vernal *equinox* is usually marked by heavy rainstorm.

e.qui.poise /ˈek.wɪ.pɔɪz/ *n.* balance, balancing force

موازنه، توازن، تعادل؛ وزنه تعادل

The high wire acrobat used his pole as an *equipoise* to overcome the swaying caused by the wind.

e.qui.tab.le /£ ˈek.wɪ.tə.bl̩, $ -t̬ə-/ *adj.* fair, impartial

منصفانه، عادلانه؛ معقول

I am seeking an *equitable* solution to this dispute.

e.qui.ty /£ ˈek.wɪ.ti, $ -t̬i/ *n.* fairness, justice

انصاف، عدل، عدالت

Our courts guarantee *equity* to all.

e.qui.vo.cal /ɪˈkwɪv.ə.kᵊl/ *adj.* doubtful, ambiguous

دوپهلو، مبهم، گنگ

Macbeth was misled by the *equivocal* statements of the witches.

e.qui.vo.cate /ɪˈkwɪv.ə.keɪt/ *v.* to lie, to mislead, to conceal the truth

دو پهلو حرف زدن، کلی بافی کردن

She accused the minister of *equivocating*.

e.rode /£ ɪˈrəʊd, $ -ˈroʊd/ *v.* to eat away

فرسودن، فرسایش یافتن، ساییدن، خوردن

The limestone was *eroded* by the dripping water.

e.ro.tic /£ ɪˈrɒt.ɪk, $ -ˈrɑː.t̬ɪk/ *adj.* related to sexual desire and pleasure

شهوانی، شهوت‌انگیز، سکسی

The **erotic** passages in this novel should be removed.

er.rant /ˈer.ənt/ *adj.* wandering

سرگردان، آواره

The tale was about **errant**-knights who helped the weak and punished the guilty.

er.ra.tic /£ ɪˈræt.ɪk, $ -ˈræt̬-/ *adj.* odd, unpredictable

عجیب و غریب، غیرعادی؛ آشفته، در هم برهم

Investors become anxious when the stock market appears **erratic**.

er.ro.ne.ous /£ ɪˈrəʊ.ni.əs, $ -ˈroʊ-/ *adj.* wrong, mistaken

غلط، نادرست

I thought my answer was correct, but it was **erroneous**.

e.ru.dite /ˈer.ʊ.daɪt/ *adj.* learned, scholar

دانشمند، عالم، فاضل؛ عالمانه

He is the author of an **erudite** book on Scottish history.

e.ru.di.tion /ˌer.ʊˈdɪʃ.ᵊn/ *n.* great learning

علم، دانش، فضل

He tried to display his **erudition**.

es.ca.pade /ˈes.kə.peɪd/ *n.* prank, flighty conduct

ماجراجویی؛ شیطنت، بدجنسی

The headmaster could not regard this latest **escapade** as a boyish joke.

es.chew /ɪsˈtʃuː/ *v.* to avoid

اجتناب کردن، دوری جستن، پرهیز کردن

We won't have discussions with this group unless they **eschew** violence.

e.so.te.ric /£ ˌiː.səʊˈter.ɪk, $ ˌes.ə-/ *adj.* very unusual, known only to the chosen few

محرمانه، سرّی؛ اختصاصی، خصوصی

Those who had access to his *esoteric* discussions were impressed by the scope of his thinking.

es.pi.on.age /ˈes.pi.ə.nɑːʒ/ *n.* spying

جاسوسی

The U. S. government developed a system of *espionage* which penetrated every household.

es.pouse /esˈpaʊz/ *v.* to adopt, to support

طرفداری کردن، حمایت کردن، پشتیبانی کردن

He always tries to *espouse* feminism.

esprit do corps /£ esˌpriː.dəˈkɔːʳ, $ -ˈkɔːr/ *n.* comradeship spirit

احساس همبستگی، روح فداکاری و صمیمیت، روحیهٔ گروهی

His leadership kept the team's *esprit do corps* intact during difficult periods.

e.strange /ɪˈstreɪndʒ/ *v.* to alienate

از هم جدا کردن، جدایی انداختن بین

The wife was *estranged from* her husband and sought a divorce.

eth.e.re.al /£ ɪˈθɪə.ri.əl, $ -ˈθɪr.i-/ *adj.* light, heavenly, fine

لطیف، قشنگ، محشر؛ اثیری

Visitors were impressed by her *ethereal* beauty.

eth.nic /ˈeθ.nɪk/ *adj.* relating to races

قومی، نژادی

Intolerance between *ethnic* groups is deplorable.

eth.nol.o.gy /£ eθˈnɒl.ə.dʒi, $ -ˈnɑː.lə-/ *n.* study of races

قوم‌شناسی
Sociology is one aspect of the science of **ethnology**.

et.y.mol.ogy /£ ˌet.ɪˈmɒl.ə.dʒi, $ -ˈmɑː.lə-/ *n.* study of the origin and history of words

ریشه‌شناسی
To the student of **etymology**, the dictionary is a tremendous source of information.

eu.gen.ic /juˈdʒen.ɪk/ *adj.* related to the improvement of race

مربوط به اصلاح نژاد
It is easier to apply **eugenic** principles to the raising of racehorses.

eu.gen.ics: *n.* علم اصلاح نژادی

eu.log.is.tic /ˌjuː.ləˈdʒɪs.tɪk/ *adj.* praising

ستایش‌آمیز، تحسین‌آمیز؛ پر از مدح و ثنا، پر از مدّاحی
The speech was **eulogistic** rather than critical in tone.

eu.log.ist: *n.* مدّاح، مدیحه‌سرا

eu.log.ize مدح گفتن؛ ستایش کردن

eu.phem.i.sm /ˈjuː.fə.mɪ.zᵊm/ *n.* mild expression

حُسن تعبیر
The expression "He passed away" is a **euphemism** for "He died".

eu.pho.ni.ous /£ juːˈfəʊ.ni.əs, $ -ˈfoʊ-/ *adj.* pleasing in sound

خوش آهنگ، خوش‌آوا، خوش الحان
Italian and Spanish are **euphonious** languages and therefore easily sung.

eu.than.a.si.a /ˌjuː.θəˈneɪ.ʒə/ *n.* mercy killing

قتل ترحمی، قتل نجات‌بخش، بِه‌کشی

Many people support *euthanasia* for terminally ill patients who wish to die.

ev.an.es.cent /£ ˌiːvəˈnesᵊnt, $ ˌev.ə-/ *adj.* vanishing, fleeting

زودگذر، گذرا، ناپایدار

The *evanescent* post-war economic boom was quickly followed by a deep recession.

e.vas.ive /ɪˈveɪ.sɪv/ *adj.* not frank, eluding

طفره‌جویانه، طفره‌آمیز؛ گنگ، دو پهلو؛ (جواب) سربالا

Your *evasive* answers convinced the judge that you were not telling the truth.

    take evasive action: *v.*   جا خالی دادن

    e.vade: *v.*   طفره رفتن، شانه خالی کردن از

e.vince /ɪˈvɪnts/ *v.* to show clearly

(از خود) نشان دادن، ابراز کردن

They have never *evinced* any readiness to negotiate.

e.vis.cer.ate /ɪˈvɪs.ə.reɪt/ *v.* to remove entrails

برداشتن امعاء و احشاء داخل بدن

The medicine man *eviscerated* the animal and offered the entrails to the angry gods.

e.voke /£ ɪˈvəʊk, $ -ˈvoʊk/ *v.* to call forth

به یاد آوردن، زنده کردن، برانگیختن؛ باعث شدن؛ فراخواندن

He *evoked* much criticism by his hostile manner.

ex.a.cer.bate /£ ɪɡˈzæs.ə.beɪt, $ -ɚ-/ *v.* to worsen, to embitter

بدتر کردن، خراب‌تر کردن، وخیم‌تر کردن

This attack will *exacerbate* the already tense relations between the two committees.

ex.ac.tion /ɪɡˈzækʃᵊn/ *n.* extortion

زورگویی، اجحاف؛ باج، پول زور

The colonies rebelled against the *exactions* of the mother country.

ex.alt /£ ɪgˈzɒlt, $ -ˈzɑːlt/ *v.* to praise, to raise in rank or dignity

ستایش کردن، تحسین کردن؛ ارتقاء مقام دادن

The actor was *exalted* to the rank of knighthood by the queen.

ex.alt.ed: *adj.*

متعال، والا، رفیع، عالی

ex.as.per.ate /£ ɪgˈzɑː.spə.reɪt, $ -ˈzæs.pɚ.eɪt/ *v.* to vex

کفر (کسی را) در آوردن، عصبانی کردن، خشمگین کردن

Johnny often *exasperates* his mother with his pranks.

ex.che.quer /£ ɪksˈtʃek.əʳ, $ -ɚ/ *n.* treasury

خزانهٔ دولت؛ (با E بزرگ) وزارت دارایی، وزارت خزانه‌داری

He had been chancellor of *the Exchequer* before his promotion.

ex.ci.sion /ekˈsɪʒ.ən/ *n.* act of cutting away, censorship

(پزشکی) قطع، بریدن؛ حذف، سانسور

The *excisions* have destroyed the literary value of the text.

ex.cise: *v.*

(پزشکی) بریدن، قطع کردن؛ حذف کردن

ex.co.ri.ate /£ ekˈskɔː.ri.eɪt, $ -ˈskɔːr.i-/ *v.* to flay, to abrade

پوست (چیزی را) کندن، (کفش) زدن پا

These shoes are so ill-fitting that they will *excoriate* the feet and create blisters.

ex.cul.pate /ˈek.skəl.peɪt/ *v.* to clear from blame

تبرئه کردن

He was *exculpated* of the crime when the real criminal confessed.

ex.e.cra.ble /ˈek.sə.krə.bl̩/ *adj.* very bad

افتضاح، فوق‌العاده بد؛ زشت، شنیع

I've never heard such an *execrable* performance of the concerto.

ex.e.crate /ˈek.si.kreɪt/ *v.* to curse, to express abhorrence

متنفر بودن از، نفرت داشتن از، منزجر بودن از

The world *execrates* the memory of Hitler.

ex.e.cute /ˈek.sɪ.kjuːt/ *v.* to carry out, to put into effect

اجرا کردن، به اجرا در آوردن، عمل کردن به، جامهٔ عمل پوشاندن به

Now that we have approval we may *execute* the scheme as previously agreed.

ex.e.ge.sis /ˌek.sɪˈdʒiː.sɪs/ *n.* explanation

تفسیر متون مذهبی

I can follow your *exegesis* of this passage to a limited degree.

ex.em.plar.y /£ ɪɡˈzem.plə.ri, $ -plɚ.i/ *adj.* serving as a model; outstanding

نمونه؛ سرمشق؛ عبرت‌انگیز، هشدار دهنده

Her *exemplary* behavior was praised at commencement.

ex.haus.tive /£ ɪɡˈzɔː.stɪv, $ -ˈzɑː-/ *adj.* thorough, comprehensive

کامل، جامع، تمام عیار، فراگیر

We have made an *exhaustive* study of all published tests.

ex.hort /£ ɪɡˈzɔːt, $ -ˈzɔːrt/ *v.* to urge, to persuade

ترغیب کردن، خواستن، تشویق کردن

The governor **exhorted** the prisoners not to riot.

ex.hume /£ eks'hju:m, $ eg'zu:m/ *v.* to remove from a grave

از قبر در آوردن

They **exhumed** the body after the funeral.

ex.i.gen.cy /'ek.sɪ.dʒᵊnt.si/ *n.* urgent situation

وضع اضطراری، وضعیت فوق‌العاده

In this **exigency**, we must look for aid from our allies.

ex.ig.u.ous /eg'zɪgjʊəs/ *adj.* small, minute

اندک، ناچیز، مختصر

This is the last of the old man's **exiguous** savings.

ex.o.dus /'ek.sə.dəs/ *n.* departure

خروج دسته جمعی؛ مهاجرت

The famine is causing a mass **exodus** of people from the country.

ex of.fi.ci.o /£ ˌeks.ə'fɪʃ.i.əʊ, $ -oʊ/ *adj., adv.* by virtue of one's office

به اعتبار مقام، به‌خاطر پست

She is an **ex officio** member of the finance committee because she is head of the design department.

ex.on.er.ate /£ ɪg'zɒn.ə.reɪt, $ -'zɑː.nɚ.eɪt/ *v.* to acquit, to exculpate

تبرئه کردن، بی‌گناه شناختن

I am sure this letter will **exonerate** you.

ex.or.bi.tant /£ ɪg'zɔː.bɪ.tᵊnt, $ -'zɔːr.bə.tᵊnt/ *adj.* excessive

(قیمت) گزاف، سرسام‌آور

The bill for dinner was **exorbitant**.

ex.or.cise /£ 'ek.sɔː.saɪz, $ -sɔːr-/ *v.* to drive out evil spirit

دفع کردن، با دعا و جادو (روح پلیدی) را بیرون راندن
After the priest *exorcised* the spirit, noises stopped.

ex.o.tic /£ ɪɡˈzɒt.ɪk, $ -ˈzɑː.t̬ɪk/ *adj.* not native; strange

غیر بومی، خارجی؛ نامتعارف، عجیب و غریب، غیرمعمول
Because of his *exotic* headdress, he was followed in the streets by small children.

ex.pa.ti.ate /ekˈspeɪ.ʃi.eɪt/ *v.* to talk at length

شرح و بسط دادن، به تفصیل بیان کردن
She *expatiated* on/ upon/ about her own work for the whole afternoon.

ex.pa.tri.ate /£ ekˈspæt.ri.ət, $ -ˈspeɪ.tri-/ *n.* exile

مهاجر، مقیم (کشور دیگر)
Henry James was an American *expatriate* who settled in England.

ex.pa.tri.ate: *v.*   جلای وطن کردن، ترک تابعیت کردن

ex.pe.di.ency /ɪkˈspiː.di.ᵊnt.si/ *n.* that which is advisable or practical

مصلحت، مصلحت اندیشی
I think this government operates on the basis of *expediency*.

ex.pe.di.tious.ly /ˌek.spəˈdɪʃ.ə.sli/: *adv.* rapidly and efficiently

با سرعت، با عجله
Please adjust this matter as *expeditiously* as possible.

ex.per.tise /£ ˌek.spɜːˈtiːz, $ -spɜːr-/ *n.* specialized knowledge

مهارت، تخصص
She was hired for her particular *expertise* in computer programming.

ex.pi.ate /ˈek.spi.eɪt/ *v.* to make amends for (a sin)

جبران کردن، کفارهٔ (گناه را) دادن

He tried to *expiate* his crimes by a full confession to the authorities.

ex.ple.tive /£ ɪkˈspliː.tɪv, $ ˈek.splə.tɪv/ *n.* a swear word

فحش، ناسزا، بد و بیراه

The sergeant's remarks were filled with *expletives*.

ex.pli.cit /ɪkˈsplɪs.ɪt/ *adj.* open, definite

صریح، روشن؛ بی‌پرده، عیان، آشکار

Your remarks are *explicit*; no one can misinterpret them.

ex.ploit /ˈek.splɔɪt/ *n.* a brave deed

دلاوری، قهرمانی، ماجراجویی

Did she tell you about her *exploits* during the holiday weekend?

ex.ploit /ɪkˈsplɔɪt/ *v.* to use unfairly

سوء استفاده کردن؛ بهره‌کشی کردن، استثمار کردن

Laws exist to stop companies *exploiting* their employees.

ex.ploit.a.tion: *n.* سوء استفاده، بهره‌کشی، استثمار

ex.pos.tu.la.tion /£ ɪkˌspɒs.tjʊˈleɪ.ʃ°n, $ -ˌspɑː.stjʊ-/ *n.* complaint

اعتراض، مخالفت؛ بگو مگو، مشاجره

Despite the *expostulation* of the children, we went to visit their aunt.

expostulate on/ about/ against مشاجره کردن، بگومگو کردن

ex.punge /ɪkˈspʌndʒ/ *v.* to cancel, to remove

حذف کردن؛ زدودن، محو کردن

His name has been *expunged* from the list of members.

ex.pur.gate /£ ˈek.spə.geɪt, $ -spɚ-/ *v.* to remove offensive parts of a book

هرزه‌زدایی کردن، تنقیح کردن

The book has been *expurgated* to make it suitable for children to read.

ex.tant /ɪkˈstænt/ *adj.* still in existence

موجود (سند)؛ جاری، نافذ (قانون)

Medieval customs are *extant* in some parts of Europe.

ex.tem.po.ra.ne.ous /ekˌstem.pəˈreɪ.ni.əs/ *adj.* not planned, impromptu

بدون آمادگی قبلی، فی‌المجلس، فی‌البداهه

The minister gave an *extemporaneous* speech on the education policy.

ex.ten.u.ate /ɪkˈsten.ju.eɪt/ *v.* to weaken, to mitigate

تعدیل کردن، از قبح (چیزی) کاستن

Nothing can *extenuate* such appalling behavior.

ex.tir.pate /£ ˈek.stɜː.peɪt, $ -stɚ-/ *v.* to root up

ریشه‌کن کردن، نابود کردن؛ سرکوب کردن، فرو نشاندن

The country must *extirpate* the evils of drug abuse.

ex.tol /£ ɪkˈstəʊl, $ -ˈstoʊl/ *v.* to praise highly, to glorify

تحسین کردن، ستودن، ستایش کردن

The astronauts were *extolled* as the pioneers of the Space Age.

ex.tort /£ ɪkˈstɔːt, $ -ˈstɔːrt/ *v.* to get money by threats

اخاذی کردن، با زور گرفتن، با تهدید و ارعاب گرفتن

The blackmailer *extorted* money from his victim.

ex.tra.di.tion /ˌek.strəˈdɪʃ.ən/ *n.* surrender of prisoner by one state to another

استرداد مجرم، تحویل، استرداد

They have applied for his *extradition* to Ireland.

ex.tra.dite: *v.* (مجرم) مسترد کردن، تحویل دادن

ex.tra.ne.ous /ɪkˈstreɪ.ni.əs/ *adj.* not essential; external

نامربوط، بی‌ربط؛ خارجی، بیرونی

Don't pad your paper with *extraneous* matters.

ex.tra.vert /£ ekˈstrə.vɜːt, $ -vɜːrt/ *n.* energetic, happy

آدم اجتماعی و سرزنده، آدم با نشاط

A good salesman is usually an *extravert*.

ex.tri.cate /ˈek.stri.keɪt/ *v.* to free, to disentangle

آزاد کردن، نجات دادن؛ از شرّ (چیزی) خلاص کردن

He found that he could not *extricate* himself from the trap.

ex.trin.sic /ekˈstrɪnsɪk/ *adj.* external, foreign

خارجی، بیرونی؛ غیرضروری، نامربوط

Do not be fooled by *extrinsic* causes. We must look for the intrinsic reason.

ex.trude /ɪkˈstruːd/ *v.* to force or push out

با فشار خارج کردن

Much pressure is required to *extrude* these plastics.

ex.u.ber.ant /£ ɪɡˈzjuːbªrªnt, $ -ˈzuː.bɚ-/ *adj.* abundant, effusive, lavish

فراوان، انبوه، پُر؛ شاد، سرزنده، پرنشاط

His speeches were famous for his *exuberant* language and vivid imagery.

ex.ude /£ ɪɡˈzjuːd/ *v.* to discharge, to give forth

از خود بیرون دادن، ترشح کردن

Some trees *exude* from their bark a sap that repels insects.

ex.uda.tion: *n.*   ترشح، تراوش

ex.ult /ɪgˈzʌlt/ *v.* to rejoice

شادی کردن، ذوق کردن

We *exulted* when our team won the victory.

لیستی از لغاتی که در جملات بخش E به کار رفته‌اند:

allies: *n.*	متحدین	feminism: *n.*	طرفداری از حقوق زن
appalling: *adj.*	اسفناک		
banquet: *n.*	ضیافت، جشن	garb: *n.*	لباس
bark: *n.*	پوست درخت	glacial: *adj.*	یخبندان
boom: *n.*	شکوفایی	hazard: *n.*	خطر، اتفاق
chairperson: *n.*	رییس جلسه	heated: *adj.*	داغ
clinched: *adj.*	گره‌کرده	high-pitched: *adj.*	(صدا) زیر
commencement: *n.*	جشن پایان تحصیلی	hostile: *adj.*	خصمانه
		hunch: *n.*	حدس و گمان
confess: *v.*	اعتراف کردن، اظهار کردن	inflamed: *adj.*	ملتهب
		ingredients: *n.*	مواد
convince: *v.*	متقاعد کردن	insolence: *n.*	وقاحت، بی‌شرمی
decipher: *v.*	رمزگشایی کردن، خواندن	intolerance: *n.*	تعصب
		intrinsic: *adj.*	ذاتی، درونی
deplorable: *adj.*	تأسف‌آور، زشت	investor: *n.*	سرمایه‌گذار
		liar: *n.*	دروغگو
dispute: *n.*	مشاجره، بحث	loot: *n.*	غنایم، اموال مسروقه
disputed: *adj.*	مورد مناقشه	mob: *n.*	مردم، جمعیت
don: *v.*	پوشیدن	mustard: *n.*	سُس خردل
drip: *v.*	چکیدن	object to: *v.*	اعتراض کردن به
embarrass: *v.*	خجالت‌زده کردن	pad: *v.*	شاخ و برگ دادن
encompass: *v.*	در برگرفتن	picketing: *n.*	تحریک به اعتصاب
entertain: *v.*	سرگرم کردن	pioneer: *n.*	پیشرو، پیشگام
entrails: *n.*	امعاء و احشا	plant: *n.*	کارخانه
extravagant: *adj.*	ولخرج	prank: *n.*	شوخی، مسخرگی
famine: *n.*	قحطی، گرسنگی	promote: *v.*	ایجاد کردن

pulpit: *n.*	منبر	swaying: *n.*	تکان، نوسان
rank: *n.*	درجه، رتبه	tombstone: *n.*	سنگ قبر
recession: *n.*	رکود اقتصادی	tremendous: *adj.*	عظیم، مهم
repress: *v.*	سرکوب کردن	trifle: *n.*	امر جزیی
sap: *n.*	شیره (گیاه)	virtue: *n.*	مزیت، حسن، عفت
scope: *n.*	میزان، حوزه	wan: *adj.*	رنجور، ضعیف
stand: *v.*	تحمل کردن	will: *n.*	وصیت‌نامه
stir: *v.*	به هیجان آوردن		

F   f

fab.ri.cate /ˈfæb.rɪ.keɪt/ *v.* to invent, to forge

ساختن؛ جعل کردن، به هم بافتن

He was late, so he *fabricated* an excuse to avoid trouble.

fa.cade /fəˈsɑːd/ *n.* front of the building

(ساختمان) نما، سردر؛ ظاهر، صورت ظاهر

The *facade* of the church has often been photographed by tourists.

fac.et /ˈfæs.ɪt, -et/ *n.* small plane surface, a side

(جواهر) تراش، بَر، سطح

The stonecutter decided to improve the rough diamond by providing it with several *facets*.

fa.ce.tious /fəˈsiː.ʃəs/ *adj.* humorous, jocular

طنزآمیز، خنده‌دار؛ شوخ، بذله‌گو

Your *facetious* remarks are not appropriate at this serious moment.

fa.cile /ˈfæs.aɪl/ *adj.* easy; expert

سهل‌الوصول، آسان؛ فصیح، روان

Because he was a *facile* speaker, he never refused a request to address an organization.

fac.il.i.tate /fəˈsɪl.ɪ.teɪt/ *v.* to make less difficult

تسهیل کردن، آسان کردن، راحت‌تر کردن
The new ramp will *facilitate* the entry of wheelchairs.

fac.tion /'fæk.ʃ°n/ *n.* party, clique; dissension

دسته، باند؛ تفرقه، نفاق، اختلاف
The party split on that issue and is now in danger of breaking into two or more *factions*.

fac.ti.ous: *adj.* فرقه‌ای، فرقه‌گرایانه؛ ستیزه‌جویانه

fac.ti.tious /fæk'tɪʃ.əs/ *adj.* artificial, sham

تصنعی، ساختگی، مصنوعی
Actresses often create *factitious* tears by using glycerine.

fac.to.tum /£ fæk'təʊ.təm, $ -'toʊ.təm/ *n.* handyman, a person with varied duties

مستخدم
He was a general *factotum* at the restaurant–washing dishes, cleaning the floors and polishing the furniture.

fac.ul.ty /£ 'fæk.ºl.ti, $ -ti/ *n.* mental or bodily power; teaching staff

قوهٔ ذهنی، استعداد؛ (آمریکا) عضو هیأت علمی
As he grew old, he feared he might lose his *faculties* and become useless to his employer.

fal.la.cious /fə'leɪ.ʃəs/ *adj.* misleading

اشتباه، غلط؛ گمراه‌کننده، سفسطه‌آمیز
It is quite *fallacious* to argue that traffic congestion will be reduced by building more roads.

fal.la.cy: *n.* سفسطه؛ تصور غلط، عقیدهٔ نادرست

fal.li.ble /'fæl.ɪ.bl̩/ *adj.* liable to err

جایزالخطا، اشتباه‌پذیر

The more *fallible* a politician seems to be, the more honest people think he is.

fal.low /£ ˈfæl.əʊ, $ -oʊ/ *adj.* uncultivated, not planted

(زمین) آیش

Farmers have learned that it is advisable to permit land to *lie fallow* every few years.

fal.ter /£ ˈfɒl.tər, $ ˈfɑːl.tɚ/ *v.* to lose strength, to hesitate, to stop

تضعیف شدن؛ مردد بودن، به تردید افتادن

Her friends never *faltered* in their belief in her.

fa.na.ti.ci.sm /£ fəˈnæt.ɪ.sɪ.zᵊm, $ -ˈnæṭ-/ *n.* excessive zeal

عِرق، حمیّت، غیرت؛ تعصّب

The leader of the group was held responsible even though he could not control the *fanaticism* of his followers.

fan.ci.ed /ˈfænt.si.əd/ *adj.* imagined, unreal

غیرواقع، تخیلی، موهوم

You are resenting *fancied* insults. No one has ever said such things about you.

fan.ci.er /£ ˈfænt.si.ər, $ -ɚ/ *adj.* breeder or dealer of animal

(در ترکیب) ـ باز؛ علاقمند به پرورش حیوانات و گیاهان

He is a pigeon *fancier*.

fan.ci.ful /ˈfænt.si.fᵊl/ *adj.* unreal, whimsical, visionary

دور از واقع، تخیلی؛ شگفت، عجیب و غریب

This is a *fanciful* scheme because it does not consider the facts.

fan.fare /£ ˈfæn.feər, $ -fer/ *n.* call by bugles and trumpets

بوق و کرنا؛ (موسیقی) فانفار

The exposition was opened with a *fanfare* of trumpets and firing of a cannon.

fan.tas.tic /fæn'tæs.tɪk/ *adj.* unreal, grotesque

دور از واقع، عجیب و غریب، شگفت، موهوم؛ عالی، فوق‌العاده

1) Your plans are quite *fantastic* — they can never work.
2) You look *fantastic* in that outfit.

farce /£ fɑːs, $ fɑːrs/ *n.* broad comedy, mockery

نمایش مضحک؛ مسخره‌بازی، شوخی

Nothing went right; the entire interview degenerated into a *farce*.

far.ci.cal: *adj.* خنده‌دار، مضحک

fas.ti.di.ous /fæs'tɪd.i.əs/ *adj.* difficult to please

سختگیر، مشکل‌پسند، ایرادی

The waitresses disliked to serve him dinner because of his very *fastidious* taste.

fat.al.i.sm /£ 'feɪ.tᵊl.ɪ.zᵊm, $ -tᵊl-/ *n.* belief that fate determines events

تقدیرگرایی، سرنوشت‌گرایی

With *fatalism*, he accepted the hardships that beset him.

fat.al.is.tic: *adj.* جبری، جزمی

fath.om /'fæð.əm/ *v.* to comprehend, to investigate

به کُنه (چیزی) پی بردن، فهمیدن، کشف کردن

I find his motives impossible to *fathom*.

fat.u.ous /'fæt.ju.əs/ *adj.* foolish, inane

احمقانه، ابلهانه

He is far too intelligent to utter such *fatuous* remarks.

fau.na /£ ˈfɔː.nə, $ ˈfɑː-/ *n.* animals of a period or region

حیات‌وحش، جانوران (خاص یک دوره یا منطقه)

The scientists could visualize the *fauna* of the period by examing the skeletal remains and the fossils.

faux pas /fəʊ ˈpɑː/ *n.* an error or slip

اشتباه فاحش، گاف

Your tactless remarks during dinner were a *faux pas*.

fawn /£ fɔːn, $ fɑːn/ *v.* to seek favor by groveling

چاپلوسی کردن، تملق گفتن، خود شیرینی کردن

He *fawned* over his boss in an attempt to gain approval.

fe.al.ty /ˈfiːəltɪ/ *n.* loyalty, faithfulness

وفاداری

The feudal lord demanded *fealty* of his vassals.

fea.si.ble /ˈfiːzə.bl̩/ *adj.* practical

امکان‌پذیر، عملی، ممکن

This is an entire *feasible* proposal, I suggest we adopt it.

feb.rile /£ ˈfiː.braɪl, $ ˈfeb.rɪl/ *adj.* feverish

همراه با تب، ناشی از تب، تب‌دار

In his *febrile* condition, he was subject to nightmares.

fec.und.i.ty /£ feˈkʌn.də.ti, $ -ṭi/ *n.* fertility, fruitfulness

حاصلخیزی، باروری؛ خلاقیت

The *fecundity* of his mind is illustrated by the many vivid images in his poems.

feign /feɪn/ *v.* to pretend

تظاهر کردن، خود را به ... زدن

I don't want to go out tonight; I think I shall *feign* a headache.

feint /feɪnt/ *n.* trick, shift, sham

فریب، کلک، گول، ترفند

The boxer was fooled by the opponent's *feint* and dropped his guard.

fe.li.ci.tous /£ fə'lɪs.ɪ.təs, £ fel'ɪs-, $ -təs/ *adj.* apt, suitably expressed, well chosen

بجا، به مورد؛ فصیح، بلیغ

He was famous for his *felicitous* remarks.

fell /fel/ *adj.* cruel, deadly

مهلک، کشنده، خطرناک

Henley writes of the "*fell* clutch of circumstance" in his poem "Invictus".

fel.on /'fel.ən/ *n.* person convicted of a grave crime

جنایتکار، جانی

A convicted *felon* loses the right to vote.

fel.on.y: *n.* جنایت

fer.ment /£ 'fɜː.ment, $ 'fɜːr-/ *n.* agitation, commotion

شورش، ناآرامی، طغیان، بحران

The entire country was in a state of *ferment*.

fer'ment: *v.* شورش کردن، طغیان کردن

fer.ret /'fer.ɪt/ *v.* to drive or hunt out of hiding

دنبال (چیزی) گشتن، کند و کاو کردن؛ پی بردن به

He *ferreted* out their secret.

fer.vent /£ 'fɜː.vᵊnt, $ 'fɜːr-/ *adj.* ardent, hot

مشتاق، پرشور، پرحرارت، گرم

He felt that the *fervent* praise was excessive.

fer.vid /£ 'fɜː.vɪd, $ 'fɜːr-/ *adj.* ardent, fervent

مشتاق، پرشور، پرحرارت، گرم

His *fervid* enthusiasm inspired all of us to undertake the dangerous mission.

fer.vor /£ ˈfɜː.vəʳ, $ ˈfɝː.vɚ/ *n.* glowing ardor

شور، اشتیاق

There is growing sense of nationalist *fervor* in the state.

fes.ter /£ ˈfes.təʳ, $ -tɚ/ *v.* to generate pus

چرک کردن، عفونت کردن

His finger began to *fester*.

fes.tive /ˈfes.tɪv/ *adj.* joyous, celebratory

شادی‌بخش، مسرّت بخش؛ شاد، شادمان

Their wedding in the park was a *festive* occasion

fête /feɪt/ *v., n.* to honor at a festival

جشن گرفتن، مقدم کسی را گرامی داشتن؛ جشن

The returning hero was *fêted* at a community supper and dance.

fe.tid /£ ˈfet.ɪd, $ ˈfeṭ-/ *adj.* malodorous

بدبو، متعفن

The neglected wound became *fetid*.

fe.tish /£ ˈfet.ɪʃ, $ ˈfeṭ-/ *n.* object believed to have magical powers

بت، شیء جادویی

The native wore a *fetish* around his neck to ward off evil spirits.

fet.ter /£ ˈfet.əʳ, $ ˈfeṭ.ɚ/ *v., n.* to shackle, to chain

غل و زنجیر کردن؛ غل و زنجیر

The prisoner was *fettered* to the wall.

fi.as.co /£ fiˈæs.kəʊ, $ -koʊ/ *n.* total failure

شکست کامل، مایهٔ آبروریزی

The whole show was a *fiasco*—the lights wouldn't work, one actor forgot his lines and another fell off the stage.

fi.at /ˈfiːæt/ *n.* command

حکم، فرمان، دستور

The decision was arrived at not by reasoned argument but by prime ministerial *fiat*.

fick.le /ˈfɪk.l/ *adj.* changeable, faithless

بی‌ثبات، دمدمی مزاج، متلون

He discovered she was *fickle*.

fic.ti.tious /fɪkˈtɪʃ.əs/ *adj.* imaginary

ساختگی، تخیلی، خیالی

Many of the incidents in his book are *fictitious*.

fi.del.i.ty /£ fɪˈdel.ə.ti, $ -ţi/ *n.* loyalty

وفاداری، پایبندی

They have shown great *fidelity* to their grand leader.

fi.du.ci.ary /fɪˈdjuːʃɪərɪ/ *adj.* holding in trust

امانتی، قیمومیتی

In his will, he stipulated that the bank act in a *fiduciary* capacity until his children became of age.

fig.ment /ˈfɪg.mənt/ *n.* invention, imaginary thing

توهم، خیال، ساخته و پرداختهٔ ذهن

That incident is *a figment* of your *imagination*.

filch /fɪltʃ/ *v.* to steal, to pinch, to nick

کِش رفتن، دزدیدن، بلند کردن

The boys *filched* apples from the fruit stand.

fil.i.al /ˈfɪl.i.əl/ *adj.* related to a son or daughter

فرزندی، (مربوط به) فرزند یا فرزندان

Many children forget their *filial* obligation and disregard the wishes of their parents.

fi.na.le /fɪˈnɑː.li/ *n.* conclusion

(موسیقی) پایانه، فینال؛ پایان، آخر

It is not until we reach the *finale* of this play that we can understand the author's message.

fi.nesse /fɪˈnes/ *n.* delicate skill

ظرافت، نکته‌سنجی

She has handled these difficult negotiations with tremendous *finesse*.

fin.ick.y /ˈfɪn.ɪ.ki/ *adj.* too particular, fussy

بهانه‌گیر، ایرادی، بدقلق

The old lady was *finicky*.

fi.nite /ˈfaɪ.naɪt/ *adj.* limited

محدود، متناهی؛ معین

It is difficult for humanity with its *finite* existence to grasp the infinite.

fire.brand /£ ˈfaɪə.brænd, $ ˈfaɪr-/ *n.* hothead, trouble maker

اخلال‌گر، آشوبگر، آتش‌افروز

The police tried to keep track of all the local *firebrands* when the President came to town.

fis.sure /£ ˈfɪʃ.ər, $ -ɚ/ *n.* crevice

شکاف، چاک، درز، تَرَک

The mountain climbers secured footholds in tiny *fissures* in the rock.

fit.ful /'fɪt.fᵊl/ *adj.* spasmodic, intermittent

نامنظم، بریده بریده

After several *fitful* attempts, he decided to postpone the start of the project.

flac.cid /'flæk.sɪd, 'flæs.ɪd/ *adj.* soft rather than firm, weak, flabby

ضعیف؛ نرم، شل

His sedentary life had left him with *flaccid* muscles.

fla.gel.late /'flædʒ.ə.leɪt/ *v.* to whip, to flog

تازیانه زدن، شلاق زدن؛ به باد انتقاد گرفتن

The Romans used to *flagellate* criminals with a whip that had three knotted strands.

flagg.ing /flægɪŋ/ *adj.* weak, drooping

ضعیف، خسته

The encouraging cheers of the crowd lifted the team's *flagging* spirits.

fla.grant /'fleɪ.grᵊnt/ *adj.* conspicuously wicked

شرم‌آور، وقیحانه؛ بی‌حیا

We cannot condone such *flagrant* violations of the rules.

flail /fleɪl/ *n., v.* to thresh grain by hand; to strike

خرمن‌کوب، کوبیدن؛ زدن، کتک زدن

In medieval times, warriors *flailed* their foe with a metal ball attached to a handle.

flair /£ fleəʳ, $ fler/ *n.* natural aptitude

استعداد؛ ابتکار؛ شمّ

The head of the department has a great *flair* for public speaking.

flam.boy.ant /flæmˈbɔɪ.ənt/ *adj.* ornate, showy

پرزرق و برق، رنگارنگ

His clothes were rather ***flamboyant*** for such a serious occasion.

flaunt /£ flɔːnt, $ flɑːnt/ *v.* to show sth in order to get admiration

به رخ کشیدن، پز (چیزی را) دادن

She is not one of those actresses who ***flaunt*** their physical charms.

flay /fleɪ/ *v.* to strip off skin; to plunder

پوست (کسی را) کندن؛ انتقاد شدید کردن، به باد انتقاد گرفتن

1) The criminal was condemned to be ***flayed*** alive.
2) My dad will ***flay*** me alive.

fleck /flek/ *v., n.* to spot, to mark

خال خال کردن، لکه لکه کردن؛ خال، لکه

Her cheeks, ***flecked*** with tears, were testimony to the hours of weeping.

fledg.ling /ˈfledʒ.lɪŋ/ *adj.* inexperienced

جوجهٔ پر در آورده؛ نوپا، نورسته، تازه‌کار

It is necessary to provide these ***fledgling*** poets with an opportunity to present their work.

fleece /fliːs/ *n.* wool coat of a sheep

پشم گوسفند

They shear sheep of their ***fleece***, which then comb into separate strands of wool.

fleece /fliːs/ *v.* to rob, to plunder

چاپیدن، لخت کردن، سر کیسه کردن

That restaurant really *fleeced* us.

flick /flɪk/ *n., v.* a light stroke; to hit with quick blow

تکان، ضربه، تلنگر؛ تکان دادن، تلنگر زدن

The horse went faster when it was given a quick *flick* of the whip.

flinch /flɪntʃ/ *v.* to hesitate, to shrink

به خود لرزیدن، خود را باختن؛ شانه خالی کردن، خود را پس کشیدن

He did not *flinch* in the face of danger but fought back bravely.

flip.pan.cy /ˈflɪp.ᵊnt.si/ *v.* trifling gaiety

شوخی، مسخره‌بازی

Your *flippancy* at this moment is offensive.

floe /£ fləʊ, $ floʊ/ *n.* mass of floating ice

تخته یخ شناور

The ship made slow progress as it battered its way through the ice *floes*.

flo.ra /£ ˈflɔː.rə, $ ˈflɔːr.ə/ *n.* plants of a region or era

گیاهان مخصوص یک ناحیه یا یک دوره

Because she was a botanist, she spent most of her time studying the *flora* of the desert.

flo.rid /£ ˈflɒr.ɪd, $ ˈflɔːr-/ *adj.* flowery, ruddy, too red

(چهره) سرخ، گلگون

His complexion was even more *florid* than usual because of his anger.

flo.til.la /fləˈtɪl.ə/ *n.* small fleet

گروه کوچکی از قایق‌ها

It is always an exciting moment when the fishing *flotilla*

returns to port.

flot.sam /£ ˈflɒt.sᵊm, $ ˈflɑːt-/ *n.* drifting wreckage

تکه پاره، تخته پاره، آت و آشغال آب آورده

We wandered along the shore, stepping over the *flotsam and jetsam* that had washed up in the night.

flout /flaʊt/ *v.* to reject, to mock

(قانون) نقض کردن، سرپیچی کردن از؛ نادیده گرفتن

The headstrong youth *flouted* all authority, he refused to be curbed.

fluc.tu.a.tion /ˌflʌk.tjuˈeɪ.ʃᵊn/ *n.* wavering

نوسان، تغییر، افت و خیز

A certain amount of *fluctuation* in quality is unavoidable.

flu.enc.y /ˈfluː.ənt.si/ *n.* smoothness of speech

فصاحت، روانی؛ راحتی، سهولت

He spoke French with *fluency* and ease.

flus.ter /£ ˈflʌs.tərʳ, $ -tɚ/ *v.* to confuse

دستپاچه کردن، مضطرب کردن

The teacher's sudden question *flustered* him and he stammered his reply.

flut.ed /£ ˈfluː.tɪd, $ ˈfluː.t̬ɪd/ *adj.* having vertical parallel grooves

(معماری) قاشقی تراش، خیاره‌دار

All that remained of the ancient building were the *fluted* columns.

flux /flʌks/ *n.* continuous change

تغییر مداوم، بی‌ثباتی

Our plans are in a state of *flux* at the moment.

foi.ble /ˈfɔɪ.bl̩/ *n.* weakness, slight fault

ضعف، نقطه ضعف

We can overlook the *foibles* of our friends.

foil /fɔɪl/ *v., n.* to defeat, to frustrate

ناکام کردن، خنثی کردن، عقیم گذاشتن

An attempted coup against the country's military ruler was *foiled* yesterday.

foil /fɔɪl/ *n.* contrast, comparison

وجه تقابل، وجه مقایسه، نقطه مقابل

Her husband's strength acts as a *foil* to her hastiness.

foist /fɔɪst/ *v.* to force someone to accept, to palm off

تحمیل کردن، انداختن به، قالب کردن

Parents should not try to *foist* their values *on* their children.

fo.ment /£ fəʊˈment, $ foʊ-/ *v.* to stir up, to instigate

(آشوب و غیره) به راه انداختن، بر پا کردن، ایجاد کردن

The song was banned on the grounds that it might *foment* racial tension.

fool.hard.y /£ ˈfuːlˌhɑː.di, $ -ˌhɑːr-/ *adj.* rash, foolishly brave

احمقانه، جسورانه؛ کله‌خر، احمق

Don't be *foolhardy*. Get the advice of experienced people before undertaking this venture.

fop.pish /£ ˈfɒp.ɪʃ, $ ˈfɑː.pɪʃ/ *adj.* vain about dress and appearance

سوسول، سوسول مآب، ژیگول

He tried to imitate the *foppish* manner of the young

men of the court.

for.ay /£ ˈfɒr.eɪ, $ ˈfɔːr-/ *n.* raid

حمله، شبیخون، یورش

The soldiers *made* the first *foray* into enemy-occupied territory.

for.bear.ance /£ fɔːˈbeə.rᵊnts, $ fɔːr-/ *n.* patience

صبر، شکیبایی؛ خویشتن‌داری؛ گذشت، چشم‌پوشی

He thanked his employees for the *forbearance* they showed.

for.bear: *v.* گذشت کردن، چشم پوشی کردن

fo.ren.sic /fəˈren.zɪk/ *adj.* suitable to debate or courts of law

دادگاهی، (مربوط به) دادگاه،(در خور) دادگاه یا قانون

In his best *forensic* manner, the lawyer addressed the jury.

fore.sight /£ ˈfɔː.saɪt, $ ˈfɔːr-/ *n.* ability to foresee future happenings, prudence

آینده‌نگری، دوراندیشی، مآل اندیشی

She had the *foresight* to sell her house just before house prices came down.

for.mal.i.ty /£ fɔːˈmæl.ə.ti, $ -t̬i/ *n.* adherence to established rules

رسمیت؛ تشریفات، تکلّف

Signing this is a mere *formality*; it does not obligate you in any way.

for.mi.dab.le /£ fɔːˈmɪ.də.bl̩, $ fɔːr-/ *adj.* threating, causing fear, very difficult

هولناک، رعب‌انگیز؛ (دشمن) سرسخت، قوی؛ سخت، دشوار

We must not treat the battle lightly because we are facing a *formidable* foe.

for.te /£ 'fɔː.teɪ, $ 'fɔːr-/ *n.* a strong ability

نقطهٔ قدرت، هنر، تخصص

His *forte* is after-dinner speeches.

for.ti.tude /£ 'fɔː.tɪ.tjuːd, $ 'fɔːr.tə.tuːd/ *n.* bravery, courage

تحمل، بردباری؛ شجاعت، جسارت

He was awarded the medal for his *fortitude* in the battle.

for.tu.i.tous /£ fɔː'tjuː.ɪ.təs, $ fɔːr'tuː.ə.təs/ *adj.* accidently, by chance; good

تصادفی، شانسی؛ مبارک، میمون

Accepting the job was a *fortuitous* move and her career blossomed.

fos.ter /£ 'fɒs.təʳ, $ 'fɑː.stɚ/ *v.* to rear; to encourage

پرورش دادن؛ ترویج کردن، تشویق کردن

They are trying to *foster* an interest in classical music in my children.

fra.cas /'fræk.ɑː/ *n.* brawl, mêlée

دعوا، کتک کاری

The police stopped the *fracas* in the bar and arrested the belligerents.

frac.tious /'fræk.ʃəs/ *adj.* annoyed, unruly

بدعنق، بداخلاق؛ چموش

I don't have much patience in dealing with *fractious* teenagers.

frail.ty /£ 'feɪl.ti, $ -t̬i/ *n.* weakness

ضعف، سستی؛ نقطه ضعف

Even during his last few months of *frailty* he kept up his writing.

fran.chise /'fræn.tʃaiz/ *n.* right granted by authority

امتیاز؛ اجازه؛ نمایندگی

They lost the *franchise* when they failed to meet the required standard of service.

fran.tic /£ 'fræn.tɪk, $ -tɪk/ *adj.* wild, out of control

پُر تب و تاب، پُر هیجان؛ مضطرب، سراسیمه، هراسان

Exams always drive him *frantic*; he gets so nervous.

fraud.u.lent /£ 'frɔː.djʊ.lᵊnt, $ 'frɑː-/ *adj.* cheating, deceitful

جعلی، تقلبی؛ ریاکارانه

The government seeks to prevent *fraudulent* advertising.

fraught /£ frɔːt, $ frɑːt/ *adj.* filled, full of

مملو از، آکنده از، پُر از

The enterprise was *fraught* with danger.

fray /freɪ/ *n.* brawl

نزاع، مشاجره، دعوا

Members of the royal family rarely enter the political *fray*.

free.boot.er /ˈfriːbuːtər/ *n.* buccaneer

دزد، غارتگر، چپاولگر

This place is frequented by pirates, *freebooter*, and other plunderers.

fre.ne.tic /£ frəˈnet.ɪk/ *adj.* frenzied, frantic

پُر تب و تاب، پُر جوش و خروش، پُر هیجان

His *frenetic* activities convinced us that he had no

organized plan of operation.

fren.zied /ˈfren.ziːd/ *adj.* madly excited

عنان گسیخته، هیجان‌زده؛ دیوانه‌وار

As soon as they smelled smoke, the *frenzied* animals milled about in their cages.

fres.co /£ ˈfres.kəʊ, $ -koʊ/ *n.* painting on plaster

نقاشی دیواری

Michelangelo's famous *frescoes* are in the Sistine Chapel in Rome.

fret /fret/ *v.* to be annoyed, to worry

نگران بودن، ناراحت بودن، بی‌تابی کردن

Don't *fret*—I'm sure he's OK.

fric.tion /ˈfrɪk.ʃən/ *n.* clash in opinion

اختلاف نظر، برخورد؛ اصطکاک

At this time, we cannot afford to have any *friction* in our group.

frieze /friːz/ *n.* ornamental band on a wall

کتیبه (معماری)

The *frieze* of the church was adorned with sculpture.

frig.id /ˈfrɪdʒ.ɪd/ *adj.* intensely cold

خشک، بی‌روح؛ سرد، بسیار سرد، یخ‌زده

Alaska is in the *frigid* zone.

frit.ter /£ ˈfrɪt.ər, $ ˈfrɪt̬.ɚ/ *v.* to waste

تلف کردن، هدر دادن، ضایع کردن

She *fritters* so much money (away) on expensive make-up.

friv.o.li.ty /£ frɪˈvɒl.ə.ti, $ -ˈvɑː.lə.t̬i/ *n.* lack of seriousness

You should not treat such a serious subject with *frivolity*. سبک‌سری، سر به هوایی، بی‌خیالی

friv.o.lous: *adj.* سبک‌سر، بی‌خیال

fro.lic.some /£ ˈfrɒl.ɪk.səm, $ ˈfrɑː.lɪk-/ *adj.* gay, prankish

شاد، شنگول، بازیگوش

The *frolicsome* puppy tried to lick the face of its master.

fruc.ti.fy /ˈfrʌktɪfaɪ/ *v.* to bear fruit

بار دادن، به ثمر نشستن

This tree should *fructify* in three years.

fru.gal.i.ty /£ fruːˈɡæl.ə.ti, $ -t̬i/ *n.* thrift

قناعت، صرفه‌جویی، امساک

In these difficult days, we must live with *frugality*.

fru.i.tion /fruːˈɪʃ.ən/ *n.* bearing of fruit, fulfillment

تحقق، ثمر، نتیجه

The idea *came to fruition* with an exhibition of student's work.

fru.strate /frʌsˈtreɪt/ *v.* to defeat, to thwart

خنثی کردن، ناکام کردن، عقیم گذاشتن؛ مأیوس کردن

They *frustrated* the dictator's plan to seize control of the government.

ful.crum /ˈfʊl.krəm/ *n.* support on which a lever rests

تکیه‌گاه، نقطهٔ اتکا

A pair of weighing scales balances on a *fulcrum*.

ful.min.ate /ˈfʊl.mɪ.neɪt/ *v.* to explode, to thunder

به باد انتقاد گرفتن، تاختن، پرخاش کردن

The people against whom he *fulminated* were innocent of any wrongdoing.

ful.some /ˈfʊl.səm/ *adj.* excessive

اغراق‌آمیز، تملق‌آمیز، چاپلوسانه

His *fulsome* praise of the dictator annoyed his listeners.

func.tion.ar.y /ˈfʌŋk.ʃ°n.ri/ *n.* official

کارمند، کارگذار

As a high-ranking party *functionary*, he speaks Russian fluently.

fu.ner.e.al /£ fjuːˈnɪə.ri.əl, $ -ˈnɪr.i-/ *adj.* sad, solemn

ماتم‌زده، غمزده، غمگین، حزن‌آور

This music is rather *funereal*.

fu.ror /£ ˈfjʊːrɔːʳ, $ -rɔːr/ *n.* frenzy, great excitement

جنجال، غوغا، هیاهو

The government's decision to raise taxes has caused a great *furor*.

fur.tive /£ ˈfɜː.tɪv, $ ˈfɜːr.tɪv/ *adj.* stealthy

دزدکی، پنهانی، مخفیانه

The boy took a *furtive* look at his classmate's test paper.

fu.sion /ˈfjuːʒ°n/ *n.* union, coalition

ائتلاف، ادغام

The opponents organized a *fusion* of disgruntled groups.

fu.tile /£ ˈfjuː.taɪl, $ -təl/ *adj.* fruitless, ineffective

بیهوده، بی‌فایده، بی‌ثمر، بی‌حاصل

It's quite *futile* trying to reason with him — he just won't listen.

لیستی از لغاتی که در جملات بخش F به کار رفته‌اند:

act: *v.*	اقدام کردن، عمل کردن	degenerate: *v.*	تبدیل شدن
adopt: *v.*	پذیرفتن	disgruntled: *adj.*	ناراضی
appropriate: *adj.*	مناسب	disregard: *v.*	نادیده گرفتن
approval: *n.*	رضایت	encouraging: *adj.*	دلگرم‌کننده
attempted: *adj.*	نافرجام	enthusiasm: *n.*	علاقه
ban: *v.*	قدغن کردن، تحریم کردن	evil spirits: *n.*	ارواح خبیث
batter: *v.*	درب و داغون کردن	excessive: *adj.*	زیاده از حد
belligerent: *n.*	پرخاشگر، ستیزه‌جو	exhibition: *n.*	نمایش، ارائه
		exposition: *n.*	نمایشگاه
beset: *v.*	گریبانگیر شدن	foe: *n.*	دشمن
blossom: *v.*	رونق پیدا کردن، شکفتن	fool: *v.*	فریب دادن
		foothold: *n.*	جا پا
botanist: *n.*	گیاه‌شناس	frequent: *v.*	رفت و آمد کردن
cannon: *n.*	توپ	grasp: *v.*	درک کردن
capacity: *n.*	مقام؛ ظرفیت	grounds: *n.*	بهانه، دلیل، موجب
cheers: *n.*	تشویق، بچه‌ها متشکریم!	hastiness: *n.*	تعجیل
		headstrong: *adj.*	سرسخت، قُد
clutch: *n.*	چنگ	incident: *n.*	اتفاق، حادثه
complexion: *n.*	چهره، سیما	infinite (the): *n.*	ذات لایتناهی، خداوند
condemn: *v.*	محکوم کردن		
condone: *v.*	پذیرفتن	inspire: *v.*	روحیه دادن
congestion: *n.*	تراکم	jetsam: *n.*	آشغال دریا
convicted: *adj.*	محکوم	knotted: *adj.*	گره‌دار
convince: *v.*	متقاعد کردن	lick: *v.*	لیسیدن
coup: *n.*	کودتا	lift: *v.*	بالا بردن
curb: *v.*	کنترل کردن، محدود کردن	meet: *v.*	برآوردن

mill about: v.	پریشان و سرگردان بودن	shear	چیدن پشم گوسفند
motive: n.	انگیزه	spirits: n.	روحیه
neglected: adj.	کهنه	split: v.	دو دستگی ایجاد کردن
nightmare: n.	کابوس	stand: n.	بساط، دکه
obligate: v.	تعهد ایجاد کردن	stipulate: v.	تصریح کردن
obligation: n.	وظیفه	stammer: v.	با لکنت گفتن
opponent: n.	رقیب، مخالف	strand: v.	رشته، لا
outfit: n.	پیراهن زنانه	subject: n.	دستخوشِ
overlook: v.	نادیده گرفتن	tactless: adj.	نسنجیده، نابجا
pirate: n.	دزد دریایی	tension: n.	کشمکش، تنش
plunderer: n.	غارتگر	territory: n.	قلمرو، حیطه
puppy: n.	توله (سگ، گربه)	track: n.	رد، اثر
pus: n.	چرک	tremendous: adj.	زیاد
racial: adj.	نژاد پرستی، نژادی	unavoidable: adj.	اجتناب ناپذیر
ramp: n.	پلکان متحرک	undertake: v.	قبول کردن
remarks: n.	اظهارات	utter: v.	بیان کردن
request: n.	درخواست، تقاضا	vain: adj.	مغرور
resent: v.	بد آمدن، آزرده خاطر شدن	vassal: n.	رعیت
		venture: n.	کار مخاطره‌آمیز
		violation: n.	تخطی
rough: adj.	سخت	visualize: v.	تجسم کردن
scales: n.	وزنه	vivid: adj.	زنده
scheme: n.	طرح	ward off: v.	از خود دور کردن
secure: v.	بستن، مصون ساختن	warrior: n.	سلحشور
sedentary	زمین‌گیر، مقیم	whip: n.	شلاق، تازیانه

G g

gad.fly /gæd.ˈflaɪ/ *n.* animal-biting fly; an irritating person

خرمگس؛ آدم خرده‌گیر، عیبجو

Like a *gadfly*, he irritated all the guests at the hotel.

gain.say /ˌgeɪnˈseɪ/ *v.* to deny

انکار کردن، تردید کردن در

He could not *gainsay* the truth of the report.

gait /geɪt/ *n.* manner of walking or running, speed

طرز راه رفتن

He was tall and portly and walked with a slow stiff *gait*.

gal.ax.y /ˈgæl.ək.si/ *n.* very large group of stars; distinguished assembly

کهکشان؛ جمعیتی از شخصیت‌های برجسته

The *galaxy* of Hollywood superstars is rapidly disappearing.

gall /£ gɔːl, $ gɑːl/ *n.* bitterness; insolence

وقاحت، بی‌شرمی؛ زخم زبان، سرکوفت

The knowledge of his failure filled him with *gall* .

gall: *v.* تحقیر کردن، خرد کردن، (احساسات) جریحه‌دار کردن

gal.le.on /ˈgæl.i.ən/ *n.* large sailing ship

کشتی بزرگ بادبانی

The Spaniards pinned their hopes on the *galleon*, the large warship.

gal.van.ize /ˈgæl.və.naɪz/ *v.* to stir up, to stimulate by shock

تحریک کردن، برانگیختن، به هیجان آوردن

The entire nation was *galvanized* into strong military activity by the news of the attck on Pearl Harbor.

gam.bit /ˈgæm.bɪt/ *n.* opening tactic in chess

(شطرنج) گامبی، قربانی

The player was afraid to accept his opponent's *gambit*.

gam.bol /ˈgæm.bᵊl/ *v., n.* to leap palyfully

بالا و پایین پریدن، جست و خیز کردن؛ ورجه وورجه

Watching children *gamboling* in the park is a pleasant experience.

game.ly /ˈgeɪm.li/ *adj.* in a plucky manner, bravely

شجاعانه، باشهامت، دلیرانه

"I'll look after the baby," he said *gamely*.

game.ster /ˈgeɪm.stəʳ/ *n.* gambler

قمارباز

He is an inveterate *gamester*.

gam.ut /ˈgæm.ət/ *n.* whole range of things

طیف، گستره، دامنه

Jonson has *run* the *gamut* of hotel work, from porter to owner of a large chain of hotels.

gape /geɪp/ *v., n.* to open widely

از هم باز شدن، دهان باز کردن؛ با دهان باز نگاه کردن به

The huge pit *gaped* before him; if he stumbled, he would fall in.

gar.ble /£ ˈgɑː.bl̩, $ ˈgɑːr-/ *v.* to change meaning by distortion, to mix up

تحریف کردن، مخدوش کردن

Because the report was *garbled* it confused many readers who were not familiar with the facts.

gar.goyle /£ ˈgɑː.gɔɪl, $ ˈgɑːr-/ *n.* a stone object in the shape of the head of an ugly creature

ناودان کله اژدری

The *gargoyles* at the top of Norte Dame look down over Paris.

gar.ish /£ ˈgeə.rɪʃ, $ ˈger.ɪʃ/ *adj.* unpleasantly bright, gaudy

رنگ وارنگ، زرق و برق‌دار

He was wearing *garish* Bermuda shorts and training shoes.

gar.ner /£ ˈgɑː.nəʳ, $ ˈgɑːr.nɚ/ *v., n.* to gather, to store up

گردآوری کردن، جمع‌آوری کردن؛ جمع‌آوری

He hoped to *garner* the world's literature in one library.

gar.nish /£ ˈgɑː.nɪʃ, $ ˈgɑːr-/ *v., n.* to decorate (food)

تزیین کردن (غذا)؛ تزیین

Parsley was used to *garnish* the boiled potato.

gar.ru.li.ty /£ gærˈuː.lɪ.ti, $ -lə.t̬i/ *n.* talkativeness

پرحرفی، پرگویی، وّراجی

The man asked the doctor to make him deaf because of his wife's *garrulity*.

gar.ru.lous: *adj.* پرحرف، وّراج

ga.stro.no.my /£ gæsˈtrɒn.ə.mi, $ -ˈtrɑː.nə-/ *n.* science of preparing and serving good food

هنر آشپزی، خوراک شناسی

The food writer Elizabeth David introduced ***gastronomy*** to many Britons.

gauche /£ gəʊʃ, $ goʊʃ/ *adj.* clumsy, awkward

بی‌ظرافت، ناشیانه؛ بی‌دست و پا، دست و پا چلفت

She had grown from a ***gauche*** teenager to a self-assured young woman.

gaunt /£ gɔːnt, $ gɑːnt/ *adj.* lean, very thin

تکیده، لاغر، نحیف، لاغر مردنی

Hunger had made her face ***gaunt*** and grey.

gaunt.let /£ ˈgɔːnt.lət, $ ˈgɑːnt-/ *n.* leather glove

دستکش

She put on a helmet and a leather jacket and ***gauntlets*** before getting on the motor bike.

throw down the gauntlet	به مبارزه دعوت کردن
pick up the gauntlet	مبارزه را پذیرفتن

ga.zette /gəˈzet/ *n.* a newspaper

روزنامهٔ رسمی

He reads the ***gazettes*** regularly.

gen.e.al.o.gy /ˌdʒiː.niˈæl.ə.dʒi/ *n.* record of one's family, lineage

تبارشناسی؛ شجره، شجره‌نامه

I have been studying the ***genealogy*** of my family.

gen.er.al.i.ty /£ ˌdʒen.əˈræl.ɪ.ti, $ -ə.t̬i/ *n.* vague statement

کلی‌گویی، کلی‌بافی

This report is filled with ***generalities***; you must be more specific.

ge.ne.ric /dʒə'ner.ɪk/ *adj.* characteristic of a class or species

کلی، عام، ژنریک

The plays all fit within the ***generic*** definition of "comedy".

ge.ni.al.i.ty /£ ˌdʒi:.ni'æl.ɪ.ti, $ -ə.ṭi/ *n.* cheerfulness, kindliness, sympathy

صمیمیت، مهربانی، محبت

This restaurant is famous because of the ***geniality*** of the owner who tries to make everyone happy.

gen.re /'ʒɑ̃:.rə, 'ʒɒn/ *n.* form

(هنر و غیره) نوع، ژانر

What ***genre*** does the book fall into — comedy or tragedy?

gen.teel /£ dʒen'tɪəl, $ -'ti:l/ *adj.* well-bred, elegant

متشخص، اشراف مآب، محترم

We are looking for a man with a ***genteel*** appearance.

gen.til.i.ty /£ dʒen'tɪl.ɪ.ti, $ -ə.ṭi/ *n.* those of gentle birth, refinement

نزاکت، ادب

Her family was proud of its ***gentility***.

gen.try /'dʒen.tri/ *n.* the people of high social class

اشراف

At the time, the local ***gentry*** was / were resisting the changes.

gen.u.flect /'dʒen.jʊ.flekt/ *v.* to bend the knee as in worship

زانو زدن، کرنش کردن

Aa a proud democrat, he refused to ***genuflect*** to any man.

ger.mane /£ dʒɜ:'meɪn, $ dʒɜ:r-/ *adj.* relevant

Her remarks could not have been more ***germane*** to the discussion.

ger.mi.nal /ˈdʒɜːmɪnᵊl/ *adj.* in the first stage of growth

آغازین، ابتدایی، اولیه، مقدماتی

Such an idea is ***germinal***; it will influence thinkers for many generations.

ger.mi.nate /£ ˈdʒɜː.mɪ.neɪt, $ ˈdʒɜːr-/ *v.* to sprout

روییدن، رویاندن؛ خلق کردن، ایجاد کردن

The beans will only ***germinate*** if the temperature is warm enough.

ger.ry.man.der /£ ˈdʒer.iˌmæn.dəʳ, $ -dɚ/ *v.* to change voting district lines

(انتخابات) تقسیمات کشوری را به نفع یک حزب تغییر دادن

The state legislature ***gerrymandered*** this area in order to favor the majority party.

ges.tate /dʒesˈteɪt/ *v.* to evolve

تکامل یافتن، دوران تکوینی خود را طی کردن

While the scheme was being ***gestated*** by the conspirators, they were silent about their intentions.

ges.ti.cu.la.tion /dʒesˌtɪk.jʊˈleɪ.ʃᵊn/ *n.* motion, gesture

حرکات سر و دست؛ ایما و اشاره

Operatic performers are trained to make exaggerated ***gesticulations***.

gha.stly /£ ˈɡɑːst.li, $ ˈɡæst-/ *adj.* horrible

هولناک، مخوف، فجیع؛ وحشتناک

The murdered man was a ***ghastly*** sight.

gib.ber /£ ˈdʒɪb.ər, $ -ɚ/ v. to speak foolishly

تته پته کردن، مهمل گفتن؛ ور ور کردن

Stop *gibbering*, man, and tell us what you saw.

gib.bet /ˈdʒɪb.ɪt/ n. gallows

چوبهٔ دار

The bodies of the highwaymen were left dangling from the *gibbet*.

gibe /dʒaɪb/ v. to mock

دست انداختن، مسخره کردن، خندیدن به

She *gibed at* the way he ran his business.

gig /gɪg/ n. two-wheeled carriage

درشکهٔ یک اسبه

They drove down the street in their new *gig*.

gin.ger.ly /£ ˈdʒɪn.dʒə.li, $ -dʒɚ-/ adv. very carefully

محتاطانه، با احتیاط، آرام، یواش، آهسته

To separate egg whites, first crack the egg *gingerly*.

gist /dʒɪst/ n. essence

لبّ مطلب، جان کلام، موضوع اصلی

She was asked to give the *gist* of the essay in two sentences.

glaze /gleɪz/ v., n. to cover with a thin and shiny surface

لعاب دادن؛ لعاب

The freezing rain *glazed* the streets and made driving hazardous.

glean /gliːn/ v. to gather leavings

خوشه‌چینی کردن، جمع‌آوری کردن؛ برداشت کردن

The peasants were permitted to *glean* the wheat left in

the fields.

glean.ings: *n.*   مطالب، نکات

glib /glɪb/ *adj.* fluent, slick

                                             چرب‌زبان، زبان باز

He is a ***glib*** speaker.

gloam.ing /£ ˈgləʊ.mɪŋ, $ ˈgloʊ-/ *n.* twilight

                                             شامگاه، شفق

The snow began to fall in the ***gloaming*** and continued all through the night.

gloat /£ gləʊt, $ gloʊt/ *v.* to feel or express great pleasure

                 احساس غرور کردن، به خود نازیدن؛ شاد شدن

She won't stop ***gloating*** *over/ about* her new job.

glos.sa.ry /£ ˈglɒs.ᵊr.i, $ ˈglɑː.sɚ-/ *n.* a list of words or phrases in a text

                                                   واژه‌نامه

I have found the ***glossary*** in this book very useful.

glos.sy /£ ˈglɒl.i, $ ˈglɑː.si/ *adj.* smoth and shining

                                     براق، درخشنده، درخشان

I want this photograph printed on ***glossy*** paper.

glow.er /£ ˈglaʊ.əʳ, $ -ɚ/ *v.* to scowl, to look very angry

                 چشم غرّه رفتن، چپ چپ نگاه کردن

The angry boy ***glowered*** *at* his father.

glut /glʌt/ *v.* to overstock, to fill to excess

           (بازار) پُر کردن، اشباع کردن، بیش از حد عرضه کردن

The manufacturers ***glutted*** the market and could not find purchasers.

glu.tin.ous /£ ˈgluː.tɪ.nəs, $ -tɪ-/ *adj.* sticky, viscous

چسبناک، چسبنده

Rice turns into a soft **glutinous** mass when cooked.

glut.ton.ous /£ ˈglʌt.ᵊn.əs, $ ˈglʌt̬-/ *adj.* greedy for food

(آدم) شکمباره، شکمو، پُرخور، حریص

The **gluttonous** boy ate all the cookies.

gnarled /£ nɑːld, $ nɑːrld/ *adj.* twisted

گره‌دار، کج و کوله

The **gnarled** oak tree had been a landmark for years.

gnome /£ nəʊm, $ noʊm/ *n.* dwarf, underground spirit

جن کوتوله

In medieval mythology **gnomes** were the special guardians of subterranean mines.

goad /£ gəʊd, $ goʊd/ *v.* to urge on

وادار کردن، واداشتن؛ تحریک کردن، ترغیب کردن

Will the pressure be enough to **goad** the nations into using less fossil fuels?

gorge /£ gɔːdʒ, $ gɔːrdʒ/ *v.* to stuff oneself

تا خرخره خوردن، شکمی از عزا در آوردن

The gluttonous guest **gorged** *himself with* food as if he had not eaten for days.

go.ry /£ ˈgɔː.ri, $ ˈgɔːr.i/ *adj.* bloody

خونین، پُر از خون و خونریزی

The audience shuddered as they listened to the details of the **gory** massacre.

gos.sam.er /£ ˈgɒs.ə.məʳ, $ ˈgɑː.sə.mɚ/ *adj.* sheer, like cobwebs

نازک، لطیف، مثل تار عنکبوت

The bride wore a delicate **gossamer** veil.

gouge /gaʊdʒ/ *v.* to tear out, to make a hole

کندن، سوراخ کردن

He drove into some railings and *gouged* a hole in the back of his car.

gour.mand /£ gɔː'mãːd, $ 'gʊr.mɑːnd/ *n.* a person who enjoys eating large amount of food

(آدم) شکم‌پرست، شکمو، شکمباره، پُرخور

The *gourmand* liked the French cuisine.

gour.met /£ 'gɔː.meɪ, $ 'gʊr.meɪ/ *n.* a person who knows a lot about food and cooking

غذاشناس، خبره در خوراک

The *gourmet* stated that this was the best onion soup he had ever tasted.

gran.a.ry /£ 'græn.ᵊr.i, $ -'ɚ-/ *n.* storehouse for grain

انبار غلّه

We are thankful to God, for our crops were good and our *granaries* are full.

gran.dil.o.quent /græn'dɪl.ə.kwᵊnt/ *adj.* pompous, bombastic

پر تکلّف، پرطمطراق

The politician could never speak simply, he was always *grandiloquent*.

gran.di.ose /£ 'græn.di.əʊs, £ -əʊz, $ -oʊs/ *adj.* imposing, impressive

خودنمایانه، متکبرانه، با ابهت

His *grandiose* manner impressed those who met him for the first time.

gran.u.late /'græn.jʊ.leɪt/ *v.* to form into grains

دانه دانه کردن، به‌صورت ذرات در آوردن
Sugar that has been *granulated* dissolves more readily than lump sugar.

gran.ule: *n.* دانه، ذره

gra.tis /£ ˈgrɑːtɪs, $ ˈgræt̬.əs/ *adv.* free

مجانی، رایگان

I'll give it to you, *gratis*.

gra.tu.i.tous /£ grəˈtjuː.ɪ.təs, $ -ˈtuː.ə.t̬əs/ *adj.* not necessary, with no cause

بی‌جهت، بی‌خود، بی‌دلیل، ناحق، بیجا

A lot of viewers complained that there was too much *gratuitous* violence in the film.

gra.tu.i.ty /£ grəˈtjuː.ə.ti, $ -ˈtuː.ə.t̬i/ *n.* tip

انعام، پاداش

The guides sometimes receive *gratuities* from the tourists.

gre.ga.ri.ous /£ grɪˈgeə.ri.əs, $ -ˈger.i-/ *adj.* sociable

اجتماعی، معاشرتی، خونگرم

He was not *gregarious* and preferred to be alone most of the time.

grim.ace /ˈgrɪ.məs, grɪˈmeɪs/ *n.* a facial distortion to show feeling such as pain

شکلک، اخم، ادا؛ شکلک درآوردن، اخم کردن

His *grimace* indicated his displeasure.

gris.ly /ˈgrɪz.li/ *adj.* ghastly, unpleasant

فجیع، هولناک، وحشتناک

The newspaper described a series of *grisly* murders.

gro.tesque /£ grəʊtesk, $ groʊ-/ *adj.* fantastic, comically hideous

مضحک، مسخره؛ زشت، کریه

On Halloween people enjoy wearing *grotesque* costume.

grot.to /£ ˈgrɒt.əʊ, $ ˈgrɑː.toʊ/ *n.* small cavern

غار، غار مصنوعی

The Blue *Grotto* in Capri can be entered only by small boats.

grov.el /£ ˈgrɒv.ᵊl, $ ˈgrɑː.vᵊl/ *v.* to crawl or creep on ground

به خاک افتادن، به پای(کسی) افتادن، التماس کردن

Even though we have been defeated, we do not have to *grovel* before our conquerors.

grudg.ing /ˈgrʌdʒ.ɪŋ/ *adj.* unwilling, reluctant

با اکراه، با بی‌میلی، زورکی

He won the *grudging* respect of his boss.

gru.el /£ groəl, $ ˈgruː.əl/ *n.* liquid food made by boiling oatmeal

آش جو، سوپ جو

While he was in prison, he was served a meagre diet of rice, bread and *gruel*.

gru.el.ing /£ ˈgroə.lɪŋ, $ ˈgruː.lɪŋ/ *adj.* exhausting

سخت، خسته‌کننده، توان‌فرسا، دشوار، طاقت‌فرسا

The Marathon is a *grueling* race.

grue.some /ˈgruː.səm/ *adj.* grisly

فجیع، وحشتناک، هولناک

People screamed when his *gruesome* appearance was flashed on the screen.

gruff /grʌf/ *adj.* rough-mannered, unfriendly

(صدا، لحن) خشن، تند

She spoke to me in a *gruff* voice.

guf.faw /£ gʌfˈɔː, $ -ˈɑː/ *n.* boisterous laughter

قهقهه، شلیک خنده

The loud *guffaws* came from the closed room.

guile /gaɪl/ *n.* deceit, duplicity

نیرنگ، تزویر، مکر

He achieved his high position by *guile* and treachery.

guile.less: *adj.* بی‌ریا، صادق، یکرنگ

guise /gaɪz/ *n.* appearance; costume

ظاهر، سیما، قیافه؛ لباس؛ در قالبِ

In the *guise* of a plumber, the detective investigated the murder case.

gul.li.ble /ˈgʌl.ə.bl̩/ *adj.* easily deceived

ساده‌لوح، زودباور، هالو

He preyed upon *gullible* people.

gust.a.tor.y /£ ˈgʌs.tə.tʳr.i, $ -tɔː.ri/ *adv.* affecting the sense of taste

چشایی، (مربوط به) ذائقه

This food has great *gustatory* appeal because of the spices it contains.

gust.o /£ ˈgʌs.təʊ, $ -toʊ/ *n.* enjoyment, enthusiasm

شور و شوق، ذوق و شوق، هیجان

They sang with such *gusto* that they compensated for the play's weakness.

gust.y /ˈgʌs.ti/ *adj.* windy

توفانی،(باد) تند و شدید

The *gusty* weather made sailing precarious.

gut.tur.al /£ ˈgʌt.ᵊr.əl, $ ˈgʌt̬.ɚ-/ *adj.* produced at the back of the throat

حلقی، پسکامی؛ (صدا) بم

Two Egyptians were arguing outside the room, their voices loud and *guttural*.

لیستی از لغاتی که در جملات بخش G به‌کار رفته‌اند:

Britions: *n.*	انگلیسی‌ها	lump sugar: *n.*	قند حبه‌ای
compensate: *v.*	جبران کردن	massacre: *n.*	قتل‌عام دسته‌جمعی
complain: *v.*	گله کردن	meagre: *adj.*	کم، ناکافی
conspirator: *n.*	توطئه‌گر	mine: *n.*	معدن، نقب
costume: *n.*	لباس	parsley: *n.*	جعفری
crack: *n.*	شکاف	peasant: *n.*	روستایی
cuisine: *n.*	پخت و پز، غذا	pin: *v.*	دوختن
dangle: *v.*	آویزان بودن	pit: *n.*	گودال
delicate: *adj.*	ظریف	plucky: *adj.*	با شهامت
displeasure: *adj.*	نارضایتی	porter: *n.*	دربان، باربر
dissolve: *v.*	حل شدن	portly: *adj.*	تنومند، قوی هیکل
drive into: *v.*	زدن به	precarious: *adj.*	خطرناک
exaggerated: *adj.*	مبالغه‌آمیز	prey: *v.*	به دام انداختن
favor: *v.*	پشتیبانی کردن	purchaser: *n.*	خریدار
gluttonous: *adj.*	شکمو	railings: *n.*	نرده آهنی
hazardous: *adj.*	خطرناک	self-assured: *adj.*	متکی به خود
helmet: *n.*	کلاه	shudder: *v.*	به خود لرزیدن
highwayman: *n.*	راهزن	stiff: *adj.*	شق
indicate: *v.*	نشان از ... بودن	stumble: *v.*	سکندری خوردن
intention: *n.*	قصد	subterranean: *adj.*	زیرزمینی
inveterate: *adj.*	کهنه‌کار	treachery: *n.*	ریاکاری
irritate: *v.*	ناراحت کردن	veil: *n.*	روبنده
landmark: *n.*	نشان، راهنما	violence: *n.*	خشونت
local: *adj.*	محلی، موضعی	wheat: *n.*	گندم

H h

hack.les /ˈhæk.l̩z/ *n.* hairs on back and neck of a dog

موی پشت و گردن سگ

The dog's *hackles* rose and began to growl as the sound of footsteps grew louder.

hack.neyed /ˈhæk.nɪd/ *adj.* commonplace, trite

کهنه، قدیمی، تکراری، بی‌مزه

The English teacher criticized his story because of his *hackneyed* plot.

hag.gard /£ ˈhæg.əd, $ -ərd/ *adj.* tired and odd looking, wasted away

خسته، فرسوده، با چشمان گود افتاده، زرد و رنجور

She was looking a bit *haggard* as if she hadn't slept for days.

hag.gle /ˈhægl/ *v.* to argue about prices

چانه زدن، چک و چانه زدن

It's traditional that you *haggle* over/ about the price of things in the market.

hal.cy.on /ˈhæl.si.ən/ *adj.* calm, peaceful

خوش، شاد

In those *halcyon* days, people were not worried about

sneak attacks and bombing.

hale /ˈheɪl/ *adj.* healthy

سرحال، تندرست

After a brief illness, he was *hale* again.

hal.lowed /£ ˈhæl.əʊd, $ -oʊd/ *adj.* blessed, consecrated

مقدس، متبرکه

He was laid to rest in *hallowed* ground.

hal.luc.in.a.tion /həˌluː.sɪˈneɪ.ʃᵊn/ *n.* delusion

توهم، خیال

I think you were frightened by the *hallucination* which you created in your own mind.

ham.per /£ ˈhæm.pəʳ, $ -pɚ/ *v.* to obstruct

دست و بال (کسی را) بستن، جلو (چیزی را) گرفتن، مشکل کردن

The party agreed not to *hamper* the efforts of the leaders to secure a lasting peace.

hap /hæp/ *n.* chance, luck

شانس، اقبال، بخت

In his poem "*Hap*", Hardy objects to the part chance plays in our lives.

hap.haz.ard /£ ˌhæpˈhæz.əd, $ -ɚd/ *adj.* by chance, random

اتفاقی، تصادفی

He tackled the problem in a typically *haphazard* manner.

hap.less /ˈhæp.ləs/ *adj.* unfortunate

نگون‌بخت، بخت برگشته، شوربخت

This *hapless* creature had never known a moment's pleasure.

ha.ran.gue /həˈræŋ/ *n.* noisy speech

نطق آتشین

In his lengthy *harangue*, the principal berated the offenders.

har.ass /ˈhær.əs/ *v.* to annoy by repeated attacks

به ستوه آوردن، عاجز کردن، ایجاد مزاحمت کردن

He was *harassed* by his creditors.

har.bing.er /£ ˈhɑː.bɪn.dʒəʳ, $ ˈhɑːr.bɪn.dʒɚ/ *n.* forerunner

پیام‌آور، منادی، پیک

The crocus is an early *harbinger* of spring.

har.bor /£ ˈhɑː.bəʳ, $ ˈhɑːr.bɚ/ *v.* to hide, to protect

پنهان کردن، پناه دادن

The church *harbored* illegal aliens who were political refugees.

harp /£ hɑːp, $ ˌhɑːr-/ *v.* to repeat, to complain

مدام (چیزی را) تکرار کردن، ور زدن

He's always *harping* about lack of discipline.

har.ri.dan /£ ˈhær.ɪ.dən, $ ˈher-/ *n.* hag, a nagging woman

پیرزن بدخلق، پیرزن نق نقو

He's got an absolute *harridan* of a mother-in-law.

har.row /£ ˈhær.əʊ, $ ˈher.oʊ/ *v.* to break up ground after plowing; to torture

کلوخ شکن انداختن؛ عذاب دادن

I don't want to *harrow* you by asking you to recall the details of your unpleasant experience.

har.ry /ˈhær.ɪ/ *v.* to raid

چپاول کردن، غارت کردن، حمله کردن

The guerrilla band *harried* the enemy nightly.

haugh.ti.ness /£ ˈhɔː.tɪ.nəs, $ ˈhɑː.t̬ɪ-/ n. pride, arrogance

تکبّر، غرور، نخوت

I resent his **haughtiness** because he is no better than we are.

hau.teur /£ əʊˈtɜːʳ, $ hoʊˈtɜːr/ n. haughtiness

تکبّر، غرور، نخوت

He presided over the first day of the meeting with his customary **hauteur**.

haw.ser /£ ˈhɔː.zə, $ ˈhɑː.zɚ/ n. large rope

طناب کلفت، طناب سیمی، کابل

The ship was tied to the pier by a **hawser**.

haz.ard.ous /£ ˈhæz.ə.dəs, $ -ɚ-/ adj. dangerous

پُرخطر، مخاطره‌آمیز، خطرناک

Your occupation is too **hazardous** for insurance companies to consider your application.

haz.y /ˈheɪ.zi/ adj. slightly obscure

مه‌آلود، غبارآلود

In **hazy** weather, you cannot see the top of this mountain.

heck.le /ˈhek.l̩/ v. to interrupt sth with unfriendly questions

(سخنرانی) با سؤال قطع کردن، اخلال ایجاد کردن

A few angry locals started **heckling** (the speaker).

heck.ler: n. اخلال‌گر

he.don.i.sm /ˈhed.ᵊn.ɪ.zᵊm/ n. belief that pleasure is the sole aim in life

لذت‌گروی، لذت‌گرایی؛ لذت‌جویی، خوش گذرانی

Asceticism and **hedonism** are opposing philosophies of

human behavior.

heed.less /ˈhiːd.ləs/ *adj.* not noticing, disregarding

بی‌اعتنا، بی‌توجه

He drove on, **heedless** of the warnings placed at the side of the road.

he.gi.ra /ˈhedʒɪrə/ *n.* flight

هجرت

The Prophet began his **hegira** when he was 53 years old.

hei.nous /ˈhiːnəs/ *adj.* hatefully bad, atrocious

فجیع، شریر

Hitler's **heinous** crimes will never be forgotten.

her.bi.vor.ous /£ hɜːˈbɪv.ºr.əs, $ hɜːrˈbɪv.ɚ-/ *adj.* grain-eating

علف‌خوار، گیاه‌خوار

Some **herbivorous** animals have two stomachs for digesting their food.

her.e.sy /ˈher.ə.si/ *n.* opinion contrary to popular belief, opinion contrary to church dogma

بدعت، بدعت‌گذاری

He was threatened with excommunication because his remarks were pure **heresy**.

her.e.tic /ˈher.ə.tɪk/ *n.* a person who is guilty of heresy

بدعت‌گذار

She was branded a **heretic** and burned at the stake.

her.met.ic.ally /£ hɜːˈmet.kli, $ hɚˈmet̬-/ *adv.* sealed airtight

بدون هوا

The disk is housed in a **hermetically** sealed unit to protect it from dust.

her.mi.tage /£ ˈhɜː.mɪ.tɪdʒ, $ ˈhɜːr.mɪ.t̬ɪdʒ/ *n.* home of a hermit

گوشهٔ عزلت، منزلگاه معتکف

Even in his remote ***hermitage*** he could not escape completely from the world.

het.er.og.en.eous /£ ˌhet.ər.əˈdʒiː.ni.əs, $ ˌhet̬.ə.roʊ-/ *adj.* dissimilar

جوراجور، مختلف، نامتجانس، ناهمگن

There was a wonderfully ***heterogeneous*** gathering of people at the party.

hew /hjuː/ *v.* to cut to pieces with ax or sword

تکه تکه کردن، ضربه زدن

The cavalry rushed into the mêlée and ***hewed*** the enemy with their swords.

hi.a.tus /£ haɪˈeɪ.təs, $ -t̬əs/ *n.* gap, pause

وقفه؛ خلأ؛ گسستگی

Tourists are once again visiting the city after a brief ***hiatus*** caused by the war.

hi.ber.nal /ˈhaɪ.bə.nʌl/ *adj.* wintry

زمستانی

Bears prepare for their long ***hirbernal*** sleep by overeating.

hi.ber.nate /£ ˈhaɪ.bə.neɪt, $ -bɚ-/ *v.* to sleep throughout the winter

به خواب زمستانی رفتن

The turtle ***hibernates*** in a shallow burrow for six months of the year.

hier.ar.chy /£ ˈhaɪə.rɑːki, $ ˈhaɪr.ɑːr-/ *n.* a system divided into ranks

سلسله مراتب؛ مقامات

There's a very rigid social **hierarchy** in their society.

hier.o.glyph.ics /£ ˌhaɪə.rəˈglɪf.ɪks, $ -roʊ/ *n.* picture writing

خط تصویری

The discovery of the Rosetta Stone enabled scholars to read the ancient Egyptian **hieroglyphics**.

hi.la.ri.ty /£ hɪˈlær.ə.ti, $ -ler.ə.t̬i/ *n.* a lot of laughter, biosterous mirth

قهقههٔ شادی

This **hilarity** is improper on this solemn day of mourning.

hi.la.ri.ous: *adj.* (مهمانی) شاد، گرم، پُر سر و صدا

hind.most /ˈhaɪnd.moʊst/ *adj.* furthest behind

عقب‌ترین؛ دورترین

The coward could always be found in the **hindmost** lines whenever a battle was being waged.

hire.ling /£ ˈhaɪə.lɪŋ, $ ˈhaɪr-/ *n.* one who serves someone else for gain

مزدور

He's not the boss, he's just a **hireling** employed to do the dirty work.

hir.sute /£ ˈhɜː.sjuːt, $ ˈhɜːr.suːt/ *adj.* hairy

پُرمو، مودار، پشمالو

He was a **hirsute** individual with a heavy black beard.

hi.stri.on.ic /£ ˌhɪs.triˈɒn.ɪk, $ -ˈɑː.nɪk/ *adj.* theatrical

نمایشی، تئاتری

He was proud of his **histrionic** ability and wanted to play the role of Hamlet.

hi.stri.on.ics: *n.*   نمایش، بازیگری

hoar.y /£ ˈhɔː.ri, $ ˈhɔːr.i/ *adj.* white with age

مو سفید، سالخورده

The man was *hoary* and wrinkled.

hoax /£ həʊks, $ hoʊks/ *n., v.* trick, practical joke

شوخی سرکاری، کلک، حقه؛ دست انداختن، سر به سر گذاشتن، گول زدن

Embarrassed by the *hoax*, he reddened and left the room.

hol.o.caust /£ ˈhɒl.ə.kɔːst, $ ˈhɑː.lə.kɑːst/ *n.* destruction by fire

انهدام با حریق، قتل عام با حریق

Citizens of San Francisco remember that the destruction of the city was caused not by the earthquake but by the *holocaust* that followed.

the Holocaust: *n.*   یهودکشی (قتل عام یهودیان در دوران نازیسم)

hol.ster /£ ˈhəʊl.stər, $ ˈhoʊl.stɚ/ *n.* pistal case

جلد تپانچه

He carried a *holster* and pistol under his arm.

hom.age /£ ˈhɒm.ɪdʒ, $ ˈhɑː.mɪdʒ/ *n.* honor; tribute

ادای احترام؛ تقدیر

In her speech she tried to *pay homage* to a great man.

home.spun /£ ˈhəʊm.spʌn, $ ˈhoʊm-/ *adj.* simple and ordinary

ساده، معمولی؛ دست ریس

Homespun wit like *homespun* cloth was often coarse and plain.

hom.i.ly /£ ˈhɒm.ɪ.li, $ ˈhɑː.mə-/ *n.* sermon, serious warning

موعظه، هشدار

His speeches were always *homilies*, advising his listeners to repent and reform.

ho.mo.gen.eous /£ ˌhɒm.əˈdʒiː.ni.əs, £ ˌhəʊ.mə-, $ ˌhoʊ.moʊˈdʒiː-/ *adj.* of the same kind

متجانس، همگن؛ شبیه، همانند، یک دست

The population of the village has remained remarkably *homogeneous*.

hom.o.ge.ne.i.ty: *n.* تجانس. همگنی. یکدستی

hone /£ həʊn, $ hoʊn/ *v., n.* to sharpen; to make perfect

آماده کردن؛ تیز کردن؛ سنگ تیغ تیزکنی

The bone had been *honed* to a point.

hood.wink /ˈhʊd.wɪŋk/ *v.* to deceive, to delude

کلک زدن، گول زدن، نیرنگ زدن

He *hoodwinked* us *into* agreeing.

hor.ta.to.ry /ˈhɔːtətəri/ *adj.* encourging, exhortive

دلگرم کننده، امیدبخش

The crowd listened to his *hortatory* statements with ever growing excitement.

hor.ti.cul.tur.al /£ ˌhɔː.tɪˈkʌl.tʃʳr.ᵊl, $ ˌhɔːr.təkʌl.tʃɚ.əl/ *adj.* related to cultivation of gardens

(مربوط به) باغبانی یا باغداری

He has begun to read books dealing with *horticultural* matters.

hos.tel.ry /£ ˈhɒs.tᵊl.ri, $ ˈhɑː.stᵊl-/ *n.* inn, bar

میکده، مسافرخانه

Travelers interested in economy should stay at *hostelries* rather than fashionable hotels.

hov.el /£ ˈhɒv.ᵊl, $ ˈhɑː.vᵊl/ *n.* a small wretched house, shack
کلبه، آلونک، زاغه
The house was little more than a *hovel* and totally uninhabitable.

hov.er /£ ˈhɒv.əʳ, $ ˈhɑː.vɚ/ *v.* to hang about, to wait nearby
پلکیدن، معطل ماندن، بودن
The police helicopter *hovered* above the accident.

hub.bub /ˈhʌb.ʌb/ *n.* confused uproar
سر و صدا، همهمه، جار و جنجال
The marketplace was a scene of *hubbub* and excitement.

hu.bris /ˈhjuː.brɪs/ *n.* very great pride, arrogance
غرور بیجا، بلند پروازی احمقانه، تکبّر، خودپسندی
Filled with *hubris*, Lear refused to heed his friends' warnings.

hue /hjuː/ *n.* color
رنگ
In the Caribbean waters there are fish of every *hue*.

hu.mane /hjuːˈmeɪn/ *adj.* kind, showing sympathy
انسانی؛ محبت‌آمیز، دوستانه
His *humane* and considerate treatment of the unfortunate endeared him to all.

hum.drum /ˈhʌm.drʌm/ *adj.* dull, monotonous
یکنواخت، خسته‌کننده
After his years of adventure, he could not settle down to a *humdrum* existence.

hu.mid /ˈhjuː.mɪd/ *adj.* damp
مرطوب

He could not stand the *humid* climate and moved to a drier area.

hu.mil.i.ty /£ hjuːˈmɪl.ɪ.ti, $ -ə.t̬i/ *n.* humbleness of spirit

تواضع، فروتنی، افتادگی

He spoke with a *humility* and lack of pride which impressed his listeners.

hum.mock /ˈhʌm.ək/ *n.* small hill

تپهٔ کوچک، تل، پشته

The ascent of the *hummock* is not difficult and the view from the hilltop is ample reward for the effort.

hu.mus /ˈhjuː.məs/ *n.* dark organic part of soil

خاک برگ

In order to improve his garden, he spread *humus* over his lawn and flower beds.

hurt.le /£ ˈhɜː.tl̩, $ ˈhɜːr.t̬l̩/ *v.* to rush headlong

با سرعت رفتن؛ پرتاب شدن

The runaway train *hurtled* towards disaster.

hus.band.ry /ˈhʌz.bən.dri/ *n.* thrift, frugality; agriculture

عقل معاش؛ کشاورزی

He accumulated his small fortune by diligence and *husbandry*.

hy.brid /ˈhaɪ.brɪd/ *n., adj.* mixed breed, mongrel

حیوان دو رگه؛ گیاه پیوندی؛ دورگه

The garden strawberry is a large-fruited *hybrid*.

hy.dro.pho.bi.a /ˌhaɪ.drəʊˈfəʊ.bi.ə, $ -droʊˈfoʊ-/ *n.* fear of water; rabies

آب هراسی؛ (بیماری) هاری

A dog that bites a human being must be observed for symptoms of **hydrophobia**.

hy.per.bo.le /£ haɪˈpɜː.bᵊl.i, $ -ˈpɜːr-/ *n.* overstatement, exaggeration

اغراق، مبالغه، غلوّ

The salesman is guilty of **hyperbole** in describing his product.

hy.per.bo.re.an /ˌhaɪpəbˈriːən, -ˈbɔːriən/ *adj.* arctic, cold

(مربوط به) قطب شمال، سرد

The **hyperborean** blasts brought snow and ice to the countryside.

hy.per.crit.i.cal /£ ˌhaɪ.pəˈkrɪt.ɪ.kᵊl, $ -pɚˈkrɪt̬-/ *adj.* too eager to find mistakes

خرده‌گیر، عیب‌جو

You are **hypercritical** in your demands for perfection; we all make mistakes.

hyp.o.chon.dri.ac /£ ˌhaɪ.pəʊˈkɒn.dri.æk, $ -poʊˈkɑːn-/ *n.* person unduly worried about his health

بیماری هراس

She is a well-known **hypochondriac**, complaing of everything.

hyp.o.crit.i.cal /£ ˌhɪp.əʊˈkrɪt.ɪ.kᵊl, $ -əˈkrɪt̬-/ *adj.* deceiving

ریاکار، دورو؛ ریاکارانه، مزورانه

These accusations of corruption are **hypocritical**.

hyp.o.thet.i.cal /£ ˌhaɪ.pəʊˈθet.ɪ.kᵊl, $ -poʊˈθet̬-/ *adj.* based on assumption or hypothesis

فرضی

This is only a *hypothetical* example, but it will help us to consider the problem.

لیستی از لغاتی که در جملات بخش H به کار رفته‌اند:

accumulate: *v.*	جمع‌کردن	mêlée: *n.*	ازدحام، جنگ و دعوا
alien: *n.*	غریبه	mourning: *n.*	سوگواری، عزاداری
ascent: *n.*	صعود	offender: *n.*	متخلف
asceticism: *n.*	زهد، پارسایی	part: *n.*	نقش
berate: *v.*	پرخاش کردن	pier: *n.*	اسکله
blast: *n.*	توفان، وزش	plain: *adj.*	ساده
brand: *v.*	مارک زدن	play: *v.*	ایفا کردن، بازی کردن
burrow: *n.*	سوراخ، نقب	preside: *v.*	ریاست جلسه را به‌عهده داشتن
cavalry: *n.*	سواره نظام		
cloth: *n.*	پارچه	recall: *v.*	به یاد آوردن
coarse: *adj.*	زبر، خشن	repent: *v.*	توبه کردن
considerate: *adj.*	از روی لطف	resent: *v.*	بد آمدن، متنفر بودن
corruption: *n.*	فساد	reward: *n.*	دستمزد
creditor: *n.*	طلبکار	runaway: *adj.*	از کنترل خارج شده
crocus: *n.*	گل زعفران		
customary: *adj.*	همیشگی	sealed: *adj.*	مهر و موم شده
diligence: *n.*	جدیّت، سخت‌کوشی	secure: *v.*	تضمین کردن
		shallow: *adj.*	کم عمق
endear: *v.*	عزیز کردن	sneak: *adj.*	ناجوانمردانه
excommunication: *n.*	تکفیر	solemn: *adj.*	جدّی، رسمی
fortune: *n.*	ثروت	stake: *n.*	چوبه دار
growl: *v.*	خُرخُر کردن	symptom: *n.*	اثر، نشان
guerrilla: *n.*	چریک	tackle: *v.*	برخورد کردن
house: *v.*	نگهداری کردن	treatment: *n.*	برخورد
improper: *adj.*	نامناسب	uninhabitable: *adj.*	غیرقابل سکونت
locals: *n.*	اهالی محل		

wrinkled: *adj.* چین و چروک‌دار

wit: *n.* شوخ طبعی، بذله‌گویی

I i

ich.thy.ol.o.gy /ɪk.θɪ'ɒlə.dʒɪ/ *n.* study of fish

ماهی‌شناسی

Jacques Cousteau's programs about sea-life have advanced the cause of *ichthyology*.

i.con /£ 'aɪ.kɒn, $ -kɑ:n/ *n.* religious image, idol

تصویر، نقاشی، شمایل؛ نماد تصویری

The *icons* on the walls of the church were painted in the thirteenth century.

i.con.o.clas.tic /£ aɪˌkɒn.ə'klæs.tɪk, $ -kɑː.nə-/ *adj.* attacking cherished traditions

سنت شکنانه، نوآورانه، انقلابی

George Bernard shaw's *iconoclastic* plays often startled people.

id.e.ol.og.y /£ ˌaɪ.di'ɒl.ə.dʒi, $ -'ɑː.lə-/ *n.* ideas of a group of people

مرام، مسلک، مکتب، ایدئولوژی

That *ideology* is dangerous to this country because it embraces undemocratic philosophies.

id.i.om /'ɪd.i.əm/ *n.* special usage in language

اصطلاح؛ گویش؛ نحوه بیان

I could not understand their *idiom* because literal translation made no sense.

id.i.o.syn.cra.sy /ˌɪd.i.əˈsɪŋ.krə.si/ *n.* peculiarity, eccentricity

خصیصهٔ فردی، خصلت فردی، ویژگی فردی

One of his personal *idiosyncrasies* was his habit of rinsing all cutlery given him in a restaurant.

id.i.o.syn.crat.ic: *adj.* فردی، غیرعادی، غیر متعارف

i.dol.a.try /ˈaɪdᵊltri/ *n.* worship of idols, excessive admiration

بت‌پرستی؛ پرستش، ستایش

Such *idolatry* of singers is typical of excessive enthusiasm of youth.

id.yl.lic /ɪˈdɪl.ɪk/ *adj.* charmingly carefree, simple

آرام، آرام‌بخش، باصفا، خوش و خرّم

Far from the city, she led an *idyllic* existence in her rural retreat.

ig.ne.ous /ˈɪg.ni.əs/ *adj.* produced by fire, volcanic

(مربوط به) آتش، آتشی؛ آذرین، آتشفشانی

Lava, pumice, and other *igneous* rocks are found in great abundance around Naples.

ig.no.ble /£ ɪgˈnəʊ.bl̩, $ -ˈnoʊ/ *adj.* unworthy, of lowly origin

پست، فرومایه؛ شرم‌آور، ننگین؛ بی‌شرمانه

This plan is inspired by *ignoble* motives and I must, therefore, oppose it.

ig.no.min.i.ous /ˌɪg.nəˈmɪn.i.əs/ *adj.* disgraceful

ننگین، شرم‌آور، خفت‌بار

The country smarted under the *ignominious* defeat and

dreamed of the day when it would be victorious.

'ig.no.min.y: *n.* رسوایی، فضاحت؛ عمل ننگین، کار شرم‌آور

il.lim.it.a.ble /ˌɪl.iːmɪtᵊbl/ *adj.* infinite

لایتناهی، بی‌کران، بی‌پایان

Man, having explored the far corners of the earth, is now reaching out into ***illimitable*** space.

il.lu.sion /ɪˈluː.ʒᵊn/ *n.* misleading vision

تصور غلط، خیال باطل؛ خطای ادراک، خطای حسی

It is easy to create an optical ***illusion*** in which lines of equal length appear different.

il.lu.so.ry: *adj.* واهی، غیرواقعی؛ فریبنده

il.lu.sive: *adj.* واهی، غیرواقعی؛ فریبنده

im.be.cil.i.ty /£ ˈɪm.bə.siːlɪti, $ -sɪl-/ *n.* weakness of mind

کودنی، خنگی، خرفتی؛ عمل احمقانه، حماقت

I am amazed at the ***imbecility*** of the readers of these trashy magazines.

im.bibe /ɪmˈbaɪb/ *v.* to drink in

مشروب خوردن؛ جذب کردن، در بر گرفتن

The dry soil ***imbibed*** the rain quickly.

im.brog.lio /£ ɪmˈbrəʊ.li.əʊ, $ -ˈbroʊ.li.oʊ/ *n.* a complicated situation, perplexity

مخمصه، گرفتاری، تنگنا

He was called in to settle the ***imbroglio*** but failed to bring harmony to the situation.

im.brue /ɪmˈbruː/ *v.* to drench, to stain with blood

آلودن، آغشتن (مخصوصاً با خون)

As the investigator of the murder, he is as much ***imbrued*** in blood as the actual assassin.

im.bue /ɪmˈbjuː/ *v.* to saturate, to fill

آکندن، پر کردن

She *imbued* him *with* a feeling of self-worth.

im.mac.u.late /ɪˈmæk.jʊ.lət/ *adj.* pure, spotless

تمیز، پاکیزه؛ بی‌عیب و نقص، کامل

1) He was dressed in an *immaculate* white suit.
2) He gave an *immaculate* performance as the aging hero.

imminent /ˈɪm.ɪ.nənt/ *adj.* near at hand, impending

قریب‌الوقوع، نزدیک، در راه

The *imminent* battle will determine our success or failure in this conflict.

im.mo.bi.li.ty /£ ˌɪm.əʊˈbɪl.ə.ti, $ -oʊˈbɪl.ə.t̬i/ *n.* state of being immovable

بی‌حرکتی، عدم تحرک؛ ثبات

Modern armies cannot afford the luxury of *immobility*.

im.mo.late /ˈɪm.ə.leɪt/ *v.* to offer as a sacrifice

(کسی را) قربانی کردن، کشتن؛ (خود را) سوزاندن

The tribal king offered to *immolate* his daughter to quiet the angry gods.

im.mune /ɪˈmjuːn/ *adj.* exempt

مصون، ایمن، در امان

He was fortunately *immune from* the disease and could take care of the sick.

im.mure /£ ɪˈmjʊəʳ, $ -ˈmjʊr/ *v.* to imprison, to shut up in confinement

زندانی کردن، محبوس کردن
Before the examination, the student *immured* himself in his room and concentrated upon his studies.

im.mut.ab.le /£ ɪˈmjuː.tə.bl̩, $ -tə-/ *adj.* unchangeable

تغییرناپذیر، ثابت، ابدی
Scientists are constantly seeking to discover the *immutable* laws of nature.

im.pair /£ ɪmˈpeəʳ, $ -ˈper/ *v.* to worsen, to diminish in value

تضعیف کردن؛ آسیب رساندن، صدمه زدن
This arrest will *impair* his reputation in the community.

im.pale /ɪmˈpeɪl/ *v.* to pierce

سوراخ کردن؛ به صلابه کشیدن
He was *impaled* by the spear hurled by his adversary.

im.pal.pab.le /ɪmˈpæl.pə.bl̩/ *adj.* intangible, imperceptible

دور از ذهن، غیرقابل فهم؛ ناملموس
When I awoke, a few *impalpable* images and sensations were all I could remember of the dream.

im.par.tial /£ ɪmˈpɑː.ʃəl, $ -ˈpɑːr-/ *adj.* fair, not biased

منصفانه، بی‌طرفانه؛ بی‌طرف، منصف
It is very interesting to have an *impartial* observer's account of the dispute.

im.passe /£ æmˈpæs, $ ˈɪm.pæs/ *n.* inescapable predicament

بن‌بست، آنپاس
The dispute had *reached at* an *impasse* as neither side would compromise.

im.pas.sive /ɪmˈpæs.ɪv/ *adj.* without feeling; not affected by pain

خونسرد؛ بی‌احساس؛ بی‌رگ، بی‌غم

The American Indian has been incorrectly depicted as an *impassive* individual.

im.peach /ɪmˈpiːtʃ/ *v.* to charge with crime in office, to indict

اعلام جرم کردن، متهم کردن؛ استیضاح کردن

The angry congressman wanted to *impeach* the President.

im.pec.ca.ble /ɪmˈpek.ə.bl̩/ *adj.* faultless

بی‌عیب، کامل، بی‌نقص؛ منزه، پاک

He was proud of his *impeccable* manners.

im.pe.cun.i.ous /ˌɪm.pəˈkjuː.ni.əs/ *adj.* without money

مفلس، بی‌چیز

Now that he was wealthy, he gladly contributed to funds to assist the *impecunious* and the disabled.

im.pede /ɪmˈpiːd/ *v.* to interfere with, to delay

جلوگیری کردن، مانع شدن، سدّ راه شدن

A series of accidents *impeded* the launching of the space shuttle.

im.ped.i.ment /ɪmˈped.ɪ.mənt/ *n.* hindrance

مانع، مشکل؛ اختلال، نقص

She had a speech *impediment* that prevented her speaking clearly.

im.pend.ing /ɪmˈpen.dɪŋ/ *adj.* nearing, approaching

در راه، قریب‌الوقوع، نزدیک

The entire country was saddened by the news of his *impending* death.

im.pen.i.tent /£ ɪmˈpen.ɪ.tᵊnt, $ -tᵊnt/ *adj.* not repentant

فاقد احساس پشیمانی

We could see by his brazen attitude that he was *impenitent*.

im.pe.ri.ous /£ ɪmˈpɪə.ri.əs, $ -ˈpɪr.i-/ *adj.* arrogant or domineering

مغرور، متکبّر؛ سلطه‌جو؛ آمرانه، مستبدانه

She sent them away with an *imperious* wave of the hand.

im.per.me.ab.le /£ ɪmˈpɜː.mi.ə.bl̩, $ -ˈpɜːr-/ *adj.* not allowing liquid or gas to go through, impervious

نفوذناپذیر، ناتراوا، مقاوم

This new material is *impermeable* to liquids.

im.per.tin.ent /£ ɪmˈpɜː.tɪ.nənt, $ -ˈpɜːr.tᵊn.ᵊnt/ *adj.* rude, insolent

گستاخانه، بی‌ادبانه؛ گستاخ، پُر رو، بی‌ادب

I regard your remarks as *impertinent* and resent them.

im.per.turb.ab.il.i.ty /£ ˌɪm.pəˈtɜː.bə.bɪlɪti, $ -pɚˈtɜːr-/ *adj.* calmness

خونسردی، آرامش، خودداری

We are impressed by his *imperturbability* in this critical moment.

    im.per.turb.ab.le: *adj.*   آرام، خونسرد، خوددار

im.per.vi.ous /£ ɪmˈpɜː.vi.əs, $ -ˈpɜːr-/ *adj.* not penetrable

نفوذناپذیر، ناتراوا؛ مقاوم، سرسخت، تأثیرناپذیر

You cannot change their habits for their minds are *impervious* to reasoning.

im.pet.u.ous /ɪmˈpet.ju.əs/ *adj.* violent, hasty, rash

عجولانه، شتاب‌زده، نسنجیده

We tried to curb his *impetuous* behavior because we felt in his haste he might offend some people.

im.pe.tus /£ ˈɪm.pɪ.təs, $ -pə.t̬əs/ *n.* moving force

نیروی حرکتی، نیرو؛ انگیزه

The two automobiles that collided were traveling with great *impetus*.

im.pi.e.ty /£ ɪmˈpaɪ.ə.ti, $ -t̬i/ *n.* wickeness, lack of respect for God

ناسپاسی، حق ناشناسی؛ بی‌دینی، لامذهبی

The church accused him of *impiety* and had all his writings burned.

im.pi.ous: *adj.*   بی‌دین، لامذهب؛ ناسپاس، حق ناشناس

im.pinge /ɪmˈpɪndʒ/ *v.* to have an effect, to infringe

تأثیر گذاشتن، تأثیر سوء گذاشتن، لطمه زدن؛ تجاوز کردن (به حقوق/ حریم دیگران)

The government's spending limits will *impinge on* the education budget.

im.plac.ab.le /ɪmˈplæk.ə.bl̩/ *adj.* unable to be changed

سرسخت، سازش‌ناپذیر؛ ریشه‌دار، عمیق

She has long been the *implacable* enemy of the party.

im.plaus.ib.le /£ ɪmˈplɔː.zɪ.bl̩, $ -ˈplɑː.zə-/ *adj.* unbelievable; unlikely

باور نکردنی؛ غیرواقعی، دور از حقیقت؛ ناپذیرفتنی

Though her alibi seemed *implausible*, it in fact turned out to be true.

im.ple.ment /ˈɪm.plɪ.mənt/ *v., n.* to use, to supply what is needed; tool

به انجام رساندن، تحقق بخشیدن؛ ابزار، وسیله

The changes to the national health system will be *implemented* next year.

im.pli.ca.tion /ˌɪm.plɪˈkeɪ.ʃᵊn/ *n.* indirect suggestion

معنی ضمنی، اشاره غیرمستقیم

She accused the party, and by *implication*, accused its leader.

im.ply: *v.*   به‌طور ضمنی بیان کردن، تلویحاً گفتن؛ اشاره داشتن بر
im.plied: *adj.*   تلویحی، ضمنی

im.pli.cit /ɪmˈplɪs.ɪt/ *adj.* understood but not stated

ضمنی، تلویحی؛ بی‌چون و چرا

It is *implicit* that you will come to our aid if we are attacked.

im.pol.i.tic /£ ɪmˈpɒl.ɪ.tɪk/ *adj.* not wise

بیجا، نامعقول، نسنجیده

I think it is *impolitic* to raise this issue at the present time because the public is too angry.

im.pon.der.ab.le /£ ɪmˈpɒn.dᵊr.ə.bl̩, $ -ˈpɑːn-/ *adj.* unable to be guessed or evaluated

غیر قابل پیش‌بینی، غیرقابل محاسبه

The impact on the environment of this massive oil spillage is *imponderable*.

im.port /£ ˈɪm.pɔːt, $ -pɔːrt/ *n.* significance

معنا، مفهوم؛ اهمیت

I feel that you have not grasped the full *import* of the message sent to us by enemy.

im'port: *v.* معنی دادن، دلالت داشتن بر

im.por.tun.ate /£ ɪmˈpɔː.tjʊ.nət, $ -ˈpɔːr.tʃə.nɪt/ *adj.*
demanding, urging

مصرّ، سمج؛ مصرانه، با سماجت

He tried to hide from his ***importunate*** creditors until his allowance arrived.

im.por.tune /£ ˌɪm.pəˈtjuːn, $ ˌɪm.pɔːrˈtuːn/ *v.* to beg earnestly

سماجت کردن، اصرار کردن، تحت فشار قرار دادن

I must ***importune*** you to work for peace at this time.

im.pos.ture /£ ɪmˈpɒs.tjəʳ, $ -ˈpɑː.stjɚ/ *n.* assuming a false identity

شیّادی، ظاهرسازی

She was imprisoned for her ***imposture*** of a doctor.

im.po.tent /£ ˈɪm.pə.tᵊnt, $ -tᵊnt/ *adj.* weak, ineffective

ناتوان، عاجز، بی‌نتیجه، بی‌ثمر

He found himself ***impotent*** in resisting the craving for a cigarette.

im.pov.er.ished /£ ɪmˈpɒv.ᵊr.ɪʃt, $ -ˈpɑː.vɚ-/ *adj.* poor

ضعیف، بی‌مایه؛ فقیر، فقرزده

The loss of their farm left the family ***impoverished*** and hopeless.

im.pre.cate /ˌɪm.prəˈkeɪt/ *v.* to curse

فحش دادن، ناسزا گفتن؛ لعنت کردن، نفرین کردن

To ***imprecate*** Hitler's atrocities is not enough; we must insure against any future practice of genocide.

im.preg.na.ble /ɪmˈpreg.nə.bl̩/ *adj.* strong enough to be secure against attack

مصون، آسیب ناپذیر، تسخیرناپذیر، شکست‌ناپذیر
Until the development of the airplane, the fort was considered *impregnable*.

im.promp.tu /£ ɪmˈprɒmp.tʃuː, $ -tuː/ *adj.* without previous preparation

بدون برنامه‌ریزی (قبلی)، فی‌البداهه
His listeners were amazed that such a presentation could be made in an *impromptu* speech.

im.pro.pri.e.ty /£ ˌɪm.prəˈpraɪ.ə.ti, $ -t̬i/ *n.* state of being inappropriate

نامناسب بودن، زشتی
Because of the *impropriety* of his costume, he was denied entrance into the dining room.

im.prov.i.dent /£ ɪmˈprɒv.ɪ.dᵊnt, $ -ˈprɑː.və-/ *adj.* thriftless

بی‌حساب و کتاب، ولخرج؛ ناماٰل اندیش
He was constantly being warned to mend his *improvident* ways and begin to "save for a rainy day".

im.pro.vise /ˈɪm.prə.vaɪz/ *v.* to compose on the spur of the moment

بداهه‌گویی کردن، فی‌البداهه گفتن؛ سرهم(بندی) کردن
I hadn't prepared a speech so I suddenly had to *improvise*.

im.pru.dent /ɪmˈpruː.dᵊnt/ *adj.* lacking caution, injudicious

بی‌احتیاط، بی‌فکر؛ نسنجیده، عجولانه
The report criticizes the banks for being *imprudent* in their lending.

im.pugn /ɪmˈpjuːn/ *v.* to doubt, to challenge, to gainsay

زیر سؤال بردن، مورد تردید قرار دادن

I cannot *impugn* your honesty without evidence.

im.pun.i.ty /ˌɪm.pjuː.nɪ.ti, $ -ə.t̬i/ *n.* freedom from punishment

بخشودگی (از مجازات)، مصونیت

The ability to carry out bomb attacks with *impunity* has shocked the French people.

im.put.a.tion /ˌɪm.pjʊˈteɪ.ʃᵊn/ *n.* charge, reproach

اتهام، بهتان، افترا

You cannot ignore the *imputations* in his speech that you are the guilty party.

im.pute /ɪmˈpjuːt/ *v.* to attribute, to ascribe

نسبت دادن، اسناد کردن

In his arrogance he would always *impute* stupidity *to* those who disagreed with him.

in.ad.ver.tence /£ ˌɪn.ədˈvɜː.tᵊnts, $ -ˈvɜːr.t̬ᵊnts/ *n.* oversight, carelessness

بی‌دقتی، بی‌توجهی، بی‌مبالاتی

By *inadvertence*, he omitted two questions on the examination.

in.a.li.en.a.ble /ɪˈneɪ.li.ə.nə.bl̩/ *adj.* not to be taken away, nontransferable

لاینفک، غیرقابل انتقال، غیرقابل واگذاری

The Declaration of Independence mentions the *inalienable* rights that all of us possess.

in.ane /ɪˈneɪn/ *adj.* silly, senseless

مزخرف، بی‌معنی؛ احمقانه، ابلهانه

Such comments are *inane* because they do not help us

solve our problem.

in.an.i.ty: *n.* حماقت، کار احمقانه، کار بی‌معنی

in.an.i.mate /ɪˈnæn.ɪ.mət/ *adj.* lifeless

بی‌جان، فاقد حیات؛ بی‌روح، ملال‌آور

She was asked to identify the still and *inanimate* body.

in.ar.ti.cu.late /£ ˌɪn.ɑːˈtɪk.jʊ.lət, $ -ɑːr-/ *adj.* speechless

فاقد قدرت بیان، خاموش، لال

When it comes to expressing their emotion, most men are hopelessly *inarticulate*.

in.can.des.cent /ˌɪŋ.kænˈdes.ᵊnt/ *adj.* strikingly bright, glowing with heat

گداخته، ملتهب؛ برافروخته، برآشفته

1) If you leave on an *incandescent* light bulb, it quickly grows too hot to touch.
2) He was absolutely *incandescent* with rage.

in.can.ta.tion /ˌɪŋ.kænˈteɪ.ʃᵊn/ *n.* chanting of magic spells

سحر، جادو، ورد؛ افسون

A fire was lit and the shamans and elders chanted *incantations* over the offerings.

in.ca.pa.ci.tate /ˌɪŋ.kəˈpæs.ɪ.teɪt/ *v.* to disable, to remove the ability

از توان انداختن، ناتوان کردن، عاجز کردن

Rubber bullets are intended to *incapacitate* people rather than kill them.

in.car.cer.ate /£ ɪŋˈkɑː.sᵊr.eɪt, $ -ˈkɑːr.sə.reɪt/ *v.* to imprison

محبوس کردن، زندانی کردن

The warden will *incarcerate* the felon.

in.car.nate /£ ɪŋˈkɑː.nət, $ -ˈkɑːr-/ *adj.* in human form

به شکل انسان، مجسم

One survivor described his torturers as devils *incarnate*.

in.car.nation /£ ˌɪn.kɑːˈneɪ.ʃən, $ -kɑːr-/ *n.* act of assuming a human body.

مظهر، تجسم، عینیّت، تجسّد

1) She is the *incarnation* of everything I hate about politics.
2) The *incarnation* of Jesus Christ is a basic tenet of Christian theology.

in.cen.di.ar.y /£ ɪnˈsen.di.ər.i, $ -er.i/ *n., adj.* designed to cause fire; arsonist

(بمب) آتش‌زا؛ (آدم) حریق‌آفرین، آتش‌افروز

1) The fire department chiefs were certain that the fire had been set by an *incendiary*.
2) He was accused by placing an *incendiary* bomb in a litter bin.

in.cen.tive /£ ɪnˈsen.tɪv, $ -t̬ɪv/ *n.* motive, spur

انگیزه، محرک؛ دلگرمی، شوق

Students who dislike school must be given an *incentive* to learn.

in.ces.sant /ɪnˈses.ənt/ *adj.* never stopping, uninterrupted

بی‌وقفه، پیوسته، دائماً، مدام

Having endured weeks of *incessant* bombardment, they surrendered as soon as they had the opportunity.

in.cho.ate /£ ɪŋˈkəʊ.eɪt, $ -ˈkoʊ-/ *adj.* elementary, recently or partly formed

خام، ابتدایی، تازه شروع شده
She had a child's *inchoate* awareness of language.

in.ci.dence /ˈɪnt.sɪ.dᵊnts/ *n.* the rate at which something happens

وقوع؛ میزان بروز، شیوع
There is a higher *incidence* of left-handedness among boys than girls.

in.ci.den.tal /£ ˌɪnt.sɪˈden.tᵊl, $ -t̬ᵊl/ *adj.* not essential, minor

جزئی، فرعی، غیرضروری
There are always a lot of *incidental* expenses when you go on foreign trips.

in.cip.i.ent /ɪnˈsɪp.i.ᵊnt/ *adj.* just beginning

آغازین، در مرحلهٔ شروع
The disease is curable if it is treated at an *incipient* stage.

in.ci.sive /ɪnˈsaɪ.sɪv/ *adj.* cutting, sharp

بُرنده، گزنده؛ صریح، بی‌پرده
His *incisive* remarks made us see the fallacy in our plans.

in.cite /ɪnˈsaɪt/ *v.* to arouse, to action, to encourage

تحریک کردن، برانگیختن، موجب شدن
She was expelled for *inciting* her classmates *to* rebel against their teachers.

in.clem.ent /ɪŋˈklem.ᵊnt/ *adj.* stormy, unkind

نامساعد، توفانی
This afternoon's match has had to be cancelled due to *inclement* weather.

in.clu.sive /ɪŋˈkluː.sɪv/ *adj.* tending to include all

All our prices are *inclusive* of V(alue) A(dded) T(ax).

in.cog.ni.to /£ ˌɪŋ.kɒgˈniː.təʊ, $ -kɑːgˈniː.t̬oʊ/ *adj.*, *adv.* with identity concealed

ناشناس، با هویت جعلی؛ بهطور ناشناس

The prince often travels abroad *incognito*.

in.co.her.ence /£ ˌɪŋ.kəʊˈhɪə.rənts, $ -koʊˈhɪr.ᵊnts/ *n.* lack of relevance

عدم انسجام، گسیختگی

The recession, he said, was a direct result of the *incoherence* of the governments economic policy.

in.co.her.ent: *adj.*   فاقد انسجام؛ نامربوط، پرت و پلا

in.com.mo.di.ous /ɪn.kəˈməʊdɪəs/ *adj.* not spacious

(جا) تنگ، ناراحت

In their *incommodious* quarters, they had to improvise for closet space.

in.com.pat.i.ble /£ ˌɪŋ.kəmˈpæt.ɪ.bl̩, $ -ˈpæt̬.ə-/ *adj.* inharmonious

ناسازگار، مغایر، در تضاد(با)

The married couple argued incessantly and finally decided to separate because they were *incompatible*.

in.con.gru.i.ty /£ ˌɪŋ.kəŋˈgruː.ə.ti, $ -kənˈgruː.ə.t̬i/ *n.* lack of harmony, absurd

ناهماهنگی، ناسازگاری، عدم تناسب

The *incongruity* of his wearing sneakers with formal attire amused the observers.

in.con.gru.ous: *adj.*   ناسازگار، ناهماهنگ، خارج از تناسب

in.con.se.quen.tial /£ ɪŋˌkɒnt.sɪˈkwen.tʃ°l, $ -ˌkɑːnt-/ *adj.* not important, insignigicant

کم اهمیت، پیش پا افتاده؛ غیرمنطقی

Most of what she said was pretty ***inconsequential***.

in.con.ti.nent /£ ɪŋˈkɒn.tɪ.nənt, $ -ˈkɑːn.tə-/ *adj.* unable to control one's bladder or bowels

فاقد قدرت نگهداری شکم

Many of our elderly patients are ***incontinent***.

in.con.tro.ver.ti.ble /£ ˌɪŋˈkɒn.trəˈvɜː.tɪ.bl̩, $ -ˌkɑːn.trəˈvɜːr.t̬ə/ *adj.* indisputable

مسلّم، محقّق، غیرقابل انکار

We must yield to the ***incontrovertible*** evidence which you have presented and free your client.

in.cor.po.re.al /£ ˌɪŋ.kɔːˈpɔː.ri.əl, $ ˌɪn.kɔːrˈpɔːr.i-/ *adj.* immaterial

غیرمادی، غیرجسمانی، مجرد

We must devote time to the needs of our ***incorporeal*** mind as well as our corporeal body.

in.cor.ri.gi.ble /£ ɪŋˈkɒr.ɪ.dʒə.bl̩, $ -ˈkɔːr-/ *adj.* uncorrectable

اصلاح ناپذیر، درست نشدنی

Because he was an ***incorrigible*** criminal, he was sentenced to life imprisonment.

in.cre.du.li.ty /ˌɪn.krɪˈdjuː.lɪ.ti/ *n.* a tendency to disbelief

ناباوری، شک

He felt a sense of ***incredulity***, anger and pain at the accusation made against him.

in.cred.u.lous: *adj.*

حاکی از ناباوری؛ شکاک

in.cre.ment /ˈɪn.krɪ.mənt/ *n.* increase, raise

افزایش، رشد؛ اضافهٔ حقوق

You will receive annual salary *increments* every September.

in.crim.i.nate /ɪnˈkrɪm.ɪ.neɪt/ *v.* to accuse, to make someone seem guilty

(به جرمی) متهم کردن، مقصّر دانستن؛ پای(کسی را) به میان کشیدن

A secret report *incriminating* the company was leaked last week.

in.cu.bate /ˈɪn.kjʊ.beɪt/ *v.* to hatch, to scheme, to plan

جوجه در آوردن؛ روی تخم خوابیدن؛ در سر پروردن

1) The female bird *incubates* the eggs for about 16 days while the male brings food.

2) She's always *incubating* new sales promotions.

in.cu.bus /ˈɪŋkjʊ.bəs/ *n.* nightmare

کابوس، بختک

The *incubus* of financial worry helped bring on his nervous breakdown.

in.cul.cate /ˌɪŋ.kʌlˈkeɪt/ *v.* to teach

آموختن، القا کردن، ملکهٔ ذهن کردن

Our football coach has worked hard to *inculcate* a team spirit *in/ into* the players.

in.cum.bent /ɪŋˈkʌm.bənt/ *n.* officeholder

مقام مسئول، صاحب مقام، دارندهٔ پست اداری

The present *incumbent* of the position is due to retire next month.

in.cur /£ ɪŋˈkɜːʳ, $ -ˈkɜːr/ *v.* to bring upon oneself

به بار آوردن، موجب شدن، ایجاد کردن

His parents refused to pay any future debts he might *incur*.

in.cur.sion /£ ɪŋˈkɜː.ʒᵊn, $ -ˈkɜːr-/ *n.* temporary invasion

یورش، حمله، هجوم

Terrorist forces made several *incursions* into occupied areas during the fighting.

in.de.fat.i.ga.ble /£ ˌɪn.dɪˈfæt.ɪ.gə.bl̩, $ -ˈfæt̬-/ *adj.* tireless

خستگی ناپذیر، نستوه

He was *indefatigable* in his constant efforts to raise funds for the Red Cross.

in.dem.ni.fy /ɪnˈdem.nɪ.faɪ/ *v.* to make secure against loss

غرامت پرداختن، خسارت دادن، تاوان دادن

The city will *indemnify* all home owners whose property is spoiled by this project.

in.den.ture /£ ɪnˈden.tʃəʳ, $ -tʃɚ/ *v.* to bind as servant or apprentice to master

به شاگردی کسی در آوردن

He was *indentured* to a coach-builder.

in.dict /ɪnˈdaɪt/ *v.* to charge with a crime

متهم کردن، به محاکمه کشیدن

If the grand jury *indicts* the suspect, he will go to trial.

in.di.gen.ous /ɪnˈdɪdʒ.ɪ.nəs/ *adj.* native to a particular region

بومی

Tobacco is one of the *indigenous* plants which the early explorers found in this country.

in.di.gent /ˈɪn.dɪ.dʒᵊnt/ *adj.* very poor

تهیدست، مسکین، فقیر
Because he was *indigent*, he was sent to the welfare office.

in.dig.ni.ty /£ ɪnˈdɪg.nɪ.ti, $ -nə.ţi/ *n.* a loss of respect, offensive treatment

بی‌احترامی، بی‌حرمتی، توهین، تحقیر
They were subjected to various *indignities* and discomforts throughout the voyage.

in.dig.nant: *adj.* عصبانی، برآشفته

in.dis.pu.ta.ble /£ ˌɪn.dɪˈspjuː.tə.bḷ, $ -ţə-/ *adj.* too certain to be disputed

غیرقابل بحث، بی‌چون و چرا
In the face of these *indisputable* statements, I withdraw my complaint.

in.dis.sol.u.ble /£ ˌɪn.dɪˈsɒl.jʊ.bḷ, $ -ˈsɑːl.jə-/ *adj.* permanant, impossible to take apart

ثابت، پایدار، همیشگی؛ تجزیه‌ناپذیر
The links between the two nations are *indissoluble*.

in.dite /ɪnˈdaɪt/ *v.* to write, to compose

نوشتن، تألیف کردن
Fitz Gerald *indited* many letters.

in.dol.ence /ˈɪn.dᵊl.ᵊnts/ *n.* laziness

سستی، تنبلی، بی‌حالی
After a sudden burst of activity the team lapsed back into *indolence*.

in.dol.ent: *adj.* تنبل، سست، بی‌حال

in.dom.i.ta.ble /£ ɪnˈdɒm.ɪ.tə.bḷ $ -ˈdɑː.mə.ţə-/ *adj.*

unconquerable

شکست‌ناپذیر، تزلزل‌ناپذیر؛ راسخ
The founders of our country had *indomitable* willpower.

in.du.bi.ta.bly /£ ɪnˈdjuː.bɪ.tə.bli, $ -ˈduː.bɪ.t̬ə-/ *adv.* beyond a doubt

مسلماً، یقیناً، بی‌تردید، به‌طور قطع
Because his argument was *indubitably* valid, the judge accepted it.

in.duc.tive /ɪnˈdʌk.tɪv/ *adj.* proceeding from the specific to the general

استقرایی؛ القایی
The discovery of the planet Pluto is an excellent example of *inductive* reasoning.

in.dul.gent /ɪnˈdʌl.dʒənt/ *adj.* humouring, yielding

اهل تسامح، آسان‌گیر، بیش از اندازه نرم
He had been a strict father but was *indulgent to/ towards* his grandchildren.

in.e.bri.e.ty /ˌɪnɪːˈbraɪətɪ/ *n.* habitual intoxication

دائم‌الخمری، مستی، میخوارگی
Because of his *inebriety*, he was discharged from his position.

in.ef.fa.ble /ɪˈnef.ə.bl̩/ *adj.* cannot be expressed in speech, unutterable

وصف‌ناپذیر، غیر قابل بیان
Such *ineffable* joy must be experienced; it cannot be described.

in.ef.fec.tu.al /ˌɪn.ɪˈfek.tju.ᵊl/ *adj.* not effective

بی‌نتیجه، بی‌حاصل، بی‌ثمر

Because the candidate failed to get across his message to the public, his campaign was *ineffectual*.

in.e.luc.ta.ble /ɪn.ɪˈlʌktəbᵊl/ *adj.* irresistable, not to be escaped

گریزناپذیر، محتوم، حتمی

He felt that his fate was *ineluctable* and refused to make any attempts to improve his lot.

in.ept /ɪˈnept/ *adj.* unsuited, absurd

نابجا، نامناسب؛ نالایق، بی‌عرضه

The constant turmoil in the office proved that he was an *inept* administrator.

in.ep.ti.tude: *n.*

نابجایی؛ بی‌عرضگی، بی‌لیاقتی

in.e.quit.y /£ ɪˈnek.wɪ.ti, $ -ṭi/ *n.* unfairness

بی‌انصافی، بی‌عدالتی

Women protested the basic *inequity* of a system that gives greater financial rewards to men.

in.er.tia /£ ɪˈnɜː.ʃə, $ -ˈnɜːr-/ *n.* lack of activity or interest

رخوت، بی‌علاقگی، سستی، کاهلی

Our *inertia* in this matter may prove disastrous; we must move to aid our allies immediately.

in.ex.or.a.ble /£ ɪˈnek.sᵊr.ə.bl̩, $ -sɚ-/ *adj.* relentless, unyielding

مصمم، سرسخت

After listening to the pleas for clemency, the judge was *inexorable* and gave the convicted man the maximum punishment.

in.fal.li.ble /ɪnˈfæl.ɪ.bl̩/ *adj.* unerring

بری از اشتباه، بدون خطا

We must remember that none of us is *infallibe*.

in.fa.mous /ˈɪn.fə.məs/ *adj.* notoriously bad

شرم‌آور، ننگین؛ انگشت‌نما، بدنام، رسوا

The list included the *infamous* George Drake, a double murderer.

in.fan.tile /£ ˈɪn.fən.taɪl, $ -tᵊl/ *adj.* childish, extremely immature

کودکانه، بچه‌گانه

When will he outgrow such *infantile* behavior?

in.fer /£ ɪnˈfɜːʳ, $ -ˈfɜːr/ *v.* to conclude, to deduce

استنباط کردن، پی بردن، دریافتن

What do you *infer* from his refusal?

in.fer.ence: *n.*   استنباط، استنتاج، دریافت
in.fer.en.ti.al: *adj.*   استنباطی، استنتاجی

in.fer.nal /£ ɪnˈfɜː.nəl, $ -ˈfɜːr-/ *adj.* related to hell, devilish, very bad

جهنمی، دوزخی؛ شیطانی؛ لعنتی

1) He described a journey through the *infernal* world.
2) We've been having *infernal* weather.

in.fi.del /£ ˈɪn.fɪ.dᵊl, £ -del, $ -fə.del/ *n.* unbeliever

بی‌دین، کافر، لامذهب

He lived among *infidels*.

in.fin.it.es.i.mal /ˌɪn.fɪ.nɪˈtes.ɪ.məl/ *adj.* very small

اندک، ناچیز، بسیار کم

The amounts of radioactivity were *infinitesimal* and

seemed to present no danger.

in.fir.mi.ty /£ ɪnˈfɜː.mə.ti, $ -ˈfɜːr.mə.t̬i/ *n.* weakness

نقطه ضعف؛ ضعف، عیب، نقص

His greatest *infirmity* was lack of willpower.

in.flat.ed /ɪnˈfleɪtəd/ *adj.* enlarged with air or gas

متورم، ورم کرده، پرباد، بادکرده

After the balloons were *inflated*, they were distributed among the children.

in.flux /ˈɪn.flʌks/ *n.* flowing into

سرازیر شدن، هجوم، سیل

The *influx* of refugees into the country has taxed the relief agencies severely.

in.frac.tion /ɪnˈfræk.ʃən/ *n.* violation

(قانون و مقررات) تخلف، تخطی، نقض

Because of his many *infractions* of school regulations, he was suspended by the dean.

in.fringe /ɪnˈfrɪndʒ/ *v.* to violate, to encroach

(قانون) نقض کردن، زیر پا گذاشتن، تخطی کردن

The prisoners complained that their rights were being *infringed*.

in.ge.nue /£ ˈæn.ʒeɪ.nuː, $ ˈæn.ʒə-/ *n.* an artless girl

(فیلم یا نمایش) دختر ساده، دختر معصوم

She plays a charming *ingenue* who arrived in Paris hoping to be a dancer.

in.ge.nu.ous: *adj.*

صاف و ساده، بی‌ریا

in.grate /ˈɪn.ɡreɪt/ *n.* ungrateful person

(آدم) ناسپاس، نمک‌نشناس، حق نشناس

After all I've done for you, **ingrate**!

in.gra.ti.ate /ɪŋˈgreɪt.ʃiː.eɪt/ *v.* to try to make oneself liked

خود شیرینی کردن پیشِ، خود را سبک کردن پیشِ

He tried to *ingratiate himself* into her parent's good graces.

in.her.ent /£ ɪnˈher.ənt, £ -ˈhɪə.rənt, $ -ˈhɪr.ənt/ *adj.* firmly established by nature or habit

ذاتی، فطری

There are dangers *inherent* in almost every sport.

in.hib.it /ɪnˈhɪb.ɪt/ *v.* to prohibit, to restrain

جلوگیری کردن، باز داشتن، مانع شدن

Some officers were *inhibited* from speaking by the presence of more senior officers.

in.hi.bi.tion: *n.*

منع، بازداری

in.i.mi.cal /ɪˈnɪm.ɪ.kəl/ *adj.* unfriendly, hostile

مخالف، دشمن؛ مُخل، مضرّ

She felt that they were *inimical* and were hoping for her downfall.

in.im.i.ta.ble /£ ɪˈnɪm.ɪ.tə.bl̩, $ -t̬ə-/ *adj.* matchless, not able to be imitated

بی‌همتا، بی‌نظیر، تقلیدناپذیر

We admire Hafiz for his *inimitable* use of language; he is one of a kind.

in.iq.ui.tous /£ ɪˈnɪk.wɪ.təs, $ -t̬əs/ *adj.* unjust, wicked

رذل؛ ظالمانه، بی‌رحمانه

I cannot approve of the *iniquitous* methods you used to gain your present position.

ink.ling /ˈɪŋ.klɪŋ/ *n.* hint

اشاره؛ تصور مبهم

I didn't have the slightest *inkling* that she was unhappy.

in.nate /ɪˈneɪt/ *adj.* inborn

ذاتی، فطری، سرشتی

His *innate* talent for music was soon recognized by his parents.

in.noc.u.ous /£ ɪˈnɒk.ju.əs, $ -ˈnɑː.kju-/ *adj.* harmless

بی‌ضرر، بی‌خطر؛ خالی از غرض، غیر مغرضانه

Let him drink it; it is *innocuous*.

in.no.va.tion /ˌɪn.əʊˈveɪ.ʃən/ *n.* change, introduction of something new

تغییر، پیشرفت؛ نوع‌آوری؛ ابداع

He loved *innovations* just because they were new.

in.nu.en.do /£ ˌɪn.juˈen.dəʊ, $ -doʊ/ *n.* hint, insinuation

کنایه، اشاره، زخم زبان

The newspaper *innuendos* about his private life eventually made him resign.

in.op.por.tune /£ ɪˈnɒp.ə.tjuːn, $ ɪˈnɑː.pɚ.tuːn/ *adj.* untimely; poorly chosen

بدموقع، بی‌موقع؛ نامناسب

I made a rather *inopportune* remark about divorce.

in.or.di.nate /£ɪˈnɔː.dɪ.nət, $ ˌɪnˈɔːr-/ *adj.* excessive, unrestrained

بیش از اندازه، مفرط، زیاده از حد

She had an *inordinate* fondness for candy.

in.sa.tia.ble /ɪnˈseɪ.ʃə.bl̩/ *adj.* not easily satisfied, greedy

His thirst for knowledge was *insatiable*; he was always in the library.

ارضا نشدنی؛ سیری‌ناپذیر

in.scrut.a.ble /£ ɪnˈskruː.tɪ.bl̩, $ -tə-/ *adj.* incomprehensible

His motives were *inscrutable*.

اسرارآمیز، مرموز، غیرقابل درک، سر در نیافتنی

in.sen.sate /ɪnˈsen.seɪt/ *adj.* without feeling

He lay there as *insensate* as a log.

بی‌احساس، بی‌عاطفه؛ بی‌روح، بی‌جان

in.sid.i.ous /ɪnˈsɪd.i.əs/ *adj.* treacherous, stealthy, sly

The fifth column is *insidious* because it works secretly within our territory for our defeat.

موذی، مکار، حیله‌گر؛ موذیانه، مکارانه

in.sin.u.ate /ɪnˈsɪn.ju.eɪt/ *v.* to hint, to imply

What are you trying to *insinuate* by that remark?

تلویحاً گفتن، به کنایه گفتن

in.sip.id /ɪnˈsɪp.ɪd/ *adj.* tasteless, dull

I am bored by your *insipid* talk.

بی‌مزه؛ بی‌روح، کسل‌کننده

in.sol.ent /ˈɪnt.sᵊl.ənt/ *adj.* contemptuously rude

I resent your *insolent* manner.

بی‌شرمانه، گستاخانه؛ وقیح، بی‌حیا

in.sol.ven.cy /£ ɪnˈsɒl.vᵊnt.si, $ -ˈsɑːl-/ *n.* bankruptcy

The company could not sell its products and was driven into *insolvency*.

ورشکستگی

in.som.ni.a /£ ɪnˈsɒm.ni.ə, $ -ˈsɑːm-/ *n.* inability to sleep

She went to the doctor's because she was *suffering from insomnia*.

بی‌خوابی

in.sou.ci.ant /ɪnˈsuː.si.ənt/ *adj.* indifferent, without concern or care

بی‌خیال، بی‌قید، راحت

Your *insouciant* attitude indicates that you do not understand the gravity of the situation.

in.sti.gate /ˈɪn.stɪ.geɪt/ *v.* to start, to provoke

باعث شدن، راه انداختن، موجب شدن

I am afraid that this statement will *instigate* a revolt.

in.su.lar /£ ˈɪn.sjʊ.ləʳ, $ -lɚ/ *adj.* like an island; narrow-minded

جزیره مانند؛ تنگ‌نظرانه، کوته‌فکرانه

Theirs is a very *insular* culture, protected as it is from outside influence.

in.su.per.a.ble /£ ɪnˈsjuː.pᵊr.ə.bl̩, $ -ˈsuː.pɚ-/ *adj.* insurmountable, invincible

سخت، برطرف شدنی، حل نشدنی؛ غیرقابل عبور

The hospitals now face *insuperable* difficulties with too few staff and too little money.

in.sur.gent /£ ɪnˈsɜː.dʒᵊnt, $ -ˈsɜːr-/ *adj., n.* rebellious

شورشی؛ (آدم) سرکش

We will not discuss reforms until the *insurgent* troops have returned to their homes.

in.te.grate /£ˈɪn.tɪ.greɪt, $ -tə-/ *v.* to combine, to make whole

تلفیق کردن، یکی کردن، یکپارچه کردن

He tried to *integrate* all their activities into one program.

in.te.gri.ty: *n.* یکپارچگی، انسجام؛ صداقت، درستی

in.tel.lect /£ ˈɪn.tᵊl.ekt, $ -tə-/ *n.* higher mental powers

نیروی عقلانی، خرد، عقل

He thought college would develop his *intellect*.

in.tel.li.gent.si.a /ɪnˌtel.ɪˈdʒent.si.ə/ *n.* the intelligent and educated classes

روشنفکران

He preferred discussions about sports and politics to the literary conversation of the *intelligentsia*.

in.ter /£ ɪnˈtɜːʳ, $ -ˈtɜːr/ *v.* to bury

دفن کردن، به خاک سپردن

They are going to *inter* the body tomorrow.

in.ter.ment: *n.* خاک‌سپاری، تدفین

in.ter.dict /ɪn.təˈdɪkt/ *v.* to prohibit, to forbid

قدغن کردن، ممنوع کردن؛ باز داشتن، ممانعت کردن

Civilized nations must *interdict* the use of nuclear weapons if we expect our society to live.

ˈin.ter.dict: *n.* ممنوعیت، حکم نهی

in.ter.dic.tion: *n.* حکمِ نهی، ممنوعیت؛ (حقوقی) حَجْر

in.ter.im /£ ˈɪn.tᵊr.ɪm, $ -tɚ-/ *n., adj.* meantime

ضمن، اثنا، حین؛ موقتی

An *interim* government was set up in Afghanistan.

in the interim در ضمن، تا آنموقع

in.ter.lo.cu.tor.y /£ ˌɪn.təˈlɒk.jʊ.tᵊr.ɪ, $ -tɚˈlɑː.kjə.tɚɪ/ *adj.* conversational; not final

شفاهی؛ موقت، مقدماتی

This ***interlocutory*** decree is only a temporary setback; the case has not been settled.

in.ter.min.a.ble /£ ɪnˈtɜː.mɪ.nə.bl̩, $ -ˈtɜːr-/ *adj.* endless

طولانی، خسته‌کننده، بی‌پایان

Although his speech lasted for only 20 minutes, it seemed ***interminable*** to his bored audience.

in.ter.mit.tent /£ ˌɪn.təˈmɪt.ᵊnt, $ -t̬ɚˈmɪt̬-/ *adj.* periodic, on and off

ادواری، متناوب

Our picnic was marred by ***intermittent*** rains.

in.ter.ne.cine /ˌɪn.təˈniː.saɪn/ *adj.* mutually destructive

(جنگ، نزاع و غیره) خانمان‌برانداز برای هر دو طرف؛ خونین

The island had been torn by ***internecine*** *strife/ conflict.*

in.ter.stice /£ ɪnˈtɜː.stɪs, $ -ˈtɜːr-/ *n.* chinks, crevices

درز، شکاف

The mountain climber sought to obtain a foothold in the ***interstices*** of the cliff.

in.ti.mate /£ ˈɪn.tɪ.meɪt, $ -t̬ə-/ *v.* to hint, to suggest

فهماندن، با اشاره حالی کردن، تلویحاً گفتن

She ***intimated*** rather than stated her preferences.

    in.ti.ma.cy: *n.*   صمیمیت، نزدیکی

    in.ti.mate: *adj.*   صمیمی، نزدیک

in.ti.mi.da.tion /ɪnˌtɪm.ɪˈdeɪ.ʃᵊn/ *n.* fear, threat

ارعاب، تهدید

The campaign of violence and ***intimidation*** *against* them intensifies daily.

in.trac.ta.ble /£ ɪnˈtræk.tə.bl̩, $ -t̬ə-/ *adj.* unruly, very difficult

سرکش، نافرمان؛ بغرنج، دشوار، سخت

The horse was *intractable* and refused to enter the starting gate.

in.tran.si.gence /ɪnˈtræn.zɪ.dʒ°nts, £ -ˈtrɑːn-/ *n.* refusing to compromise

سازش‌ناپذیری، سرسختی، انعطاف‌ناپذیری

The collapse of the talks is being blamed on the union's *intransigence*.

in.tran.si.gent: *adj.*   سازش ناپذیر، سرسخت

in.trep.id /ɪnˈtrep.ɪd/ *adj.* fearless

نترس، جسور

For his *intrepid* conduct in battle, he was promoted.

in.trin.sic /ɪnˈtrɪn.zɪk/ *adj.* essential, inherent

ذاتی؛ درونی، داخلی

Although the *intrinsic* value of this award is small, I shall always cherish it.

in.tro.vert /£ ˈɪn.trə.vɜːt, $ -vɜːrt/ *n.* shy or reserved person

درون‌گرا؛ تودار، خوددار

He has been an *introvert* since his wife's death.

in.trude /ɪnˈtruːd/ *v.* to enter as an uninvited person, to trespass

سرزده وارد شدن؛ (خود را) به زور وارد کردن، (خود را) تحمیل کردن

He hesitated to *intrude on* their conversation

in.tru.sion: *n.*   تجاوز؛ مزاحمت

in.tu.i.tion /£ ˌɪn.tjuːˈɪʃ.°n, $ -tuː-/ *n.* quick and ready insight

شمّ، بصیرت؛ الهام

She claimed to know the truth *by intuition*.

in.tu.i.tive: *adj.* شمّی؛ حدسی: باطنی، درونی

in.un.date /'ɪn.ʌn.deɪt/ *v.* to overflow, to flood

زیر آب بردن، غرق کردن

The tremendous waves *inundate* the town.

in.ure /£ ɪn'jʊə, $ -'jʊr/ *v.* to accustom, to harden

عادت کردن، خو گرفتن به

You'll just have to *inure yourself to* the criticism.

in.val.i.date /ɪn'væl.ɪ.deɪt/ *v.* to destroy, to weaken

از اعتبار انداختن، باطل کردن

Last year, the decision was *invalidated* by a federal appeal court.

in.vec.tive /£ ɪn'vek.tɪv, $ -tɪv/ *n.* abuse, curse

دشنام، ناسزا، فحش؛ توهین، اهانت، فحاشی

He had expected criticism but not the *invective* which greeted his proposal.

in.veigh /ɪn'veɪ/ *v.* to denounce, to utter invective

به باد انتقاد گرفتن، حمله کردن؛ دشنام دادن، ناسزا گفتن

There were politicians who *inveighed against* immigrants to get votes.

in.vei.gle /ɪn'veɪ.gl̩, -'viː-/ *v.* to lead astray, to wheedle

اغوا کردن؛ وسوسه کردن

He was *inveigled into* joining the club.

in.verse /£ ɪn'vɜːs, $ -'vɜːrs/ *adj.* opposite

معکوس، وارونه

There is an *inverse* ratio between the strength of light and its distance.

in.vet.er.ate /£ ɪn'vet.ᵊr.ət, $ -'veṭ.ɚ/ *adj.* deep-rooted, habitual

ریشه‌دار؛ کهنه کار، قدیمی، قهّار
Every member of the family is an *inveterate* talker.

in.vid.i.ous /ɪnˈvɪd.ɪ.əs/ *adj.* unfair, harmful

مغرضانه، غرض‌آلود، تبعیض‌آمیز
We disregarded her *invidious* remarks because we realized how jealous she was.

in.vin.ci.ble /ɪnˈvɪn.sɪ.bl̩/ *adj.* unconquerable, impossible to defeat

شکست‌ناپذیر؛ سرسخت، مصرّ
When you're young, you think you are *invincible*.

in.vi.o.la.bil.i.ty /£ ɪnˌvaɪə.ləˈbɪl.ɪ.ti, $ -ə.t̬i/ *n.* safety of violation or desecration

مصونیت از تعرض، تخطی ناپذیری، حرمت، تقدّس
They respected the *inviolability* of her faith and did not try to change her manner of living.

in.voke /£ ɪnˈvəʊk, $ -ˈvoʊk/ *v.* to ask for, to call upon

کمک خواستن، طلب یاری کردن؛ متوسل شدن به
She *invoked* her advisor's aid in filling out her financial aid forms.

in.vul.ne.ra.ble /£ ɪnˈvʌl.nᵊr.ə.bl̩, $ -nɚ-/ *adj.* incapable of injury

آسیب‌ناپذیر، مصون؛ خدشه‌ناپذیر
Achilles was *invulnerable* except in his heel.

i.o.ta /£ aɪˈəʊ.tə, $ -ˈoʊ.t̬ə/ *n.* very small quantity

ذره، سر سوزن، یک جو
He hadn't an *iota* of common sense

i.ras.ci.ble /ɪˈræs.ə.bl̩/ *adj.* easily angered, irritable

His ***irascible*** temper frightened me.

i.rate /aɪˈreɪt/ *adj.* angry

تندخو، عصبی

غضب‌آلود، غضبناک

She was so ***irate*** that she could scarcely speak to him.

i.ri.des.cent /ˌɪr.ɪˈdes.ᵊnt/ *adj.* showing many bright colors

رنگین‌کمانی، قوس و قزح‌سان

He admired the ***iridescent*** hues of the oil that floated on the surface of the water.

irk.some /£ ˈɜːk.səm, $ ˈɜːrk-/ *adj.* tedious, boring

آزاردهنده، آزارنده؛ خسته‌کننده، کسالت‌آور

The vibration can become ***irksome*** after awhile.

i.ron.i.cal /£ aɪəˈrɒn.ɪ.kᵊl, $ aɪˈrɑː.nɪ.kᵊl/ *adj.* resulting in an unexpected and contrary manner

طعنه‌آمیز، طنزآمیز؛ شگفت‌آور

It is ***ironical*** that his success came when he least wanted it.

i.rony: *n.*

طنز، طعنه؛ رویداد شگفت

ir.rec.on.cil.a.ble /ˌɪr.ek.ᵊnˈsaɪ.lə.bl̩/ *adj.* impossible to deal with

سازش‌ناپذیر؛ ناسازگار

The talks have become ***irreconcilable*** with both sides refusing to compromise any further.

ir.rel.e.vant /ɪˈrel.ɪ.vᵊnt/ *adj.* unrelated, not applicable

نامربوط، بی‌ارتباط

This statement is ***irrelevant*** and should be disregarded by the jury.

ir.re.med.i.a.ble /ˌɪrɪˈmiː.di.ə.bl̩/ *adj.* incurable, uncorrectable

جبران‌ناپذیر، جبران نشدنی

The error he made was *irremediable*.

ir.rep.a.ra.ble /ɪˈrep.rə.bl̩/ *adj.* impossible to repair

ترمیم ناپذیر، اصلاح‌ناپذیر، جبران‌ناپذیر

Your apology cannot atone for the *irreparable* damage you have done to his reputation.

ir.rev.er.ent /£ ɪˈrev.ᵊr.ᵊnt, $ ˈ-ɚ-/ *adj.* lacking proper respect

حاکی از بی‌حرمتی، گستاخانه

The worshippers resented his *irreverent* remarks about their faith.

ir.rev.o.ca.ble /ɪˈrev.ə.kə.bl̩/ *adj.* unalterable

قطعی، نهایی؛ لغو نشدنی، برگشت‌ناپذیر، غیر قابل فسخ

Let us not brood over past mistakes since they are *irrevocable*.

i.so.tope /£ ˈaɪ.sə.təʊp, $ -toʊp/ *n.* varying form of an element

ایزوتوپ

The study of the *isotopes* of uranium led to the development of the nuclear bomb.

it.er.ate /ˈɪtə.reɪt/ *v.* to repeat, to utter a second time

تکرار کردن

I will *iterate* the warning I have previously given to you.

i.tin.er.ant /£ àɪˈtɪn.ᵊr.ᵊnt, $ ˈ-ɚ-/ *adj.* wandering, traveling

سیّار

He was an *itinerant* peddler and traveled throughout the country.

i.tin.er.ar.y /£ aɪˈtɪn.ᵊr.ᵊr.i, $ -ə.rer/ plan of a trip
برنامهٔ مسافرت
Several tour companies have changed their announced *itineraries*.

لیستی از لغاتی که در جملات بخش I به کار رفته‌اند:

agency: *n.*	شرکت		قاتل دو نفر
alibi: *n.*	ادله و شواهد	felon: *n.*	جانی
allowance: *n.*	مستمری	grasp: *v.*	متوجه شدن، دریافتن
appeal: *n.*	استیناف	(of a) kind: *adj.*	بی‌نظیر
assassin: *n.*	آدمکش	lapse back: *v.*	پس رفتن
attire: *n.*	جامه	leak: *v.*	درز کردن
award: *n.*	لوح تقدیر، جایزه	leave on: *v.*	روشن گذاشتن
bladder: *n.*	مثانه	log: *n.*	چوب خشک
bowels: *n.*	روده	mar: *v.*	ضایع کردن
breakdown: *n.*	اختلال، قطع	offering: *n.*	نذری، هدیه
bring on: *v.*	سبب شدن	plea: *n.*	درخواست
brood: *v.*	غصه خوردن	predicament: *n.*	گرفتاری
cherished: *adj.*	عزیز و به یاد ماندنی	pumice: *n.*	سنگ پا
		rage: *n.*	خشم
chirp: *v.*	جیرجیر کردن	rainy day: *n.*	روز مبادا
clemency: *n.*	عفو	relief: *adj.*	پشتیبانی
coach-builder: *n.*	مربی‌پرور	retreat: *n.*	خلوتگاه
convicted: *adj.*	محکوم	rinse: *v.*	آب کشیدن
craving: *n.*	میل و هوس	rural: *adj.*	روستایی
cricket: *n.*	جیرجیرک	setback: *n.*	بدبیاری، شکست
curb: *v.*	کنترل کردن	severely: *adv.*	شدیداً
cutlery: *n.*	قاشق و چنگال	smart: *v.*	زجر کشیدن
dean: *n.*	مدیر مدرسه	sneakers: *n.*	کفش ورزشی
decree: *n.*	حکم	spillage: *n.*	نشت، ریزش
(the) disabled: *n.*	معلولین	still: *adj.*	بی‌حرکت، راکد
double murderer: *n.*		(be) subjected to: *v.*	

tenet: *n.*	اعتقاد
warden: *n.*	رییس زندان
welfare: *n.*	رفاه
willpower: *n.*	اراده

suspend: *v.*	در معرضِ ... قرار گرفتن، موقتاً اخراج کردن، معلق شدن
talker: *n.*	حرّاف، وراج
tax: *v.*	به‌ستوه آوردن

J j

jad.ed /ˈdʒeɪ.dɪd/ *adj.* fatigued, surfeited

سیر، زده، دلزده، خسته

He looked for exotic foods to stimulate his *jaded* appetite.

jar.gon /£ ˈdʒɑː.gən, $ ˈdʒɑːr-/ *n.* language used by special group

لوتر (= زبان خاص یک گروه)

We tried to understand the *jargon* of the peddlers in the market-place.

jaun.diced /£ ˈdʒɔːn.dɪst, $ ˈdʒɑːn-/ *adj.* yellowed, prejudiced

یرقانی، مبتلا به یرقان؛ مغرضانه، بدبینانه، غرض‌آلود

Sadly, the child developed a *jaundiced view* of personal relationships.

jaunt /£ dʒɔːnt, $ dʒɑːnt/ *n.* trip, short journey

گردش، سفر

He took a quick *jaunt* to Atlantic city.

jaun.ty /£ ˈdʒɔːn.ti, $ ˈdʒɑːn.t̬i/ *adj.* stylish, perky, carefree

شیک، تر و تمیز؛ شنگول، سرحال، شاد

She wore her beret at a *jaunty* angle.

je.june /dʒɪˈdʒuːn/ *adj.* lacking interest, barren

خسته‌کننده، یکنواخت، ملال‌آور

The plot of the play is *jejune* and fails to capture the interest of the audience.

jeo.par.dy /£ ˈdʒep.ə.di, $ -ɚ-/ *n.* exposure to death or danger

خطر، مخاطره

The lives of thousands of birds are *in jeopardy* as a result of oil spillage.

jeo.par.dize: *v.*   به خطر انداختن

jet.ti.son /£ ˈdʒet.ɪ.sᵊn, $ ˈdʒet̬-/ *v.* to throw away or get rid of something or someone

دور انداختن؛ کنار گذاشتن، دست برداشتن از

The company has been forced to *jettison* 200 employees because of financial problems.

jin.go.i.sm /£ ˈdʒɪŋ.gəʊ.ɪ.zᵊm, $ -goʊ-/ *n.* extremely aggressive patriotism

وطن‌پرستی افراطی

Patriotism can turn into *jingoism* and intolerance very quickly.

jo.cose /£ dʒəˈkəʊs, $ dʒoʊˈkoʊs/ *adj.* giving to joking, playful

شوخی‌آمیز، خنده‌دار

His *jocose* manner was unsuitable for such a solemn occasion.

joc.u.lar /£ ˈdʒɒk.jʊ.lərʳ, $ ˈdʒɑː.kjə.lɚ/ *adj.* said or done in jest

شوخی‌آمیز، خنده‌دار؛ شوخ، شوخ طبع

Do not take my *jocular* remarks seriously.

joc.und /ˈdʒɒ.kənd/ *adj.* merry

شاد، خوش، سرخوش

In such a *jocund* company, I gazed - and gazed but little thought.

ju.bil.a.tion /ˌdʒuː.bɪˈleɪ.ʃən/ *n.* rejoicing

شعف، شادمانی؛ جشن و سرور

There was *jubilation* in the crowd as the winning goal was scored.

ju.bilant: *adj.* سرمست، شادمان

ju.di.cious /dʒuːˈdɪʃ.əs/ *adj.* wise, having sound judgment

عاقلانه، حساب شده؛ با شعور، عاقل

We should try and make *judicious* use of the resources available to us.

jug.ger.naut /£ ˈdʒʌg.ə.nɔːt, $ -ɚ.nɑːt/ *n.* powerful force

نیروی مخرب، مصیبت، بلای خانمان سوز

Nothing could survive in the path of the *juggernaut*.

junc.ture /£ ˈdʒʌŋk.tʃəʳ, $ -tʃɚ/ *n.* crisis, joining point

وضع، موقعیت؛ اتصال، پیوند

At this critical *juncture*, let us think carefully before determining the course we shall follow.

junk.et /ˈdʒʌŋ.kɪt/ *n.* a merry feast or picnic

مسافرت تفریحی (با هزینهٔ دولت)

David's *gone* off *on* another one of those *junkets* to Paris this weekend.

jun.ta /ˈdʒʌn.tə, ˈhʊn-/ *n.* group of men joined in political intrigue

حکومت نظامیان، گروه توطئه

The military *junta* has / have today broadcast an appeal for calm.

ju.ris.pru.dence /£ ˌdʒʊə.rɪˈspruː.dənts, $ ˌdʒʊr.ɪ-/ *n.* science of law

علم حقوق؛ رویّهٔ قضایی؛ فقاهت

He was more a student of *jurisprudence* than a practitioner of the law.

ju.ris.pru.dent: *n.* فقیه

jux.ta.pose /£ ˌdʒʌk.stəˈpəʊz, $ -ˈpoʊz/ *v.* to place side by side

برابر هم گذاشتن، کنار هم قرار دادن، مقایسه کردن

Comparison will be easier if you *juxtapose* the two objects.

jux.ta.po.si.tion: *n.* هم‌کناری، تقابل

لیستی از لغاتی که در جملات بخش J به کار رفته‌اند:

appeal: *n.*	تقاضا	jettison: *v.*	کنار گذاشتن
beret: *n.*	کلاه بره	peddler: *n.*	دوره‌گرد
company: *n.*	همنشینی	solemn: *adj.*	جدی، رسمی
exotic food: *n.*		spillage: *n.*	نشت، ریزش

غذایی که آدم تا بحال نخورده باشد

K k

ka.lei.do.scope /£ kəˈlaɪ.də.skəʊp, $ -skoʊp/ *n.* a tube-like device you look through to see different patterns of light

شهر فرنگ، زیبابین

The street bazzar was a *kaleidoscope* of colours, smells and sounds.

ken /ken/ *n.* range of knowledge

فهم، دانش

I cannot answer your question since this matter is *beyond my ken*.

kin.dred /ˈkɪn.drəd/ *n., adj.* related, similar in nature or character

وابسته؛ مشابه، نزدیک؛ قرابت؛ هم فکر

Tom Sawyer and Huck Finn were two *kindred* spirits.

ki.net.ic /£ kɪˈnet.ɪk, $ -ˈneṭ-/ *adj.* producing motion

جنبشی

The source of the *kinetic* energy needed to propel the vehicle.

ki.osk /£ ˈkiː.ɒsk, $ -ɑːsk/ *n.* summerhouse, open pavilion

اطاقک، دکه، باجه، کیوسک

She waited at the subway *kiosk*.

kis.met /ˈkɪs.met, ˈkɪz-/ *n.* fate

قسمت، سرنوشت، تقدیر

Kismet is the Arabic word for "fate".

kith /kɪθ/ *n.* familiar friends

دوستان

He always helped both his *kith* and *kin*.

klep.to.ma.ni.ac /£ ˌklep.təʊˈmeɪ.ni.æk, $ -toʊ-/ *n.* a person who has a compulsive desire to steal

شخص مبتلا به جنون دزدی

They discovered that the wealthy customer was a *kleptomaniac*.

knav.er.y /ˈneɪvᵊri/ *n.* rascality

بدجنسی، شیطنت؛ نادرستی

We cannot condone such *knavery* in public officials.

knave: *adj.*

بدجنس، نادرست

knead /niːd/ *v.* to mix, to work dough

خمیر کردن؛ ورز دادن؛ ماساژ دادن

Her hands grew strong from *kneading* bread.

knell /nel/ *n.* tolling of a bell at a funeral

(صدای) ناقوس مرگ، نشان پایان چیزی

The curfew tolls the *knell* of parting day.

knoll /£ nəʊl, $ noʊl/ *n.* little round hill

پشته، تپهٔ کوچک، کپه

A grassy *knoll* was visible through the trees.

لیستی از لغاتی که در جملات بخش K به کار رفته‌اند:

condone: *v.*	چشم‌پوشی کردن	knell: *n.*	ناقوس
curfew: *n.*	منع عبور و مرور	parting: *adj.*	جدایی
kin: *n.*	آشنایان	propel: *v.*	پیش راندن

L l

lab.y.rinth /ˈlæb.ɪ.rɪnθ/ *n.* maze

مارپیچ، ماز، هزار تو

Tom and Betty were lost in the ***labyrinth*** of secret caves.

lab.y.rin.thine: *adj.* مازی شکل؛ مارپیچی

lac.er.ate /£ ˈlæs.ᵊr.eɪt, $ -ə.reɪt/ *v.* to mangle, to tear

مجروح کردن، دریدن؛ آزردن، جریحه‌دار کردن

Her body was ***lacerated*** in the automobile crash.

lach.ry.mose /£ ˈlæk.rɪ.məʊs, $ -moʊs/ *adj.* producing tears

گریان، دارای چشم‌های گریان؛ پر سوز و گداز

His voice has a ***lachrymose*** quality which is more appropriate at a funeral than a class reunion.

lack.a.dai.si.cal /ˌlæk.əˈdeɪ.zɪ.kᵊl/ *adj.* lacking spirit, lazy

بی‌علاقه، بی‌ذوق و شوق؛ تنبل، وارفته

He was ***lackadaisical*** and indifferent about his part in the affair.

lack.ey /ˈlæk.i/ *n.* footman or servant

نوکر، غلام حلقه به گوش

He treats us all like his ***lackeys***.

lack.lus.tre /£ ˈlæk.lʌs.təʳ, $ -tɚ/ *adj.* dull

خسته‌کننده، بی‌روح، ملال‌آور

We were disappointed by the *lacklustre* performance.

la.con.ic /£ ləˈkɒn.ɪk, $ -ˈkɑː.nɪk/ *adj.* brief and to the point

موجز، مختصر و مفید؛ گزیده‌گو، کم‌گو

Will Roger's *laconic* comments on the news made him world famous.

lag.gard /£ ˈlæg.əd, $ -ɚd/ *adj., n.* slow, sluggish

کند، تنبل، کم تحرک؛ آدم تنبل، وامانده

The sailor had been taught not to be *laggard* in carrying out orders.

lag: *v.* عقب ماندن، عقب افتادن

la.gniappe /læ.njʌp/ *n.* trifling present given to a customer

هدیه و یا انعام ناچیز از طرف فروشنده

The butcher threw in some bones for the dog as a *lagniappe*.

la.goon /ləˈguːn/ *n.* shallow body of water near a sea

مرداب، تالاب

They enjoyed their swim in the calm *lagoon*.

la.i.ty /£ ˈleɪ.ə.ti, $ -t̬i/ *n.* laymen

افراد غیر روحانی؛ افراد غیر حرفه‌ای

The *laity* are all the people who are involved with a church but are not priests.

lam.bent /ˈlæm.bənt/ *adj.* flickering, softly radiant

درخشان؛ آرام، ملایم

They sat quietly before the *lambent* glow of the fireplace.

lam.i.nat.ed /£ ˈlæm.ɪ.neɪ.tɪd, $ -t̬ɪd/ *adj.* consisting of thin layers of plastic

ورقه ورقه؛ چند لایه؛ سلفون‌دار

The recipe cards are **laminated** so they can be wiped clean.

lam.poon /læm'pu:n/ *v., n.* to ridicule, to criticize in an amuzing way

هجو کردن؛ هجو

The relationship was mercilessly **lampooned** in all the papers.

lan.guid /'læŋ.gwɪd/ *adj.* weary, lacking energy, listless

بی‌حال، سست، بی‌دل و دماغ، وارفته

Her siege of illness left her **languid** and pallid.

lan.guish /'læŋ.gwɪʃ/ *v.* to lose strength, to lose animation

ضعیف شدن، تحلیل رفتن؛ غم خوردن، حسرت (چیزی را) خوردن

He has been **languishing** in jail *for* the past twenty years.

lan.guor /£ 'læŋ.gəʳ, $ -gɚ/ *n.* lassitude, depression

ضعف، سستی، رخوت، دل مردگی، بی‌حوصلگی

His friends tried to overcome the **languor** into which he had fallen by taking him to parties.

lank /læŋk/ *adj.* long and thin

لاغر، استخوانی

Gaunt, **lank**, Abraham Lincoln was a striking figure.

lap.i.dar.y /'læpɪdərɪ/ *n.* worker in precious stones

جواهرساز، گوهرتراش

He employed a **lapidary** to cut the large diamond.

lar.cen.y /£ 'lɑː.sᵊn.i, $ 'lɑːr-/ *n.* theft

(حقوقی) سرقت

Because of the prisoner's record, the district attorney

refused to reduce the charge from grand *larceny* to petit *larceny*.

lar.gess /£ lɑːˈʒes, $ lɑːr-/ *n.* generous gift

بذل و بخشش، گشاده‌دستی، صدقه

Lady Bountiful distributed *largess* to the poor.

las.ci.vi.ous /ləˈsɪv.i.əs/ *adj.* lustful

شهوت‌انگیز، شهوانی

The *lascivious* books were confiscated and destroyed.

las.si.tude /£ ˈlæs.ɪ.tjuːd, $ -tuːd/ *n.* weariness, languor

بی‌حالی، کسالت، بی‌حوصلگی؛ خستگی، سستی

The hot, tropical weather created a feeling of *lassitude* and encouraged drowsiness.

la.tent /ˈleɪ.tᵊnt/ *adj.* hidden, dormant

نهفته، پنهان، نهان

His *latent* talent was discovered by accident.

lat.er.al /£ ˈlæt.rᵊl, $ ˈlæt̬.ɚ.ᵊl/ *adj.* coming from the side

جانبی، کناری

In order to get good plant growth, the gardener must pinch off all *lateral* shoots.

lat.i.tude /£ ˈlæt.ɪ.tjuːd, $ ˈlæt̬.ɪ.tuːd/ *n.* freedom to behave

آزادی (عمل)

I think you have permitted your son too much *latitude* in this matter.

laud.a.ble /£ ˈlɔː.də.bl̩, $ ˈlɑː-/ *adj.* praiseworthy, commendable

درخور تحسین، قابل تمجید، قابل ستایش

His *laudable* deeds will be remembered by all whom he aided.

laud.a.tory /£ ˈlɔː.də.tri, $ ˈlɑː-/ *adj.* expressing praise

تحسین‌آمیز، تحسین برانگیز

The critic's *laudatory* comments helped to make her a star.

lave /læv/ *v.* to wash

شستن

The running water will *lave* away all stains.

lav.ish /ˈlæv.ɪʃ/ *adj.* liberal, wasteful

گشاده‌دست، ولخرج؛ بی‌بند و بار؛ بیش از حد، فراوان، زیاد

The actor's *lavish* gifts pleased her.

lech.er.ous /£ ˈletʃ.ᵊr.əs, $ -ɚ-/ *adj.* impure in thought and act, lustful

هرزه، شهوت‌ران، شهوت‌پرست

In the film he plays a *lecherous* soldier.

lech.er.y: *n.*

هرزگی، شهوت‌رانی، شهوت‌پرستی

lec.tern /£ ˈlek.tən, $ -tɜːrn/ *n.* reading desk

تریبون، میز خطابه

The speaker arranged her papers on the *lectern*.

lee.way /ˈliː.weɪ/ *n.* room to move, feedom

آزادی عمل

We need some *leeway* if we are to act effectively.

leg.a.cy /ˈleg.ə.si/ *n.* a gift made by a will; anything handed down from the past

ارث، میراث؛ یادگار

Part of my *legacy* from my parents is an album of family photographs.

leg.end /ˈledʒ.ᵊnd/ *n.* explanation

شرح؛ نوشتهٔ روی سکه، مدال، نقشه و غیره

The *legend* at the bottom of the map made it clear which symbols stood for public camp sites.

leg.er.de.main /ledʒ.əʳdə'meɪn/ *n.* sleight of hand

تردستی، شعبده‌بازی؛ حقه‌بازی، فریب‌کاری

The magician demonstrated his renowned *legerdemain*.

len.i.enc.y /'liː.ni.ənt.si/ *n.*

نرمش، ملایمت؛ ارفاق، تساهل، آسان‌گیری

The defending lawyer asked for *leniency* on the grounds of her client's youth.

len.i.ent: *adj.* ملایم، با مدارا، باگذشت؛ آسان‌گیر

le.o.nine /'liː.ə.naɪn/ *n.* like a lion

شیر مانند

He was *leonine* in his rage.

le.sion /'liːʒºn/ *n.* an injury to a person's body

زخم؛ ضایعه، آسیب

There were photographs showing *lesions to* backs and thighs.

le.thal /'liː.θºl/ *adj.* deadly, dangerous

مهلک، کشنده؛ خطرناک

It is unwise to leave *lethal* weapons where children may find them.

leth.ar.gic /£ lə'θɑː.dʒɪk, $ -'θɑːr/ *adj.* drowsy, dull

کسالت‌آور؛ خواب آلوده، بی‌حال، خموده، کسل

The stuffy room made him *lethargic*.

lev.i.ty /£ 'lev.ɪ.ti, $ -ți/ *n.* lightness

سبک‌سری، جلفی

Such **levity** is improper on this serious occasion.

lewd /luːd/ *adj.* lustful, dirty

هرزه، مستهجن، زشت؛ شهوت‌انگیز، شهوانی

They found his **lewd** stories objectionable.

lex.i.con /ˈlek.sɪ.kən/ dictionary

فرهنگ لغت؛ واژگان

I cannot find this word in any **lexicon** in the library.

lex.i.co.lo.gy: *n.*   واژه‌شناسی، واژگان‌شناسی
lex.i.cogra.phy: *n.*   فرهنگ‌نویسی
lex.i.co.gra.ph.er: *n.*   فرهنگ‌نویس

li.ais.on /£ liˈeɪ.zɒn, $ -ɑːn/ *n.* officer who acts as go-between for two armies

رابط، ارتباط

As the **liaison**, he had to avoid offending the leaders of the two armies.

li.ba.tion /laɪˈbeɪ.ʃən/ *n.* drink

شراب، مشروب، می

He offered a **libation** to the thirsty prisoner.

li.bel.ous /ˈlaɪ.bəl.əs/ *adj.* defamatory, injurious to the good name of a person

افتراآمیز؛ بدنهن، فحاش

He sued the newspaper because of its **libelous** story.

lib.er.tine /£ ˈlɪb.ə.tiːn, $ -ɚ-/ *n.* debauched person, roué

مرد لاابالی، زن باره

Although she was aware of his reputation as a **libertine**, she felt she could reform him.

li.bid.in.ous /lɪˈbɪd.ɪ.nəs/ *adj.* lustful

شهوانی، شهوی

They objected to his *libidinous* behavior.

li.bid.o /£ lɪˈbiː.dəʊ, $ -doʊ/ *n.* a person's sexual energy

شهوت، سائق جنسی

The pills claimed to be able to increase one's *libido*.

li.bret.to /£ lɪˈbret.əʊ, $ -ˈbret̬.oʊ/ *n.* text of an opera

اُپرانامه

The composer is remembered more frequently than the author of its *libretto*.

li.cen.tious /laɪˈsen.tʃəs/ *adj.* wanton, lewd

بی‌بند و بار، هرزه، شهوت‌ران

The *licentious* monarch helped bring about his country's downfall.

lieu /lju:, lu:/ *n.* instead of

به جایِ

They accepted his check *in lieu of* cash.

lil.li.pu.tain /ˌlɪl.ɪˈpjuː.ʃᵊn/ *adj.* extremely small

کوچک، ریز، مینیاتوری

The model was built on a *lilliputain* scale.

lim.ber /£ ˈlɪm.bəʳ, $ -bɚ/ *adj.* flexible

نرم، انعطاف پذیر

Hours of ballet classes kept him *limber*.

lim.ber: *v.*   نرمش کردن، (خود را) گرم کردن

lim.bo /£ ˈlɪm.bəʊ, $ -boʊ/ *n.* uncertainty

برزخ؛ بوته فراموشی؛ دو دلی

Until we've got official permission to go ahead with the plans we're in *limbo*.

lim.pid /ˈlɪm.pɪd/ *adj.* clear, transparent

شفاف، صاف

A *limpid* stream ran through his property.

lin.e.a.ments /ˈlɪn.ɪ.ə.mənts/ *n.* features of the face

(چهره) خطوط، مشخصات

She quickly sketched the *lineaments* of his face.

li.on.ize /ˈlaɪ.ə.naɪz/ *v.* to treat as a celebrity

تکریم کردن، عزّت گذاشتن

She enjoyed being *lionized* and adored by the public.

liq.uid.ate /ˈlɪk.wɪ.deɪt/ *v.* to clear up, to settle accounts

تسویه کردن؛ پرداختن؛ نقد کردن

She was able to *liquidate* all his debts in a short period of time.

list.less /ˈlɪst.ləs/ *adj.* lacking in spirit or energy

بی‌حال، بی دل و دماغ، بی‌حوصله

We had expected him to be full of enthusiasm and were surprised by his *listless* attitude.

lit.a.ny /ˈlɪt.ᵊn.i/ *n.* supplicatory prayer

دعا

A *litany* is a long Christian prayer in which some parts are spoken by the priest and other parts are spoken by the worshippers.

lithe /laɪð/ *adj.* flexible, supple

دارای بدن نرم؛ نرم، انعطاف‌پذیر

He had the *lithe*, athletic body of a ballet dancer.

lit.i.ga.tion /£ ˌlɪt.ɪˈgeɪ.ʃᵊn, $ ˌlɪt̬-/ *n.* lawsuit

دعوا، پرونده؛ دادخواهی، اقامه دعوا

Try to settle this amicably; I do not want to start *litigation*.

lit.i.gate: *v.* اقامهٔ دعوا کردن، دادخواهی کردن

li.to.tes /laɪˈtəʊ.tiːz/ *n.* understatement for emphasis

کاربرد جمله یا معنی منفی برای تأکید معنای مخالف آن

To say, "He little realizes", when we mean that he does not realize at all, is an example of *litotes*.

liv.id /ˈlɪv.ɪd/ *adj.* lead-colored, black and blue; enraged

کبود، رنگ پریده؛ خشمگین، عصبانی

His face was so *livid* with rage that we were afraid he might have an attack of apoplexy.

loath /£ ləʊθ, £ ləʊð, $ loʊθ/ *adj.* averse, reluctant

بی‌میل، بیزار، مخالف

They were both *loath* for him to go.

loathe /£ ləʊð, $ loʊð/ *v.* to detest, to abhor

متنفر بودن، بیزار بودن

From an early age the brothers have *loathed* each other.

lode /£ ləʊd, $ loʊd/ *n.* metal-bearing vein

رگه (معدن فلز)

If this *lode* which we have discovered extends for any distance, we have found a fortune.

lofty /£ ˈlɒf.ti, $ ˈlɑːf.ti/ *adj.* very highly

رفیع، بلند، والا؛ متکبرانه، مغرورانه

They used to tease him about his *lofty* ambitions.

loit.er /£ ˈlɔɪ.tɚ, $ -t̬ɚ/ *v.* to hang around, to linger

پرسه زدن، پلکیدن، ول گشتن

The policeman told him not to *loiter* in the alley.

loll /£ lɒl, $ lɑːl/ *v.* to lounge about

لمیدن، لم دادن، ولو شدن

They **lolled** around in their chairs watching television.

lon.ge.vi.ty /£ lɒn'dʒev.ə.ti, £ ˌlɒŋ'ev-, $ lɑːn'dʒev.ə.t̬i/ *n.* long life

عمر طولانی

The old man was proud of his **longevity**.

lope /£ ləʊp, $ loʊp/ *v., n.* to gallop slowly

شلنگ تخته انداختن؛ خرامیدن؛ شلنگ تخته اندازی، خرامش

The lion **loped** across the grass.

lo.qua.cious /£ ləʊ'kweɪ.ʃəs, $ loʊ'kweɪ-/ *adj.* talkative

پرحرف، پرچانه، وراج

She is very **loquacious** and can speak on the telephone for hours.

lo.qua.ci.ty: *n.*
پرحرفی، پرچانگی

lout /laʊt/ *n.* a young man who behaves in a rude and offensive way

لات، اوباش

The delivery boy is an awkward **lout**.

lu.bric.i.ty /luːˈbrɪs.ɪ.tɪ/ *n.* slipperiness, evasiveness

جواب سر بالا؛ طفره‌روی

He exasperated the reporters by his **lubricity**.

lu.cent /ˈluːs.ənt/ *adj.* shining

درخشان، روشن

The moon's **lucent** rays silvered the river.

lucid /ˈluːsɪd/ *adj.* bright, easily understood

روشن، واضح، قابل فهم

His explanation was **lucid** and to the point.

lu.cra.tive /£ ˈluː.krə.tɪv, $ -t̬ɪv/ *adj.* profitable

سودآور

He turned his hobby into a *lucrative* profession.

lu.cre /£ ˈluː.kəʳ, $ -kɚ/ *n.* money

پول

Preferring *lucre* to fame, he wrote stories of popular appeal.

lu.di.crous /ˈluː.dɪ.krəs/ *adj.* laughable, trifling

مضحک

Let us be serious, this is not a *ludicrous* issue.

lu.gu.bri.ous /luːˈguː.bri.əs/ *adj.* mournful

ماتم‌زده، اندوهگین؛ غم‌انگیز

He always has such a *lugubrious* look on his face.

lu.min.ous /ˈluː.mɪ.nəs/ *adj.* shining, issuing light

نورانی، درخشان؛ شب‌نما

You should always wear *luminous* clothing when riding a bicycle at night.

lu.nar /£ ˈluː.nəʳ, $ -nɚ/ *adj.* relating to the moon

قمری، (مربوط به) ماه

A *lunar* month is the period of time (about 29.5 days) which the moon takes to go round the Earth.

lu.rid /£ ˈljʊə.rɪd, $ ˈlʊr.ɪd/ *adj.* shocking, sensational; colorful

تکان‌دهنده، هولناک؛ رنگ وارنگ، اجق وجق

1) The newspapers contained *lurid* accounts of the bombing.

2) Their living-room is decorated with *lurid* purple wallpaper.

lus.cious /ˈlʌʃ.əs/ *adj.* pleasing to taste or smell

لذیذ، خوش‌مزه؛ آبدار، رسیده

The ripe peach was *luscious*.

lus.ter /£ ˈlʌs.təʳ, $ -tɚ/ *n.* shine, gloss

درخشش، برق، جلا

Restore the lost *luster* to your car with new "Carshine".

lu.strous /ˈlʌs.trəs/: *adj.* shining

برّاق، درخشان؛ شاداب، سرزنده

The TV advert says this conditioner will give you *lustrous* hair.

lux.u.ri.ant /£ lʌgˈʒʊə.ri.ənt, $ -ˈʒʊr.i-/ *adj.* abundant; fertile; ornate

پُر، پرپشت، فراوان؛ بارور، غنی؛ مجلل، لوکس

1) This stretch of land was once covered with *luxuriant* forest, but is now bare.
2) Her *luxuriant* hair fell around her shoulders.

lux.u.ri.ance: *n.* پُری، پرپشتی؛ انبوهی، سرسبزی

لیستی از لغاتی که در جملات بخش L به کار رفته‌اند:

advert: *n.*	آگهی	hastily: *adv.*	با عجله
alley: *n.*	کوچه	improvise: *v.*	دست و پا کردن
apoplexy: *n.*	سکته مغزی	pallid: *adj.*	رنگ پریده
attorney: *n.*	وکیل مدافع	pinch off: *v.*	هَرَس کردن
conditioner: *n.*	حالت دهنده	rage: *n.*	عصبانیت
confiscate: *v.*	توقیف کردن	roué: *n.*	فاسق، فاجر، زن‌باز
exasperate: *v.*	کفر کسی را بالا آوردن	siege: *n.*	دوران کسل کننده
		striking: *adj.*	جالب
figure: *n.*	شخصیت	stuffy: *adj.*	دم کرده، خفه
gaunt: *adj.*	لاغر	tease: *v.*	سر به سر کسی گذاشتن

M m

ma.ca.bre /məˈkɑː.brə/ *adj.* causing shock, disgust and fear; gruesome

هولناک، وحشتناک، تکان‌دهنده

Even the police were horrified at the *macabre* nature of the killings.

mac.er.ate /ˈmæs.ə.reɪt/ *v.* to soften by putting and leaving in liquid

خیساندن؛ خیس خوردن

Paper will *macerate* if it is left in water.

Mach.i.a.vel.li.an /ˌmæk.jəˈvel.i.ən/ *adj.* crafty, double - dealing

ماکیاولی‌وار؛ حقه‌باز، حیله‌گر، ترفندباز

He is not accustomed to the *Machiavellian* maneuverings of foreign diplomats.

mach.in.a.tion /ˌmæʃ.ɪˈneɪ.ʃən, ˌmæk-/ *n.* scheme, secret plans

توطئه، دسیسه؛ توطئه چینی

Who knows what *machinations* lay behind this deal?

mad.ri.gal /ˈmæd.rɪ.gəl/ *n.* pastoral song

آوازگروهی؛ ترانه، شعر عاشقانه

His program of folk songs included several *madrigal* which he sang to the accompaniment of a lute.

mael.strom /£ ˈmeɪl.strɒm, $ -strɑːm/ *n.* whirlpool, tumult

گرداب؛ مهلکه

1) The canoe was tossed about in the *maelstrom*.
2) The country is gradually being sucked into the *maelstrom* of civil war.

mag.na.nim.ous /mægˈnæn.ɪ.məs/ *adj.* very generous and honorable

بخشنده، سخاوتمند، گشاده‌دست

Arsenal's manager was *magnanimous* in victory, and praised the losing team.

magnate /ˈmæg.nət/ *n.* a very rich and successful person in business

شخص موفق و ثروتمند، آدم مهم

He was once a well-known shipping *magnate*.

mag.ni.lo.quent /mægˈnɪləkwənt/ *adj.* boastful, pompous

(کلام) پر طمطراق، مطنطن، مغلّق

The reporters ridiculed the *magniloquent* speeches of the defense attorney.

mag.ni.tude /£ ˈmæg.nɪ.tjuːd, $ -tuːd/ *n.* greatness, extent

عظمت، بزرگی؛ اهمیت

They don't seem to grasp the *magnitude* of the problem.

maim /meɪm/ *v.* to mutilate, to injure

علیل کردن، معلول کردن، نقص عضو کردن

The hospital could not take care of all who had been wounded or *maimed* in the railroad accident.

mal.a.droit /ˌmæl.əˈdrɔɪt/ *adj.* clumsy, bungling

ناشیانه؛ خراب‌کاری

In his usual *maladroit* way, he managed to upset the cart and spill the food.

mal.aise /mælˈeɪz/ *n.* uneasiness, distress

ناراحتی، دل‌مردگی؛ کسالت

They spoke of the feeling of moral and spiritual *malaise*; the lack of will to do anything.

mal.con.tent /ˈmæl.kən.ˌtent/ *n.* person dissatisfied with existing state of the affairs

ناراضی (سیاسی)

He was one of the few *malcontents* in congress; he usually voiced his objections to the Presidential program.

mal.e.dic.tion /ˌmæl.ɪˈdɪk.ʃᵊn/ *n.* curse

نفرین، لعن؛ بدگویی

The witch uttered *maledictions* against her captors.

mal.e.fac.tor /£ ˈmæl.ɪ.fæk.tər, $ -t̬ɚ/ *n.* criminal

جنایتکار، تبهکار، مجرم

We must try to bring these *malefactors* to justice.

mal.ev.o.lent /məˈlev°l.ənt/ *adj.* wishing evil

بدخواه، مغرض، شریر؛ مغرضانه، موذیانه

We must thwart his *malevolent* schemes.

mal.i.cious /məˈlɪʃ.əs/ *adj.* bearing ill-will

مغرضانه، بدخواهانه؛ بدخواه، خبیث، مغرض

The *malicious* neighbor spread the gossip.

ma.lign /məˈlaɪn/ *v., adj.* to speak evil of, to defame

بدگویی کردن از، تهمت زدن به؛ بدخواهانه، مغرض، بد سرشت

Because of her hatred of the family, she *maligns* all who are friendly to them.

ma.lig.nant /məˈlɪg.nənt/ *adj.* having an evil influence

شرور، خبیث؛ بدخیم

This is a *malignant* disease; we may use drastic measures to stop its spread.

ma.lin.ger.er /£ məˈlɪŋ.gᵊr.əʳ, $-gɚ.ɚ / *n.* one who feigns illness to escape duty

تمارض‌کننده، بیمارنما

The captain ordered the sergeant to punish all *malingerers*.

mall /£ mɔːl, $ mɑːl/ *n.* public walk

مرکز خرید پیاده

There are plans to build a new *mall* in the middle of town.

mal.le.a.ble /ˈmæl.i.ə.bl̩/ *adj.* easily changed into a new shape

چکش‌خوار، نرم؛ انعطاف‌پذیر

Gold is a *malleable* metal.

mam.mal /ˈmæm.ᵊl/ *n.* any animal in which the female gives birth to babies

پستاندار

Humans, dogs, elephants are all *mammals*, but birds and crocodiles are not.

mam.moth /ˈmæm.əθ/ *adj.* gigantic, extremely large

غول‌پیکر، عظیم، بزرگ

Cleaning up the city-wide mess is going to be a *mammoth* task.

man.date /'mæn.deɪt/ *n.* order, charge

حکم، فرمان؛ اختیار، تفویض اختیار

At the forthcoming elections, the government will be seeking a fresh *mandate* from the people.

man.da.to.ry /£ 'mæn.də.tri, $ -tɔːr.i/ *adj.* which must be done, obligatory

اجباری، ضروری، الزام‌آور

Athletes must undergo a *mandatory* drugs test before competing in the championship.

man.gy /'meɪn.dʒi/ *adj.* shabby, wretched

ژولیده، کثیف، زشت؛ فرسوده؛ نخ‌نما

We finally threw out the *mangy* rug that the dog had destroyed.

ma.ni.a.cal /mə'naɪə.kᵊl/ *adj.* raving mad

مانیایی؛ دیوانه‌وار، جنون‌آمیز

His *maniacal* laughter frightened us.

man.i.fest /'mæn.ɪ.fest/ *adj.* clear, understandable

آشکار، روشن، هویدا

His evil intentions were *manifest* and yet we could not stop him.

man.i.fest.o /£ ˌmæn.ɪ'fes.təʊ, $ -toʊ/ *n.* declaration, statement of policy

بیانیه، مانیفست

This statement may be regarded as the *manifesto* of the party's policy.

man.i.fold /£ 'mæn.ɪ.fəʊld, $ -foʊld/ *adj.* numerous, varied

بسیار، متعدد؛ متنوع؛ چندجانبه

I cannot begin to tell you how much I appreciate your *manifold* kindnesses.

ma.ni.pu.late /mə'nɪp.jʊ.leɪt/ *v.* to operate with the hands

ماهرانه به کار بردن، با مهارت کنترل کردن

How do you *manipulate* these puppets?

man.u.mit /ˌmæn.jʊ.mɪt/ *v.* to emancipate, to free from bondage

آزاد کردن، رهایی بخشیدن

Enlightened slave owners were willing to *manumit* their slaves and thus put an end to the evil of slavery.

ma.raud.er /£ mə'rɔː.dəʳ, $ -'rɑː.dɚ/ *n.* raider, intruder

سارق؛ مهاجم؛ مزاحم؛ چپاولگر

The sounding of the alarm frightened the *marauders*.

ma.raud: *v.* غارت کردن، دستبرد زدن

mari.tal /£ 'mær.ɪ.tᵊl, $ -tᵊl/ *adj.* connected with marriage

(مربوط به) زناشویی

The program discussed the main causes of *marital* breakdown.

ma.ri.time /'mær.ɪ.taɪm/ *adj.* nautical

دریایی؛ (مربوط به) کشتیرانی؛ ساحلی

The *maritime* provinces depend on the sea for their wealth.

mar.red /£ mɑːʳd, $ mɑːrd/ *adj.* damaged, disfigured

خراب، صدمه دیده، آسیب دیده

She had to refinish the *marred* surface of the table.

mar: *v.* خراب کردن، ضایع کردن

mar.row /£ 'mær.əʊ, $ -oʊ/ *n.* soft tissue filling the bones

مغزِ استخوان، مغزِ قلم

The frigid cold chilled the traveler to the *marrow*.

mar.su.pi.al /£ mɑː'suː.pi.əl, $ mɑːr-/ *n.* a family of mammals that nurse their offspring in a pouch

(حیوان) کیسه‌دار

The most common *marsupial* in Australia are koalas, wombats and kangaroos.

mar.tial /£ 'mɑː.ʃᵊl, $ 'mɑːr-/ *adj.* warlike

جنگی، نظامی، رزمی

The sound of *martial* music is always inspiring.

mar.ti.net /£ ˌmɑː.tɪ'net, $ ˌmɑːr.t̬ɪ-/ *n.* strict disciplinarian

آدم مقرراتی، آدم سخت‌گیر یا خشک

The commanding officer was a *martinet* who observed each regulation to the letter.

mas.ti.cate /'mæs.tɪ.keɪt/ *v.* to chew

جویدن

We must *masticate* our food carefully and slowly in order to avoid stomach disorders.

ma.ter.nal /£ mə'tɜː.nᵊl, $ -'tɜːr-/ *adj.* motherly

مادری؛ مادرانه

Many animals display *maternal* instincts only while their offspring are young and helpless.

ma.tri.arch /£ 'meɪ.tri.ɑːk, $ -ɑːrk/ *n.* a female leader; a powerful woman in a family

سالارزن

The *matriarch* ruled her gypsy tribe with a firm hand.

ma.tri.cide /'mæt.rɪ.saɪd/ *n.* a crime in which a person kills his/her mother

مادرکُشی

A crime such as *matricide* is inconceivable.

ma.trix /'meɪ.trɪks/ *n.* mold; development

قالب، چارچوب؛ شبکه؛ ماتریس

Europe is remaking itself politically within the *matrix* of the European Community.

maud.lin /£ 'mɔːd.lɪn, $ 'mɑːd-/ *adj.* effusively sentimental

احساساتی (افراطی)

I do not like such *maudlin* pictures. I call them tear-jerkers.

maul /£ mɔːl, $ mɑːl/ *v.* to handle roughly; to attack

با خشونت رفتار کردن؛ به باد انتقاد گرفتن؛ زخمی کردن، دریدن

1) The rock star was *mauled* by his overexcited fans.
2) The family's pet dog *mauled* their three-year-old son.

maun.der /'mɔːn.dər/ *v.* to talk incoherently

پرت و پلا گفتن، شرو ور گفتن، وِر زدن

You do not make sense; you *maunder* and garble your words.

mau.so.le.um /£ ˌmɔː.zəˈliː.əm, $ ˌmɑː-/ *n.* monumental tomb

آرامگاه، مرقد

His body was placed in the family *mausoleum*.

mauve /£ məʊv, $ moʊv/ *adj.* pale purple

ارغوانی روشن (رنگ)

The *mauve* tint in the lilac bush was another indication that spring had finally arrived.

mav.er.ick /£ 'mæv.ər.ɪk, $ '-ɚ-/ *n.* independent and unortho-

mawk.ish 313 **me.di.ate**

dox

(آدم) تکرو، خودمدار، یاغی

She is widely regarded as a political ***maverick***.

mawk.ish /£ ˈmɔː.kɪʃ, $ ˈmɑː-/ *adj.* sickening, insipid

احساساتی، پر سوز و گداز، سوزناک

Your ***mawkish*** sighs fill me with disgust.

max.im /ˈmæk.sɪm/ *n.* proverb, a truth pithily stated

مَثَل، ضرب‌المثل؛ شعار

He often preaches the ***maxim*** of "use it or lose it".

may.hem /ˈmeɪ.hem/ *n.* injury to body

(حقوقی) معلول کردن عمدی، صدمهٔ جانی؛ جار و جنجال، قشقرق

The riot was marked by ***mayhem*** with its attendant loss of life and limb.

mea.ger /£ ˈmiː.gəʳ, $ -gɚ/ *adj.* scanty, inadequate

کم، ناکافی، نابسنده

His salary was far too ***meager*** for him to afford to buy a new car.

me.an.der /£ miˈæn.dəʳ, $ -dɚ/ *v.* to wind or turn in its course

پیچ خوردن، با پیچ و خم گذشتن؛ از این شاخ به آن شاخ پریدن

The stream ***meanders*** in a leisurely way through the valley.

med.dle.some /ˈmed.l̩.səm/ *adj.* interfering

فضول، مداخله‌گر

He felt his marriage was suffering because of his ***meddlesome*** mother-in-law.

med.dle: *v.* دخالت کردن، فضولی کردن

me.di.ate /ˈmiː.di.eɪt/ *v.* to help settle a dispute

میانجی‌گری کردن، پا در میانی کردن، نسبت به حل مشکلی اقدام کردن؛ تعدیل کردن

Let us **mediate** our differences rather than engage in a costly strike.

me.di.o.cre /£ ˌmiː.diˈəʊ.kəʳ, $ -ˈoʊ.kɚ/ *adj.* not very good, ordinary

معمولی، متوسط، پیش پا افتاده

We were disappointed because he gave a rather **mediocre** performance in this role.

med.i.ta.tion /ˌmed.ɪˈteɪ.ʃən/ *n.* reflection, thought

تفکر، تعمق، اندیشه

She reached her decision only after much **meditation**.

med.i.tate: *v.* تأمل کردن، تعمق کردن

med.ley /ˈmed.li/ *n.* mixture

آمیزه، مخلوط

He played a **medley** of popular tunes for them to sing.

meg.a.lo.ma.ni.a /ˌmeg.ə.ləˈmeɪ.ni.ə/ *n.* mania for doing grandiose things

خود بزرگ بینی؛ جنون خود بزرگ بینی

Those who build the world's tallest skyscraper suffer from **megalomania**.

mé.lange /melˈɑːʒ/ *n.* medley, miscellany

آمیزه، مخلوط، ترکیب

The area is a **mélange** of shops, offices and homes.

mêlée /ˈmel.eɪ/ *n.* fight; a large noisy uncontrolled crowd

ازدحام، جمعیت، شلوغی؛ کتک کاری، بزن بزن، جنگ و دعوا

We lost sight of each other in the **mêlée**.

mel.li.flu.ous /mel'ɪf.lu.əs/ *adj.* sounding pleasant and flowing

خوش آهنگ، دلنشین، گوش‌نواز

Italian is a *mellifluous* language.

me.men.to /£ mem'en.təʊ, $ -toʊ/ *n.* token, reminder

یادگاری

Take this book as a *memento* of your visit.

mem.or.i.a.lize /£ mə'mɔː.ri.əlɪz, $ -'mɔːr.i-/ *v.* to commemorate

یاد (کسی یا چیزی را) گرامی داشتن، خاطره (کسی یا چیزی را) زنده نگه‌داشتن

Let us *memorialize* his great memory by dedicating this library in his honor.

men.da.cious /men'deɪ.ʃəs/ *adj.* lying, false

غلط، نادرست، دروغ

Some of these statements are misleading and some downright *mendacious*.

men.di.cant /'men.dɪ.kənt/ *n.* beggar

گدا

High unemployment has caused the number of homeless people and *mendicants* to rise in the city.

men.i.al /'miː.ni.əl/ *adj.* low; suitable for servants

حقیر، پست، بی‌اهمیت

In my last job I did *menial* work like washing dishes and cleaning floors.

men.tor /£ 'men.tɔːʳ, $ -tɔːr/ *n.* teacher, guide

معلم، مربی؛ مشاور، رایزن

The older writer was her *mentor* and friend, encouraging

her to write.

mer.can.tile /£ ˈmɜː.kən.taɪl, $ ˈmɜːr-/ *adj.* of trade or business

بازرگانی، تجاری؛ (مربوط به) تجارت

The 18th century saw a rise in the *mercantile* class all over Europe.

mer.cen.ar.y /£ ˈmɜː.sən.ri, $ ˈmɜːr-/ *adj., n.* wanting money; hired soldier

(سرباز) مزدور؛ پولکی، پول‌دوست، مادّی

I am certain that your action was prompted by *mercenary* motives.

mer.cu.ri.al /£ mɜːˈkjʊə.ri.əl, $ mɜːrˈkjʊr.i-/ *adj.* fickle, changing

دمدمی، متغیر، ناپایدار

He was of a *mercurial* temperament and therefore unpredictable.

me.re.tri.cious /ˌmer.ɪˈtrɪʃ.əs/ *adj.* flashy, tawdry

پر زرق و برق، فریبنده، غلط‌انداز

Her jewels were inexpensive but not *meretricious*.

me.sa /ˈmeɪsə/ *n.* high, flat-topped hill

تپهٔ بلند با قله صاف

The *mesa*, rising above the surrounding desert, was the most conspicuous feature of the area.

mes.mer.ize /ˈmez.mə.raɪz/ *v.* to hypnotize, to have someone's attention completely

مسحور کردن، شیفته کردن

The audience was completely *mesmerized* by her singing voice.

met.al.lur.gi.cal /£ ˌmet.əlˈɜː.dʒɪ.kəl, $ ˌmet.əlˈɜːr-/ *adj.* related

met.a.mor.phos.is 317 **meth.od.i.cal**

to the art of removing metal from ores

(مربوط به) فلزشناسی، فلز شناختی

During the course of his *metallurgical* research, the scientist developed a steel alloy of tremendous strength.

met.a.mor.phos.is /£ ˌmet.əˈmɔː.fə.sɪs, $ ˌmet̬.əˈmɔːr-/ *n.* change of form

دگردیسی، دگرگونی؛ مسخ؛ استحاله

The *metamorphosis* of caterpillar to butterfly is typical of many such changes in animal life.

met.a.phor /£ ˈmet.ə.fɔːʳ, $ ˈmet̬.ə.fɔːr/ *n.* implied comparison

استعاره

"He soared like an eagle" is an example of a simile; " He is an eagle in flight", a *metaphor*.

met.a.phys.ic.al /£ ˌmet.əˈfɪz.ɪ.kəl, $ ˌmet̬-/ *adj.* related to speculative philosophy

متافیزیکی، مابعدطبیعی؛ انتزاعی، مجرد

The modern poets have gone back to the fanciful poems of the *metaphysical* poets of the 17th century for many of their images.

met.a.phys.ics: *n.* (فلسفهٔ) مابعدالطبیعه، متافیزیک

mete /miːt/ *v.* to measure, to distribute

مقرر کردن، تعیین کردن

He tried to be impartial in his efforts to *mete out* justice.

meth.od.i.cal /£ məˈθɒd.ɪ.kəl, $ -ˈθɑː.dɪ-/ *adj.* systematic

با قاعده، منظم، روشمند

An accountant must be *methodical* and maintain order among his financial records.

me.ti.cu.lous /məˈtɪkjʊ.ləs/ *adj.* excessively careful

بسیار دقیق، مو شکاف

He was *meticulous* in checking his accounts.

me.trop.ol.is /£ məˈtrɒp.ᵊl.ɪs $ -ˈtrɑː.pᵊl-/ *n.* large city

کلان شهر، شهر بزرگ؛ مرکز، پایتخت

Singapore has been rebuilt as a *metropolis* of skyscrapers, shopping areas and hotels.

met.tle /£ ˈmet.l̩, $ ˈmet̬-/ *n.* courage, spirit

طاقت، توان؛ شجاعت، جرأت؛ روحیه

The German athletes *showed/ proved* their *mettle* in the final round.

mi.as.ma /miˈæz.mə/ *n.* odor of decaying matter

بوی عفن؛ فضای ناسالم، جوّ مسموم

A *miasma* of pollution hung in the air above Mexico City.

mi.cro.co.sm /£ ˈmaɪ.krəʊˌkɒz.ᵊm, $ -kroʊ.kɑː.zᵊm/ *n.* small world

عالم صغیر، دنیای کوچک؛ نمونه، تجسم

The audience was selected to create a *microcosm* of American society.

mien /miːn/ *n.* appearance, demeanor

چهره، قیافه، رفتار

His aristocratic *mien* and smart clothes singled him out.

mi.grant /ˈmaɪ.grənt/ *adj., n.* wandering, changing habitat

مهاجر

These *migrant* birds return every spring.

mi.gra.tor.y: *adj.*

مهاجر، (مربوط به) مهاجرت

mi.lieu /£ mɪˈljɜː, $ miːlˈjɜː/ *n.* surroundings or setting

محیط (اجتماعی، فرهنگی)

It is a study of the social and cultural *milieu* in which Michelangelo lived and worked.

mil.it.ant /ˈmɪl.ɪ.tᵊnt/ *adj., n.* combative, bellicose

ستیزه‌جو، جنگ طلب؛ خشن؛ سخت‌گیر، سرسخت؛ مبارز، رزمنده

Militant union extremists are threatening to bring down the government.

mil.it.ate /ˈmɪl.ɪ.teɪt/ *v.* to work against

جلوگیری کردن از، عمل کردن (علیه)

Your record of lateness and absence will *militate against* your chances of promotion.

mil.len.ni.um /mɪˈlen.i.əm/ *n.* thousand-year period

هزاره

Big celebrations had been planned for the arrival of the *millennium*.

mim.ic.ry /ˈmɪm.ɪ.kri/ *n.* imitation

تقلید، ادا؛ همرنگی استتاری

I've never had much of a talent for *mimicry*.

min.ar.et /ˌmɪn.əˈret/ *n.* slender tower attached to a mosque

مناره، منار

From the balcony of the *minaret* we obtained an excellent view of the town.

min.a.to.ry /ˈmɪn.ə.tə.ri/ *adj.* threatening

تهدیدآمیز، مهیب، هیبت‌انگیز

All abusive and *minatory* letters received by the mayor were examined by the police.

minc.ing /'mɪntsɪŋ/ *adj.* delicate; dainty

ظریف، دقیق و حساس؛ (حرف زدن و راه رفتن) با ناز و ادا، با غمزه

1) She found herself irritated by the interviewer's *mincing* way of asking questions.
2) She walked across the stage with *mincing* steps.

min.ion /'mɪn.jən/ *n.* servile dependent

مستخدم، پادو، زیردست

He was always accompanied by several of his *minions* because he enjoyed their subservience and flattery.

mi.nu.ti.ae /mɪ'nu:.ʃi.aɪ/ *n.* small and often unimportant details

جزئیات

She would have liked to ignore the *minutiae* of daily living.

mi.rage /mɪ'rɑ:ʒ/ *n.* unreal reflection, optical illusion

سراب

A common *mirage* is a sheet of water that seems to appear on a road in hot weather.

mire /£ maɪəʳ, $ maɪr/ *v., n.* to entangle, to stick in swampy ground

در گل فرو رفتن، در گل گیر کردن؛ گِلابه، گل و لای؛ مهلکه، مخمصه

Their rear wheels became *mired* in the mud.

mirth /£ mɜ:θ, $ mɜ:rθ/ *n.* merriment, laughter

شور و شادی، خوشی، شادمانی، نشاط

Her impersonations of our teachers were a source of considerable *mirth*.

mis.ad.ven.ture /£ ˌmɪs.əd'ven.tʃəʳ, $ -tʃɚ/ *n.* mischance, ill luck

بخت بد، بدِ حادثه، سوء اتفاق؛ حادثه، پیشامد ناگوار

The young explorer met death by **misadventure**.

mis.an.thrope /£ ˈmɪs.ᵊn.θrəʊp, £ ˈmɪz-, $ -θroʊp/ *n.* one who hates mankind

مردم گریز، مردم بیزار

We thought the hermit was a **misanthrope** because he shunned our society.

mis.ap.pre.hen.sion /ˌmɪs.æp.rɪˈhen.tʃᵊn/ *n.* misunderstanding, error

سوء تفاهم، درک غلط، برداشت غلط

To avoid **misapprehension**, I am going to ask all of you to repeat the instruction.

mis.ce.ge.nation /mɪsɪdʒɪˈneɪʃᵊn/ *n.* intermarriage between races

زناشویی نا هم‌نژاد، زناشویی میان نژادی

Some states passed laws against **miscegenation**.

mis.cel.lany /mɪˈsel.ə.ni/ *n.* mixture of writings on various subjects

مجموعه؛ جُنگ

This is an interesting **miscellany** of 19th century prose.

mis.cel.la.ne.ous: *adj.*   متنوع، گوناگون، جور واجور

mis.chance /£ mɪsˈtʃɑːnts, $ -ˈtʃænts/ *n.* ill luck

بخت بد، بدحادثه، سوء اتفاق؛ بدبختی

By **mischance**, he lost his week's salary.

mis.con.strue /ˌmɪs.kənˈstruː/ *v.* to misjudge, to interpret incorrectly

اشتباه فهمیدن، غلط تعبیر کردن

I think you've **misconstrued** what I was trying to say.

mis.cre.ant /ˈmɪs.kri.ənt/ *n.* one who does not obey rules, wretch, villain

آدم خلاف کار، آدم شرور، آدم رذل

The penalties for dropping litter are too low to discourage **miscreant**.

mis.de.mean.or /£ ˌmɪs.dɪˈmiː.nər, $ -nɚ/ *n.* minor crime

(حقوقی) جنجه، بزه، خلاف

The culprit pleaded guilty to a **misdemeanor** rather than face a trial for a felony.

mis.giv.ing /mɪsˈgɪv.ɪŋ/ *n.* doubt about a future event

نگرانی، دو دلی، سوء ظن، دلشوره

Many teachers expressed serious **misgivings** about the new exams.

mis.hap /ˈmɪs.hæp/ *n.* accident

بدبیاری، رویداد بد، اتفاق ناگوار، اتفاق سوء

With a little care you could have avoided this **mishap**.

mis.nom.er /£ ˌmɪsˈnəʊ.mər, $ -ˈnoʊ.mɚ/ *n.* wrong name, incorrect designation

نام غلط، اسم بی‌مسمّا

It's something of a **misnomer** to refer to these inexperienced boys as soldier.

mis.o.gyn.y /£ mɪˈsɒdʒ.ɪ.ni, $ -ˈsɑː.dʒɪ-/ *n.* hatred of marriage

تنفر از ازدواج، ازدواج ستیزی

He remained a bachelor not because of **misogyny** but because of ill fate; his fiancee died before the wedding.

mis.o.gyn.ist: *n.* (آدم) زن بیزار، ضدِ زن

mis.sile /£ 'mɪs.aɪl, $ -ᵊl/ *n.* object to be thrown or projected

موشک، پرتابه، پرانه

Scientists are experimenting with guided *missiles*.

mis.sive /'mɪs.ɪv/ *n.* letter

مکتوب، نامه، پیام نوشتاری

The ambassador received a *missive* from the Secretary of State.

mite /maɪt/ *n.* very small object or creature; small coin

موجودات ریز؛ پول ناچیز، چندر غاز

The criminal was so heartless that he even stole the widow's *mite*.

mit.i.gate /£ 'mɪt.ɪ.geɪt, $ 'mɪt̬-/ *v.* to appease

تسکین دادن، آرام کردن؛ تخفیف دادن، سبک کردن

Nothing he did could *mitigate* her wrath; she was unforgiving.

mne.mon.ic /£ nɪ'mɒn.ɪk, $ -'mɑː.nɪk/ *adj.* pertaining to memory

وابسته به حافظه، یادافزا، یادیار

He used *mnemonic* tricks to master new words.

mo.bile /£ 'məʊ.baɪl, $ 'moʊ.bᵊl/ *adj.* movable, not fixed

متحرک، سیّار

The *mobile* blood bank operated by the Red Cross visited our neighborhood today.

mo.bil.i.ty: *n.* تحرک، جنبش

mode /£ məʊd, $ moʊd/ *n.* prevailing style

شیوه، سبک، روال، نحوه، طرز، راه

She was not used to their lavish *mode* of living.

mod.i.cum /£ ˈmɒd.ɪ.kəm, $ ˈmɑː.dɪ-/ *n.* limited quantity

اندک، کم، ذره، خرده، چکه

Although his story is based on a *modicum* of truth, most of the events are fictitious.

mod.ish /£ ˈməʊ.dɪʃ, $ ˈmoʊ-/ *adj.* fashionable

مد، مد روز، بابِ روز

She always discarded all garments which were no longer *modish*.

mod.u.la.tion /£ ˌmɒd.jʊˈleɪ.ʃᵊn, $ ˌmɑː.dʒə-/ *n.* toning down, changing from one key to another

تنظیم، تعدیل، میزان؛ (موسیقی) تغییر مایه یا پرده

When she spoke, it was with quiet *modulation* of voice.

mo.gul /£ ˈməʊ.gᵊl, $ ˈmoʊ-/ *n.* powerful person

آدم مقتدر؛ (مجازی) غول

The oil *moguls* made great profits when the price of gasoline rose.

moi.e.ty /ˈmɔɪ.ɪ.ti/ *n.* half, part

نیم، نیمه، نصف؛ سهم، بخش

There is a *moiety* of the savage in her personality which is not easily perceived by those who do not know her well.

mol.e.cule /£ ˈmɒl.ɪ.kjuːl, $ ˈmɑː.lɪ-/ *n.* simplest unit of a chemical substance

مولکول؛ ذرّه

In chemistry, we study how atoms and *molecules* react to form new substances.

mol.li.fy /£ ˈmɒl.ɪ.faɪ, $ ˈmɑː.lɪ-/ v. to soothe

نرم کردن، آرام کردن، دلجویی کردن، خشم (کسی را) فرو نشاندن

We tried to *mollify* the hysterical child by promising her many gifts.

molt /£ məʊlt, $ moʊlt/ v. to shed or cast off hair or feathers

(حیوانات) پوست انداختن، مو ریختن، پر ریختن

The male robin *molted* in the spring.

mol.ten /£ ˈməʊl.tᵊn, $ ˈmoʊl-/ adj. melted

مذاب، آب شده، گداخته، تفتیده

The city of Pompeii was destroyed by volcanic ash rather than by *molten* lava flowing from Mount Vesuvius.

mo.men.tous /£ məˈmen.təs, $ -ṭəs/ adj. very important

بسیار مهم، جدّی، حسّاس، حیاتی

On this *momentous* occasion, we must be very solemn.

mo.men.tum /£ məˈmen.təm, $ -ṭəm/ n. quantity of motion of a moving body, impetus

اندازۀ حرکت؛ تکانۀ حرکت؛ شدّت

The car lost *momentum* as it tried to ascend the steep hill.

mon.ar.chy /£ ˈmɒn.ə.ki, $ ˈmɑː.nɚ-/ n. government under a single ruler

سلطنت، پادشاهی؛ کشور پادشاهی

England today remains a *monarchy*.

mon.as.tic /məˈnæs.tɪk/ adj. related to monks

(مربوط به) راهب یا راهبان؛ (مربوط به) صومعه یا دیر

Wanting to live a religious life, he took his *monastic* vows.

mon.e.ta.ry /ˈmʌn.ɪ.tri/ *adj.* related to money

پولی

She was in complete charge of all ***monetary*** matters affecting the household.

mon.o.lith.ic /£ ˌmɒn.əˈlɪθ.ɪk, $ ˌmɑː.nə-/ *adj.* solidly uniform

همگن، یکپارچه؛ سخت، انعطاف‌ناپذیر

The patriots sought to present a ***monolithic*** front.

mon.o.the.i.sm /£ ˌmɒn.əʊˈθiː.ɪ.zᵊm, $ ˌmɑː.noʊ-/ *n.* belief in one God

یکتاپرستی، توحید

Abraham was the first to proclaim his belief in ***monotheism***.

mon.o.to.ny /£ məˈnɒt.ᵊn.i, $ -ˈnɑː.t̬ᵊn-/ *n.* sameness leading to boredom

یکنواختی، عدم تنوع

He took a clerical job, but soon grew to hate the ***monotony*** of his daily routine.

mon.u.men.tal /£ ˌmɒn.jʊˈmen.tᵊl, $ ˌmɑː.nǰʊˈmen.t̬ᵊl/ *adj.* massive

عظیم، بزرگ؛ جاویدان، ماندنی، ماندگار

Writing a dictionary is a ***monumental*** task.

mood.i.ness /ˈmuː.dɪ.nəs/ *n.* fits of depression or gloom

بی‌حوصلگی، کج خلقی، ترشرویی، بد اخلاقی

We could not discover the cause of his recurrent ***moodiness***.

moor /£ mɔːʳ, £ mʊəʳ, $ mʊr/ *n.* marshly wasteland

زمین بایر، بوته‌زار، خلنگ‌زار

These **moors** can only be used for hunting; they are too barren for agriculture.

moot /muːt/ *adj.* debatable

قابل بحث، گفتمان پذیر

Our tariff policy is a **moot** subject.

mor.a.to.ri.um /£ ˌmɒr.əˈtɔː.ri.əm, $ ˌmɔːr.əˈtɔːr.i-/ *n.* legal delay of payment

اجازهٔ دیرکرد، استمهال؛ ضرب‌الاجل، مهلت قانونی

We declare a **moratorium** and delay collection of debts for six months.

mor.bid /£ ˈmɔː.bɪd, $ ˈmɔːr-/ *adj.* gloomy, gruesome

بیمار، بیمارگون؛ بد اندیشانه؛ وحشتناک

The poet demonstrates his **morbid** devotion to his dead wife by sleeping next to her grave.

mor.dant /£ ˈmɔː.dənt, $ ˈmɔːr-/ *adj.* biting, sarcastic, stinging

نیشدار، گزنده؛ تلخ

Actors feared the critic's **mordant** pen.

mo.res /£ ˈmɔː.reɪz, $ ˈmɔːr.eɪz/ *n.* customs

آداب و رسوم، شعائر

The **mores** of Mexico are those of Spain with some modification.

mor.i.bund /£ ˈmɒr.ɪ.bʌnd, $ ˈmɔːr-/ *adj.* at the point of death

نزدیک به موت، در حال احتضار

The doctors called the family to the bedside of the **moribund** patient.

mo.rose /£ məˈrəʊs, $ -ˈroʊs/ *adj.* ill-humored, sullen

ترشرو، عبوس، بدخلق، عنق

When we first meet Hamlet, we find him *morose* and depressed.

mor.ti.cian /£ mɔːˈtɪʃ.ᵊn, $ mɔːr-/ *n.* undertaker

مدیر بنگاه کفن و دفن، مأمور کفن و دفن

The *mortician* prepared the corpse for burial.

mor.ti.fy /£ ˈmɔː.tɪ.faɪ, £ -tə-, $ ˈmɔːr.tə-/ *v.* to humiliate, to punish the flesh

تحقیر کردن، سرافکنده کردن؛ به خود سختی دادن

She was so *mortified* by her blunder that she ran to her room in tears.

mote /£ məʊt, $ moʊt/ *n.* small speck

ذره، دانه، یک جو

The tinest *mote* in the eye is very painful.

mo.tif /£ məʊˈtiːf, $ moʊ-/ *n.* theme; pattern

درون‌مایه، مضمون؛ نقش و نگار، طرح

1) The *motif* of betrayal and loss is crucial in all these stories.

2) We chose some curtains with a flower *motif*.

mot.ley /£ ˈmɒt.li, $ ˈmɑːt-/ *adj.* parti-colored, mixed

گوناگون، جور واجور، قر و قاطی؛ رنگ وارنگ

There is a *motley* collection of old furniture in the house we're renting at the moment.

mot.tled /£ ˈmɒt.ld, $ ˈmɑː.t̬ld/ *adj.* spotted

خال‌مخالی، لکه لکه

When he blushed, his face took on a *mottled* hue.

moun.te.bank /ˈmaʊn.tɪ.bæŋk/ *n.* charlatan, boastful pretender

دغل‌کار، شارلاتان، شیاد
The patent medicine man was *mountebank*.

mud.dle /'mʌd.l/ *v.* to confuse, to mix up

آشفته کردن، گیج کردن، پریشان کردن
His thoughts were *muddled* and chaotic.

mug.gy /'mʌg.i/ *adj.* warm and damp

شرجی، گرم و مرطوب، دَمدار
August in New York City is often *muggy*.

mug.wump /'mʌg.wu:mp/ *n.* defector from a party

(سیاسی) مستقل، ناوابسته
When he refused to support his party's nominees, he was called a *mugwump* and deprived of his seniority privileges in Congress.

mulct /'mʌlkt/ *v., n.* to defraud a person of something

کلاه سر کسی گذاشتن، با حیله (از چنگ کسی) در آوردن؛ کلاهبرداری
The lawyer was accused of trying to *mulct* the boy of his legacy.

mul.ti.fa.ri.ous /£ ˌmʌl.tɪˈfeə.ri.əs, $ -tɪˈfer.i-/ *adj.* varied, greatly diversified

متنوع، گوناگون، مختلف
As a career woman and mother, she was constantly busy with the *multifarious* activities of her daily life.

mul.ti.form /£ 'mʌl.tɪ.fɔ:m $ -fɔ:rm/ *adj.* having many forms

چندگونه، چند شکل، چند ریخت
Snowflakes are *multiform* but always hexagonal.

mul.ti.lin.gual /£ ˌmʌl.tiˈlɪŋ.gwəl, $ -tɪ-/ *adj.* having many languages

چندزبانه

Because they are bordered by so many countries, the Swiss people are **multilingual**.

mul.ti.pli.ci.ty /£ ˌmʌl.tɪˈplɪs.ɪ.ti, $ -ṭəˈplɪs.ə.ṭi/ *n.* state of being numerous

تعدد، کثرت، فراوانی؛ تنوع، گوناگونی

There is a **multiplicity** of fashion magazines to choose from.

mun.dane /mʌnˈdeɪn/ *adj.* wordly

مادّی، دنیوی، این جهانی

He was concerned only with **mundane** matters.

mu.ni.fi.cent /mjuːˈnɪf.ɪ.sᵊnt/ *adj.* very generous

بخشنده، کریم، گشاده‌دست، سخاوتمند؛ سخاوتمندانه

The **munificent** gift was presented to the bride.

murk.i.ness /£ ˈmɜː.ki.nəs, $ ˈmɜːr-/ *n.* darkness, gloom

تیرگی، تاریکی، کدری، ظلمت

The **murkiness** and fog of the waterfront that evening depressed me.

muse /mjuːz/ *v.* to ponder

با خود اندیشیدن، به‌خود گفتن؛ در فکر غوطه‌ور شدن، در بحر تفکر فرو رفتن

For a moment he **mused** about the beauty of the scene.

musk.y /ˈmʌs.ki/ *adj.* having the odor of musk

مُشکین، مُشکبار

She left a trace of **musky** perfume behind her.

must.y /ˈmʌs.ti/ *adj.* stale; spoiled by age

بیات، کپک‌زده، نم کشیده؛ قدیمی، کهنه

The attic was dark and **musty**.

mu.ta.ble /mjuːtᵊbl̩/ *adj.* changing in form, fickle

تغییرپذیر، قابل تغییر

His opinions were *mutable* and easily influenced by anyone who had any powers of persuasion.

mu.ti.late /£ ˈmjuːtɪ.leɪt, $ -tᵊl.eɪt/ *v.* to maim

قطع عضو کردن، مُثله کردن

The torturer threatened to *mutilate* his victim.

mu.ti.nous /£ ˈmjuːtɪ.nəs, $ -tɪ-/ *adj.* unruly, rebellious

یاغی، شورشی

The captain had to use force to quiet his *mutinous* crew.

my.o.pic /£ maɪˈɒp.ɪk, $ -ˈɑː.pɪk/ *adj.* nearsighted

نزدیک‌بین؛ کوته‌بین، کوته‌نظر، فاقد چشم بصیرت

In thinking only of your present need and ignoring the future, you are being rather *myopic*.

my.o.pi.a: *n.*   نزدیک‌بینی؛ کوته‌بینی

my.ri.ad /ˈmɪr.i.əd/ *n.* large number

هزاران؛ هزارها؛ بی‌شمار

Myriad of mosquitoes from the swamps invaded our village every twilight.

لیستی از لغاتی که در جملات بخش M به کار رفته‌اند:

abusive: *adj.*	فحش‌آمیز	gypsy: *adj.*	کولی، کولی‌وار
ascend: *v.*	بالا رفتن، صعود کردن		(مربوط به) کولی
attendant: *adj.*	ملتزم	hermit: *n.*	معتکف، گوشه‌گیر
attic: *n.*	اتاق زیر شیروانی	hue: *n.*	رنگ
attorney: *n.*	وکیل مدافع	impersonation: *n.*	تقلید
blunder: *n.*	اشتباه فاحش، گاف	inconceivable: *adj.*	بعید، محال
captor: *n.*	اسیر کننده	inspiring: *adj.*	روحیه‌بخش
cart: *n.*	گاری	lateness: *n.*	تأخیر
championship: *n.*		lilac: *n.*	گُل یاس
	مسابقات قهرمانی	limb: *n.*	عضو بدن
chill: *v.*	سرما دادن	lute: *n.*	(ساز) عود
clerical: *adj.*	(کار) دفتری	manager: *n.*	گرداننده، مدیر
cold: *n.*	سرما	mania: *n.*	جنون، شیدایی
conspicuous: *adj.*	چشمگیر	patriot: *n.*	وطن‌پرست
culprit: *n.*	مجرم	persuation: *n.*	ترغیب، وسوسه
disgust: *n.*	چِندِش، نفرت	plead guilty: *v.*	
disorder: *n.*	ناراحتی، اختلال		اقرار به جرم کردن
downright: *adj.*	محض	promotion: *n.*	ارتقاء
enlightened: *adj.*	روشنفکر	recurrent: *adj.*	همیشگی، راجعه
fan: *n.*	طرفدار (پر و پا قرص)	riot: *n.*	آشوب
felony: *n.*	جنایت	robin: *n.*	(پرنده) سینه سرخ
flattary: *n.*	تملق، چاخان	Secretary of State: *n.*	
frigid: *adj.*	بسیار سرد		وزیر امور خارجه (در امریکا)
garble: *v.*	تحریف کردن	shun: *v.*	دوری جستن
gossip: *n.*	شایعات	single out: *v.*	از بقیه جدا کردن
grandiose: *adj.*	عظیم	soar: *v.*	اوج گرفتن

spill: *v.* ریختن (به زمین)
steep: *adj.* با شیب تند، شیب‌دار
subservience: *n.* اطاعت، چاپلوسی
suck: *v.* در خود فرو بردن، کشیدن
swamp: *n.* باتلاق

tariff: *n.* تعرفه
thwart: *v.* نقش بر آب کردن
toss about: *v.* این سو و آن سو انداختن
trial: *n.* محاکمه
vow: *n.* قسم، عهد
wrath: *n.* خشم

N n

na.dir /£ ˈneɪ.dɪəʳ, $ -dɚ/ *n.* the lowest point

نهایت اُفت، حضیض

The defeat was the ***nadir*** of her career.

na.ï.ve.té /£ naɪˈiː.vɪ.ti, $ -vəˈtiː/ *n.* trust based on lack of experience

سادگی، ساده‌دلی، ساده لوحی

He demonstrated such a ***naïveté*** about political issues.

nar.cis.sist /£ ˈnɑː.sɪ.sɪst, $ ˈnɑːr.sə-/ *n.* self-centered person, conceited

خود شیفته (انسان)

A ***narcissist*** is his own best friend.

nar.cis.si.sm: *n.*   خودشیفتگی

nar.cis.sis.tic: *adj.*   خود شیفتگی (مربوط به)

nas.cent /ˈnæs.ᵊnt/ *adj.* incipient, coming into being

در مراحل آغازی، در حال تولد، نوپا، نورسته، نو شکفته

He is a member of a ***nascent*** political party.

na.tal /ˈneɪ.tᵊl/ *adj.* related to birth

تولد (مربوط به)

He refused to celebrate his ***natal*** day.

nau.se.ate /£ ˈnɔː.zi.eɪt, $ ˈnɑː-/ *v.* cause to become sick, to fill with disgust

دچار تهوع کردن؛ متنفر کردن، حال (کسی را) بههم زدن
The foul smell began to *nauseate* him.

nau.ti.cal /£ ˈnɔː.tɪ.kᵊl, $ ˈnɑː.t̬i-/ *adj.* related to ships or navigation

دریایی، (مربوط به) دریانوردی
You are looking very *nautical* in your navy blue sweater.

nave /neɪv/ *n.* main body of a church

شبستان کلیسا
The *nave* of the cathedral is empty at this hour.

neb.u.lous /ˈneb.jʊ.ləs/ *adj.* cloudy, hazy

ابری، ابرآلود، مهآلود؛ مبهم، گنگ، آشفته
Your theories are too *nebulous*; please clarify them.

ne.crol.o.gy /nekrəʊˈlɒʊ.dʒi/ *n.* list of the dead; obituary notice

لیست متوفیان؛ آگهی ترحیم
The *necrology* of those buried in this cemetry is available in the office.

nec.ro.man.cy /£ ˈnek.rəʊ.mænt.si, $ -rə-/ *n.* black magic, dealing with the dead

احضار ارواح، سحر، جادوگری، ارتباط با مردگان
Because he was able to perform feats of *necromancy*, the natives thought he was in league with the devil.

ne.fa.ri.ous /£ nəˈfeə.ri.əs, $ -ˈfer.i-/ *adj.* very wicked

شیطانی، اهریمنی؛ بدجنس، شریر
He was universally feared because of his many *nefarious* deeds.

ne.ga.tion /nɪˈgeɪ.ʃ°n/ *n.* denial

انکار، نفی؛ نقیض؛ جواب منفی

She was unable to present any *negation* of his evidence.

neg.li.gence /ˈneg.lɪ.dʒ°nts/ *n.* carelessness

بی‌توجهی، بی‌مبالاتی، مسامحه، غفلت

My mother accuses me of *negligence* unless I phone her everyday.

nem.e.sis /ˈnem.ə.sɪs/ *n.* a cause of punishment or defeat

عقوبت، مکافات، کیفر اعمال

The tax increases proved to be the President's political *nemesis* at the following election.

ne.o.phyte /£ ˈniː.əʊ.faɪt, $ -oʊ-/ *n.* beginner; recent convert

تازه وارد، تازه‌کار، مبتدی؛ نوآیین، نوکیش

This mountain slope contains slides that will challenge experts as well as *neophytes*.

nep.o.ti.sm /ˈnep.ə.tɪ.z°m/ *n.* favoritism (to a relative)

پارتی‌بازی، تبارگماری

Government was dismissed following revelations about corruption, *nepotism* and political incompetence.

net.tle /£ ˈnet.l̩, $ ˈneṭ-/ *v., n.* to annoy, to vex

آزردن، سر به سر کسی گذاشتن؛ گزنه

Do not let him *nettle* you with his sarcastic remarks.

nex.us /ˈnek.səs/ *n.* connection

ارتباط، پیوند، وسیلهٔ ارتباط

I fail to see the *nexus* which binds these two widely separated events.

nib /nɪb/ *n.* beak, pen point

نوک، نوک قلم، سر قلم
The *nibs* of fountain pens often became clotted and corroded.

ni.ce.ty /£ ˈnaɪ.sə.ti, $ -ṭi/ *n.* precision, minute distinction

ظرافت، نکته‌سنجی، باریک‌بینی؛ (جمع) جزئیات
I cannot distinguish between such *niceties* of reasoning.

nig.gard.ly /£ ˈnɪg.əd.li, $ -ɚd-/ *adj.* meanly stingy, parsimonious

خسیس، کنس، ناخن خشک؛ ناچیز، اندک، کم
The *niggardly* pittance the widow receives from the government cannot keep her from poverty.

nig.gle /ˈnɪg.l/ *v.* to spend too much time on minor points, to carp

نق زدن، غُر زدن، کفری کردن، آزار دادن
Let's not *niggle* over details.

nig.gling: *adj.* خسته‌کننده؛ جزئی، پیش پا افتاده، بی‌اهمیت

ni.hil.i.sm /£ ˈnɪh.ɪ.lɪ.zᵊm, $ ˈnaɪ.ə.lɪ-/ *n.* denial of traditional values, skepticism

پوچ‌انگاری، هیچ‌گرایی، نیست‌انگاری
Nihilism holds that existence has no meaning.

nir.va.na /£ nɪəˈvɑː.nə, $ nɚ-/ *n.* in Buddhist teachings, freedom from all sufferings

(آیین هندو) آرامش ابدی، سعادت ابدی
In Buddhism *nirvana* is achieved by removing all personal desires.

noc.tur.nal /£ nɒkˈtɜː.nəl, $ nɑːkˈtɜːr-/ *adj.* done at night

شبانه

Mr Jones obtained a watchdog to prevent the *nocturnal* raids on his chicken coops.

no.isome /ˈnɔɪ.səm/ *adj.* foul smelling, unwholesome

زننده، مشمئزکننده، ناخوشایند، نفرت‌انگیز

I never could stand the *noisome* atmosphere surrounding the slaughter houses.

no.mad.ic /£ nəʊˈmæd.ɪk, $ noʊ-/ *adj.* wandering

چادرنشین؛ خانه به دوش، آواره

Several *nomadic* tribes of Indians would hunt in this area each year.

no.men.cla.ture /£ nəʊˈmeŋ.klə.tʃəʳ, $ ˈnoʊ.men.kleɪ.tʃɚ/ *n.* terminology; system of names

اسامی، نام‌گذاری، اصطلاحات

She struggled to master scientific *nomenclature*.

non.age /£ ˌnɒn.ədʒə, $ ˌnɑː.nə.dʒe/ *n.* immaturity

(حقوقی) صِغَر، صغر سن

She was embarrassed by the *nonage* of her contemporaries who never seemed to grow up.

non.cha.lance /£ ˈnɒn.tʃəl.ənts, $ ˌnɑː.nʃəˈlɑːnts/ *n.* lack of interest, indifference

بی‌تفاوتی، خونسردی، بی‌علاقگی

Beneath his apparent *nonchalance* he is as nervous and excited as the rest of us.

non.com.mit.tal /£ ˌnɒŋ.kəˈmɪt.ᵊl, $ ˌnɑːŋ.kəˈmɪt̬-/ *adj.* neutral, undecided

بی‌طرف؛ غیرمتعهد؛ پیمان‌گریز

She was very *noncommittal* about my suggestion.

non.en.ti.ty /£ nɒn'en.tɪ.ti, $ nɑː'nen.t̬ə.t̬i/ *n.* a person without strong character, ideas or influence

آدم بی‌کفایت، آدم بی سر و پا، آدم حقیر، هیچ کاره

How could such a *nonentity* become chairman of the company?

non.plus /£ ˌnɒm'plʌs, $ ˌnɑːm-/ *v.* to bring to a halt by confusion

متعجب کردن، مبهوت کردن، حیرت‌زده کردن

I was completely *nonplussed* by his sudden appearance.

non se.qui.tur /£ ˌnɒn 'sek.wɪ.təʳ, $ ˌnɑːn 'sek.wɪ.t̬ɚ/ *n.* a statement which does not correctly follow from the meaning of the previous statement

نتیجهٔ کاذب؛ استدلال غلط

Your term paper is full of *non sequitur;* I cannot see how you reached the conclusions you state.

nose.gay /'nəʊz.geɪ/ *n.* fragrant bouquet

دسته گل (کوچک و خوشبو)

These spring flowers will make an attractive *nosegay*.

nos.tal.gia /£ nɒs'tæl.dʒə, $ nɑː'stæl-/ *n.* homesick, longing for the past

نوستالژی، دلتنگی برای وطن، احساس غربت، حسرت گذشته، غم غربت

The first settlers found so much work to do that they had little time for *nostalgia*.

no.to.ri.ous /£ nəʊ'tɔː.ri.əs, $ noʊ'tɔːr.i-/ *adj.* famous for sth bad

بدنام، رسوا، انگشت‌نما

He was *notorious* as a gambler and rake.

nov.el.ty /£ 'nɒv.ᵊl.ti, $ 'nɑː.vᵊl.ti/ *n.* newness, something new

تازگی، نوظهوری؛ چیز تازه / بدیع

The *novelty* of his surroundings soon wore off.

nov.ice /£ 'nɒv.ɪs, $ 'nɑː.vɪs/ *n.* beginner

تازه‌کار، مبتدی؛ نوآموز، تازه وارد

Even a *novice* can do good work if he follows these simple directions.

no.xious /£ 'nɒk.ʃəs, $ 'nɑːk-/ *adj.* harmful

زیانمند، مضر؛ سمّی، مسموم‌کننده

We must trace the source of these *noxious* gases before they asphyxiate us.

nu.ance /£ 'njuː.ɑːnts, $ 'nuː-/ *n.* shade of difference in color or meaning

فرق جزیی، تفاوت ظریف، اختلاف مختصر

The unskilled eye of the layman has difficulty in discerning the *nuance* of color in the paintings.

nu.bile /£ 'njuː.baɪl, $ 'nuː-/ *adj.* marriageable

(دختر) دم بخت، شوهر دادنی؛ جذاب، لوند

She was worried about finding suitable husbands for her five *nubile* daughters.

nu.ga.tor.y /£ 'njuː.gə.tᵊr.i, $ 'nuː.gə.tɔːr-/ *adj.* worthless, futile

بی‌اعتبار، بی‌ارزش، بی‌اهمیت، بیهوده

This agreement is *nugatory* for no court will enforce it.

nu.mis.ma.tist /£ ˌnjuː.mɪz'mæt.ɪst, $ ˌnuː.mɪz'mæt̬-/ *n.* person who collects coins

سکه‌شناس

The *numismatist* had a splendid collection of antique

coins.

nup.tial /ˈnʌp.tʃ°l/ *adj.* related to marriage

زناشویی، (مربوط به) ازدواج، (مربوط به) عروسی
Their *nuptial* ceremony was performed in Golden Gate Park.

nur.ture /£ ˈnɜː.tʃəʳ, $ ˈnɜːr.tʃɚ/ *v.* to bring up, to feed, to educate

پرورش دادن، تربیت کردن، تعلیم دادن
We must *nurture* the young so that they will develop into good citizens.

nu.tri.ent /£ ˈnjuː.tri.ᵊnt, $ ˈnuː-/ *adj., n.* providing nourishment

مقوّی، مغذی؛ مادهٔ غذایی
During the convalescent period, the patient must be provided with *nutrient* foods.

nu.tri.tion /£ njuːˈtrɪʃ.ᵊn, $ nuː-/ *n.* act of nourishing with food

تغذیه؛ علم تغذیه، تغذیه‌شناسی
Good *nutrition* is essential if patients are to make a quick recovery.

لیستی از لغاتی که در جملات بخش N به‌کار رفته‌اند:

asphyxiate: *v.*	خفه کردن	rake: *n.*	فاسق
clotted: *adj.*	جرم گرفته، کلفت	revelation: *n.*	افشاگری
convalescent: *adj.*	نقاهت	sarcastic: *adj.*	کنایه‌دار
coop: *n.*	قفس	wear off: *v.*	تازگی خود را از دست دادن
corroded: *adj.*	خورده شده		
discern: *v.*	تشخیص دادن	tax: *v.*	به‌ستوه آوردن
incompetence: *n.*	عدم کفایت	tenet: *n.*	اعتقاد
layman: *n.*	آدم غیرحرفه‌ای، آدم عادی	warden: *n.*	رئیس زندان
		welfare: *n.*	رفاه
pittance: *n.*	حقوق ناچیز	willpower: *n.*	اراده

O o

oaf /£ əʊf, $ oʊf/ *n.* stupid, awkward person

(مرد) خنگ، دست و پا چلفتی، خرفت، احمق، گنده‌بک

He called the unfortunate waiter a clumsy *oaf*.

ob.du.rate /£ ˈɒb.djʊ.rət, $ ˈɑːb.dʊr.ɪt/ *adj.* stubborn

لجوج، خود رأى، یک دنده، سرسخت

He was *obdurate* in his refusal to listen to our complaints.

o.bei.sance /£ əʊˈbeɪ.sᵊnts, $ oʊ-/ *n.* bow

کرنش، تعظیم

She *made* an *obeisance* as the king and queen entered the room.

ob.e.lisk /ˈɒb.ə.lɪsk/ *n.* sided tapering pillar

تک ستون (سنگی) یاد بود

Cleopatra's Needle is an *obelisk* in Central Park, New York City.

o.bese /£ əʊˈbiːs, $ oʊ-/ *adj.* very fat

فربه، خیلی چاق، خپل

It is advisable that *obese* people try to lose weight.

ob.fus.cate /£ ˈɒb.fʌs.keɪt, $ ˈɑːb.fə.skeɪt/ *v.* to confuse, to muddle

(مطلبی را) پیچاندن، غامض جلوه دادن، گیج کردن، پیچیده‌تر کردن
Do not **obfuscate** the issues by dragging in irrelevant arguments.

o.bit.u.a.ry /£ əʊˈbɪtʃ.ʊə.ri, $ oʊˈbɪtʃ.u.er.i/ *n.* death notice

آگهی فوت، آگهی درگذشت
I first learned of his death when I read the **obituary** in the newspaper.

ob.jec.tive /£ əbˈdʒek.tɪv, $ -t̬ɪv/ *adj.* not influenced by emotions; fair

بی‌طرف، بی‌غرض؛ منصفانه؛ واقع‌بین
Even though he was her son, she tried to be **objective** about his behavior.

ob.jec.tive /£ əbˈdʒek.tɪv, $ -t̬ɪv/ *n.* goal, aim

هدف، منظور، غایت
A degree in medicine was her ultimate **objective**.

ob.jur.gate /ˈɒb.dʒɜː.ɡeɪt/ *v.* to scold, to rebuke severely

سخت سرزنش کردن، سخت پرخاش کردن
I am afraid he will **objurgate** us publicly for this offence.

ob.jur.ga.tion: *n.* سرزنش، پرخاش
ob.jur.ga.to.ry: *adj.* سرزنش‌آمیز، پرخاشگرانه

ob.la.tion /əˈbleɪ.ʃən/ *n.* the Eucharist; pious donation

عشاء ربانی؛ نذر، خیرات
The wealthy man offered **oblations** so that the church might be able to provide for the needy.

ob.lig.a.to.ry /£ əˈblɪɡ.ə.tər.i, $ -tɔːr-/ *adj.* binding, required

اجباری؛ ضروری، الزام‌آور

It is **obligatory** that books borrowed from the library be returned within the weeks.

o.blige: *v.*   متعهد ساختن، ملزم ساختن، مجبور کردن

ob.li.ga.tion: *n.*   تعهد اخلاقی، وظیفه، دِیْن

o.blique /£ əŏ'bli:k, $ oū-/ *adj.* slanting, indirect

اریب، کج، مایل، غیرمستقیم

He gave her an **oblique** glance which she interpreted as a warning.

o.bliq.u.ity: *n.*   انحراف، کجی

o.blit.e.rate /£ ə'blɪt.ᵊr.eɪt, $ -'blɪt̬.ə.reɪt/ *v.* to destroy completely

محو کردن، ویران کردن، از میان بردن

The tidal wave **obliterated** several island villages.

o.bliv.ion /ə'blɪv.i.ən/ *n.* forgetfulness

فراموشی، نسیان؛ بی‌خبری، ناهشیاری

His works had fallen into a state of **oblivion**; no one bothered to read them.

ob.lo.quy /'ɒb.lə.kwɪ/ *n.* slander, disgrace, infamy

هتاکی، فحش، ناسزا؛ رسوایی، بی‌حرمتی، آبروریزی

I resent the **obloquy** that you are casting upon my reputation.

ob.nox.ious /£ əb'nɒk.ʃəs, $ -'nɑːk-/ *adj.* offensive

زننده، نفرت‌انگیز، نامطبوع

I find your behavior **obnoxious**; please amend your manners.

ob.se.qui.ous /əb'siː.kwi.əs/ *adj.* slavishly attentive, servile, sycophantic

متملق، بله قربانگو، چاپلوس، بادمجان دور قاب چین
Nothing is more disgusting to me than the *obsequious* demeanor of the people who wait upon you.

ob.ses.sion /əb'seʃ.ᵊn/ *n.* fixed idea, continued brooding

نگرانی دایمی، مشغلهٔ ذهنی، وسواس فکری
This *obsession* with the supernatural has made him unpopular with his neighbors.

ob.ses.sive: *n., adj.*   آدم وسواسی؛ وسواسی، ناشی از وسواس

ob.so.lete /£ ˌɒb.sᵊl'i:t, $ ˌɑ:b-/ *adj.* outmoded

منسوخ، قدیمی، کهنه، مهجور، غیرمستعمل
That word is *obsolete*; do not use it.

ob.ste.tri.cian /£ ˌɒb.stə'trɪʃ.ᵊn, $ ˌɑ:b-/ *n.* specialist in delivery of babies

متخصص زایمان، ماما، پزشک متخصص زایمان
Her *obstetrician* could not be present at the birth.

ob.strep.er.ous /£ əb'strep.ᵊr.əs, $ ɑ:b'strep.ɚ.əs/ *adj.* noisy, boisterous

غیرقابل کنترل، پر سر و صدا، شلوغ، عربده‌جو، مهار گسیخته
The crowd became *obstreperous* and shouted their disapproval of the proposals made by the speaker.

ob.trude /əb'tru:d/ *v.* to push into prominence

(نظر خود را) تحمیل کردن؛ بزرگ جلوه دادن؛ سرزده وارد شدن
The members of the group object to the manner in which you *obtrude* your opinions into matters of no concern to you.

ob.tru.sion: *n.*   مزاحمت

ob.tru.sive: *adj.*   خودنما؛ مزاحم، فضول

ob.tuse /£ əb'tjuːs, $ -'tuːs/ *adj.* blunt, stupid

احمق، کند ذهن، کودن، خنگ

Because he was so *obtuse*, he could not follow the teacher's reasoning and asked foolish questions.

ob.vi.ate /£ 'ɒb.vi.eɪt, $ 'aːb-/ *v.* to make unnecessary, to get rid of

برطرف کردن، رفع کردن، از سر راه برداشتن

I hope this contribution will *obviate* any need for further collections of funds.

Oc.ci.dent /£ 'ɒk.sɪ.dᵊnt, $ 'aːk.sə-/ *n.* the west

غرب، کشورهای غربی

It will take time for *the Occident* to understand the ways and customs of the Orient.

oc.ci.den.tal: *adj.*

غربی، (مربوط به) غرب

oc.cult /£ 'ɒk.ʌlt, $ 'aː.kʌlt/ *adj.* mysterious, secret, supernatural

پوشیده، سری، ماوراءالطبیعه، غیبی

The *occult* rites of the organization were revealed only to members.

oc.u.list /£ 'ɒk.jʊ.lɪst, $ 'aː.kjə-/ *n.* optometrist, ophthalmologist

متخصص چشم، چشم‌پزشک

In many states, an *oculist* is the only one who may apply medicinal drops to the eyes for the purpose of examining them.

o.di.ous /£ 'əʊ.di.əs, $ 'oʊ-/ *adj.* hateful

نفرت‌انگیز، چندش‌آور

I find the task of punishing you most *odious*.

o.di.um /£ ˈəʊ.di.əm, $ ˈoʊ-/ *n.* dislike, repugnance

نفرت، تنفر، انزجار

I cannot express the *odium* I feel at your heinous actions.

o.dor.if.er.ous /əʊ.dəˈrɪf.ər.əs/ *adj.* giving off an odor

معطر، عطرآگین

The *odoriferous* spices stimulated his jaded appetite.

o.dor.ous /ˈəʊ.də.r.əs/ *adj.* having an odor

معطر، عطرآگین، خوشبو؛ بودار

This variety of hybrid tea-rose is more *odorous* than the one you have in your garden.

of.fal /£ ˈɒf.ᵊl, $ ˈɑːfᵊl/ *n.* waste, garbage

آشغال، پس‌مانده

In America, we discard as *offal* that which could feed families in less fortunate parts of the world.

of.fi.cious /əˈfɪʃ.əs/ *adj.* meddlesome, excessively trying to please

ریاست مآب، امر و نهی کن، بد منصب

We were tired of being pushed around by *officious* civil servants.

o.gle /£ ˈəʊ.gl, $ ˈoʊ-/ *v.* to glance coquettishly at, to make eyes at

چشم‌چرانی کردن، هیز نگاه کردن به

Most women dislike being *ogled* (at).

ol.fac.to.ry /£ ɒlˈfæk.tᵊr.i, $ ɑːlˈfæk.ter.i/ *adj.* concerning the sense of smell

ol.ig.ar.chy /£ ˈɒl.ɪ.gɑː.ki, $ ˈɑːlɪ.gɑːr-/ *n.* government by a few

الیگارشی، جرگه سالاری

Do you think *oligarchy* is preferable to dictatorship?

om.i.nous /£ ˈɒm.ɪ.nəs, $ ˈɑː.mə-/ *adj.* threatening

شوم، بدشگون؛ تهدیدآمیز

Those black clouds look a bit *ominous*.

om.nip.o.tent /£ ɒmˈnɪp.ə.tᵊnt, $ ɑːmˈnɪp.ə.tənt/ *adj.* all-powerful

مقتدر، قدرتمند؛ (با حروف بزرگ) قادر متعال

The monarch regarded himself as *omnipotent* and responsible to no one for his acts.

om.ni.pres.ent /£ ˌɒm.nɪˈprez.ᵊnt, $ ˌɑːm-/ *adj.* universally present, ubiquitous

همه جا حاضر، حاضر در همه جا، موجود در همه جا

She has been *omnipresent* in the media since the song went to number one in the charts.

om.ni.sci.ent /£ ɒmˈnɪs.i.ənt, $ ɑːmˈnɪʃ.ᵊnt/ *adj.* all-knowing

(صفت خدا) عالم مطلق؛ دانای کل، عالم کل

Christians and Muslims believe that God is *Omniscient*.

om.niv.o.rous /£ ɒmˈnɪv.ᵊr.əs, $ ɑːmˈnɪv.ɚ-/ *adj.* eating both plant and animal food

همه چیز خوار

Some animals, including man, are *omnivorous*; others are either carnivorous or herbivorous.

on.er.ous /£ ˈəʊ.nᵊr.əs, £ ˈɒn.ᵊr-, $ ˈɑː.nɚ-/ *adj.* burdensome

سنگین، شاق، پرزحمت

He asked for an assistant because his work load was too *onerous*.

on.o.mat.o.poe.ia /£ ˈɒn.əʊˌmæt.əˈpiː.ə, $ ˌɑː.noʊˌmæt̬.oʊ-/ *n.* words formed in imitation of natural sounds

نام‌آوا (در زبان‌شناسی)

Words like "hiss" and "cuckoo" are illustrations of *onomatopoeia*.

on.slaught /£ ˈɒn.slɔːt, $ ˈɑːn.slɑːt/ *n.* vicious attack

حملهٔ شدید و بی‌امان

They survived an *onslaught* by tribesmen.

o.nus /£ ˈəʊ.nəs, $ ˈoʊ-/ *n.* burden, responsibility

وظیفه، مسئولیت، تعهد، بار

The *onus* of bringing up five children lies with her.

o.pal.es.cent /£ ˈəʊ.pəlˈes.ənt, $ ˌoʊ-/ *adj.* iridescent

رنگین کمانی، قزح‌سان، دارای تابش قوس قزحی

The Ancient Mariner admired the *opalescent* sheen on the water.

o.paque /£ əʊˈpeɪk, $ oʊ-/ *adj.* dark, not transparent

تیره، مات، کدر، تار، تیره

I want something *opaque* placed in this window so that no one will be able to watch me.

o.pi.ate /£ ˈəʊ.pi.ət, $ ˈoʊ-/ *n.* sleep producer, deadener of pain

داروی مخدر، افیون، عامل تخدیر

By such *opiate*, he made the people forget their difficulties and accept their unpleasant circumstances.

op.por.tune /£ ˈɒp.ə.tjuːn, $ ˌɑː.pɚˈtuːn/ *adj.* timely, well-chosen

بجا، به‌موقع؛ مناسب

Your arrival was most **opportune**.

op.por.tun.i.sm: *n.*   فرصت‌طلبی
op.por.tun.ist: *n.*   فرصت‌طلب

op.pro.bri.ous /£ əˈprəʊ.bri.əs, $ -ˈproʊ-/ *adj.* disgraceful

توهین‌آمیز، اهانت آمیز، تحقیرآمیز، شرم‌آور

I find your conduct so **opprobrious** that I must exclude you from classes.

op.pro.bri.um: *n.*   اهانت، سرزنش؛ رسوایی، ننگ، خفت

op.ti.cian /£ ɒpˈtɪʃ.ən, $ ɑːp-/ *n.* maker and seller of eyeglasses

عینک‌ساز، عینک فروش؛ بینایی سنج

The patient took the prescription given him by his oculist to the **optician**.

op.ti.mal /£ ˈɒp.tɪ.məl, $ ˈɑːp-/ *adj.* most favorable

مطلوب‌ترین، مناسب‌ترین، بهترین

If you wait for the **optimal** moment to act, you may never begin your project.

op.ti.mum: *n.*   بهترین وضعیت، بهینه

op.ti.mist /£ ˈɒp.tɪ.mɪst, $ ˈɑːp.tə-/ *n.* person who looks on the bright side

(آدم) خوش‌بین، امیدوار

The pessimist says the glass is half-empty; the **optimist** says it is half-full.

op.ti.mi.sm: *n.*   خوش‌بینی، آیین خوش‌بینی

op.to.me.trist /£ ɒpˈtɒm.ə.trɪst, $ ɑːpˈtɑː.mə-/ *n.* one who fits glasses to remedy visual defects

چشم‌پزشک، متخصص بینایی سنج

Although an *optometrist* is qualified to treat many eye disorders, he may not use medicines or surgery in his examinations.

op.u.lence /£ ˈɒp.jʊ.lənts, $ ˈɑːpjʊ-/ *n.* wealth

ثروت؛ رفاه، فراوانی و توانگری، ناز و نعمت

Visitors from Europe are amazed at the *opulence* of this country.

o.pus /£ ˈəʊ.pəs, $ ˈoʊ-/ *n.* work of art, a piece of music

اثر هنری، قطعه موسیقیایی، اثر موسیقیایی

He showed us his latest *opus*, a rather awful painting of a vase of flowers.

or.a.to.ri.o /£ ˌɒr.əˈtɔː.ri.əʊ, $ ˌɔːr.əˈtɔːr.i.oʊ/ *n.* dramatic poem set to music

اُراتوریو، تصنیف موزیکال با موضوع مذهبی

The Glee Club decided to present an *oratorio* during their recital.

or.din.ance /£ ˈɔː.dɪ.nənts, $ ˈɔːr.dᵊn.ᵊnts/ *n.* decree

امر، حکم، فرمان؛ (مجازی) مقررات

Passing a red light is a violation of a city *ordinance*.

o.ri.en.ta.tion /£ ˌɔː.ri.enˈteɪ.ʃᵊn, $ ˌɔːr.i-/ *n.* act of finding oneself in society

تشخیص موقعیت، درک وضعیت؛ جهت‌یابی؛ آشنایی، خوگیری

The job is open to everyone, irrespective of political *orientation*.

o.ri.en.tate: *v.* علاقمند کردن به، آشنا ساختن با

or.i.fice /£ ˈɒr.ɪ.fɪs, $ ˈɔːr.ə-/ *n.* mouthlike opening

دهانه، دهان، منفذ

Blood flowed from his facial *orifices*.

or.nate /£ ɔːˈneɪt, $ ɔːr-/ *adj.* highly decorated

پر زرق و برق، پر زر و زیور، مزین، آراسته؛ (سبک ادبی) متکلّف

That style of architecture is too *ornate* for my taste.

or.ni.thol.o.gist /£ ˌɔː.nɪˈθɒl.ə.dʒɪst, $ ˌɔːr.nəˈθɑː.lə-/ *n.* scientific student of birds

پرنده شناس

His drawings of bird life have been of interest to the *ornithologists*.

or.ni.thol.o.gy: *n.* پرنده‌شناسی

o.ro.tund /ˈɒ.rə.tʌnd/ *adj.* having a resonant quality, inflated speech

(صدا) پرطنین؛ مُغلّق، مطنطن

The politician found that his *orotund* voice was an asset when he spoke to his constituents.

or.thog.ra.phy /£ ɔːˈθɒɡ.rə.fi, $ ɔːˈθɑː.ɡrə-/ *n.* correct spelling

املای صحیح؛ نظام خط

Many of us find English *orthography* difficult to master because most of the words are not written phonetically.

os.cil.late /£ ˈɒs.ɪ.leɪt, $ ˈɑː.sᵊl.eɪt/ *v.* to swing back and forth, to waver

نوسان کردن، در نوسان بودن؛ مردد بودن، دو دل بودن

He *oscillates* between political extremes.

os.si.fy /£ ˈɒs.ɪ.faɪ, $ ˈɑː.sə-/ *v.* to change or harden into bone

سخت شدن، استخوانی شدن؛ متحجر شدن/کردن

Years of easy success had *ossified* the company's thinking.

os.ten.si.ble /£ ɒsˈtentsɪbl̩, $ ɑːˈstent-/ *adj.* apparent, pretended

ظاهری، صوری

The *ostensible* goal was to clean up the government corruption, but their real aim was to unseat the government.

os.ten.ta.tious /£ ˌɒs.tenˈteɪ.ʃəs, $ ˌɑː.stən-/ *adj.* showy, pretentious

تجملی، پر زرق و برق؛ متظاهرانه

They criticized the *ostentatious* lifestyle of their leader.

o.stra.cize /£ ˈɒs.trə.saɪz, $ ˈɑː.strə-/ *v.* to exclude from public favor, to ban

منزوی کردن، طرد کردن، قبول نکردن، نپذیرفتن، از خود راندن

He was *ostracized* by his colleagues for refusing to support the strike.

o.stra.ci.sm: *n.*

طرد، انزوا

oust /aʊst/ *v.* to expel, to drive out

برکنار کردن، معزول کردن، اخراج کردن

He was *ousted* from his position as chairman.

o.vert /£ əʊˈvɜːt, $ oʊˈvɜːrt/ *adj.* open to view

علنی، آشکار، واضح

The *overt* aim of the proposal is to improve productivity.

o.ver.ween.ing /£ ˌəʊ.vəˈwiːnɪŋ, $ ˌoʊ.vɚ-/ *adj.* arrogant, presumptuous

خودپسندانه؛ افراطی، زیاده از حد، خارج از حد اعتدال

His ***overweening*** pride in his accomplishments was not justified.

o.vine /ˈəʊ.vaɪn/ *adj.* like a sheep

گوسفندوار، گوسفند مانند

How ***ovine*** these true believers were, following their shepherds thoughtlessly.

o.void /ˈəʊ.vɔɪd/ *adj.* egg-shaped

تخم‌مرغی، بیضی شکل، بیضی

At Easter she had to cut out hundreds of brightly colored ***ovoid*** shapes.

لیستی از لغاتی که در جملات بخش O به کار رفته‌اند:

amend: *v.*	اصلاح کردن	herbivorous: *adj.*	گیاه‌خوار
appetite: *n.*	اشتها	irrespective (of): *adj.*	بدون توجه (به)
asset: *n.*	نعمت، موهبت		
carnivorous: *adj.*	گوشتخوار	jaded: *adj.*	دلزده، سیر، خسته
constituent: *n.*	رأی دهنده	remedy: *v.*	درمان کردن
defect: *n.*	عیب، نقص	rites: *n.*	مراسم
demeanor: *n.*	رفتار	sheen: *n.*	درخشندگی
drag in: *v.*	پیش کشیدن	stimulate: *v.*	تحریک کردن
heinous: *adj.*	زشت	unseat: *v.*	از قدرت ساقط کردن

P p

pach.y.derm /£ ˈpæk.ɪ.dɜːm, $ -dɜːrm/ *n.* thick-skinned animal

جانور پوست کلفت (مانند کرگدن و فیل)

The elephant is probably the best known *pachyderm*.

pac.i.fist /ˈpæs.ɪ.fɪst/ *n.* one opposed to force, antimilitarist

صلح‌طلب، صلح‌دوست، طرفدار صلح و مخالف جنگ

The *pacifist* urged that we reduce our military budget and recall our troops stationed overseas.

pad.dock /ˈpæd.ək/ *n.* saddling enclosure at race track; lot for exercising horses

محل تربیت اسب، محوطهٔ آماده کردن اسب‌ها پیش از مسابقه

The *paddock* is located directly in front of the grandstand so that all may see the horses being saddled and the jockeys mounted.

pae.an /ˈpiː.ən/ *n.* song of praise or joy

سرود پیروزی یا نیایش

They sang *paeans* for their safe arrival.

pains.tak.ing /ˈpeɪnzˌteɪ.kɪŋ/ *adj.* showing hard work, taking great care

پر زحمت، موشکافانه؛ بسیار دقیق

The new high-frequency word list is the result of

painstaking efforts on the part of our research staff.

pal.at.a.ble /£ ˈpæl.ə.tə.bl̩, $ -tə-/ *adj.* agreeable, pleasing to the taste

خوشمزه، لذیذ، خوشایند، خوش طعم، مطبوع

Paying taxes can never be made *palatable*.

pa.la.ti.al /pəˈleɪ.ʃᵊl/ *adj.* magnificent

مجلل، با شکوه، کاخ مانند، قصر مانند

He proudly showed us his *palatial* home.

pa.la.ver /£ pəˈlɑː.vəʳ, $ -ˈlæv.ɚ/ *n.* discussion, misleading speech, chatter

جار و جنجال، داد و قال، الم شنگه؛ جرّ و بحث

What a *palaver* there was about paying the bill!

pal.ette /ˈpæl.ət/ *n.* board on which painter mixes pigments

تخته رنگ نقاشی، تخته شستی

At the present time, art supply stores are selling a paper *palette* which may be discarded after use.

pal.let /ˈpæl.ɪt/ *n.* small and poor bed

تختخواب ناراحت و بدون فنر؛ تشک کاهی

The weary traveler went to sleep on his straw *pallet*.

pal.li.ate /ˈpæ.lɪ.eɪt/ *v.* to ease pain; to make less guilty or offensive

(بهطور موقت) تسکین دادن درد؛ کوچک نشان دادن (جرم)

Doctors must *palliate* that which they cannot cure.

pal.li.a.tion: *n.* تسکین

pal.lid /ˈpæl.ɪd/ *adj.* pale, wan

رنگ پریده، زرد، کمرنگ

You look a bit *pallid* – do you feel all right?

pal.pa.ble /ˈpæl.pə.bl̩/ *adj.* tangible, easily perceptible

ملموس، محسوس؛ آشکار، مشهود، واضح

I cannot understand how you could overlook such a *palpable* blunder.

pal.pi.tate /£ ˈpæl.pɪ.teɪt, $ -pə-/ *v.* to throb, to flutter

(قلب) تپش داشتن، تند زدن؛ لرزیدن

As he became excited, his heart began to *palpitate* more and more erratically.

pal.try /£ ˈpɔːl.tri, $ ˈpɑːl-/ *adj.* insignificant, petty

بی‌ارزش، بی‌اهمیت، بی‌مقدار؛ ناچیز، کم، اندک

This is a *paltry* sum to pay for such a masterpiece.

pan.a.ce.a /ˌpæn.əˈsiː.ə/ *n.* cure-all, remedy for all diseases

نوشدارو، دوای هر درد

There's no single *panacea* for the country's economic ills.

pan.de.mo.ni.um /£ ˌpæn.dəˈməʊ.ni.əm, $ -ˈmoʊ-/ *n.* wild tumult

غوغا، آشوب، اغتشاش، هیاهو، قشقرق

There was *pandemonium* when the news was announced.

pan.der /£ ˈpæn.də, $ -dɚ/ *v.* to cater to the low desires of others

(امیال و غیره) ارضا کردن، به امیال یا خواسته‌های (کسی) تسلیم شدن

Books which *pander to* man's lowest instincts should be banned.

pan.e.gyr.ic /ˌpæn.əˈdʒɪr.ɪk/ *n.* formal praise

مدیحه

The modest hero blushed as he listened to the *panegyric* uttered by the speakers about his valorous act.

pan.o.ply /ˈpæn.ə.pli/ *n.* full set of armor

زره کامل سراسری

The medieval knight in full *panoply* found his movements limited by the weight of his armor.

pan.o.ram.a /£ ˌpæn.əˈrɑː.mə, $ -əˈræm.ə/ *n.* comprehensive view

دورنما، منظرهٔ باز، چشم‌انداز

From the summit there is a superb *panorama* of the Alps.

pan.to.mime /£ ˈpæn.tə.maɪm, $ -t̬ə-/ *n.* acting without dialogue

نمایش بدون کلام، نمایش صامت، پانتومیم

Because he worked in *pantomime*, the clown could be understood wherever he appeared.

pa.py.rus /£ pəˈpaɪə.rəs, $ -ˈpaɪ-/ *n.* ancient paper made from stem of papyrus plant

کاغذ پاپیروس؛ گیاه پاپیروس

The ancient Egyptians were among the first to write on *papyrus*.

par.a.ble /£ ˈpær.ə.bl̩, $ ˈper-/ *n.* short, simple story teaching a moral

داستان تمثیلی، حکایت، داستان

Let us apply to our own conduct the lessons that Sa'di's *parables* teach.

par.a.digm /£ ˈpær.ə.daɪm, $ ˈper-/ *n.* model, example, pattern

الگو، نمونه، مدل

Some of these educators are hoping to produce a change in the current cultural *paradigm*.

par.a.dox /£ ˈpær.ə.dɒks, $ ˈper.ə.dɑːks/ *n.* a contradictory statement

گفتهٔ متناقض، بیان متناقض، تناقض‌گویی، ضد و نقیض

It is a ***paradox*** that the French eat so much rich food and yet have a relatively low rate of heart disease.

pa.ra.dox.i.cal: *adj.*   (دارای) تضاد/تناقض، متناقض، متضاد

par.a.gon /£ ˈpær.ə.gɒn, $ ˈper.ə.gɑːn/ *n.* model of perfection

نمونه، نمونهٔ کامل، نمونهٔ عالی، مظهر

The class disliked him because the teacher was always pointing to him as a ***paragon*** of virtue.

par.al.lel.i.sm /£ ˈpær.ə.lel.ɪzm, $ ˈper-/ *n.* similarity

تشابه، مشابهت، برابری، همانندی

Don't exaggerate the ***parallelism*** between the two cases.

pa.ra.me.ter /£ pəˈræm.ɪ.tər, $ -ə.tɚ/ *n.* limit, independent variable

پارامتر، حد، اندازه، محدودیت، شاخص

We have to work within the ***parameter*** of time and budget.

par.a.mour /£ ˈpær.ə.mɔːr, ˈper.ə.mur/ *n.* illicit lover

معشوقه

She sought a divorce on the grounds that her husband had a ***paramour*** in another town.

par.a.noi.a /£ ˌpær.əˈnɔɪ.ə, $ ˌper-/ *n.* mental illness which is chronic form of insanity

پارانویا؛ بدگمانی، کج خیالی

There's a lot of ***paranoia*** about crime at the moment.

par.a.noid: *n.*   بیمار پارانویایی؛ بدگمان؛ (فکر، تصور و غیره) بی‌اساس،

واهی

par.a.pet /£ ˈpær.ə.pet, $ ˈper-/ *n.* low wall at edge of roof or balcony

دیواره (بالکن، پل، پشت بام)؛ سنگر، خاکریز، جان پناه

We sat down on the *parapet* and looked down over the city.

par.a.pher.na.li.a /£ ˌpær.ə.fəˈneɪ.li.ə, $ ˌper.ə.fɚˈneɪ.ljə/ *n.* equipment, odds and ends

وسایل، لوازم و متعلقات، ساز و برگ

His desk was cluttered with paper, pen, ink and other *paraphernalia* of the writing craft.

pa.ra.phrase /£ ˈpær.ə.freɪz, $ ˈper-/ *v., n.* to restate a passage in one's own words

به بیان دیگر گفتن، تعبیر کردن؛ بیانِ دیگر، تعبیر

In 250 words or less, *paraphrase* this article.

par.a.site /£ ˈpær.ə.saɪt, $ ˈper-/ *n.* animal or plant living on another, toady, sycophant

انگل؛ طفیلی، آدم سربار

The older drugs didn't deal effectively with the malaria *parasite*.

    live as a *parasite* on society   سربار/ طفیلی جامعه بودن
    par.a.si.tic: *adj.*   انگلی، طفیلی وار
    par.a.si.ti.cal.ly: *adv.*   انگل وار، به شکل طفیلی

pa.ri.ah /pəˈraɪə/ *n.* social outcast

(آدم) رانده شده از جامعه، مطرود، منفور

I am not a *pariah* to be shunned and ostracized.

par.i.ty /£ ˈpær.ə.ti, $ ˈper.ə.t̬i/ *n.* equality, close resemblance

برابر، تساوی، یکسانی

I find your analogy inaccurate because I do not see the *parity* between the two illustrations.

par.lance /£ ˈpɑː.lənts, $ ˈpɑːr-/ *n.* language, idiom

زبان، اصطلاح، بیان، گفتگو

All this legal *parlance* confuses me; I need an interpreter.

par.ley /£ ˈpɑː.li, $ ˈpɑːr-/ *n., v.* conference

مذاکره، گفتگو؛ مذاکره کردن (با دشمن در مورد شرایط صلح)

The peace *parley* has not produced the anticipated truce.

par.o.dy /£ ˈpær.ə.di, $ ˈper-/ *n., v.* humorous imitation, travesty

(ادبیات) تقلید شوخی‌آمیز؛ ادا، مضحکه؛ تقلید (از سبک دیگری) کردن

We enjoyed the clever *parodies* of popular songs which the chorus sang.

par.ox.y.sm /£ ˈpær.ɒk.sɪ.zᵊm, $ ˈper.ək-/ *n.* fit or attack of pain, laughter, rage

طغیان، غلیان (درد، خشم و نظایر آن) ، حمله

He went into a *paroxysm* of rage.

par.ri.cide /£ ˈpær.ɪ.saɪd, $ ˈper.ə-/ *n.* murder of a father

قتل پدر، پدرکُشی

The jury was shocked by the details of this vicious *parricide*.

par.ry /£ ˈpær.i, $ ˈper-/ *v.* to ward off a blow

(حمله، ضربه) دفع کردن؛ از جواب دادن طفره رفتن

He was content to wage a defensive battle and tried to *parry* his opponent's thrusts.

par.si.mo.ni.ous /£ ˌpɑː.sɪˈməʊ.ni.əs, $ ˌpɑːr.səˈmoʊ-/ *adj.*

stingy, excessively frugal

خسیس، ممسک، کنس

His ***parsimonious*** nature did not permit him to enjoy any luxuries.

par.si.mo.ny: *n.*   خسّت، امساک، صرفه‌جویی

par.ti.al.i.ty /£ ˌpɑː.ʃiˈæl.ə.ti, $ ˌpɑːr.ʃiˈæl.ə.t̬i/ *n.* inclination, bias

طرفداری، جانبداری، تبعیض، غرض‌ورزی

He judged the case without ***partiality***.

par.tial: *adj.*   مغرض، جانبدار؛ جزئی

partially: *adv.*   مغرضانه، جانبدارانه؛ به‌طور ناقص. به‌طور جزئی

par.ti.san /£ ˌpɑː.tɪˈzæn, $ ˈpɑːr.t̬ɪ.zən/ *adj.* one-sided, prejudiced, committed to a party

تعصب‌آمیز، کورکورانه؛ متعصب؛ حامی پر و پا قرص، مرید، طرفدار

You must listen to both points of view and try not to be ***partisan***.

par.tu.ri.tion /£ ˌpɑː.tjʊəˈrɪʃ.ᵊn, $ ˌpɑːr.tuːˈrɪʃ-/ *n.* delivery, childbirth

زایمان، وضع حمل

The difficulties anticipated by the obstetricians at ***parturition*** did not materialize; it was a normal delivery.

par.ve.nu /£ ˈpɑː.və.nuː, $ ˈpɑːr-/ *n.* upstart, newly rich person

تازه به دوران رسیده، نوکیسه

Although extremely wealthy, he was regarded as a ***parvenu*** by the aristocratic members of society.

pas.sé /£ pɑːˈseɪ, $ pæsˈeɪ/ *adj.* old-fashioned, past the prime

کهنه، قدیمی، از مُد افتاده

His style is *passé* and reminiscent of the Victorian era.

pas.sive /ˈpæs.ɪv/ *adj.* not active, acted upon

منفعل، بی‌تفاوت، بی‌اعتنا، منفی

Mahatma Gandhi urged his followers to pursue a program of *passive* resistance as he felt that it was more effective than violence.

pas.si.vi.ty: *n.* عدم تحرک، بی‌حالی، بی‌تفاوتی

pas.tiche /£ pæsˈtiːʃ, $ pɑːˈstiːʃ/ *n.* imitation of another's style

(هنر) اثر تقلیدی، هنر تقلیدی

The film is a skillful, witty *pastiche* of 'Jaws'.

pas.to.ral /£ ˈpɑː.stᵊr.ᵊl, $ ˈpæs.tɚ-/ *adj.* rural

روستایی، چوپانی؛ ساده، بی‌پیرایه

In these stories of *pastoral* life, we find an understanding of the daily tasks of country folk.

pa.tent /£ ˈpeɪ.tᵊnt, $ ˈpæt.ᵊnt/ *adj.* open for the public to read, obvious

واضح، آشکار، روشن

It was *patent* to anyone that she disliked the idea.

pa.thet.ic /£ pəˈθet.ɪk, $ -ˈθet̬-/ *adj.* causing sadness, compassion, pity-touching

رقت‌انگیز، تأثرآور، اسف‌انگیز، غم‌انگیز

Everyone in the auditorium was weeping by the time he finished his *pathetic* tale about the orphaned boy.

pa.the.ti.cal.ly: *adv.* به‌طور اسف‌باری، به‌طور رقت‌انگیزی

path.o.log.i.cal /£ ˌpæθ.əˈlɒdʒ.ɪ.kᵊl, $ -ˈlɑː.dʒɪ-/ *adj.* related to disease

آسیب‌شناختی، مربوط به علم تشخیص امراض؛ بیمارگونه؛ بی‌دلیل

1) The students study the *pathological* aspects of this disease.

2) I have got a *pathological* fear of heights.

pa.thol.o.gy: *n.* آسیب‌شناسی

pa.thol.og.ist: *n.* آسیب‌شناس

pa.thos /£ ˈpeɪ.θɒs, $ -θɑːs/ *n.* tender sorrow, pity, evoking pity

تأثّر، غم‌انگیزی، رقت‌باری، اسفناکی؛ حالتِ رقت‌بار

There is a *pathos* in his performance which he never lets slide into sentimentality.

pat.i.na /£ ˈpæt.ɪ.nə, $ -ᵊn.ə/ *n.* green crust on old bronze works

زنگار؛ لایه، پوشش؛ جلا، درخشندگی

Judging by the *patina* on his bronze statue, we can conclude that this is the work of a medieval artist.

pat.ois /ˈpæt.wɑː/ *n.* local or provincial dialect

لهجه، گویش

He speaks the local *patois*.

pa.tri.arch /£ ˈpeɪ.tri.ɑːk, $ -ɑːrk/ *n.* father or ruler of a family or tribe

مرد خانواده؛ رئیس قبیله، بزرگ خاندان؛ ریش سفید

In many primitive tribes, the leader and lawmaker was the *patriarch*.

pa.tri.ar.chy: *n.* (نظام) مرد سالاری، (نظام) پدرسالاری

pa.tri.ar.chal: *adj.* مرد سالار؛ پدر سالار

pa.tri.ar.chate: *n.* مقام اسقفی؛ دوره اسقفی

pat.ri.cide /£ ˈpæt.rɪ.saɪd, $ ˈpæt.rə-/ *n.* murder of a father

پدرکُشی؛ پدرکش

The words parricide and **patricide** have exactly the same meaning.

pat.ri.mo.ny /ˈpæt.rɪ.mə.nɪ/ *n.* inheritance from father

ارث پدری؛ موقوفهٔ کلیسا

As predicted by his critics, he spent his *patrimony* within two years of his father's death.

pat.ri.mo.ni.al: *adj.* موروثی، ارثی

pa.tron.ize /£ ˈpæt.rə.naɪz, $ ˈpeɪ.trə-/ *v.* to support, to act superior toward

حمایت کردن، مورد لطف و مرحمت قرار دادن، تشویق کردن

Experts in a field sometimes appear to *patronize* people who are less knowledgeable of the subject.

pa.tron: *n.* حامی، مشوّق، پشتیبان

pau.ci.ty /£ ˈpɔː.sɪ.ti, $ ˈpɑː.sə.t̬i/ *n.* scarcity

کمی، کمبود، قلّت

There is a *paucity* of information on the ingredients of many cosmetics.

pec.ca.dil.lo /£ ˌpek.əˈdɪl.əʊ, $ -oʊ/ *n.* slight offense, a small fault

لغزش، خطا، اشتباه، معصیت کوچک

The President's sexual *peccadillo* were widely known about.

pe.cu.ni.a.ry /£ pɪˈkjuː.njᵊr.i, $ -ni.er-/ *adj.* related to money

پولی، مالی، مادّی

I never expected a *pecuniary* reward for my work in this activity.

ped.a.gogue /£ ˈped.ə.ɡɒɡ, $ -ɡɑːɡ/ *n.* teacher, dull and formal teacher

معلم سخت‌گیر و خشک، معلم مقرراتی

He could never be a stuffy *pedagogue*; his classes were always lively and filled with humor.

ped.ant /'ped.ᵊnt/ *n.* learned bore

آدم ملانقطی؛ آدم فضل فروش

His insistence that the book be memorized marked the teacher as a *pedant* rather than a scholar.

ped.ant.ry: *n.* فضل‌فروشی؛ خرده‌گیری

pe.dan.tic /£ pəˈdæn.tɪk, $ pedˈæn-/ *adj.* showing off learning, bookish

ناشی از فضل فروشی؛ خرده‌گیرانه؛ مقرراتی؛ خشک

What you say is *pedantic* and reveals an unfamiliarity with the realities of life.

pe.dan.ti.cal.ly: *adv.* از روی فضل فروشی

pe.des.tri.an /pəˈdes.tri.ən/ *adj.* ordinary, unimaginative

خالی از لطف و هیجان، بی‌روح، خشک؛ معمولی

Unintentionally boring, he wrote page after page of *pedestrian* prose.

pe.di.a.tri.cian /ˌpiː.di.əˈtrɪʃ.ᵊn/ *n.* expert in children's disease

پزشک اطفال، متخصص کودکان

The family doctor advised the parents to consult *pediatrician* about their child's ailment.

pe.di.at.rics: *n.* پزشکی / طب اطفال

pe.di.at.ric: *adj.* مربوط به پزشکی / طب اطفال

ped.i.ment /'ped.ɪ.mənt/ *n.* triangular gablelike decoration on a building

(معماری) سنتوری
The *pediment* of the building was filled with sculptures and adorned with elaborate scrollwork.

pe.jor.a.tive /£ prˈdʒɒr.ə.tɪv, $ -ˈdʒɔːr.ə.t̬ɪv/ *adj.* having a negative or degrading effect

تحقیرآمیز، توهین‌آمیز؛ منفی، بد
His use of *pejorative* language indicated his contempt for his audience.

pell-mell /ˌpelˈmel/ *adv., adj.* in confusion, disorderly

سراسیمه، شتاب‌زده، با عجله؛ درهم برهم، قروقاتی
The excited students dashed *pell-mell* into the stadium to celebrate the victory.

pel.lu.cid /pɪˈljuː.sɪd/ *adj.* transparent, limpid, easy to understand

شفاف، بلورین؛ واضح، سلیس، روان، روشن
After reading these stodgy philosophers, I find his *pellucid* style very enjoyable.

pen.ance /ˈpen.ənts/ *n.* self-imposed punishment for sin

توبه؛ عذاب؛ مجازات، جریمه
1) They are doing *penance for* their sins.
2) As a *penance*, she said she would buy them all a box of chocolate.

pen.chant /£ ˈpɑ̃ːŋ.ʃɑ̃ːŋ, $ ˈpen.tʃənt/ *n.* strong inclination, liking

میل شدید، علاقهٔ وافر، رغبت
He had a *penchant for* sculpture.

pen.dant /ˈpen.dənt/ *n.* a piece of jewellery which is worn round the neck, with an object hanging from it

گردنبند

She was wearing a crystal *pendant*.

pen.dent /ˈpen.dᵊnt/ *adj.* hanging from or over something

معلق، آویزان

Her *pendent* errings glistered in the light.

pen.dul.ous /£ ˈpen.djʊ.ləs, $ -dʒə.ləs/ *adj.* hanging, suspended

آویخته، آویزان، معلق

The *pendulous* chandeliers swayed in the breeze and gave the impression that they were about to fall from the ceiling.

pen.i.tent /ˈpen.ɪ.tᵊnt/ *adj.* regretting sth wrong you have done

نادم، توبه‌کار، پشیمان، شرمسار از گناه

When he realized the enormity of his crime, he became remorseful and *penitent*.

pen.i.tence: *n.* پشیمانی، ندامت، توبه

pen.i.ten.ti.al: *adj.* نادم، تائب، پشیمان

pen.sive /ˈpentˌsɪv/ *adj.* thoughtful, dreamily thoughtful

غرقه در فکر، توأم با تفکر؛ غمگین، محزون

The *pensive* youth gazed at the painting for a long time and then sighed.

pen.sive.ly: *adv.* فکورانه؛ با تأمل؛ غمگنانه

pe.num.bra /pɪˈnʌm.brə/ *n.* partial shadow (in an eclipse)

نیم سایه، سایه روشن

During an eclipse, we can see an area of total darkness and a lighter area which is the *penumbra*.

pe.nu.ri.ous /pɪ'njʊə.rɪ.əs/ adj. stingy, parsimonious; extremely poor

خسیس، ممسک؛ فقیر، تنگدست، تهیدست

He was a *penurious* man, averse to spending money even for the necessities of life.

pen.u.ry: *n.* فقر، تنگدستی، مسکنت، تهیدستی

pe.on /'piːən/ *n.* unskilled laborer, drudge

کارگر ساده و روزمزد، حمّال

He was doomed to be a *peon*, to live a lowly life of drudgery and toil.

per.cus.sion /£ pə'kʌʃ.ᵊn, $ pɚ-/ *adj.* striking one object against another sharply

کوبش، ضربه، ضربت؛ سازهای کوبه‌ای

The drum is a *percussion* instrument.

per.di.tion /£ pə'dɪʃ.ᵊn, $ pɚ-/ *n.* damnation; complete ruin

عذاب ابدی، نابودی، فنا

He was damned to eternal *perdition*.

per.e.grin.a.tion /ˌper.ə.grɪ'neɪ.ʃᵊn/ *n.* journey

مسافرت، سفر، سیاحت، جهانگردی

His *peregrination* in foreign lands did not bring understanding.

per.empt.o.ry /£ pə'remp.tᵊr.i, $ -tɚ-/ *adj.* demanding and leaving no choice

آمرانه، تحکم‌آمیز؛ واجب‌الاجراء، بی‌چون و چرا، نهایی

I resent your *peremptory* attitude.

per.empt.or.i.ly: *adv.* با تحکم. آمرانه

per.en.ni.al /pə'ren.i.əl/ *n.*, *adj.* something long-lasting

گیاه چند ساله؛ پایدار، درازمدت؛ دایم، دایمی

These plants are hardy *perennials* and will bloom for many years.

per.fid.i.ous /£ pə'fɪd.i.əs, $ pɚ-/ *adj.* basely false

پیمان شکن، فریبکار، خائن؛ غلط، گمراه کننده

Your *perfidious* gossip is malicious and dangerous.

per.fi.dy: *n.* خیانت، خیانتکاری، پیمانشکنی

per.force /£ pə'fɔːs, $ pɚ'fɔːrs/ *adv.* of necessity

بناچار، بالاجبار، ناگزیر

I must *perforce* leave, as my train is about to start.

per.funct.o.ry /£ pə'fʌŋk.tᵊr.i, $ pɚ'fʌŋk.tɚ.i/ *adj.* superficial, listless, not thorough

سطحی، ظاهری، سرسری، فرمالیته

Her smile was *perfunctory*.

per.i.gee /'per.i.dʒiː/ *n.* point of moon's orbit when it is nearest to the earth

(اخترشناسی) حضیض زمینی، نزدیکترین نقطه به زمین

The rocket was launched as the moon approached its *perigee*.

pe.ri.me.ter /£ pə'rɪm.ɪ.təʳ, $ -'rɪm.ə.tɚ/ *n.* outer boundary

پیرامون، محیط؛ دور، اطراف

To find the *perimeter* of any quadrilateral, we add the four sides.

per.i.pa.tet.ic /£ ˌper.ɪ.pə'tet.ɪk, $ -'teṭ-/ *adj.* walking about, moving

سیّار

Many schools can only afford to employ *peripatetic*

music teachers.

per.i.phe.ry /£ pəˈrɪf.ᵊr.i, $ -ˈrɪf.ɚ.i/ *n.* edge, especially of a round surface

حاشیه، کنار، اطراف

Houses have been built on the *periphery* of the factory site.

per.i.pher.al: *adj.* حاشیه‌ای، کناری؛ پیرامونی

per.jur.y /£ ˈpɜː.dʒᵊr.i, $ ˈpɜːr.dʒɚ-/ *n.* false testimony while under oath

(حقوقی) شهادت دروغ

He was indicted for *perjury*.

per.jue: *v.* (حقوقی) شهادت دروغ دادن
per.jur.er: *n.* (حقوقی) شاهد دروغگو، شهادت دهندهٔ دروغگو

per.me.a.ble /£ ˈpɜː.mi.ə.bl̩, $ ˈpɜːr-/ *adj.* porous, allowing passage through

نفوذپذیر، تراوا

Glass is *permeable* to light.

per.me.a.bil.i.ty: *n.* نفوذپذیری، تراوایی

per.me.ate /£ ˈpɜː.mi.eɪt, $ ˈpɜːr-/ *v.* to pass through, to spread

نفوذ کردن، نشت کردن، تراویدن؛ (به همه جا) پخش شدن؛ فراگرفتن، سایه انداختن بر

The odor of frying onions *permeated* the air.

per.me.a.tion: *n.* نفوذ، تراوش، پخش، نشت

per.ni.cious /£ pəˈnɪʃ.əs, $ pɚ-/ *adj.* very destructive

مضر، خطرناک، مهلک، زیانمند، زیان‌آور

He argued that these books had a *pernicious* effect on young and susceptible minds.

per.ni.cious.ly: *adv.* به گونه‌ای زیان آور

per.o.ra.tion /per.əˈreɪ.ʃᵊn/ *n.* conclusion of an oration

پایان و نتیجه سخنرانی، خاتمهٔ نطق، نتیجه‌گیری

We had to listen to the *peroration* on the evils of drink.

per.pe.trate /£ ˈpɜː.pə.treɪt, $ ˈpɜːr-/ *v.* to commit an offense

مرتکب شدن (جنایت و غیره)

Only an insane person could *perpetrate* such a horrible crime.

per.pe.tra.tion: *n.* ارتکاب

per.pe.trat.or: *n.* مرتکب، مقصر، مسبِّب، گناهکار

per.pet.u.al /£ pəˈpetʃ.u.əl, $ pɚˈpetʃ-/ *adj.* everlasting

دائمی، پیوسته، همیشگی، مداوم؛ ابدی، جاودانی

He was irritated by their *perpetual* complaints.

per.qui.site /ˈpɜː.kwɪ.zɪt/ *n.* any gain above stipulated salary

فوق‌العاده شغل، عایدی اضافه بر حقوق ثابت؛ (جمع) مزایای جنبی

The *perquisites* attached to this job make it even more attractive than the salary indicates.

per.si.flage /ˈpɜː.sɪ.flɑːʒ/ *n.* banter, flippant conversation

شوخی کنایه‌دار، مزاح، ریشخند

This *persiflage* is not appropriate when we have such serious problems to discuss.

per.son.a.ble /£ ˈpɜː.sᵊn.ə.bl̩, $ ˈpɜːr-/ *adj.* attractive

خوش سیما، خوش قیافه

The salesman was a very *personable* young man.

per.spi.ca.cious /£ ˌpɜː.spɪˈkeɪ.ʃəs, $ ˌpɜːr-/ *adj.* having insight, penetrating, astute

زیرک، با ذکاوت، با فراست، تیزهوش، تیزبین

It was very *perspicacious of* you to find the cause of the trouble so quickly.
per.spi.cac.i.ty: *n.* ذکاوت، فراست و تیزبینی
per.spic.u.ous /pə'spɪkjʊəs/ *adj.* plainly expressed

واضح، روشن، سلیس

His *perspicuous* comments eliminated all possibility of misinterpretation.
per.spi.cu.i.ty: *n.* وضوح، روشنی، سلاست
pert /£ pɜːt, $ pɜːrt/ *adj.* impertinent, forward

وقیحانه، گستاخانه، بی‌ادبانه، گستاخ، پررو، بی‌حیا، پررو

I think your *pert* remarks call for an apology.
per.tin.a.cious /£ ˌpɜːtɪ'neɪ.ʃəs, $ ˌpɜːr.tᵊn'eɪ-/ *adj.* stubborn, persistent

مُصِرّ، یک‌دنده، سمج، مصمم؛ مصرّانه

He is bound to succeed because his *pertinacious* nature will not permit him to quit.
per.tin.a.ci.ty: *n.* سماجت، اصرار، عزم، اراده
per.tin.ent /£ 'pɜːtɪ.nənt, $ 'pɜːr.tᵊn.ᵊnt/ *adj.* suitable, to the point

مربوط، بجا، مناسب

The lawyer wanted to know all the *pertinent* details.
per.tin.ence: *n.* ربط، ارتباط، وابستگی
per.turb /£ pə'tɜːb, $ pɚ'tɜːrb/ *v.* to disturb greatly

نگران کردن، مضطرب کردن

I am afraid this news will *perturb* him.
per.tur.ba.tion: *n.* اضطراب، نگرانی
per.us.al /pə'ruː.zᵊl/ *n.* reading

مرور، بررسی

I am certain that you have missed important details in your rapid **perusal** of this document.

per.use: *v.*   به‌دقت خواندن، مطالعه کردن، بررسی کردن

per.vas.ive /£ pəˈveɪ.sɪv, $ pɚ-/ *adj.* spread throughout, permeating

نافذ، فراگیر، منتشرشده

The **pervasive** odor of mothballs clung to the clothes and didn't fade away until they had been thoroughly aired.

per.vade: *v.*   منتشر شدن در، پخش شدن در، پُر کردن

per.verse /£ pəˈvɜːs, $ pɚˈvɜːrs/ *adj.* stubborn, intractable

مصر در خطاکاری، لجوج، لجباز؛ گمراه، منحرف

You are being unnecessarily **perverse**.

per.ver.sely: *adv.*   لجوجانه، عمداً
per.ver.se.ness: *n.*   انحراف، لجاجت
per.ver.si.ty: *n.*   انحراف، لجاجت

per.ver.sion /£ pəˈvɜː.ʃən, $ pɚˈvɜːr-/ *n.* corruption, turning from right to wrong

انحراف؛ انحراف جنسی؛ تحریف

Her account was a **perversion** of the truth.

pes.sim.i.sm /ˈpes.ɪ.mɪ.zəm/ *n.* belief that life is basically bad or evil, gloominess

بدبینی؛ آیین بدبینی

His **pessimism** has the effect of depressing everyone.

pes.sim.ist: *n.*   آدم بدبین
pes.sim.is.tic: *adj.*   بدبینانه

pes.ti.len.tial /ˌpes.tɪˈlen.ʃəl/ *adj.* causing plague, baneful

People were afraid to explore the **pestilential** swamp.
طاعون‌زا، کشنده، مهلک

pes.ti.lence: *n.* طاعون، بیماری مسری خطرناک
pes.ti.len.tial.ly: *adv.* به‌طور کشنده
pet.ri.fy /'pet.rə.faɪ/ *v.* to turn to stone
به‌سنگ تبدیل کردن/شدن؛ سر جای خود میخ‌کوب کردن
His sudden and unexpected appearance seemed to **petrify** her.

pet.ri.fi.ca.tion: *n.* سنگ شدگی؛ رکود، سکون، تحجر
pe.tul.ant /'pet.jʊ.lᵊnt/ *adj.* touchy, peevish
زودرنج، کج خلق، بد خلق، بهانه‌گیر، ایرادی
The feverish patient was **petulant** and restless.

pet.ul.ance: *n.* زودرنجی، تندی و بی‌حوصلگی، بد عنقی، بد خلقی
pet.ul.ant.ly: *adv.* از روی بی‌حوصلگی، با کج خلقی، با بد خلقی
phar.i.sa.ic.al /ˌfærɪˈseɪkəl/ *adj.* self-righteous, hypocritical
جزم‌اندیش، حق به جانب، ریاکار، زهدفروش
Lippman has pointed out that those who do not attempt to explain the moral code they advocate are often regarded as **pharisaical** and ignored.

phar.i.see: *n.* زاهد ریاکار، آدم زهدفروش
phial /faɪəl/ *n.* small bottle
شیشه، بطری کوچک (برای دارو یا عطر)
Even though it is small, this **phial** of perfume is expensive.

phil.an.der /fɪˈlæn.dᵊr/ *v.* to make love, to flirt
لاس زدن، عشقبازی کردن، بازی کردن با
Do not **philander** or trifle with my affections because

love is too serious.

phil.an.der.er: *n.*   اهل لاسیدن، زن‌باز، دختر‌باز

phil.an.throp.ist /£ fɪˈlænt.θrə.pɪst, $ fə-/ *n.* lover of mankind, doer of good

آدم بشردوست، آدم خیّر، آدم نوع‌دوست

As he grew older, he became famous as a *philanthropist* and benefactor of the needy.

phil.an.thro.py: *n.*   بشردوستی، نوع‌دوستی

phil.an.thro.pic: *adj.*   نوع دوستانه

phil.is.tine /£ ˈfɪl.ɪ.staɪn, $ -stiːn/ *n., adj.* narrow minded person; un-cultured person

آدم بی‌فرهنگ، آدم کوته‌فکر؛ کوته فکر، بی‌فرهنگ، هنر ستیز

We need more men of culture and enlightment; we have too many *philistine* among us.

phil.ol.o.gy /£ fɪˈlɒl.ə.dʒi, $ -ˈlɑː.lə-/ *n.* study of language

لغت‌شناسی، زبان‌شناسی، متن‌شناسی

The professor of *philology* advocated the use of Esperanto as an international language.

phil.o.log.i.cal: *adj.*   مربوط به زبان شناسی / لغت‌شناسی

phil.o.log.ist: *n.*   متن‌شناس، نسخه‌شناس، لغت‌شناس

phleg.mat.ic /£ flegˈmæt.ɪk, $ -ˈmæt̬-/ *adj.* calm, not easily disturbed

آرام، خونسرد، خویشتن‌دار

The nurse was a cheerful but *phlegmatic* person.

pho.bi.a /£ ˈfəʊ.bi.ə, $ ˈfoʊ.bjə/ *n.* morbid fear

ترس بیمارگونه، هراس بی‌مورد، فوبیا

His fear of flying was more than mere nervousness; it was

a real *phobia*.

phys.i.og.no.my /£ ˌfɪz.iˈɒn.ə.mi, $ -ˈɑː.nə-/ *n.* face

چهره، قیافه؛ قیافه‌شناسی؛ (جغرافیا) عوارض طبیعی

He prided himself on his ability to analyze a person's character by studying his *physiognomy*.

phys.i.o.log.i.cal /£ ˌfɪz.i.əˈlɒdʒ.ɪ.kᵊl, $ -ˈlɑː.dʒɪ-/ *adj.* related to the science of the function of living organisms

فیزیولوژیکی، مربوط به‌مطالعهٔ عملکرد اندام‌های زنده

To understand this disease fully, we must examine not only its *physiological* aspects but also its psychological elements.

phys.i.ol.o.gy: *n.*   فیزیولوژی

phys.i.ol.o.gist: *n.*   متخصص فیزیولوژی، متخصص علم اندام

pic.a.resque /pɪk.əˈresk/ *adj.* related to the rogues in literature

(سبک ادبی) پیکارسک (= ماجراهای افراد فرومایه / پست)

Moll Flanaders has been hailed as one of the best *picaresque* novels in the English language.

pie.bald /£ ˈpaɪ.bɔːld, $ -bɑːld/ *adj., n.* spotted, mottled

اسب سفید و سیاه، اسب ابلق؛ خال‌دار، خال‌مخالی

You should be able to identify this horse easily as it is the only *piebald* horse in the race.

pied /paɪd/ *adj.* variegated, multicolored

رنگارنگ، ملون، سیاه و سفید، خال‌مخالی

The *Pied Piper* of Hamelin got his name from the multicolored clothing he wore.

pil.lage /ˈpɪl.ɪdʒ/ *v., n.* to plunder

pil.lo.ry /£ ˈpɪl.ªr.i, $ -ɚ.i/ *v.* to punish by placing in a wooden frame; to expose to public scorn

به یغما بردن، غارت کردن، چپاول کردن؛ غارت، چپاول، تاراج
The enemy *pillaged* the quiet village and left it in ruins.
pil.lag.er: *n.* غارتگر، چپاولگر، تاراج‌گر

pil.lo.ry /£ ˈpɪl.ªr.i, $ -ɚ.i/ *v.* to punish by placing in a wooden frame; to expose to public scorn

بوسیله قاپوق تنبیه کردن؛ ریشخند کردن، به باد انتقاد گرفتن
Even though he was mocked and *pilloried*, he maintained that he was correct in his belief.
pil.lo.ry: *n.*

قاپوق (وسیله شکنجه چوبی که سر و دست‌های مجرم از سوراخ‌های آن گذرانده می‌شد)

pin.ion /ˈpɪn.jən/ *v.* to restrain

دست یا کَتِ (کسی را) بستن، مانع حرکت (کسی) شدن
They *pinioned* his arms against his body but left his legs free so that he could move about.

pin.na.cle /ˈpɪn.ə.kl̩/ *n.* peak

(کوه) قله، نوک
We could see the morning sunlight illuminate the *pinnacle* while the rest of the mountain lay in shadow.

pi.ous /ˈpaɪ.əs/ *adj.* devout, high-minded

دیندار، متدین، مذهبی، باتقوی، پرهیزگار
The *pious* parents gave their children a religious upbringing.
pi.e.ty: *n.* تقوی، پرهیزکاری

pi.quant /ˈpiː.kənt, -kɑːnt/ *adj.* having a pleasant taste

(مزه) تند و مطبوع؛ خوشایند
Bland vegetables are often served with a *piquant* sauce.
pi.quan.cy: *n.* (مزه) تند و مطبوع؛ خوشایندی

pique /piːk/ *n., v.* irritation, resentment; to irritate

رنجش، دلخوری، آزردگی؛ آزردن، دلخور کردن، رنجاندن

1) She showed her *pique* by her refusal to appear with the other contestants at the end of the contest.
2) He was *piqued* to discover that he hadn't been invited.

pith.y /ˈpɪθ.i/ *adj.* concise, meaty

موجز، پرمغز، پرمعنی

I enjoy reading his essays because they are always compact and *pithy*.

pit.tance /£ ˈpɪt.ᵊnʦ, $ ˈpɪt̬-/ *n.* a small allowance or wage

مقرری ناچیز، حقوق ناچیز، حقوق بخور و نمیر، شندرغاز

He could not live on the *pittance* he received as a pension and had to look for an additional source of revenue.

pla.cate /£ pləˈkeɪt, $ ˈpleɪ.keɪt/ *v.* to pacify, to conciliate

(کسی را) آرام کردن، فرو نشاندن خشم، تسکین دادن

The teacher tried to *placate* the angry mother.

pla.ca.ble: *adj.* قابل تسکین

plac.id /ˈplæs.ɪd/ *adj.* peaceful, calm

آرام و راحت، خونسرد؛ خونسردانه

After his vacation in this *placid* section, he felt soothed and rested.

plac.id.ly: *adv.* به آرامی، با خونسردی
pla.cid.i.ty: *n.* آرامش، خونسردی

pla.giar.i.sm /£ ˈpleɪ.dʒᵊr.ɪ.zᵊm, $ -dʒɚ.ɪ-/ *n.* theft of another's ideas or writings

سرقت ادبی، انتحال

The editor recognized the *plagiarism* and rebuked the culprit who had presented the manuscript as original.

pla.giar.ize: *v.*   سرقت ادبی کردن، انتحال کردن

pla.giar.ist: *n.*   سارق ادبی

plain.tive /£ ˈpleɪn.tɪv, $ -t̬ɪv/ *adj.* mournful

محزون، غم‌انگیز، حزن‌انگیز، اندوهگین

The dove has a *plaintive* and melancholy call.

plat.i.tude /£ ˈplæt.ɪ.tjuːd, $ ˈplæt̬.ə.tuːd/ *n.* trite remark, commonplace statement

حرف تکراری، حرف کلیشه‌ای، شعار

We shall have to listen to more *platitudes* about the dangers of overspending.

plat.i.tud.i.nous: *adj.*   تکراری، کلیشه‌ای؛ بی‌مزه، مبتذل

pla.ton.ic /£ pləˈtɒn.ɪk, $ -ˈtɑː.nɪk/ *adj.* purely spiritual; theoretical

پاک، بی‌آلایش؛ صوری

Although a member of the political group, he took only a *platonic* interest in its ideals and gools.

plau.dit.o.ry /£ ˈplɔː.dɪt.ər.i, $ ˈplɑː-/ *adj.* approving, applauding

تحسین‌برانگیز، رضایت‌مندانه

The theatrical company reprinted the *plauditory* comments of the critics in its advertisement.

plaus.i.ble /£ ˈplɔː.zə.bl̩, $ ˈplɑː-/ *adj.* reasonable, believeable

پذیرفتنی، قابل قبول، باور کردنی، معقول

She could find no *plausible* explanation for its disappearance.

plaus.i.bly: *adv.* به‌طور معقولی، به‌طور قابل قبولی
plaus.i.bi.li.ty: *n.* قابلیت پذیرش، اعتبار، صحت
ple.be.ian /pləˈbiː.ən/ *adj.* common, related to common people

عامی؛ عامیانه؛ پست، دون‌پایه
His speeches were aimed at the *plebeian* minds and emotions.

pleb.i.scite /£ ˈpleb.ɪ.sɪt, $ -ə.saɪt/ *n.* referendum

همه پرسی، رأی‌گیری عمومی
A *plebiscite* was held to decide the fate of the country.

ple.nary /£ ˈpliː.nə.ri, $ -nɚ.i/ *adj.* complete, full

(اختیار، قدرت) نامحدود، مطلق، تام
The union leader was given *plenary* power to negotiate a new contract with the employers.

plen.i.po.ten.tia.ry /£ ˌplen.ɪ.pəʊˈtent.ʃˀr.i, $ -poʊˈtent.ʃi.er-/ *adj., n.* fully empowered

تام‌الاختیار، دارای اختیار تام؛ تام، مطلق؛ نمایندهٔ تام‌الاختیار
The minister was given *plenipotentiary* powers in the trade negotiations.

plen.i.tude /ˈplen.ɪtjuːd/ *n.* abundance, completeness

فراوانی، وفور، پُری
Looking in the party, we admired the *plenitude* of fruits and pickles we had preserved during the summer.

pleth.o.ra /£ ˈpleθ.ˀr.ə, $ -ɚ.ə/ *n.* excess, overabundance

کثرت، زیادی؛ بیش از اندازه؛ ازدیاد، کثرت
She offered a *plethora* of reasons for her shortcomings.

plumb /plʌmp/ *adj., n., v.* checking perpendicularity; vertical

عمودی، راست، صاف؛ شاغول؛ با شاغول سنجیدن
Before hanging wallpaper it is advisable to drop a **plumb** line from the ceiling as a guide.

pod.i.a.trist /£ pəʊˈdaɪ.ə.trɪst, $ pɒdˈdaɪ-, $ pəˈdaɪ-/ *n.* doctor who treats ailments of the feet

متخصص پا، پا پزشک
He consulted a *podiatrist* about his fallen arches.

pod.i.a.try: *n.* پا پزشکی

po.di.um /£ ˈpəʊ.di.əm, $ ˈpoʊ-/ *n.* pedestal, raised platform

سکو؛ تریبون
The audience applauded as the conductor made his way to the *podium*.

poi.gnant /ˈpɔɪ.njənt/ *adj.* keen, piercing, severe

عمیق، شدید؛ دردناک، غم‌انگیز
Her *poignant* grief left her pale and weak.

poi.gnan.cy: *n.* حزن، اندوه، غم

po.lem.ic /pəˈlem.ɪk/ *n.* controversy, argument

(سخنرانی یا مقاله) بحث‌انگیز؛ مشاجره، بگومگو، مجادله
He *launched into* a fierce *polemic* against the government's policies.

po.lem.ic.ist: *n.* اهل جدل، اهل مجادله

pol.i.tic /£ ˈpɒl.ɪ.tɪk, $ ˈpɑː.lə-/ *adj.* expedient, prudent, well-devised

عاقلانه، معقول، به صلاح، سنجیده، مناسب
When the fight began, he thought it *politic* to leave.

pol.i.ty /ˈpɒl.ɪ.ti/ *n.* form of government of nation or state

حکومت، نوع حکومت؛ واحد سیاسی

Our ***polity*** should be devoted to the concept that the government should strive for the good of all citizens.

po.ly.gam.ist /pəˈlɪg.ə.mɪst/ *n.* one who has more than one spouse at a time

مرد چند زنه

He was arrested as a ***polygamist*** when his two wives filed complaints about him.

po.ly.ga.my: *n.* چند همسری، تعدد زوجات، چند زنی
po.ly.gam.ous: *adj.* (مربوط به) چند زنی

pol.y.glot /£ ˈpɒl.ɪ.glɒt, $ ˈpɑː.lɪ.glɑːt/ *adj., n.* speaking several languages

چند زبانه؛ شخص چند زبانه

New York city is a ***polyglot*** community because of the thousands of immigrants who settle there.

pon.der.ous /£ ˈpɒn.dᵊr.əs, $ ˈpɑːn.dɚ-/ *adj.* weighty, unwieldy

سنگین، وزین؛ یغور؛ بی‌روح، خشک

His humor lacked the light touch; his jokes were always ***ponderous***.

por.tent /£ ˈpɔː.tent, $ ˈpɔːr-/ *n.* sign, omen, forewarning

نشان، علامت، گواه، فال بد

The report reveals some worrying economic ***portents*** for the coming year.

por.ten.tous: *adj.* بدیمن، شوم، بدشگون

port.ly /£ ˈpɔːt.li, $ ˈpɔːrt/ *adj.* stately, stout

تنومند، قوی هیکل

He arrived at the restaurant, a ***portly*** figure in a tight-fitting jacket and bow tie.

pos.ter.i.ty /£ pɒsˈter.ə.ti, $ pɑːˈster.ə.t̬i/ *n.* future generation, descendants

نسل‌های آینده، آیندگان

We hope to leave a better world to *posterity*.

post.hu.mous /£ ˈpɒs.tjʊ.məs, $ ˈpɑːs.tʃə-/ *adj.* after death

بعد از مرگ، پس از مرگ؛ (کتاب و غیره) منتشر شده پس از مرگ نویسنده

It was only after the *posthumous* publication of his last novel that the critics recognized his great talent.

post.pran.di.al /£ pəʊstˈpræn.di.əl, $ poʊst-/ *adj.* after dinner

بعد از غذا، پس از صرف غذا

The most objectionable feature of these formal banquets is the *postprandial* speech.

pos.tu.late /£ ˈpɒs.tjʊ.leɪt, $ ˈpɑː.stjə-/ *n., v.* self-evident truth; to assume as true

اصل، فرض، شرط لازم؛ اصل قرار دادن، بدیهی فرض کردن

We must accept these statements as *postulate* before pursuing our discussions any further.

po.ta.ble /ˈpəʊ.tə.bᵊl/ *adj.* suitable for drinking

نوشیدنی، قابل شرب، آشامیدنی

They are doing extensive research in ways of making sea water *potable*.

po.tent /£ ˈpəʊ.tᵊnt, $ ˈpoʊ.t̬ᵊnt/ *adj.* powerful, persuasive, greatly influential

(استدلال) محکم، قانع‌کننده؛ قوی؛ مؤثر

The jury was swayed by the highly *potent* testimony of the crime's sole eyewitness.

po.ten.cy: *n.*   قوّت؛ توانایی؛ توان جنسی

po.ten.tate /£ ˈpəʊ.tˀn.teɪt, $ ˈpoʊ.tˀn-/ *n.* monarch, sovereign
فرمانروای مطلق، حاکم، پادشاه
The *potentate* spent more time at Monte Carlo than he did at home with his people.

po.ten.tial /£ pəʊˈten.tʃˀl, $ poʊ-/ *adj.* expressing possibility
ممکن، احتمالی؛ بالقوه
She is widely regarded as a *potential* Olympic gold medallist.

po.ten.tial.ly: *adv.* بالقوه

po.ten.ti.al.i.ty: *n.* امکان؛ استعداد، توانایی؛ نیرو، قوه

po.tion /£ ˈpəʊ.ʃˀn, $ ˈpoʊ-/ *n.* liquid medicine or poison
معجون، دارو، اکسیر
The magician displayed his charms and *potions*.

pot.pour.ri /£ ˌpəʊ.pəˈri, $ ˌpoʊ-/ *n.* heterogeneous mixture, of dried plants and things
قدحِ گل، انواع گل خشک؛ آمیزه، ملغمه
He offered a *potpourri* of folk songs from many lands.

poul.tice /£ ˈpəʊl.tɪs, $ ˈpoʊl.tɪs/ *n.*, *v.* warm medicated dressing
مرهم، ضماد؛ مرهم گذاشتن
The heat from the *poultice* increases the flow of blood to the injury.

prac.ti.ca.ble /£ ˈpræk.tɪ.kə.bl̩, $ -tɪ-/ *adj.* feasible
عملی، ممکن، قابل اجرا؛ مفید، قابل استفاده
The board of directors decided that the plan was *practicable* and agreed to undertake the project.

prac.ti.ca.bi.li.ty: *n.* عملی بودن، امکان

prac.ti.cal /£ ˈpræk.tɪ.kᵊl, $ -tɪ-/ *adj.* based on experience, useful

عملی، ممکن، کاری، قابل استفاده، مفید

He was a *practical* man, opposed to theory.

prac.ti.cal.i.ty: *n.* امکان، عملی بودن
prac.ti.cal.ly: *adv.* در عمل، عملاً

prag.mat.ic /£ prægˈmæt.ɪk, $ -ˈmæt̬-/ *adj.* practical

عملی؛ عمل‌گرایانه؛ واقع‌بینانه، واقع‌گرایانه

This test should provide us with a *pragmatic* analysis of the value of this course.

prag.ma.tist: *n.* واقع‌بین؛ عمل‌گرا

prate /preɪt/ *v.* to speak foolishly, to boost idly

ورّاجی کردن، ور زدن، پرحرفی کردن، یاوه‌گویی کردن

Let us not *prate* about our quality; rather, let our virtues speak for themselves.

prat.tle /£ ˈpræt.l̩, $ ˈpræt̬-/ *v., n.* to babble

ساده و بچگانه حرف زدن، من من کردن؛ پرحرفی، ورّاجی

The little girl *prattled* endlessly about her dolls.

pre.am.ble /ˈpriːæm.bl̩, priˈæm-/ *n.* introductory statement

مقدمه، دیباچه

He launched into his statement without any *preamble*.

pre.ca.ri.ous /£ prɪˈkeə.ri.əs, $ -ˈker.i-/ *adj.* uncertain, risky

نامطمئن، بی‌ثبات؛ مخاطره‌آمیز، خطرناک

I think this stock is a *precarious* investment and advise against its purchase.

pre.ca.ri.ous.ly: *adv.* به‌طور نامطمئن/نامعلوم؛ به‌طور مخاطره‌آمیزی
pre.ca.ri.ous.ness: *n.* عدم اطمینان، بی‌ثباتی

prec.e.dent /£ ˈpres.ɪ.dᵊnt, $ -ə.dent/ *n.* something said or done earlier that serves as an example

سابقه، پیشینه

This decision sets a *precedent* for future cases of a similar nature.

pre.ced.ent /prɪˈsɪd.ənt/ *adj.* preceding in time and rank

قبل از، پیش از، قبلی، پیشین

Our discussions, *precedent* to this event, certainly did not give you any reason to believe that we would adopt your proposal.

pre.cept /ˈpriːsept/ *n.* practical rule guiding conduct

دستورالعمل، حُکم؛ اصل، قاعده؛ پند و اندرز، موعظه

"Love thy neighbor as thyself" is a worthwhile *precept*.

prec.i.pice /ˈpres.ɪ.pɪs/ *n.* cliff, dangerous position

پرتگاه؛ شیب تند

Suddenly Indiana Jones found himself dangling from the edge of *precipice*.

pre.ci.pi.tate /£ prɪˈsɪp.ɪ.teɪt, $ -ṭeɪt/ *v.* to throw headlong, to hasten

تسریع کردن، جلو انداختن

We must be patient as we cannot *precipitate* these results.

pre.ci.pi.tate /£ prɪˈsɪp.ɪ.tət, $ priːˈsɪp.ɪ.ṭɪt/ *adj., n.* headlong; rash

عجولانه، شتابزده، نسنجیده؛ رسوب؛ ته نشست

Do not be *precipitate* in this matter, investigate further.

pre.ci.pi.tate.ly: *adv.*   .   با عجله، شتاب‌زده

pre.ci.pi.tate.ness: *n.* عجله، شتاب

pre.ci.pi.tous /£ prɪˈsɪp.ɪ.təs, $ prɪˈsɪp.ɪ.t̬əs/ *adj.* steep

شیب‌دار، دارای شیب تند؛ مرتفع، بلند

This hill is difficult to climb because it is so ***precipitous***.

pre.clude /£ prɪˈkluːd, $ priː-/ *v.* to make impossible, to eliminate

جلوگیری کردن، مانع شدن، غیرممکن ساختن

This contract does not ***preclude*** my being employed by others at the same time that I am working for you.

pre.co.cious /£ prɪˈkəʊ.ʃəs, $ priːˈkoʊ-/ *adj.* developed ahead of time

قبل / پیش از موقع؛ پیشرس، استثنایی

He was a ***precocious*** child who could play the piano at the age of three.

pre.coc.i.ty: *n.* پیشرس بودن، پیشرسی؛ ذکاوت، تیزهوشی

pre.cur.sor /£ ˌpriːˈkɜː.sər, $ -ˈkɜːr.sɚ/ *n.* forerunner

پیشرو، منادی، پیام‌آور، طلیعه؛ سرآغاز، پیش درآمد

Gray and Burns were ***precursor*** of the Romantic Movement in English literature.

pred.at.o.ry /£ ˈpred.ə.tᵊr.i, $ -tɔːr-/ *adj.* plundering

(حیوانِ) شکارگر؛ غارتگر، متجاوز

The hawk is a ***predatory*** bird.

pred.at.or: *n.* حیوانِ شکارگر؛ غارتگر، متجاوز

pre.di.lec.tion /£ ˌpriː.dɪˈlek.ʃᵊn, $ ˌpred.ᵊlˈek-/ *n.* partiality, preference

اشتیاق، تمایلِ، میل، علاقه، جانبداری

Ever since she was a child, she has had a ***predilection*** for spicy foods.

pre.em.i.nent /priːˈem.ɪ.nənt/ *adj.* outstanding, superior

برجسته، شاخص، عالی، ممتاز

The king traveled to Boston because he wanted the *preeminent* surgeon to perform the operation.

pre.em.i.nence: *n.* برتری، تفوق، برجستگی

pre.em.i.nent.ly: *adv.* عمدتاً، بیشتر

pre.empt /priːˈempt/ *v.* to seize for oneself

به خود اختصاص دادن، تصاحب کردن، دست روی (چیزی) گذاشتن

Your attempt to *preempt* this land before it is offered to the public must be resented.

pre.emp.tion: *n.* پیش دستی در خرید

pref.a.to.ry /£ ˈpref.ə.tᵊr.i, $ -tɔːr-/ *adj.* introductory

مقدماتی

The chairman made a few *prefatory* remarks before he called on the first speaker.

pre.hen.sile /£ prɪˈhent.saɪl, $ priːˈhent.sɪl/ *adj.* capable of grasping or holding

(در مورد دُم یا پای حیوان) قادر به گرفتن اشیا

Monkeys use not only their arms and legs but also their *prehensile* tails in traveling through the trees.

prel.ude /ˈprel.juːd/ *n.* introduction, forerunner

مقدمه، سرآغاز، پیش درآمد

I am afraid that this border raid is the *prelude* to more serious attacks.

pre.med.i.tate /priːˈmed.ɪ.teɪt/ *v.* to plan in advance

از قبل برنامه‌ریزی کردن، از پیش تدارک دیدن، از قبل نقشه کشیدن

She had ***premeditated*** the murder for months.

prem.o.ni.tion /ˌprem.əˈnɪʃ.ᵊn, ˌpriː.məˈ-/ *n.* forewarning

دلشوره، اخطار قبلی، پیش آگاهی

My ***premonition*** was right.

prem.o.ni.to.ry: *adj.*   شوم، بد شگون، نحس، هشدار دهنده

pre.pon.der.ance /£ prɪˈpɒn.dᵊr.ᵊnts, $ -ˈpɑːn.dɚ-/ *n.* the largest part or greatest amount

فراوانی، کثرت؛ اکثریت

Small businesses appear to create the ***preponderance*** of new jobs.

pre.pon.der.ant: *adj.*   غالب، مهم‌ترین، عمده‌ترین

pre.pon.der.ant.ly: *adv.*   غالباً، عمدتاً، بیشتر

pre.pon.der.ate /£ prɪˈpɒn.dᵊr.eɪt, $ -ˈpɑːn.dɚ-/ *v.* to be superior in power

غالب بودن، بیشتر بودن، برتر بودن

Christians ***preponderate*** in the population of that part of the country.

pre.pos.ter.ous /£ prɪˈpɒs.tᵊr.əs, $ -ˈpɑːstɚ-/ *adj.* absurd, ridiculous

مضحک، مسخره‌آمیز؛ مزخرف، افتضاح

The excuse he gave for his lateness was so ***preposterous*** that everybody laughed.

pre.rog.a.tive /£ prɪˈrɒg.ə.tɪv, $ -ˈrɑː.gə.t̬ɪv/ *n.* privilege, unquestionable right

حق انحصاری، حق قانونی؛ امتیاز ویژه

It is the Prime Minister's ***prerogative*** to decide when to call an election.

pres.age /ˈpres.ɪdʒ, prɪˈseɪdʒ/ *v.* to foretell

حاکی بودن از، نشان (چیزی) بودن، از وقوع (چیزی) خبر دادن

The vultures flying overhead *presaged* the discovery of the corpse in the desert.

pre.sen.ti.ment /prɪˈzen.tɪ.mənt/ *n.* premonition

پیش‌بینی واقعهٔ ناگوار، حس پیش از وقوع، دلشوره

She had a *presentiment* of what might lie ahead.

pres.tige /presˈtiːdʒ/ *n.* estimation in the eyes of people

آبرو، حیثیت، شهرت، اعتبار، خوشنامی، قدر و منزلت

The wealthy man sought to obtain social *prestige* by contributing to popular charity.

pres.tig.ious: *adj.* صاحب نام، معتبر، با آبرو، آبرومند

pre.sumption /prɪˈzʌmp.ʃən/ *n.* arrogance, effrontery; probability

گستاخی، وقاحت، پررویی؛ احتمال، فرض

She had the *presumption* to disregard our advice.

pre.sump.tive: *adj.* احتمالی، فرضی

pre.ten.ti.ous /prɪˈten.tʃəs/ *adj.* ambitious, ostentatious

ظاهر فریب، متظاهر، پرمدعا؛ متکلف

I do not feel that your limited resource will permit you to carry out such a *pretentious* program.

pre.ten.tious.ness: *n.* تکلّف، تصنع؛ خودنمایی، تظاهر

pre.ter.nat.u.ral /£ ˌpriː.təˈnætʃ.ər.əl, $ -t̬ɚˈnætʃ.ɚ-/ *adj.* exceeding what is natural

خارق‌العاده، فوق‌طبیعی، استثنایی

Anger gave me *preternatural* strength, and I managed to force the door open.

pre.text /ˈpriː.tekst/ *n.* excuse

بهانه، عذر، دستاویز

He looked for a good ***pretext*** to get out of paying a visit to his aunt.

pre.vail /prɪˈveɪl/ *v.* to induce; to triumph over

قانع کردن، قبولاندن؛ غلبه کردن

He tried to ***prevail*** on her to type his essay for him.

prev.a.lent /ˈprev.ºl.ənt/ *adj.* widespread, generally accepted

معمول، متداول، رایج، شایع

The ***prevalent*** opinion is in favor of reform.

pre.var.i.cate /£ prɪˈvær.ɪ.keɪt, $ -ˈver-/ *v.* to lie

کلی‌بافی کردن، حقیقت را کتمان کردن، دو پهلو حرف زدن، زبان‌بازی کردن

Tell us exactly what happened and don't ***prevaricate***.

    pre.var.i.ca.tion: *n.*   کتمان حقیقت، دروغ؛ کلی‌بافی

    pre.var.i.ca.tor: *n.*   دروغ‌گو؛ زبان‌باز

prim /prɪm/ *adj.* very precise and formal, exceedingly proper

خیلی رسمی و خشک؛ سنگین، موقّر، آراسته

You can't tell that joke to her — she's much too ***prim*** and proper.

    prim.ly: *adv.*   خشک و رسمی، شق و رق

    prim.ness: *n.*   رسمیت

pri.mo.gen.i.ture /£ ˌpraɪ.məʊˈdʒen.ɪ.tʃəʳ, $ -moʊˈdʒen.ɪ.tʃɚ/ *n.* seniority by birth

(ارشد) حق پسر ارشد؛ ارشدیت، بزرگی

By virtue of ***primogeniture***, the first-born child had many privileges over his brothers and sisters.

pri.mor.di.al /£ praɪˈmɔː.di.əl, $ -ˈmɔːr-/ *adj.* rudimentary,

primeval

اصلی، اولیه، نخستین، آغازین
The universe was created out of a ***primordial*** ball of matter.

primp /prɪmp/ *v.* to dress or groom oneself with care

خود را آراستن، به سر و وضع خود رسیدن
She ***primps*** for hours before a dance.

pris.tine /£ ˈprɪs.tiːn, $ prɪˈstiːn/ *adj.* primitive, unspoiled

دست نخورده، سالم؛ بکر؛ تازه، نو
This area has been preserved in all its ***pristine*** wildness.

pri.va.tion /praɪˈveɪ.ʃ°n/ *n.* hardship

محرومیت، مشقّت، بدبختی، سختی
In his youth, he knew hunger and ***privation***.

pri.vy /ˈprɪv.i/ *adj.* secret, hidden, not public

خصوصی، محرمانه؛ آگاه، باخبر
I wasn't ***privy*** to the negotiations.

pri.vi.ly: *adv.* محرمانه، سرّی

probe /£ prəʊb, $ proʊb/ *v.* to explore with tools

جستجو کردن، به‌طور دقیق تحقیق کردن، کند و کاو کردن
The surgeon ***probed*** the wound for foreign matter before suturing it.

pro.bi.ty /£ ˈprəʊ.bɪ.ti, $ ˈproʊ.bə.t̬i/ *n.* uprightly, incorruptibility

راستی، صداقت، امانتداری
Everyone took his ***probity*** for granted; his defalcations, therefore, shocked us all.

prob.lem.a.tic /£ ˌprɒb.ləˈmæt.ɪk, $ ˌprɑː.bləˈmæt̬-/ *adj.*

perplexing, unsettled, questionable

دشوار، پیچیده؛ مسئله‌ساز، مشکل آفرین

Given the many areas of conflict still awaiting resolution, the outcome of the peace talks remains ***problematic***.

pro.bos.cis /£ prəˈbɒs.ɪs, $ proʊˈbɑː.sɪs/ *n*. nose, long snout

(فیل) خرطوم؛ اندام مکنده؛ پوزه

The elephant uses his ***proboscis*** to handle things and carry them from place to place.

pro.cli.vi.ty /£ prəˈklɪv.ɪ.ti, $ -ə.ți/ *n*. inclination, natural tendency

تمایل، میل، گرایش

He has a ***proclivity*** to grumble.

pro.cras.tin.ate /£ prəʊˈkræs.tɪ.neɪt, $ proʊ-/ *v*. to delay, to postpone

به تأخیر انداختن، پشت گوش انداختن، امروز و فردا کردن

It is wise not to ***procrastinate***; otherwise, we find ourselves bogged down in a mass of work which should have been finished long ago.

pro.cras.ti.na.tion: *n*.   تعلل، مسامحه، طفره

pro.cras.ti.nat.or: *n*.   سهل انگار، طفره‌رو

prod /£ prɒd, $ prɑːd/ *v*. to poke, to stir up, to urge

وادار کردن، واداشتن؛ سیخ زدن، سیخونک زدن

If you ***prod*** him hard enough, he'll eventually clean his room.

prod.i.gal /£ ˈprɒd.ɪ.gᵊl, $ ˈprɑː.dɪ-/ *adj*. wasteful, reckless with money

ولخرج، اسراف‌کار، مُسرف؛ دست و دلباز، سخاوتمند

The **prodigal** son squandered his inheritance.
prod.i.gal.i.ty: *n.* اسراف، ولخرجی، بخشندگی

pro.di.gious /prəˈdɪdʒ.əs/ *adj.* marvelous, enormous
حیرت‌انگیز، شگفت‌انگیز؛ عظیم، چشمگیر؛ هنگفت، کلان
He marveled at her **prodigious** appetite.
pro.di.gious.ly: *adv.* به‌طرز حیرت‌آوری، به‌طور شگفت‌انگیزی

pro.fane /prəˈfeɪn/ *v.* to violate, to desecrate
(به مقدسات) بی‌حرمتی کردن، توهین کردن
Tourists are urged not to **profane** the saintity of holy places by wearing improper garb.
pro.fan.a.tion: *n.* بی‌حرمتی، توهین

prof.li.gate /£ ˈprɒf.lɪ.gət, $ ˈprɑː.flɪ-/ *adj.* dissipated, wasteful, licentious
ولخرج، بریز و بپاش؛ بی‌بند و بار، وِل؛ اسراف‌کارانه
In this **profligate** company, he lost all sense of decency.
prof.li.ga.cy: *n.* اسراف، تبذیر

pro.fu.sion /prəˈfjuː.ʒən/ *n.* lavish expenditure, overabundent condition
کثرت، بسیاری، وفور، فراوانی، مقدار زیاد
Seldom have I seen food and drink served in such **profusion**.
pro.fuse: *adj.* فراوان، زیاد، وافر
pro.fuse.ly: *adv.* به وفور، بی حد و حصر

pro.gen.i.tor /£ prəʊˈdʒen.ɪ.tər, $ proʊˈdʒen.ɪ.tɚ/ *n.* ancestor; founder
جد، پدربزرگ، نیا؛ بنیان‌گذار
We must not forget the teachings of our **progenitor** in

our desire to appear modern.

prog.e.ny /£ ˈprɒdʒ.ə.ni, $ ˈprɑː.dʒə-/ *n.* children, offspring

اولاد، اعقاب، فرزندان، سلاله، ذرّیه

He was proud of his *progeny* but regarded George as the most promising of all his children.

prog.no.sis /£ prɒgˈnəʊ.sɪs, $ prɑːgˈnoʊ-/ *n.* prediction, prospect of recovery from disease

(پزشکی) پیش‌آگهی، پیش‌بینی؛ پیشگویی، چشم‌انداز

If the doctor's *prognosis* is correct, the patient will be in coma for at least twenty-four hours.

prog.nos.tic.ate /£ prəgˌnɒs.tɪˈkeɪt, $ prɑːgˌnɑːˈsti-/ *v.* to predict

پیش‌بینی کردن، پیشگویی کردن؛ نشانه چیزی بودن

I *prognosticate* disaster unless we change our wasteful ways.

prog.nos.ti.ca.tion: *n.* پیش‌بینی، پیشگویی

prog.nos.ti.ca.tor: *n.* پیش‌بین، پیشگو

pro.jec.tile /£ prəˈdʒek.taɪl, $ -t̬əl/ *n.* missile

موشک، پرتابه

Man has always hurled *projectiles* at his enemy whether in the form of stones or of highly explosive shells.

pro.le.ta.ri.an /£ ˌprəʊ.lɪˈteə.ri.ən, £ ˌprɒl.ɪ-, $ ˌproʊ.ləˈter.i-/ *n., adj.* member of the working class

کارگر، مزدبگیر؛ کارگری، پرولتاریایی

The aristocrats feared mob rule and thus deprived the *proletarians* of a voice in government.

pro.lif.ic /prəˈlɪf.ɪk/ *adj.* abundantly fruitful

پربار، پرمحصول؛ پرکار، فعال

He was a ***prolific*** writer and wrote as many as three books a year.

pro.lix /£ ˈprəʊ.lɪks, $ ˈproʊ-/ *adj.* verbose, drawn out

پرگو، درازگو؛ مطوّل، دارایِ اطناب

His ***prolix*** arguments irritated the jury.

   pro.lix.i.ty: *n.*   درازگویی، اِطناب

pro.mis.cu.ous /prəˈmɪs.kju.əs/ *adj.* haphazard, irregular; having a number of sexual partners

اتفاقی، بی‌قاعده، نسنجیده، درهم و برهم؛ بی‌بند و بار، هرزه (از لحاظ جنسی)

The sixties are synonymous with ***promiscuous*** sex and free living.

   prom.is.cu.i.ty: *n.*   بی‌بند و باری (جنسی)، بی‌عفتی
   pro.mis.cu.ous.ness: *n.*   بی‌قاعدگی، بی‌عفتی
   pro.mis.cu.ous.ly: *adv.*   از روی بی‌بند و باری

pro.mon.to.ry /£ ˈprɒm.ən.tri, $ ˈprɑː.mən.tɔːr-/ *n.* headland

(جغرافیا) برآمدگی، دماغه، سنگ پوز

They erected a lighthouse on the ***promontory*** to warn approaching ships.

prom.ul.gate /£ ˈprɒm.ᵊl.geɪt, $ ˈprɑː.məl-/ *v.* to announce, to spread

انتشار دادن، پخش کردن، رسماً اعلان کردن، ترویج کردن

The new law was finally ***promulgated*** in the autumn of last year.

   prom.ul.ga.tion: *n.*   اعلان، اعلام، انتشار رسمی

prone /£ prəʊn, $ proʊn/ *adj.* inclined to, prostrate

آمادۀ، مستعدِ؛ دَمَر، وارونه، دمرو

She was ***prone*** to sudden fits of anger.

prop.a.gate /£ ˈprɒp.ə.geɪt, $ ˈprɑː.pə-/ v. to multiply, to spread

تولید مثل کردن؛ زیاد شدن، تکثیر شدن؛ اشاعه دادن، رواج دادن

I am sure disease must *propagate* in such unsanitary and crowded area.

prop.a.ga.tion: n.   تولید مثل، ازدیاد، تکثیر

pro.pel.lant /£ prəˈpel.ənt/ n. substances which propel or drive forward

مادهٔ مولد فشار، نیروی محرکه

The development of our missile program has forced our scientists to seek more powerful *propellants*.

pro.pel: v.   به پیش راندن، به جلو راندن

pro.pen.si.ty /£ prəˈpen.sɪ.ti, $ -sə.t̬i/ n. natural inclination

تمایل، رغبت، گرایش، کشش

I dislike your *propensity* to belittle every contribution he makes to our organization.

proph.y.lac.tic /£ ˌprɒf.ɪˈlæk.tɪk, $ ˌprɑː.fɪˈlæk.t̬ɪk/ adj. used to prevent disease

داروی پیشگیری؛ وسیلهٔ پیشگیری؛ اقدام پیشگیرانه

Despite all *prophylactic* measures introduced by the authorities, the epidemic raged until cool weather set in.

pro.pin.qui.ty /prəˈpɪŋkwɪti/ n. nearness, kinship

قرابت، نزدیکی، همجواری، مجاورت؛ خویشاوندی

The neighbors lived *in* close *propinquity to* each other.

pro.pi.ti.ate /prəˈpɪʃ.i.eɪt/ v. to appease

خشنود کردن، استمالت کردن؛ خشم (کسی را) فرو نشاندن

The natives offered sacrifices to *propitiate* the gods.

pro.pi.ti.a.tion: n.   جلب رضایت، دلجویی، استمالت

pro.pi.ti.a.to.ry: *adj.* برای جلب خشنودی، از روی دلجویی

pro.pi.tious /prəˈpɪʃ.əs/ *adj.* kindly, favorably

مساعد، مناسب، خوش، خوب، مقتضی

I think it is advisable that we wait for a more *propitious* occasion to announce our plans.

pro.pound /prəˈpaʊnd/ *v.* to put forth for analysis

عنوان کردن، مطرح کردن، پیشنهاد کردن

In your discussion, you have *propounded* several questions; let us consider each one separately.

pro.pri.e.ty /£ prəˈpraɪə.ti, $ -ṭi/ *n.* fitness, correct conduct

ادب، نزاکت، رفتار صحیح

I want you to behave at this dinner with *propriety*; don't embarrass me.

pro.pul.sive /prəˈpʌl.sɪv/ *adj.* driving forward

(مکانیک) رانشی، پیش‌رانشی

The jet plane has a greater *propulsive* power than the engine-driven plane.

pro.pul.sion: *n.* (مکانیک) رانش، نیروی جلو برنده

pro.sa.ic /prəˈzeɪ.ɪk/ *adj.* commonplace, dull

یکنواخت، کسل‌کننده، ملال‌آور، پیش پا افتاده، بی‌لطف، بی‌روح

I do not like this author because he is so unimaginative and *prosaic*.

pro.scribe /£ prəʊˈskraɪb, $ proʊ-/ *v.* to banish, to outlaw, to ostracize

ممنوع کردن، خطرناک اعلام کردن، قدغن کردن، تحریم کردن

The sale of narcotics is *proscribed* by law.

pro.scrip.tion: *n.* منع، ممنوعیت، توقیف

pros.e.lyt.ize /£ ˈprɒs.ᵊl.ɪ.taɪz, $ ˈprɑː.sə.lɪ-/ *v.* to convert to a religion or belief

به کیش خود فراخواندن، (مذهب، مرام و غیره) تبلیغ کردن

In these interfaith meetings, there must be no attempt to *proselytize*; we must respect all points of view.

pros.o.dy /ˈprɒsədɪ/ *n.* the art of versification

عروض

This book on *prosody* contains a rhyming dictionary as well as samples of various verse forms.

pro.strate /£ prɒsˈtreɪt, $ ˈprɑː.streɪt/ *v.* to stretch out full on ground

سجده کردن، به خاک افتادن

He *prostrated* himself before the idol.

pro.stra.tion: *n.* سجده، اطاعت، تسلیم، بندگی

prot.é.gé /£ ˈprɒt.eʒ.eɪ, $ ˈprɑː.t̬eʒ-/ *n.* person under the protection of a patron

شخص تحت الحمایه دیگری، دست پرورده

As the *protégé* of the most powerful man in the country, his success is guaranteed.

pro.té.gée: *n.* دست پرورده (مؤنث)

pro.to.cal /£ ˈprəʊ.tə.kɒl, $ ˈproʊ.t̬ə.kɑːl/ *n.* diplomatic etiquette

تشریفات، پروتکل؛ یادداشت تفاهم، تفاهم‌نامه

We must run this state dinner according to *protocal* if we are to avoid offending any of our guests.

pro.to.type /£ ˈprəʊ.tə.taɪp, $ ˈproʊ.t̬ə-/ *n.* original work used as a model by others

نمونهٔ اولیه، نسخهٔ اصلی، نمونهٔ اصلی، الگوی نخستین
A *prototype* of the system was unveiled at an agricultural engineering conference in Paris last month.

pro.tract /prəˈtrækt/ *v.* to prolong

طولانی کردن، به درازا کشاندن، طول دادن
Do not *protract* this phone conversation as I expect an important business call within the next few minutes.

pro.trude /prəˈtruːd/ *v.* to stick out

بیرون زدن، درآمدن، جلو آمدن
His fingers *protruded* from the holes in his gloves.

pro.tru.sion: *n.* بیرون زدگی، جلوآمدگی
pro.tru.sive: *adj.* جلو آمده، برجسته، بیرون زده

prov.e.nance /£ ˈprɒv.ᵊn.ənts, $ ˈprɑː.vᵊn-/ *n.* origin or source of something

منشأ، اصل، اصالت، مبدأ
I am not interested in its *provenance*; I am more concerned with its usefulness than with its source.

prov.en.der /ˈprɒv.ɪn.dər/ *n.* dry food, fodder

علوفه، علیق؛ سور و سات، آذوقه
I am not afraid of a severe winter because I have stored a large quantity of *provender* for the cattle.

prov.i.dent /£ ˈprɒv.ɪ.dᵊnt, $ ˈprɑː.və-/ *adj.* displaying foresight, thrifty

آینده‌نگر، مآل اندیش، محتاط
In his usual *provident* manner, he had insured himself against this type of loss.

prov.i.dent.ly: *adv.* محتاطانه، از روی مآل‌اندیشی

pro.vin.cial /prəˈvɪn.tʃᵊl/ *adj.* related to province; limited

استانی، مربوط به استان؛ کوته‌بین، کوته‌نظر؛ دهاتی

Whenever I go to London, I feel like a *provincial*.

pro.vin.cial.i.sm: *n.* نگرش و دید شهرستانی؛ کوته فکری

pro.vi.so /£ prəˈvaɪ.zəʊ, $ -zoʊ/ *n.* stipulation

شرط، قید

He accepted, with one *proviso*.

prov.o.ca.tion /£ ˌprɒv.əˈkeɪ.ʃᵊn, $ ˌprɑː.və-/ *n.* cause for anger or retaliation

تحریک؛ عصبانیت؛ عمل تحریک‌آمیز

She loses her temper *at/ on* slightest *provocation*.

pro.voc.a.tive: *adj.* شهوت‌انگیز، تحریک‌کننده؛ بحث‌انگیز

pro.voke: *v.* عصبانی کردن؛ تحریک کردن

prox.i.mi.ty /£ prɒkˈsɪm.ɪ.ti, $ prɑːkˈsɪm.ə.t̬i/ *n.* nearness

نزدیکی، مجاورت، قرب

The deer sensed the hunter's *proximity* and bounded away.

prox.y /£ ˈprɒk.si, $ ˈprɑːk-/ *n., adj.* authorized agent

جانشین، نماینده، وکیل؛ وکالت‌نامه

Please act as my *proxy* and vote for this slate of candidates.

pru.dent /ˈpruː.dᵊnt/ *adj.* careful, cautious

آینده‌نگر، دوراندیش، محتاط، مآل اندیش، حسابگر، مقتصد

A miser hoards money not because he is *prudent* but because he is greedy.

prune /pruːn/ *v.* to cut away; to trim

حذف کردن، زواید (چیزی را) زدن، کوتاه کردن؛ هرس کردن

With the help of her editor, she was able to *prune* her manuscript into publishable form.

pru.ri.ent /£ ˈpruə.ri.ənt, $ ˈprur.i-/ *adj.* based on lascivious thoughts

هرزه، شهوانی، شهوی؛ هیز، شهوت پرست

The police attempted to close the theater where the *prurient* film was being presented.

pru.ri.ence: *n.*   هرزگی، شهوترانی، شهوانیت

pseu.do.nym /ˈsuː.də.nɪm/ *n.* pen name

اسم مستعار؛ تخلّص

Samuel Clemen's *pseudonym* was Mark Twain.

psy.che /ˈsaɪ.ki/ *n.* soul, mind

روان، روح، ذهن؛ طبیعت، ذات

It is difficult to delve into the *psyche* of a human being.

psy.chic: *adj.*	روانی، روحی
psy.chi.a.trist: *n.*	روانپزشک
psy.chi.a.try: *n.*	روانپزشکی
psy.chi.at.ric: *adj.*	(مربوط به) روانپزشکی

psy.cho.path.ic /ˌsaɪ.kəˈpæθ.ɪk/ *adj.* related to mental derangement

روان بیمار، روانی

The *psychopathic* patient suffers more frequently from a disorder of the nervous system than from a diseased brain.

psy.cho.path: *n.*   شخص روان بیمار، روان رنجور

psy.cho.sis /£saɪˈkəʊ.sɪs, $ -ˈkoʊ-/ *n.* mental disorder

روانپریشی، سایکوز

We must endeavor to find an outlet for the patient's repressed desires if we hope to combat this *psychosis*.

puer.ile /£'pjʊə.raɪl, $ 'pjʊr.ɪl/ *adj.* childish

بچگانه، کودکانه، احمقانه

His *puerile* pranks sometimes offended his serious-minded friends.

puer.il.i.ty: *n.* رفتار بچگانه، حماقت

pu.gil.ist /'pjuː.dʒɪl.ɪst/ *n.* boxer

مشت‌زن، بوکسور

The famous *pugilist* Cassius Clay changed his name to Muhammed Ali.

pug.na.cious /pʌg'neɪ.ʃəs/ *adj.* combative, disposed to fight

جنگ‌طلب، پرخاشگر، مهاجم، ستیزه‌جو

As a child he was *pugnacious* and fought with everyone.

pug.nac.i.ty: *n.* ستیزه‌جویی، پرخاشگری

pu.is.sant /'pjuː.ɪs.ᵊsnt, 'pwiː-/ *adj.* powerful, strong, potent

مقتدر، توانا، قدرتمند، بانفوذ

We must keep his friendship for he will make a *puissant* ally.

pu.is.sance: *n.* توانایی، قدرت، اقتدار، نفوذ

pul.chri.tude /'pʌl.krɪ.tjuːd/ *n.* beauty, comeliness

زیبایی، خوشگلی، قشنگی

The judges have to select this year's Miss America from a selection of female *pulchritude*.

pul.chri.tu.di.nous: *adj.* زیبا، خوشگل، قشنگ

pul.mo.na.ry /£'pʊl.mə.nə.ri, $ -ner.i/ *adj.* related to the lungs

ریوی، مربوط به شش‌ها

She is doing her research on **pulmonary** diseases.

pul.sate /£ pʌlˈseɪt, $ ˈ- -/ v. to throb

زدن، تپیدن، ضربان داشتن

We could see the blood vessels in his temple **pulsate** as he became more angry.

pul.sa.tion: n. تپش، ضربان، زنش

pum.mel /ˈpʌm.ᵊl/ v. to beat

با مشت زدن، با مشت به جانِ کسی افتادن

The child **pummeled** his mother angrily as she carried him home.

punc.ti.li.ous /pʌŋkˈtɪl.i.əs/ adj. laying stress on niceties of conduct, precise

مقید به جزء جزء امور، دقیق؛ مؤدبانه، با نزاکت، باادب

We must be **punctilious** in our planning of this affair, for any error may be regarded as a personal affront.

pun.dit /ˈpʌn.dɪt/ n. learned Hindu, any learned man

هندوی فاضل؛ کارشناس، صاحب‌نظر؛ مشاور

The **pundits** disagree on the best way of dealing with the problem.

pun.gent /ˈpʌn.dʒᵊnt/ adj. stinging, caustic

(بو و مزه) تند؛ تلخ، گزنده؛ انتقادآمیز، انتقادی

The **pungent** aroma of the smoke made me cough.

pun.gen.cy: n. (بو و مزه) تندی؛ گزندگی، تلخی
pun.gent.ly: adv. به‌طور تند و گزنده

pu.ni.tive /£ ˈpjuː.nɪ.tɪv, $ -t̬ɪv/ adj. punishing

تنبیهی، کیفری

He asked for **punitive** measures against the offender.

pu.ny /ˈpjuː.ni/ *adj.* insignificant, tiny, weak

نحیف، ضعیف؛ کوچک، فسقلی؛ غیرقابل توجه؛ مذبوحانه

Our *puny* efforts to stop the flood were futile.

pur.ga.to.ry /£ ˈpɜː.gə.tri, $ ˈpɜːr.gə.tɔːr.i/ *n.* place of spiritual expiation

عالم برزخ، اعراف، محل عذاب؛ (مجازی) جهنم

Waiting in a queue is sheer *purgatory* for him.

pur.ga.to.ri.al: *adj.*   برزخی، برزخ مانند؛ (مجازی) جهنمی

purge /£ pɜːdʒ, $ pɜːrdʒ/ *v.* to clean by removing impurities, to clear of charges

پاکسازی کردن، تصفیه کردن؛ (از گناه و غیره) تبرئه کردن، پاک کردن

Catholics go to confession to be *purged* of sin.

pur.ga.tion: *n.*   تصفیه، تزکیه، پاکسازی

pur.loin /£ pəˈlɔɪn, $ pɚ-/ *v.* to steal

دزدیدن، سرقت کردن، به‌سرقت بردن

In the story, "The *Purloined* Letter," Poe says that the best hiding place is often the most obvious place.

pur.port /£ ˈpɜː.pɔːt, $ ˈpɜːr.pɔːrt/ *n.* intention, meaning

مقصود، منظور، مفهوم، مضمون

The *purport* of the statement is that the firm is bankrupt.

pur.port: *v.*   حاکی بودن، ادعا کردن

pur.vey.or /£ pəˈveɪ.ər, $ pɚˈveɪ.ɚ/ *n.* furnisher of foodstuffs, caterer

تأمین کننده، تهیه‌کننده، عرضه‌کننده

Brown and Son are the *purveyor* of leather goods.

pur.vey: *v.*   عرضه کردن، تأمین کردن

pur.vey.ance: *n.* تدارک، تأمین، عرضه

pur.view /£ ˈpɜː.vjuː, $ ˈpɜːr-/ *n.* scope

محدودهٔ عملیات، حیطه، میدان، حوزه، گستره

These are questions that lie outside the *purview* of our inquiry.

pu.sil.lan.i.mous /ˌpjuː.sɪˈlæn.ɪ.məs/ *adj.* cowardly, fainthearted

بزدلانه، توأم با ترس، جبون

You should be ashamed of your *pusillanimous* conduct during this dispute.

pu.sil.la.ni.mi.ty: *n.* جُبن، بزدلی

pu.ta.tive /£ ˈpjuː.tə.tɪv, $ -t̬ɪv/ *adj.* supposed, reputed

مشهور، معروف، عرفی، قلمداد شده

The *putative* leader of the terrorist organization was arrested by police yesterday.

pu.trid /ˈpjuː.trɪd/ *adj.* foul, rotten, decayed

پوسیده، فاسد، گندیده؛ (مجازی) افتضاح، گند

1) We came across the *putrid* body of a fox while we were walking in the woods.
2) Why did you paint the room that *putrid* color?

put.ri.di.ty: *n.* پوسیدگی، گندیدگی

py.ro.ma.ni.ac /ˌpaɪ.rəʊˈmeɪ.ni.æk, $ -roʊ-/ *n.* person with an irresistible desire to set things on fire

دیوانهٔ ایجاد حریق، بیمار آتش‌افروز

The detectives searched the area for the *pyromaniac* who had set these costly fires.

py.ro.ma.ni.a: *n.* جنون ایجاد حریق، جنون آتش‌افروزی

لیستی از لغاتی که در جملات بخش P به کار رفته‌اند:

affront: n.	آبروریزی	light: adj.	شاد (رنگ)
anticipated: adj.	پیش‌بینی شده	lighthouse: n.	فانوس دریایی
aroma: n.	بوی خوش	materialize: v.	تحقق یافتن
blunder: n.	اشتباه فاحش، گاف	modest: adj.	متین، محجوب
chandelier: n.	چلچراغ	mothball: n.	نفتالین
cling: v.	چسبیدن	mount: v.	سوار شدن
cluttered: adj.	انباشته (از)	odor: n.	بو
culprit: n.	مجرم	ostracize: v.	طرد کردن
defalcation: n.	سوء استفاده مالی	outlet: n.	راه حل، مفرّ
delivery: n.	زایمان	pension: n.	مستمری
discart: v.	دور انداختن	pickle: n.	ترشی
drudgery: n.	کار پر زحمت، حمالی	prank: n.	شوخی، متلک
		privilege: n.	امتیاز
erect: v.	بنا کردن	rage: v.	شدت داشتن
erratically: adv.	نامنظم	rebuke: v.	سرزنش کردن
fade away: v.	از بین رفتن	reminiscent: adj.	یادآور
garb: n.	لباس	repressed: adj.	سرکوب شده
hail: v.	استقبال کردن	revenue: n.	درآمد، عایدی
hawk: n.	شاهین	scrollwork: n.	پیچک چنگ (گچبری)
hurl: v.	پرتاب کردن	sheer: adj.	محض، صرف
jockey: n.	سوارکار	shun: v.	دوری جستن
launch into: v.	پرداختن به		

slate: *n.*	toil: *n.*	کار شاق
فهرست نامزدهای انتخاباتی	touch: *n.*	شیوه
sole: *adj.* تنها	thrust: *n.*	حمله
stodgy: *adj.* کسالت‌آور	truce: *n.*	آتش‌بس موقّت
straw: *n.* کاه	unsanitary: *adj.*	غیربهداشتی
stuffy: *adj.* بدخلق	unveil: *v.*	نشان دادن
susceptible: *adj.* آسیب‌پذیر	valorous: *adj.*	شجاعانه
sway: *v.* تحت تأثیر قرار دادن؛	virtue: *n.*	حسن، خوبی
تکان خوردن	weary: *adj.*	خسته
temple: *n.* گیجگاه، معبد		

Q q

quack /kwæk/ *n., adj.* charlatan, imposter

شیّاد، شارلاتان

Do not be misled by the exorbitant claims of this *quack*.

quad.ru.ped /£ ˈkwɒd.rʊ.ped, $ ˈkwɑː.drə-/ *n.* four-footed animal

چهارپا (حیوان)

Most mammals are *quadrupeds*.

quaff /£ kwɒf, $ kwæf/ *v.* to drink with relish

لاجرعه سر کشیدن

He's always *quaffing* these strange herbal medicines.

quag.mire /£ ˈkwɒg.maɪəʳ, $ ˈkwæg.maɪr/ *n.* bog, marsh

باتلاق، لجن‌زار

Our soldiers who served in Vietnam will never forget the drudgery of marching through the *quagmires* of the delta country.

quail /kweɪl/ *v.* to cower, to lose heart

جا زدن، خود را باختن، از میدان در رفتن

He was afraid that he would *quail* in the face of danger.

qua.li.fied /£ ˈkwɒl.ɪ.faɪd, $ ˈkwɑː.li-/ *adj.* limited, restricted;

skilled, expert

محدود، مشروط، تعدیل شده؛ دارای صلاحیت؛ واجد شرایط

1) It takes three years to become **qualified**.
2) Unable to give the candidate full support, the mayor gave him only a **qualified** endorsement.

qualm /kwɑ:m/ *n.* misgiving

عذاب وجدان، دل نگرانی، دغدغهٔ خاطر؛ تردید

He felt no serious **qualms** about concealing the information from the police.

quan.dary /£ 'kwɒn.dri, $ 'kwɑ:n-/ *n.* dilemma

سر در گمی، بلاتکلیفی؛ تردید، دودلی

I've been offered a better job but at a lower salary-I'm *in a* **quandary** about what to do.

qua.ran.tine /£ 'kwɒr.ᵊn.ti:n, $ 'kwɔ:r-/ *n., v.* isolation of person or animal to prevent spread of infection

قرنطینه، دوران قرنطینه؛ قرنطینه کردن

They were kept in **quarantine** for a couple of days.

quar.ry /£ 'kwɒr.i, $ 'kwɔ:r-/ *v.* to dig into

استخراج کردن

They **quarried** blocks of marble out of the hillside.

quar.ry /£ 'kwɒr.i, $ 'kwɔ:r-/ *n.* victim, object of a hunt

معدن سنگ؛ شکار، فراری

The police closed in on their **quarry**.

quay /ki:/ *n.* dock, landing place

اسکله، بارانداز

Because of the captain's carelessness, the ship crashed into the **quay**.

quea.sy /ˈkwiːzi/ *adj.* easily nauseated, squeamish

تهوع‌آور؛ دل به هم خورده، دارای حالت تهوع، دچار حالت تهوع

Traveling on a bus makes me feel *queasy*.

quell /kwel/ *v.* to put down, to quiet

فرونشاندن، سرکوب کردن

The police used fire hoses and tear gas to *quell* the rioters.

quer.ul.ous /ˈkwer.ju.ləs/ *adj.* fretful, whining

بهانه‌گیر، ایرادی، نق نقو، کج خلق

His classmates were repelled by his *querulous* and complaining statements.

quib.ble /ˈkwɪb.l/ *v.* to play on words, to equivocate

طفره رفتن، از زیر سؤال در رفتن، با کلمات بازی کردن، کلی بافی کردن

Do not *quibble*; I want a straightforward and definite answer.

qui.es.cent /kwiˈes.ənt/ *adj.* at rest, dormant

غیرفعال، راکد، خاموش، خفته، ساکت، آرام

It is unlikely that such an extremist organization will remain *quiescent* for long.

qui.es.cence: *n.* آرامش، بی‌حرکتی، سکون، رکود

qui.et.ude /£ ˈkwaɪə.tjuːd, $ -tuːd/ *n.* tranquillity

آرامش، سکوت

He was impressed by the air of *quietude* and peace that pervaded the valley.

quin.tes.sence /kwɪnˈtes.əns/ *n.* purest and highest embodiment

جوهر، هستهٔ اصلی؛ نمونهٔ بارز، مظهر

Her book captures the *quintessence* of Renaissance humanism.

quip /kwɪp/ *n.* taunting remark

کنایه، طعنه، لطیفه، متلک

He ended his speech with a merry *quip*.

quirk /£ kwɜːk, $ kwɜːrk/ *n.* startling twist, caprice

اتفاق عجیب، رویداد شگفت؛ حادثه، اتفاق

By a *quirk* of fate, they had booked into the same hotel.

by a *quirk* of fate   از قضای روزگار

qui.xot.ic /£ kwɪkˈsɒt.ɪk, $ -ˈsɑː.t̬ɪk/ *adj.* idealistic but impractical

رؤیایی، خیالی، آرمانی

This is a vast, exciting and perhaps *quixotic* project.

quiz.zi.cal /ˈkwɪz.ɪ.kᵊl/ *adj.* comical, bantering, humorously serious

شوخ؛ شیطنت‌آمیز؛ ناباورانه، سؤال برانگیز

She gave me a *quizzical* look.

quo.rum /£ ˈkwɔː.rəm, $ ˈkwɔːr.əm/ *n.* required number of members present

اکثریت لازم، حد نصاب

Four members walked out of the session, with the result that the committee did not have a *quorum* and could not take any decisions.

لیستی از لغاتی که در جملات بخش Q به‌کار رفته‌اند:

خنده‌دار	merry: *adj.*	close in on sth.
لذت	relish: *n.*	نزدیک‌تر شدن و حمله کردن
جلسه	session: *n.*	endorsement: *n.* تأیید، حمایت
		exorbitant: *adj.* گزاف، غیرمعقول

R r

rab.id /ˈræb.ɪd, ˈreɪ.bɪd/ *adj.* like a fanatic, furious

هار؛ دیوانه‌وار، مفرط؛ افراطی، متعصب

She is a *rabid* feminist who believes that all men want to exercise power over women.

rac.on.teur /£ ˌræk.ɒnˈtɜːʳ, $ -ɑːnˈtɜːr/ *n.* storyteller

قصه‌گو

My father was a gifted *raconteur* with an unlimited supply of anecdotes.

rag.a.muf.fin /ˈræɡ.əˌmʌf.ɪn/ *n.* person wearing tattered clothes

ژنده‌پوش، بچهٔ ژنده‌پوش

He felt sorry for the *ragamuffin* who was begging for food and gave him money to buy a meal.

rail /reɪl/ *v.* to scold, to rant

سرزنش کردن، پرخاش کردن؛ تندی کردن، اوقات تلخی کردن

You may *rail at* him all you want; you will never change it.

rai.ment /ˈreɪ.mənt/ *n.* clothing, clothes

جامه، لباس، تن‌پوش

"How can I go to the ball? "asked Cinderella. "I have no

raiment to wear".

rak.ish /'reɪ.kɪʃ/ *adj.* stylish, sporty

کج؛ جلف؛ هرزه؛ سرحال و شنگول

He wore his hat at a *rakish* and jaunty angle.

ram.i.fi.ca.tion /ˌræm.ɪ.fɪ'keɪ.ʃᵊn/ *n.* branching out, subdivision

انشعاب، شعبه، شاخه؛ (به‌صورت جمع) عواقب، پیامد

We must examine all the *ramifications* of this problem.

ram.i.fy: *v.* شاخه شاخه شدن، منشعب شدن

ramp /ræmp/ *n.* slope, inclined palne

سکّو، پلکان چرخدار، شیب راهه، پلکان متحرک

The house was built with *ramps* instead of stairs to enable the man in the wheelchair to move easily from room to room and floor to floor.

ram.pant /'ræm.pᵊnt/ *adj.* rearing up on hind legs; unrestrained, increasing

(حیوان) در حال حمله؛ (بیماری) شایع؛ (گیاه) پرپشت، انبوه

The *rampant* weeds in the garden killed all the flowers which had been planted in the spring.

ram.part /£ 'ræm.pɑːt, $ -pɑːrt/ *n.* defensive mound of earth

خاکریز، بارو؛ (مجازی) حفاظ، وسیلهٔ دفاع

From the *ramparts* we watched as the fighting continued.

ran.cid /'rænt.sɪd/ *adj.* having the odor of stale fish

(روغن، کره و غیره) بوگرفته، مانده، گندیده، فاسد؛ (بو) نامطبوع

A *rancid* odor filled the ship's galley.

ran.cor /£ 'ræŋ.kəʳ, $ -kɚ/ *n.* bitterness, hatred

کینه، بغض، دشمنی دیرینه

Let us forget our **rancor** and cooperate in this new endeavor.

rank.le /'ræŋ.kl/ *v.* to irritate, to fester

دل چرکین کردن / شدن، آزار دادن، رنجاندن، عذاب دادن، عصبانی کردن

The memory of having been jilted **rankled** him for years.

rant /rænt/ *v., n.* to speak bombastically, to rave

توپ و تشر زدن، داد و هوار کردن؛ رجز خواندن، شعار دادن

I get fed up with my mother **ranting and raving** about my clothes all the time.

ra.pa.cious /rə'peɪ.ʃəs/ *adj.* excessively grasping, plundering

حریص، طماع، آزمند؛ درنده، چپاولگر

Hawks and **rapacious** birds play an important role in the balance of nature.

rap.proche.ment /£ ræp'rɒʃ.mɑ̃ːŋ, $ ˌræp.rɔːʃ'mɑ̃ːŋ/ *n.* reconciliation

آشتی دوباره، تجدید روابط حسنه

Both sides were eager to effect a **rapprochement** but did not know how to undertake a program designed to bring about harmony.

ra.re.fied /£ 'reə.rɪ.faɪd, $ 'rer.ə-/ *adj.* made less dense (of a gas)

رقیق (گاز و هوا)

The mountain climbers had difficulty breathing in the **rarefied** atmosphere.

ras.py /£ rɑːspɪ, $ ræspɪ/ *adj.* grating, harsh

گوش خراش، ناهنجار

The sergeant's **raspy** voice grated on the recruit's ears.

ra.ti.o.ci.na.tion /ˌræ.tɪˈɒsɪneɪ.ʃən/ n. reasoning

استدلال، تعقل

Poe's "The Gold Bug" is a splended example of the author's use of *ratiocination*.

ra.tion.al.ize /ˈræʃ.ən.ə.laɪz/ v. to reason, to justify an improper act

توجیه کردن، دلیل تراشی کردن، معقول جلوه دادن

Do not try to *rationalize* your behavior by blaming your companions.

rat.ion.a.liz.a.tion: n.   توجیه، دلیل تراشی

rau.cous /£ ˈrɔː.kəs, $ ˈrɑː-/ adj. harsh and shrill

(صدا) ناهنجار، گوش خراش؛ پر سر و صدا، شلوغ

His *raucous* laughter irritated me.

rav.age /ˈræv.ɪdʒ/ v., n. to plunder, to despoil

ویران کردن، چاپیدن و کشتن؛ نابودی، انهدام، ویرانی، تخریب

The marauding army *ravaged* the countryside.

rav.en.ous /ˈræv.ən.əs/ adj. extremely hungry

بسیار گرسنه؛ درنده خوی

The *ravenous* dog upset several garbage pails in its search for food.

raze /reɪz/ v. to destroy completely

منهدم کردن، با خاک یکسان کردن

The owners intend to *raze* the hotel and erect an office building on the site.

re.ac.tion.a.ry /£ riˈæk.ʃən.ər.i, $ -er-/ n., adj. recoiling from progress, retrograde

مرتجع؛ ارتجاعی

His program was **reactionary** since it sought to abolish many of the social reforms instituted by the previous administration.

realm /relm/ *n.* kingdom, sphere

قلمرو، حوزه، حیطه، گستره

The **realm** of possibilities for the new invention was endless.

re.bate /ˈriː.beɪt/ *n., v.* to discount

تخفیف، کسر قیمت؛ تخفیف دادن، بازپرداخت کردن

We offer a **rebate** of ten percent to those who pay cash.

re.buff /rɪˈbʌf/ *v.* to reject sharply, to snub

رد کردن، نپذیرفتن؛ حال کسی را گرفتن، مورد بی‌اعتنایی قرار دادن

She **rebuffed** his invitation so smoothly that he did not realize he had been snubbed.

re.cal.ci.trant /rɪˈkæl.sɪ.trənt/ *adj.* obstinately stubborn

سرسخت، کله شق، سرکش، نافرمان، متمرد، ناسازگار

Donkeys are reputed to be the most **recalcitrant** of animals.

re.cant /rɪˈkænt/ *v.* to repudiate, to withdraw previous statement

(جلوی همه) پوزش خواستن، حرف خود را پس گرفتن، اظهار ندامت کردن

Unless you **recant** your confession, you will be punished severely.

re.ca.pit.u.late /ˌriː.kəˈpɪt.ju.leɪt/ *v.* to summarize

جمع‌بندی کردن، خلاصه کردن

Let us **recapitulate** what has been said thus far before going ahead.

re.ces.sion /rɪˈseʃ.ᵊn/ *n.* withdrawal, retreat

عقب‌نشینی، پس‌روی؛ رکود اقتصادی

The *recession* of the troops from the combat area was completed in an orderly manner.

re.ci.di.vi.sm /rɪˈsɪd.ɪ.vɪ.zᵊm/ *n.* habitual return to crime

اعتیاد به ارتکاب جرم

Prison reformers in the United States are disturbed by the high rate of *recidivism*.

re.ci.pi.ent /rɪˈsɪp.i.ənt/ *n.* receiver

دریافت‌کننده، گیرنده

Although he had been the *recipient* of many favors, he was not grateful to his benefactor.

re.ci.pro.cal /rɪˈsɪp.rə.kᵊl/ *adj.* mutual, exchangeable, interacting

دو جانبه، دو طرفه، متقابل

The two nations signed a *reciprocal* trade agreement.

re.ci.pro.cate /rɪˈsɪp.rə.keɪt/ *v.* to repay in kind

تلافی کردن، متقابلاً جواب دادن، معامله به مثل کردن

If they attack us, we shall be compelled to *reciprocate* and bomb their territory.

re.cluse /rɪˈkluːs/ *n.* hermit

(آدم) خلوت‌نشین، چله‌نشین، گوشه‌نشین، عزلت‌نشین

The *recluse* lived in a hut in the forest.

re.con.cile /ˈrek.ᵊn.saɪl/ *v.* to make friendly after quarrel, to correct inconsistencies

آشتی دادن، فیصله دادن؛ تطبیق دادن، منطبق کردن

Each month we *reconcile* our checkbook with the bank

statement.

re.con.dite /ˈrekəndaɪt/ *adj.* abstruse, profound, hidden from view

مشکل، غامض، غیرقابل فهم، مبهم، سنگین، سخت

He read many *recondite* books in order to obtain the material for his scholarly thesis.

re.con.nais.sance /£ rɪˈkɒnɪsəns, $ -ˈkɑːnə-/ *n.* survey of enemy by soldiers

(نظامی) شناسایی، تجسس، اکتشاف؛ گشت اکتشافی

If you encounter any enemy soldiers during your *reconnaissance*, capture them for questioning.

re.course /£ rɪˈkɔːs, $ ˈriːkɔːrs/ *n.* resorting to help when in trouble

توسل، کمک‌گیری، ملجاء؛ راه چاره

The boy's only *recourse* was to appeal to his father for aid.

rec.re.ant /ˈrekriənt/ *n.* coward; betrayer of faith

خائن، بی‌وفا، منافق؛ ترسو

The religious people ostracized the *recreant* who had abandoned their faith.

re.cri.mi.na.tion /rɪˌkrɪmɪˈneɪʃən/ *n.* counterchanges

تهمت متقابل، اتهام متقابل

Loud and angry *recriminations* were her answer to his accusations.

rec.ti.fy /ˈrektɪfaɪ/ *v.* to correct

اصلاح کردن، تصحیح کردن

I want to *rectify* my error before it is too late.

rec.ti.tude /£ ˈrek.tɪ.tjuːd, $ -tə.tuːd/ *n.* uprightness

راستی، درستی، درستکاری، صداقت، شرافت

He was renowned for his *rectitude* and integrity.

re.cum.bent /rɪˈkʌm.bənt/ *adj.* reclining, lying down

(شخص) خوابیده، دراز کشیده

She looked at the *recumbent form* beside her.

re.cu.pe.rate /£ rɪˈkjuː.pəˈr.eɪt, $ -ˈkuː.pə.reɪt/ *v.* to recover

بهبود یافتن، شفا یافتن، خوب شدن؛ (سلامت، نیرو و غیره) باز یافتن

The doctors were worried because the patient did not *recuperate* as rapidly as they had expected.

re.cur.rect /£ rɪˈkʌr.ənt, $ -ˈkɜːr-/ *adj.* occurring again and again

مکرر، تکراری، همیشگی؛ عودکننده، راجعه

These *recurrent* attacks disturbed us and we consulted a physician.

red.o.lent /ˈred.əl.ənt/ *adj.* fragrant, odorous

خوشبو، معطر، آکنده از بویِ، پر از بویِ

Even though it is February, the air is *redolent* of spring.

re.doub.ta.ble /£ rɪˈdaʊ.tə.bl̩, $ tə-/ *adj.* formidable, causing fear

سرسخت، قوی؛ قابل احترام، با ابهت، با هیبت، با جذبه؛ مهیب

Tonight Clay faces the most *redoubtable* opponent of his boxing career.

re.dress /rɪˈdres/ *n., v.* remedy, compensation; to compensate

جبران، خسارت؛ استمالت، دلجویی؛ جبران کردن

Do you mean to tell me that I can get no *redress* for my injuries?

re.dun.dant /rɪˈdʌn.dᵊnt/ *adj.* superfluous, excessively wordy

زیادی، زاید، بیش از حد لزوم؛ پر از حشو، دارای حشو

Your composition is *redundant*, you can easily reduce its length.

reek /riːk/ *v.* to emit (odor)

بوی گند (چیزی) دادن، بوی ... دادن

His breath *reeked of* tobacco.

re.fec.tion /rɪˈfek.ʃᵊn/ *n.* slight refreshment

غذای سبک، حاضری

We stopped on the road for only a quick *refection*.

re.fec.to.ry /£ rɪˈfek.tᵊr.i, $ -tɚ-/ *n.* dining hall

(مدرسه، دانشگاه و غیره) سالن غذاخوری

In this huge *refectory*, we can feed the entire monastic order at one sitting.

re.frac.tion /rɪˈfræk.ʃᵊn/ *n.* bending of a ray of light

(نور) شکست، انکسار

You can see a *refraction* of light in action by placing a drinking straw in a glass of water.

re.frac.to.ry /rɪˈfræk.tə.ri/ *adj.* stubborn, unmanageable

(اسب) چموش؛ (کودک) سرکش، نافرمان؛ صعب‌العلاج

The *refractory* horse was eliminated from the race.

re.fur.bish /£ ˌriːˈfɜː.bɪʃ, $ -ˈfɜːr-/ *v.* to renovate, to make bright by polishing

مجدداً تر و تمیز کردن، مرمت کردن، دکور عوض کردن

The flat will be *refurbished* for the new tenants.

re.fute /rɪˈfjuːt/ *v.* to disprove

(نظریه، ادعا) تکذیب کردن، رد کردن

The barrister used new evidence to **refute** the charges and clear the defendant.

re.fu.ta.tion: *n.* تکذیب، رد، ابطال؛ انکار

re.gal /ˈriː.gᵊl/ *adj.* royal

شاهانه، سلطنتی؛ مجلل، با شکوه

He made a **regal** entrance.

re.gale /rɪˈgeɪl/ *v.* to entertain

سرگرم کردن، موجب سرگرمی (کسی) شدن؛ سور دادن

John **regaled** us with tales of his adventures in Africa.

re.gat.ta /£ rɪˈgæt.ə, $ -ˈgɑː.tə/ *n.* boat or yacht race

مسابقهٔ قایقرانی

Many boating enthusiasts followed the **regatta** in their own yachts.

re.gen.e.rate /ˌriːˈdʒen.ə.reɪt/ *v.* to reform completely, to improve, to grow again

جان تازه بخشیدن / یافتن، احیا کردن / شدن، جان تازه یافتن

The party soon **regenerate** under her leadership.

re.gen.e.ra.tion: *n.* احیا، بازسازی، تجدید حیات

re.gen.e.ra.tive: *adj.* حیات‌بخش، نشاط‌آور

reg.i.cide /ˈredʒ.ɪ.saɪd/ *n.* murder of a king or queen

قتل پادشاه یا ملکه، شاه‌کُشی، ملکه‌کُشی

The death of Mary Queen of Scots was an act of **regicide**.

re.gime /reɪˈʒiːm/ *n.* method or system of government

رژیم، حکومت، سیستم حکومتی

When he mentions the old **regime**, he refers to the government existing before the revolution.

regimen /'redʒ.ɪ.mən/ *n.* systematic plan, especially for health

رژیم غذایی، دستور غذایی

After his heart attack, the doctor put him on a strict ***regimen***.

re.ha.bi.li.tate /ˌriː.həˈbɪl.ɪ.teɪt/ *v.* to restore to proper condition

توان‌بخشی کردن، ترمیم کردن؛ مرمت کردن، نوسازی کردن

We must ***rehabilitate*** those whom we send to prison.

re.ha.bi.li.ta.tion: *n.*   توان‌بخشی؛ بازپروری؛ ترمیم

re.im.burse /£ ˌriː.ɪmˈbɜːs, $ -ˈbɜːrs/ *v.* to repay

باز پرداختن، (زیان کسی را) جبران کردن، پول (کسی را) پس دادن

Let me know what you have spent and I will ***reimburse*** you.

re.i.te.rate /£ riˈɪt.ºr.eɪt, $ -ˈɪt̬.ɚ.eɪt/ *v.* to repeat

تکرار کردن، دوباره گفتن

I shall ***reiterate*** this message until all have understood it.

re.juv.e.nate /rɪˈdʒuː.vº.eɪt/ *v.* to make young again

جوان کردن، سرحال آوردن؛ جان تازه بخشیدن، احیا کردن

The charlatan claimed that his elixir would ***rejuvenate*** the aged and the weary.

rel.e.gate /ˈrel.ɪ.geɪt/ *v.* to remove to some less prominent position, to banish

تنزل (درجه) دادن، پایین آوردن؛ تبعید کردن، منتقل کردن

If we ***relegate*** these experienced people to positions of unimportance, we shall lose the services of valuably trained personnel.

rel.e.van.cy /ˈrel.ə.vºnt.si/ *n.* relation to the matter at hand

ارتباط، ربط، مناسبت

I was impressed by the *relevancy* of your remarks.

rel.e.vant: *adj.* مربوط، مربوط به موضوع

re.lin.quish /rɪˈlɪŋ.kwɪʃ/ *v.* to abandon

رها کردن، ترک کردن، دست کشیدن؛ واگذار کردن

She *relinquished* possession of the house to her sister.

rel.ish /ˈrel.ɪʃ/ *v., n.* to enjoy

دوست داشتن، خوش آمدن، لذت بردن؛ لذت، شور و شوق

I *relish* a good joke as much as anyone else.

re.me.di.a.ble /rɪˈmiː.dɪ.ə.bəl/ *adj.* reparable, curable

قابل ترمیم، علاج‌پذیر، قابل درمان، درمان‌پذیر

Let us be grateful that the damage is *remediable*.

re.me.di.al /rɪˈmiː.di.əl/ *adj.* curative, corrective

درمانی؛ ترمیمی؛ تقویتی، جبرانی

Because he was a slow reader, he decided to take a course in *remedial* reading.

re.mi.nis.cence /ˌrem.ɪˈnɪs.ənts/ *n.* recollection

تجدید خاطرات گذشته، یادآوری

Her *reminiscence* of her experiences are so fascinating that she ought to write a book.

re.mi.nis.cent: *adj.* یادآور، تداعی‌کننده

re.miss /rɪˈmɪs/ *adj.* negligent

بی‌مبالات، سهل‌انگار، اهمال‌کار، فراموشکار

You have been very *remiss* in fulfilling your obligations.

rem.nant /ˈrem.nənt/ *n.* remainder

باقی‌مانده، پس مانده؛ ته تاقه، ته توپ

I suggest that you wait until the store places the

remnant of these goods on sale.

re.mon.strate /£ ˈrem.ᵊn.streɪt, $ rɪˈmɑːnt-/ *v.* to protest

اعتراض کردن، نکوهش کردن، شکایت کردن

I must *remonstrate* about the lack of police protection in this area.

re.morse /£ rɪˈmɔːs, $ -ˈmɔːrs/ *n.* guilt, self-reproach

پشیمانی، ندامت، دریغ

The murderer felt no *remorse* for his crime.

re.mu.ne.ra.tive /£ rɪˈmjuː.nᵊr.ə.tɪv, $ -nə.reɪ.ṭɪv/ *adj.* rewarding, compensating

پرسود، سودمند؛ باحقوق مکفی

I find my new work so *remunerative* that I may not return to my previous employment.

re.mu.ne.ra.tion: *n.*   مزد، پاداش، اجر

rend /rend/ *v.* to split, to tear apart

دریدن، پاره کردن، چاک کردن

In his grief, he tried to *rend* his garments.

rend.er /£ ˈren.dəʳ, $ -dɚ/ *v.* to deliver, to provide, to represent

ارائه دادن، عرضه کردن، تقدیم کردن

He *rendered* aid to the needy and indigent.

ren.dez.vous /£ ˈrɒn.deɪ.vuː, $ ˈrɑːn-/ *n.* meeting place

محل ملاقات، وعده‌گاه؛ قرار ملاقات، قرار

The two fleets met at the *rendezvous* at the appointed time.

ren.di.tion /renˈdɪ.ʃᵊn/ *n.* translation, artistic interpretation

ترجمه؛ ارائه، اجرا

The audience cheered enthusiastically as she completed her ***rendition*** of the aria.

ren.e.gade /ˈren.ɪ.geɪd/ *n.* deserter, apostate

مرتد؛ خائن

Because he refused to support his fellow members in their drive, he was shunned as a ***renegade***.

re.nounce /rɪˈnaʊnts/ *v.* to abandon, to discontinue, to disown

ترک کردن، صرفنظر کردن، دست کشیدن؛ از خود راندن، از خود دور کردن

Joan of Arc refused to ***renounce*** her statements even though she knew she would be burned at the stake as a witch.

ren.o.vate /ˈren.ə.veɪt/ *v.* to restore to good condition

تجدید بنا کردن، نوسازی کردن، تعمیرات اساسی کردن

They claim that they can ***renovate*** worn shoes so that they look like new ones.

re.nun.ci.a.tion /rɪˌnʌt.siˈeɪ.ʃən/ *n.* giving up, renouncing

کناره‌گیری، انصراف، چشم‌پوشی؛ ترک؛ رد

Do not sign this ***renunciation*** of your right to sue until you have consulted a lawyer.

rep.a.rable /ˈrepərəbəl/ *adj.* capable of being repaired

جبران‌پذیر، قابل اصلاح، اصلاح‌پذیر

Fortunately, the damages we suffered in the accident were ***reparable***.

re.par.a.tion /ˌrep.əˈreɪ.ʃən/ *n.* amends, compensation

خسارت، غرامت، تاوان؛ جبران

At the peace conference, the defeated country promised

to pay *reparations* to the victors.

re.par.tee /£ ˌrep.ɑːˈtiː, $ -ɑːr-/ *n.* clever reply

حاضر جوابی؛ جواب دندان شکن، جواب تر و چسبان

He was famous for his witty *repartee* and his sarcasm.

re.pel.lent /rɪˈpelᵊnt/ *adj.* driving away, unattractive

مشمئزکننده، زننده، تهوع‌آور، نفرت‌انگیز

I find his selfishness *repellent*.

re.per.cus.sion /£ ˌriː.pəˈkʌʃᵊn, $ -pɚ-/ *n.* rebound, reverberation, reaction

عواقب، پیامد، نتایج

I am afraid that this event will have serious *repercussion*.

re.per.toire /£ ˈrep.ə.twɑːʳ, $ -ɚ.twɑːr/ *n.* all the things (esp. music or plays) that someone or something knows or can perform

(موسیقی، نمایش و غیره) اپراتور؛ مجموعه آثار، گنجینه

The Royal Shakespeare Company also have many plays in their *repertoire*.

re.plen.ish /rɪˈplen.ɪʃ/ *v.* to fill up again

دوباره پرکردن؛ دوباره تهیه کردن

Does your glass need *replenishing*?

re.plete /rɪˈpliːt/ *adj.* filled to capacity

پر از، مملو از، سرشار از

This book is *replete* with humorous situations.

rep.li.ca /ˈrep.lɪ.kə/ *n.* copy

مدل، کپی، نسخهٔ بدل

The ship is an exact *replica* of the original Golden Hind.

re.pos.i.to.ry /£ rɪˈpɒz.ɪ.tᵊr.i, $ -ˈpɑː.zɪ.tɔːr-/ *n.* storehouse

مخزن، انبار، منبع

Libraries are *repositories* of the world's best thoughts.

rep.re.hen.si.ble /ˌrep.rɪˈhent.sə.bl̩/ *adj.* deserving blame

قابل انتقاد، قابل سرزنش، نکوهیده، شنیع

Your vicious conduct in this situation is *reprehensible*.

re.prieve /rɪˈpriːv/ *n., v.* temporary stay; to delay the punishment

تعلیق اجرای مجازات، لغو حکم اعدام؛ لغو کردن مجازات

He was sentenced to death but was granted a last minute *reprieve*.

rep.ri.mand /£ ˈrep.rɪ.mɑːnd, $ -rə.mænd/ *v.* to reprove severely

توبیخ کردن، مؤاخذه کردن؛ توبیخ، مؤاخذه

I am afraid that my parents will *reprimand* me when I show them my report card.

re.pri.sal /rɪˈpraɪ.zᵊl/ *n.* retaliation

تلافی، انتقام

I am confident that we are ready for any *reprisals* the enemy may undertake.

re.pro.bate /£ ˈrep.rəʊ.beɪt, $ -rə-/ *n.* person hardened in sin

آدم هرزه، آدم فاسد، آدم لاقید

You sinful old *reprobate*!

re.pro.ba.tion /re.prəˈbeɪ.ʃᵊn/ *n.* severe disapproval

نارضایتی شدید، مخالفت شدید

The students showed their *reprobation* of his act by refusing to talk with him.

re.prove /rɪˈpruːv/ *v.* to censure, to rebuke

ملامت کردن، سرزنش کردن

The principal *reproved* the students when they became unruly in the auditorium.

re.pu.di.ate /rɪˈpjuː.di.eɪt/ *v.* to disown, to disavow

زیر بار نرفتن، نپذیرفتن؛ پرداخت نکردن، ادا نکردن

He announced that he would *repudiate* all debts incurred by his wife.

re.pug.nance /rɪˈpʌg.nənts/ *n.* loathing

تنفر، نفرت، انزجار

She has a deep *repugnance* to the idea of accepting chairty.

re.pug.nant: *adj.* نفرت‌انگیز، مشمئزکننده، مهوع

re.qui.em /ˈrek.wi.əm/ *n.* a mass for the dead, dirge

موسیقی مجلس یادبود

They played Mozart's *requiem* at the funeral.

req.ui.site /ˈrek.wɪ.zɪt/ *n.* necessary requirement

ضروری، لازم، مورد لزوم، بایسته

Have you the *requisite* visa to enter Canada?

re.quite /rɪˈkwaɪt/ *v.* to repay, to revenge

جبران کردن؛ تلافی کردن، انتقام گرفتن

The wretch *requited* his benefactors by betraying them.

re.scind /rɪˈsɪnd/ *v.* to cancel

لغو کردن، فسخ کردن

Because of public resentment, the king had to *rescind* his order.

re.scis.sion /rɪˈsɪ.ʒ³n/ *n.* abrogation, annulment

لغو، نسخ، ابطال

The ***rescission*** of the unpopular law was urged by all political parties.

re.serve /£ rɪˈzɜːv, $ -ˈzɜːrv/ *n.* self-control, care in expressing oneself

خویشتن‌داری، خودداری

She was outspoken and uninhibited; he was cautious and inclined to ***reserve***.

re.served: *adj.* خویشتن‌دار، خوددار، تودار، درون‌گرا، ساکت

res.i.due /£ ˈrez.ɪ.djuː, $ -ə.duː/ *n.* remainder, balance

بقیه، مانده، باقیمانده؛ (حقوقی) باقی‌ماندهٔ ماترک

In his will, he requested that after payment of debts, taxes, and funeral expenses, the ***residue*** be given to his wife.

re.signed /rɪˈzaɪnd/ *adj.* unresisting, patiently submissive

بردبار، شکیبا، تسلیم، راضی

I am ***resigned*** to my fate.

re.sign.ed.ly: *adv.* با حالت تسلیم و رضا، با بردباری
re.sign: *v.* تحمل کردن؛ استعفا دادن
res.ig.na.tion: *n.* استعفا، کناره‌گیری؛ تسلیم و رضا

re.si.li.ent /rɪˈzɪl.i.ənt/ *adj.* elastic

کِش‌سان، ارتجاعی، فنری، انعطاف‌پذیر

Steel is highly ***resilient*** and therefore is used in manufacture of springs.

re.si.li.ence: *n.* کِش‌سانی، خاصیت ارتجاعی / فنری، انعطاف‌پذیری

res.o.nant /ˈrez.ᵊn.ənt/ *adj.* echoing, resounding

(صدا) پرطنین، رسا، قوی

His ***resonant*** voice was particulary pleasing.

res.pite /ˈres.paɪt/ *n.* delay in punishment; rest

مهلت، فرجه؛ استراحت

The judge *granted* the condemned man a ***respite*** to enable his attorneys to file an appeal.

re.splen.dent /rɪˈsplen.dᵊnt/ *adj.* brilliant, lustrous

پر زرق و برق، درخشنده، خیره‌کننده، تابناک، پر تلألو

The queen's ***resplendent*** purple robes and crown were on display in the museum.

re.spon.sive.ness /£ rɪˈspɒnt.sɪv.nəs, $ -ˈspɑːnt-/ *n.* state of reaction

پذیرش، عکس‌العمل، رغبت به پاسخگویی؛ تفاهم

The audience's ***responsiveness*** is a key part of any performance.

res.ti.tu.tion /£ ˌres.tɪˈtjuː.ʃᵊn, $ -ˈtuː-/ *n.* reparation, indemnification

جبران خسارت، خسارت، غرامت

He offered to make ***restitution*** for the window broken by his son.

res.tive /£ ˈres.tɪv, $ -t̬ɪv/ *adj.* unmanageable

بی‌قرار، ناآرام، سرکش، ناراحت

We must quiet the ***restive*** animals.

re.sur.gent /£ rɪˈsɜː.dʒᵊnt, $ -ˈsɜːr-/ *adj.* rising again after defeat

احیا شده، دوباره زنده شده، زندگی تازه گرفته؛ از نو باب شده

The ***resurgent*** nation surprised everyone by its quick recovery after total defeat.

re.sus.ci.tate /rɪˈsʌs.ɪ.teɪt/ *v.* to revive

به هوش آوردن؛ به یاد آوردن

The lifeguard tried to *resuscitate* the drowned child by applying artificial respiration.

re.tal.i.ate /rɪˈtæl.i.eɪt/ *v.* to repay in kind

تلافی کردن، مقابله به مثل کردن، دست به اقدام متقابل زدن

Fear that we will *retaliate* immediately deters our foe from attacking us.

re.ten.tive /rɪˈten.tɪv/ *adj.* having a good memory

(حافظه) قوی

The pupil did not need to spend much time in study as he had a *retentive* mind.

ret.i.cence /£ ˈret.ɪ.sᵊnts, $ ˈret̬.ə-/ *n.* reserve, inclination to be silent

توداری، کم حرفی، خودداری، سکوت

Because of the *reticence* of the key witness, the case against the defendant collapsed.

ret.i.nue /£ ˈret.ɪ.njuː, $ -ᵊn.uː/ *n.* following, attendants

ملازمین و همراهان (یک شخص مهم)

The queen's *retinue* followed her down the aisle.

re.tort /£ rɪˈtɔːt, $ -ˈtɔːrt/ *n., v.* quick, sharp reply

جوابِ تند، جواب دندان‌شکن، پرخاش؛ با تندی جواب دادن

He made a rude sign by way of *retort*.

re.trac.tion /rɪˈtræk.ʃᵊn/ *n.* withdrawal

انصراف، پس‌گیری؛ تکذیب

The newspaper printed a *retraction* for their previous error.

re.tract: *v.* پس گرفتن، تکذیب کردن

re.trench /rɪ'trentʃ/ v. to cut down, to economize
صرفه‌جویی کردن، کاستن هزینه‌ها
If they were able to send their children to college, they would have to *retrench*.

ret.ri.bu.tion /ˌret.rɪ'bjuː:.ʃᵊn/ n. vengeance, compensation
مجازات، کیفر، عقوبت، مکافات
The evangelist maintained that an angry deity would exact *retribution* from the sinners.

re.trieve /rɪ'triːv/ v. to recover, to find and bring in
یافتن، پیدا کردن، پیدا کردن و آوردن، به‌دست آوردن
The dog was intelligent and quickly learned to *retrieve* the game killed by the hunter.

ret.ro.ac.tive /£ ˌret.rəʊ'æk.tɪv, $ -roʊ-/ adj. made effective as of a prior date
(حقوقی) عطف به ماسبق شونده
Because the law was *retroactive* to the first of the year, we found he was eligible for the pension.

ret.ro.grade /£ 'ret.rəʊ.greɪd, $ -rə-/ v. to go backwards, to degenerate
سیر قهقرایی پیمودن، تنزل کردن، بدتر شدن
Instead of advancing, our civilization seems to have *retrograded* in ethics and culture.

ret.ro.spec.tive /£ ˌret.rəʊ'spek.tiv, $ -rə-/ adj. looking back on the past
ناظر به گذشته، مربوط به گذشته، ناشی از گذشته
It is only when we become *retrospective* that we can apppreciate the tremendous advances made during this

century.

rev.el.ry /ˈrev.ᵊl.ri/ *n.* boisterous merrymaking

عربده‌جویی، خوشگذرانی، عیاشی

New Year's Eve is a night of ***revelry***.

re.ver.be.rate /£ rɪˈvɜːbᵊr.eɪt, $ -ˈvɜːrbɚ.eɪt/ *v.* to echo, to resound

طنین انداختن، باز تابیدن؛ به‌لرزه در آوردن؛ پیچیدن، انعکاس داشتن

The entire valley ***reverberated*** with the sound of the church bells.

re.vere /£ rɪˈvɪəʳ, $ -ˈvɪr/ *v.* to respect, to honor

احترام قائل شدن، حرمت گذاشتن؛ گرامی داشتن، عزیز شمردن

In Asian societies, people ***revere*** their elders.

rev.e.rie /£ ˈrev.ᵊr.i, $ ˈ-ɚ-/ *n.* daydream, musing

عالم خیال، عالم رؤیا؛ خیال‌پردازی

He was awakened from his ***reverie*** by the teacher's question.

re.vile /rɪˈvaɪl/ *v.* to slander, to use verbal abuse

دشنام دادن به، فحش دادن به، ناسزا گفتن به

The judge has been ***reviled*** in the newspapers for his opinions on rape.

re.vul.sion /rɪˈvʌl.ʃᵊn/ *n.* complete dislike or repugnance

تنفر، نفرت، بیزاری، انزجار

She looked at him with ***revulsion***.

rhap.so.dize /ˈræp.sə.daɪz/ *v.* to express great enthusiasm

با احساسات زائدالوصف بیان کردن، تحسین کردن، تمجید کردن

He ***rhapsodized*** *about/ over* the joys of having children.

rhet.or.ic /£ ˈret.ᵊr.ɪk, $ ˈreṯ.ɚ-/ *n.* art of effective communication

علم معانی و بیان، هنر فصاحت و بلاغت، بدیع
All writers, by necessity, must be skilled in **rhetoric**.
rhe.tor.i.cal: *adj.*   بلاغی، حاکی از بلاغت، بدیعی
rheum.y /ruːm.ɪ/ *adj.* related to a discharge from nose and eyes

(چشم و بینی) مرطوب، نمناک
His **rheumy** eyes warned us that he was coming down with a cold.

ri.bald /ˈrɪb.ᵊld, £ ˈraɪ.bᵊld, $ ˈraɪ.bɔːld/ *adj.* wanton, profane

هرزه، شنیع، بی‌شرم، توهین‌آمیز؛ لوده
He sang a **ribald** song which offended many of us.

rife /raɪf/ *adj.* abundant, current

شایع، رایج، معمول، متداول؛ سرشار از، مملو، پُر
In the face of the many rumors of scandal, which are **rife** at the moment, it is best to remain silent.

rift /rɪft/ *n.* opening, break

شکاف، بریدگی؛ اختلاف، نفاق
The plane was lost in the stormy sky until the pilot saw the city through a **rift** in the clouds.

ri.gor /£ ˈrɪg.ər, $ -ɚ/ *n.* severity

شدت، سختی آب و هوا
Many settlers could not stand the **rigors** of the New England winters.

rime /raɪm/ *n.* white frost

شبنم یخ زده
The early morning dew had frozen and everything was

covered with a thin coat of *rime*.

ri.si.ble /£ ˈrɪz.ə.bḷ, £ ˈraɪ.zə-, $ ˈrɪz.ə-/ *adj.* inclined to laugh, ludicrous

مضحک، خنده‌دار، مسخره

His remarks were so *risible* that the audience howled with laughter.

ri.si.bil.i.ty: *n.* مسخرگی، تمسخر

ris.qué /rɪˈskeɪ/ *adj.* off-color, rude

ناشایست، وقیحانه؛ (داستان و غیره) سکسی

Please do not tell your *risqué* anecdotes at this party.

roan /£ rəʊn, $ roʊn/ *adj., n.* brown mixed with gray or white

قهوه‌ای متمایل به خاکستری یا سفید؛ اسب ابلق

You can distinguish this horse in a race because it is *roan* while all the others are bay or chestnut.

ro.bust /£ rəʊˈbʌst, $ roʊ-/ *adj.* vigorous, strong

تندرست، نیرومند و سالم، قوی؛ محکم، مستحکم

The candidate for the football team had a *robust* physique.

ro.co.co /£ rəʊˈkəʊ.kəʊ, $ rəˈkoʊ.koʊ/ *adj.* ornate, higly decorated

روکوکویی، به سبک روکوکو (سبکی فوق‌العاده پر زرق و برق)

Rococo is a delicate style of interior decoration that is characterized by the use of scrolls and the asymmetrical arrangements of curves.

rose.ate /£ ˈrəʊ.zi.ət, $ ˈroʊ.zi.ɪt/ *adj.* rosy; optimistic

گلگون؛ خوشبینانه، امیدبخش

I am afraid you will have to alter your *roseate* views in

the light of the distressing news.

ros.ter /£ ˈrɒs.tə^r, $ ˈrɑː.stɚ/ *n.* list

فهرست، صورت اسامی، فهرست نوبت کاری

They print the *roster* of plays in the season's program.

ros.trum /£ ˈrɒs.trəm, $ ˈrɑː.srəm/ *n.* pulpit

سکوی خطابه، تریبون

The crowd murmured angrily as the boss was approaching the *rostrum*.

rote /£ rəʊt, $ roʊt/ *adj.* repetitive

تکراری؛ طوطی‌وار، حفظی

He recited the passage *by rote* and gave no indication he understood what he was saying.

ro.tun.da /£ rəʊˈtʌn.də, $ roʊ-/ *n.* circular building or hall covered with a dome

ساختمان مدور (با بامِ گنبدی)

The company's headquarters are made up of a central *rotunda* and four tower blocks which surround it.

ro.tun.di.ty /£ rəʊˈtʌn.dɪ.tɪ, $ roʊ-/ *n.* roundness

چاقی، تپلی، فربهی

He emphasized the *rotundity* of the governor by describing his height and circumference.

ro.tund: *adj.* چاق و چله، تپل، فربه

rout /raʊt/ *v.* to defeat decisively, to drive out

شکست دادن، در هم شکستن، تار و مار کردن، به‌زور بیرون کردن

The reinforcements were able to *rout* the enemy.

rub.ble /ˈrʌb.l̩/ *n.* the piles of broken stone and bricks

خرده سنگ، قلوه سنگ، لاشه سنگ، آجر پاره

Ten years after world war II, some of the **rubble** left by enemy bombings could still be seen.

ru.bi.cund /£ ˈruːbɪ.kənd, $ -bə.kʌnd/ *adj.* ruddy, florid

(پوست) سرخ، قرمز، گلگون؛ سرخ‌رو، سرخ چهره

His ***rubicund*** complexion was the result of an active outdoor life.

rud.dy /ˈrʌd.i/ *adj.* reddish, healthy-looking

سرخ‌فام، گلگون، گل انداخته، قرمز

His ***ruddy*** features indicated that he had spent much time in the open.

ru.di.men.ta.ry /£ ˌruːdɪˈmen.tºr.i, £ ˈ-tri, $ -tə-/ *adj.* not developed, elementary

ناقص، رشد نکرده؛ ابتدایی، اولیه، مقدماتی

His dancing was limited to a few ***rudimentary*** steps.

rue.ful /ˈruː.fºl/ *adj.* regretful, sorrowful, dejected

غم‌انگیز، اندوهناک، تأسف‌بار، محزون

The artist has captured the sadness of childhood in his portrait of the boy with the ***rueful*** countenance.

ruf.fi.an /ˈrʌf.i.ən/ *n.* bully, scoundrel

آدم شرور، (در جمع) اراذل، اوباش، اشرار

The ***ruffians*** threw stones at the police.

ru.mi.nate /ˈruː.mɪ.neɪt/ *v.* to chew the cud; to ponder

نشخوار کردن؛ اندیشیدن، تعمق کردن، تأمل کردن

We cannot afford to wait while you ***ruminate*** upon these plants.

rum.mage /ˈrʌm.ɪdʒ/ *v., n.* to ransack, to search thoroughly

به‌دنبال چیزی گشتن، زیر و رو کردن، جستجو کردن؛ کاوش، جستجو

When we **rummaged** through the trunks in the attic, we found many souvenirs of our childhood days.

ruse /ru:z/ *n.* trick, stratagem

حیله، کلک، فریب‌کاری، حقه

You will not be able to fool your friends with such an obvious **ruse**.

rus.tic /£ ˈrʌs.tɪk, $ -tɪk/ *adj.* related to the country people, uncouth

روستایی، دهاتی؛ خشن، خالی از ظرافت

The backwoodsman looked out of place in his **rustic** attire.

rus.ti.cate /ˈrʌs.tɪ.keɪt/ *v.* to suspend a student; to move to the country, to dwell in the country

(دانشجویی را) موقتاً اخراج کردن؛ در روستا ساکن شدن، زندگی روستایی داشتن

I like city life so much that I can never understand how people can **rusticate** in the suburbs.

ruth.less /ˈru:θ.ləs/ *adj.* pitiless

بی‌عاطفه، بی‌رحم، سنگدل، ظالم

The escaped convict was a dangerous and **ruthless** murderer.

لیستی از لغاتی که در جملات بخش R به کار رفته‌اند:

واژه	معنی	واژه	معنی
aisle: n.	راهرو	howl: v.	فریاد کشیدن
aria: n.	تک‌خوانی	hut: n.	کلبه
asymmetrical: adj.	نامتقارن	incline: v.	تمایل داشتن
attire: n.	لباس، جامه	incur: v.	(قرض) بالا آوردن
attorney: n.	وکیل مدافع	indigent: adj.	تهیدست، فقیر
backwoodsman: n.	دهاتی	jaunty: adj.	سرحال، شاد
bay: n.	رنگ قهوه‌ای، اسب کهر	marauding: adj.	چپاولگر
betray: v.	خیانت کردن	monastic: adj.	ساده
cautious: adj.	محتاط	mound: n.	تلّه، پشته
chestnut: n.	رنگ خرمایی؛ اسب کهر	offend: v.	آزردن
		outspoken: adj.	رک، صریح
coat: n.	لایه	pail: n.	سطل
collapse: v.	ساقط شدن	recruit: n.	سرباز جدید/ آش‌خور
come down: v.	مریض شدن	reinforcement: n.	نیروی کمکی
convict: n.	مجرم	resentment: n.	خشم، انزجار
deity: n.	خدا	respiration: n.	تنفس
drive: n.	پیکار، مبارزه؛ سائق	scroll: n.	(معماری) نقش طوماری
deter: v.	منصرف کردن	shun: v.	طرد کردن، اجتناب کردن
eligible: adj.	مستحق، درخور	souvenir: n.	یادگاری
endeavor: n.	تلاش	stake: n.	چوبه مرگ
evangelist: n.	مبلّغ مذهبی	sue: v.	شکایت کردن
exact: v.	ایجاب کردن	trunk: n.	چمدان
file an appeal: v.	دادخواست دادن	uninhibited: adj.	بی‌پروا، صریح
		vicious: adj.	شرور
galley: n.	آشپزخانه کشتی	wretch: n.	بدبخت، فلک‌زده
game: n.	شکار؛ گوشت شکار		

S s

sac.cha.rine /£ ˈsæk.ᵊr.aɪn, $ ˈ-ɚ-/ *adj.* cloyingly sweet

خیلی شیرین، بیش از حد شیرین؛ لوس، مهوع
She tried to ingratiate herself, speaking sweetly and smiling a *saccharine* smile.

sac.er.do.tal /ˈsæk.ər.du.tɔl/ *adj.* priestly

کشیشی، (مربوط به) کشیشان
The priest decided to abandon his *sacerdotal* duties and enter the field of politics.

sac.ri.le.gious /ˌsæk.rɪˈlɪdʒ.əs/ *adj.* desecrating, profane

نشانهٔ بی‌حرمتی؛ اهانت‌آمیز، بی‌احترامی (به مقدسات)
His stealing of the altar cloth was a very *sacrilegious* act.

sac.ro.sanct /ˈsæk.rə.sæŋkt/ *adj.* most sacred, inviolable

بسیار مقدس، تغییرناپذیر، خدشه‌ناپذیر، واجب‌الحرمت
The salesman invaded the *sacrosanct* privacy of the office of the president of the company.

sa.dis.tic /səˈdɪs.tɪk/ *adj.* enjoying of cruelty to others; related to sadism

آزارگرانه، سادیستی؛ بی‌رحمانه
If we were to improve conditions in this prison, we must first get rid of the *sadistic* warden.

sa.di.sm: *n.* آزارگری، سادیسم، لذت بردن از آزار دیگر، آزارگری جنسی

saf.fron /£ ˈsæf.rɒn, $ -rən/ *adj.* orange-colored (رنگ) زعفرانی، نارنجی روشن
The Halloween cake was decorated with *saffron*-colored icing.

sa.ga /ˈsɑː.ɡə/ *n.* legend, story of heroic deed
داستان بلند، سرگذشت طولانی
This is a *saga* of the sea and the men who risk their lives on it.

sa.ga.cious /səˈɡeɪ.ʃəs/ *adj.* keen, shrewd, having insight
عاقل، خردمند، مدبّر؛ داهیانه، مدبّرانه
He is much too *sagacious* to be fooled by a trick like that.

sa.li.ent /ˈseɪ.li.ənt/ *adj.* prominent
بارز، برجسته، چشمگیر؛ تیز، رو به بیرون
One of the *salient* features of that newspaper is its excellent editorial page.

sa.line /ˈseɪ.laɪn/ *adj., n.* salty
شور، نمکی؛ آب نمک، محلول نمک
The slighty *saline* taste of this mineral water is pleasant.

sal.low /£ ˈsæl.əʊ, $ -oʊ/ *adj.* yellowish, sickly in color
رنگ پریده، زرد
We were disturbed by his *sallow* complexion.

sa.lu.bri.ous /səˈluː.bri.əs/ *adj.* healthful, respectable
اعیانی، اشرافی، آبرومند؛ پاکیزه، بهداشتی، سالم، تمیز
He does not live in a *salubrious* part of the town.

sal.u.ta.ry /£ ˈsæl.jʊ.tri, $ -ter.i/ *adj., n.* tending to improve,

sal.vage 447 **san.gui.nar.y**

wholesome

مفید، آموزنده، عبرت‌انگیز

The punishment had a *salutary* effect on the boy, as he became a model student.

sal.vage /ˈsæl.vɪdʒ/ *v., n.* to rescue from loss

نجات دادن، (آتش‌سوزی) سالم بیرون آوردن؛ عملیات نجات

All attempts to *salvage* the wrecked ship failed.

sal.ver /£ ˈsæl.vəʳ, $ -vɚ/ *n.* tray

سینی

The food was brought in on silver *salvers* by the waiters.

sanct.i.mo.ni.ous /£ ˌsæŋk.tɪˈməʊ.ni.əs, $ -tɪˈmoʊ-/ *adj.* hypocritically pious

زهدفروش؛ زهد فروشانه، زاهد مآبانه

You do not have to be so *sanctimonious* to prove that you are devout.

sanc.tion /ˈsæŋk.ʃᵊn/ *v.* to approve, to ratify

تصویب کردن، تأیید کردن؛ مجاز شمردن؛ اجازه دادن

Nothing will convince me to *sanction* the engagement of my daughter to such a worthless young man.

sang.froid /£ ˌsɒ̃ˈfwɑː, $ ˌsɑːŋ-/ *n.* coolness in a trying situation

خونسردی، آرامش، خویشتن‌داری

The captain's *sangfroid* helped to allay the fears of the passengers.

san.gui.nar.y /ˈsæŋ.gwɪ.nər.i/ *adj.* bloody

خونین؛ خونخوار، خون‌آشام، خونریز

The battle of Iwo Jima was unexpectedly *sanguinary*.

san.guine /ˈsæŋ.gwɪn/ *adj.* cheerful, hopeful

خوش‌بین، امیدوار؛ خوش‌بینانه، امیدبخش

Let us not be too *sanguine* about the outcome.

sa.pi.ent /ˈseɪ.pi.ənt/ *adj.* wise, shrewd

خردمند؛ خردمندانه، هوشمندانه

The students enjoyed the professor's *sapient* digressions more than his formal lectures.

sar.ca.sm /£ ˈsɑː.kæz.ᵊm, $ ˈsɑːr-/ *n.* scornful remarks, stinging rebuke

طعنه، گوشه و کنایه، ریشخند، تمسخر

His feelings were hurt by the *sarcasm* of his supposed friends.

sar.cas.tic: *adj.* کنایه‌دار، طعنه‌آمیز، نیشدار

sar.coph.a.gus /£ sɑːˈkɒf.ə.gəs, $ sɑːrˈkɑː.fə-/ *n.* stone coffin often highly decorated

تابوت سنگی منقوش

The display of the *sarcophagus* in the art museum impresses me as a morbid exhibition.

sar.don.ic /£ sɑːˈdɒn.ɪk, $ sɑːrˈdɑː.nɪk/ *adj.* disdainful, sarcastic, cynical

توهین‌آمیز، طعنه‌آمیز، کنایه‌وار، تمسخرآمیز

The *sardonic* humor of nightclub comedian strikes some people as amusing and others as rude.

sar.to.ri.al /£ sɑːˈtɔː.ri.əl, $ sɑːrˈtɔːr.i-/ *adj.* related to tailors or tailored clothes

(مربوط به) لباس و شیوهٔ لباس پوشیدن، پوشاکی

He was as famous for the *sartorial* splendor of his attire

as he was for his action.

sate /saɪt/ *v.* to satisfy to the full, to cloy

سیر کردن، اشباع کردن، فرونشاندن؛ دل آدم را زدن

Its hunger *sated*, the lion dozed.

sat.el.lite /£ ˈsæt.ᵊl.aɪt, $ ˈsæt̬-/ *n.* small body revolving around a larger one

ماهواره، قمر (مصنوعی)

During the first few years of the Space Age, hundreds of *satellites* were launched by Russia and the United States.

sa.ti.ate /ˈseɪ.ʃi.eɪt/ *v.* to surfeit, to satisfy fully

دلزده کردن، سیر کردن، اشباع کردن

The guests, having eaten until they were *satiated*, now listened inattentively to the speakers.

sa.ti.ate: *adj.* سیر، اشباع
sa.ti.e.ty: *n.* سیری، اشباع؛ دلزدگی

sat.ire /£ ˈsæt.aɪəʳ, $ -aɪr/ *n.* sarcasm, irony

هجونامه؛ طنز؛ هجو

His novel is a *satire on* social snobbery.

sat.u.rate /£ ˈsæt.jʊ.reɪt, $ -jʊr.eɪt/ *v.* to soak

خیس کردن؛ اشباع کردن

Their clothes were *saturated* by the rain.

sat.ur.nine /£ ˈsæt.ə.naɪn, $ ˈsæt̬.ɚ-/ *adj.* gloomy

عبوس، افسرده، اخمو، غمگین، گرفته

Do not be misled by his *saturnine* face; he is not as gloomy as he looks.

sat.yr /£ ˈsæt.əʳ, $ ˈsæt̬.ɚ/ *n.* half-human, half bestial being; pleasure-loving being

(اساطیر) خدای نیمه انسان و نیمه حیوان؛ مرد شهوت‌ران
He was like a *satyr* in his lustful conduct.

saun.ter /£ ˈsɔːn.tər, $ ˈsɑːn.tɚ/ *v.* to stroll slowly
سلانه سلانه راه رفتن، پرسه زدن، ول گشتن، پلکیدن
As we *sauntered* through the park, we stopped frequently to admire the spring flowers.

sa.vant /ˈsæ.vᵊnt/ *n.* scholar
دانشمند، محقّق، عالِم
Our faculty includes many world-famous *savants*.

sav.oir-faire /£ ˌsæv.wɑːˈfeər, $ -ˈfer/ *n.* tact, poise, sophistication
حضور ذهن، آداب دانی، کاردانی
I envy his *savoir-faire*; he always knows exactly what to do and say.

sa.vor /£ ˈseɪ.vər, $ -vɚ/ *v.*, *n.* to have a distinctive flavor, smell, or quality
مزه دادن، بو دادن؛ طعم، مزه، بو، رنگ و بو، خصلت
I think your choice of a successor *savors* of favoritism.

scan.ty /£ ˈskæn.ti, $ -ţi/ *adj.* meager, insufficient
کم، ناکافی، نه چندان زیاد
Thinking his helping of food was *scanty*, Oliver Twist asked for more.

scape.goat /£ ˈskeɪp.ɡəʊt, $ -ɡoʊt/ *n.* one that hears the blame for others
سپر بلا، بلاگردان
I was made the *scapegoat*, but it was the others who started the fire.

scav.eng.er /£ 'skæv.ɪn.dʒəʳ, $ -dʒɚ/ *n.* person that collects waste; animal that feeds on decayed matter

زباله‌گرد؛ لاشخور، مردارخوار

The Oakland *Scavenger* Company is responsible for the collection and disposal of the community's garbage.

schi.sm /'skɪz.əm/ *n.* division, split

نفاق، تفرقه، دودستگی

Let us not widen the *schism* by further bickering.

scin.til.la /sɪn'tɪl.ə/ *n.* shred, least bit

ذره، کمترین مقدار، سر سوزن

You have not produced a *scintilla* of evidence to support your argument.

scin.til.late /£ 'sɪn.tɪ.leɪt, $ -t̬əl.eɪt/ *v.* to sparkle, to flash

جرقه زدن، برق زدن؛ بامزه بودن، خوش مشرب بودن

Cynthia simply *scintillated* (=spoke and behaved very excitingly and amusingly) at the party last night.

sci.on /'saɪ.ən/ *n.* offspring

نونهال، نوباوه، فرزند، سلاله

He is the *scion* of a newspaper-publishing family and the heir to a fortune of half a billion dollars.

scourge /£ skɜːdʒ, $ skɜːrdʒ/ *n.* lash, whip, severe punishment

شلاق، تازیانه؛ بلا، مصیبت؛ تنبیه

They feared the plague and regarded it as a deadly *scourge.*

scru.pu.lous /'skruː.pjʊ.ləs/ *adj.* conscientious

شریف، صادق، درستکار؛ حساس؛ باوجدان

I can recommend him for the position because I have

found him a very *scrupulous* young man.

scru.tin.ize /£ ˈskruː.tɪ.naɪz, $ -tᵊn.aɪz/ *v.* to examine closely and critically

موشکافی کردن، به دقت بررسی کردن، مورد مدّاقه قرار دادن

Searching for flaws, the sergeant *scrutinize* every detail of the private's uniform.

scru.tin.y: *n.*   بررسی، موشکافی، مدّاقه

scul.lion /ˈskʌl.jən/ *n.* menial kitchen worker

شاگرد آشپز، پادوی آشپزخانه

Lynette was angry because she thought she had been given a *scullion* to act as her defender.

scur.ri.lous /£ ˈskʌr.ɪ.ləs, $ ˈskɜːr-/ *adj.* obscene, indecent

پر از فحاشی، آکنده از هتاکی؛ افتراآمیز، موهن

Your *scurrilous* remarks are especially offensive because they are untrue.

scut.tle /£ ˈskʌt.l̩, $ ˈskʌt̬-/ *v.* to sink by cutting holes in

(کشتی) عمداً غرق کردن

The sailors decided to *scuttle* their vessel rather than surrender it to the enemy.

se.ba.ceous /sɪˈbeɪ.ʃəs/ *adj.* oily, fatty

چرب و روغنی، چربی

The *sebaceous glands* secrete oil to the hair follicles.

se.ces.sion /sesˈeʃ.ᵊn/ *n.* withdrawal

(سیاست) جدایی، انشعاب

The *secession* of the southern states provided Lincoln with his first major problem after his inauguration.

sec.u.lar /£ ˈsek.jʊ.lər, $ -jə.lɚ/ *adj.* worldly, temporal

The church leaders decided not to interfere in *secular* matters.

se.date /sɪ'deɪt/ *adj.* composed, grave

موقر، آرام، متین؛ جدّی

The parents were worried because they felt their son was too quiet and *sedate*.

se.date: *v.* (پزشکی) مسکّن دادن به

sed.en.ta.ry /£ 'sed.ᵊn.tri, $ -ter.i/ *adj.* requiring sitting

(کار) پشت میزی؛ (مردم) زمین‌گیر، خانه‌نشین؛ غیر مهاجر

Because he had a *sedentary* occupation, he decided to visit a gymnasium weekly.

se.di.tion /sɪ'dɪʃ.ᵊn/ *n.* resistance to authority, insubordination

آشوب‌گری، فتنه‌انگیزی؛ شورش، اغتشاش

His words, though not treasonous in themselves, were calculated to arouse thoughts of *sedition*.

sed.u.lous /'sed.jʊ.ləs/ *adj.* diligent

کوشا، سخت‌کوش، جدّی؛ مجدّانه

As a scholar, he paid *sedulous* attention to details.

seethe /siːð/ *v.* to be disturbed; to boil

(از عصبانیت) به‌خود پیچیدن، ناراحت شدن، عصبانی شدن؛ جوش آوردن

She was *seething* with rage when she was told to leave.

seine /seɪn/ *n.* net for catching fish

تور ماهیگیری

When the shad run during the spring, you may see fishermen with *seines* along the banks of our coastal rivers.

sem.blance /'sem.blen*ts*/ *n.* outward appearance, guise

ظاهر، صورتِ ظاهر

The city has now returned to *some semblance* of normality after last night's celebrations.

sen.il.i.ty /£ sɪ'nɪl.ɪ.ti, $ -ə.t̬i/ *n.* old age, feeble-mindedness of old age

پیری، فرتوتی؛ اختلالاتِ پیری، خرفتی پیری

Senility is perhaps the worst prospect of old age, both for the people affected and for those who care for them.

sen.su.al /'sen*t*.sjuəl/ *adj.* carnal, voluptuous

دنیوی؛ نفسانی، جسمانی؛ شهوی، شهوت‌پرستانه، شهوت‌انگیز

Nobody knows what caused him to drop his *sensual* way of life and become so ascetic.

sen.su.ous /'sen*t*.sjuəs/ *adj.* physical, sensual

لذت‌بخش؛ شهوت‌انگیز، شورانگیز

He was stimulated by the sights, sounds, and smells about him; he was enjoying his *sensuous* experience.

sen.ten.tious /sen'ten.tʃəs/ *adj.* terse, concise

موعظه‌گرانه؛ مختصر و مفید

I found his *sententious* style particularly pleasing.

sep.tic /'sep.tɪk/ *adj.* putrid, producing putrefaction

عفونی، چرکی؛ گندیده

The hospital was in such a filthy state that we were afraid that patients would suffer from *septic* poisoning.

sep.ul.cher /£ 'sep.ᵊl.kəʳ, $-kɚ/ *n.* tomb

قبر، مقبره، مرقد

Annabel Lee was buried in the *sepulcher* by the sea.

se.qua.cious /siːˈkwʌ.ʃəs/ *adj.* eager to follow, ductile

انعطاف پذیر، تأثیرپذیر

The *sequacious* members of Parliament were only too willing to do the bidding of their leader.

se.ques.ter /£ sɪˈkwes.tər, $ -tɚ/ *v.* to retire from public life, to segregate

جدا کردن، منزوی کردن

Although he hoped to *sequester himself* in a small community, he never was able to drop his busy round of activities in the city.

ser.en.di.pi.ty /£ ˌser.ənˈdɪp.ɪ.ti, $ -ə.t̬i/ *n.* gift for finding valuable things not searched for

خوش اقبالی، بخت بلند

Many scientific discoveries are a matter of *serendipity*.

se.ren.i.ty /£ sɪˈren.ɪ.ti, $ -ə.t̬i/ *n.* calmness, placidity

آرامش، سکوت

The *serenity* of the sleepy town was shattered by a tremendous explosion.

ser.pen.tine /£ ˈsɜː.pən.taɪn, $ ˈsɜːr-/ *adj.* winding, twisting

مارپیچ، پیچ در پیچ

The car swerved at every curve in the *serpentine* road.

ser.rate /sɪˈreɪt/ *adj.* having a sawtoothed edge

دندانه دندانه، دندانه‌دار، ارّه‌ای

The beech tree is one of the many plants that has *serrate* leaves.

ser.vile /£ ˈsɜː.vaɪl, $ ˈsɜːr.vəl/ *adj.* slavish, cringing

برده‌وار، پَست؛ نوکر صفت، بیش از حد مطیع، زبون؛ بنده، اجیر

I don't like this *servile* manner.

sev.er.ance /£ 'sev.ᵊr.ənts, $ '-ɚ-/ *n.* the act of dividing or separating

جدایی، بریدگی، قطع؛ وقفه

A factory accident resulted in the *severance* of two of the worker's fingers.

 sev.er: *v.*   بریدن، جدا کردن، قطع کردن، پاره کردن

se.ver.i.ty /£ sɪ'ver.ɪ.ti, $ -ə.t̬i/ *n.* harshness, plainness

شدت، سختی؛ سختگیری؛ عبوسی

The newspapers disapproved of the *severity* of the sentence.

shack.le /'ʃæk.l̩/ *v., n.* to chain, to fetter

دست‌بند زدن، با غل و زنجیر بستن؛ سلب آزادی کردن؛ قید و بند، مانع

The criminal's ankles were *shackled* to prevent his escape.

sham /ʃæm/ *v., n.* to pretend

تظاهر کردن، ظاهرسازی کردن، وانمود کردن؛ ظاهرسازی، تظاهر، فریب‌کاری

He *shammed* sickness to get out of going to school.

sham.bles /'ʃæm.bl̩z/ *n.* state of disorder

ریخته پاشیده، به هم ریختگی، آشفتگی

By the time the police arrived, the room was a *shambles*.

sheaf /ʃiːf/ *n.* bundle

دسته، بافه، بسته کاغذ

The lawyer picked up a *sheaf* of papers as he rose to question the witness.

sheathe /ʃiːð/ *v.* to place into a case

غلاف کردن، در نیام گذاشتن

He *sheathed* his sword.

sher.bet /£ ˈʃɜː.bət. $ ˈʃɜːr/ *n.* flavored dessert ice

شربت

I prefer raspberry *sherbet* to ice cream since it is less fattening.

shib.bo.leth /ˈʃɪb.ºl.eθ/ *n.* watchword, slogan

شعار کهنه، عقیدهٔ پوسیده

We are often misled by *shibboleths*.

shim.mer /£ ˈʃɪm.əʳ, $-ɚ/ *v.* to glimmer intermittently

درخشیدن، برق زدن؛ سوسو زدن

The moonlight *shimmered* on the water as the moon broke through the clouds for a moment.

shoal /£ ʃəʊl, $ ʃoʊl/ *n.* shallow place

(دریا و غیره) جای کم عمق، قسمت کم عمق

The ship was stranded on a *shoal* and had to be pulled off by tugs.

shod.dy /£ ˈʃɒd.i, $ ˈʃɑː.di/ *adj.* sham, not genuine, inferior

بهدرد نخور، بد، با کیفیت پایین، بنجل، نامرغوب، آشغال

You will never get the public to buy such *shoddy* material.

shrew /ʃruː/ *n.* scolding woman

زن بداخلاق، زن سلیطه، سلیطه

Her former husband described her as a greedy and manipulative *shrew*.

sib.ling /ˈsɪb.lɪŋ/ *n.* brother or sister

برادر یا خواهر، همشیر

I have two brothers and a sister: three *siblings* in all.

sib.yl.line /'sɪb.əliːn/ *adj.* prophetic, oracular

غیبی، ناظر به حوادث آینده

Until their destruction by fire in 83 B.C., the *sibylline* books were often consulted by the Romans.

sib.yl: *n.*   (اساطیر یونان و روم) زنِ غیب‌گو

side.real /£ saɪˈdɪə.ri.əl, $ -ˈdɪr.i/ *adj.* relating to the stars

نجومی؛ ستاره‌ای، ستارگانی

The study of *sidereal* bodies has been greatly advanced by the new telescopes.

silt /sɪlt/ *n., v.* sediment deposited by running water

گِل و لای؛ لای گرفتن، بند آمدن

The harbor channel must be dredged annually to remove the *silt*.

si.mi.an /ˈsɪm.i.ən/ *adj.* monkeylike

مثلِ میمون، شبیه میمون، میمون‌وار، به‌شکلِ میمون

Lemurs are nocturnal mammals and have many *simian* characteristics, although they are less intelligent than monkeys.

si.mi.le /ˈsɪm.ɪ.li/ *n.* comparison

تشبیه

Her style is rich in *simile*.

si.mil.i.tude /sɪˈmɪl.ɪ.tjuːd/ *n.* similarity, using simile

شباهت، تشابه؛ تشبیه

He used to talk in *similitude*.

sim.per.ing /ˈsɪm.pər.ɪŋ/ *adj.* smirking

با لبخند تصنعی؛ احمقانه، ابلهانه

I can overlook his *simpering* manner, but I cannot ignore

his stupidity.

si.mu.late /'sɪm.jʊ.leɪt/ *v.* to feign

وانمود کردن، تظاهر کردن؛ تقلید کردن؛ شبیه‌سازی کردن

He *simulated* insanity in order to avoid punishment for his crime.

si.mu.lated: *adj.* بدل، بدلی؛ مصنوعی، ساختگی
si.mu.la.tion: *n.* تقلید؛ شبیه‌سازی

si.ne.cure /£ 'sɪn.ɪ.kjʊəʳ, $ 'saɪ.nə.kjʊr/ *n.* well-paid position with little respon-sibility

شغل تشریفاتی، شغل بی‌مسئولیت و پر درآمد

My job is no *sinecure*; I work long hours and have much responsibility.

si.new.y /'sɪn.ju.i/ *adj.* tough, strong and firm

پرعضله، عضلانی؛ خشن، ماهیچه‌ای؛ سفت؛ قوی، محکم

The steak was too *sinewy* to chew.

si.ni.ster /£ 'sɪn.ɪ.stəʳ, $ -stɚ/ *adj.* evil

شرور؛ نحس؛ شرارت‌بار

We must defeat the *sinister* forces that seek our downfall.

si.nu.ous /'sɪn.ju.əs/ *adj.* winding, bending in and out

مارپیچ، پر پیچ و خم؛ پیچ و خم‌دار

The snake moved in a *sinuous* manner.

si.roc.co /£ sɪ'rɒk.əʊ, $ -'rɑ:koʊ/ *n.* warm and sultry wind blown from Africa to Europe

سیروکو (باد گرم و مرطوبی که از آفریقا به اروپا می‌وزد)

When the *sirocco* blows, the afternoon heat is unbearable.

skep.tic /'skep.tɪk/ *n.* doubter

(آدم) شکاک؛ شک‌اندیش

In this matter, I am a *skeptic*; I want proof.

skimp /skɪmp/ *v.* to provide scantily, to live very economically

کم مصرف کردن، صرفه‌جویی کردن، با حداقل ساختن

They were forced to *skimp on* necessities in order to make their limited supplies last the winter.

skit.tish /£ 'skɪt.ɪʃ, $ 'skɪt̬-/ *adj.* lively, frisky

سرزنده و با نشاط، اهل دل؛ (اسب) چست و چالاک، چموش

He is as *skittish* as a kitten playing with a piece of string.

skul.dug.ge.ry /£ ˌskʌl'dʌg.ᵊr.i, $ '-ɚ-/ *n.* dishonest behavior

تزویر، حیله‌گری، نیرنگ‌بازی، خدعه

The investigation into municipal corruption turned up new instances of *skulduggery*.

skulk /skʌlk/ *v.* to move furtively and secretly

دزدانه راه رفتن، پاورچین پاورچین رفتن؛ پنهان شدن، قایم شدن

He *skulked* through the less fashionable sections of the city in order to avoid meeting any of his former friends.

slack.en /'slæk.ᵊn/ *v.* to slow up, to loosen

شل شدن/کردن، کند شدن/کردن، آهسته شدن/کردن

As they passed the finish line, the runners *slackened* their pace.

slake /sleɪk/ *v.* to quench, to sate

فرو نشاندن، رفع کردن

When we reached the oasis, we were able to *slake* our thirst.

slan.der /£ ˈslɑːn.dəʳ, $ ˈslæn.dɚ/ *n., v.* malicious gossip; to defame

(حقوقی) افترا، آبروریزی؛ افترا زدن

Unless you can prove your allegations, your remarks constitute *slander*.

slat.tern /£ ˈslæt.ɜːn, $ ˈslæt̬.ɚn/ *n., adj.* untidy or slovenly woman

زن شلخته، زن ولنگار، زن نامرتب

If you persist in wearing such sloppy clothes, people will call you a *slattern*.

sleaz.y /ˈsliː.zi/ *adj.* flimsy, unsubstantial

بی‌دوام، بدون استحکام؛ (مکان) کثیف

1) This is a *sleazy* material; it will not wear well.
2) This part of town is full of *sleazy* bars and restaurants.

sleep.er /£ ˈsliː.pəʳ, $ -pɚ/ *n.* something originally of little value or importance becomes very valuable

(کتاب، نمایشنامه، شخص) هر چه که پس از بی‌توجهی یک مرتبه گل می‌کند، موفقیت دیررس

Unnoticed by the critics at its publication, the eventual Paulitzer Prize winner was a classic *sleeper*.

sleight of hand /sleɪt/ *n.* dexterity

تردستی؛ ترفند، نیرنگ

The magician amazed the audience with his *sleight of hand*.

sli.ther /£ ˈslɪð.əʳ, $ -ɚ/ *v.* to slip or slide

لغزیدن، سر خوردن، لیز خوردن

She watched the passers-by as they *slithered* on the ice.

sloth /£ sləʊθ, $ sloʊθ/ *n.* laziness, no effort

کاهلی، تنبلی، لاقیدی، تن‌پروری

The report criticizes the government's *sloth* in tackling environmental problems.

slough /slʌf/ *v., n.* to cast off

پوست انداختن؛ پوست‌اندازی

Each spring, the snake *sloughs off* its skin.

slo.ven.ly /ˈslʌvənli/ *adj.* untidy, careless in work habits

شلخته، بی‌قید، ولنگار، بی‌نظم، نامرتب، ژولیده و کثیف

Those terrible overalls would make anyone look *slovenly*.

slug.gard /£ ˈslʌgəd, $ ˈslʌgərd/ *n.* lazy person

آدم سست و بی‌حال، تن لش

"You are a *sluggard*, a drone, a parasite", the angry father shouted at his lazy son.

slug.gish /ˈslʌg.ɪʃ/ *adj.* slow, lazy, lethargic

کند، کم تحرک؛ بی‌حال، وارفته؛ تنبل، کم‌کار

After two nights without sleep, she felt *sluggish*.

sluice /sluːs/ *n.* artificial channel

آب بند، کانال مصنوعی، آبراهه، کانال

This *sluice* gate is opened only in times of drought to provide water for irrigation.

smat.ter.ing /£ ˈsmæt.ər.ɪŋ, $ ˈsmæt̬.ɚ-/ *n.* slight knowledge

اطلاعات مختصر؛ اندک، کمی، یک کمی

It is better to have a more *smattering* of information about it.

smirk /£ smɜːk, $ smɜːrk/ *n., v.* conceited smile; to wear a conceited smile

پوزخند؛ پوزخند زدن

Wipe that *smirk* off your face!

smol.der /£ ˈsməʊl.dəʳ, $ ˈsmoʊl.dɚ/ *v.* to burn without flame

بدون شعله سوختن، با دود سوختن؛ (احساسات) پنهان بودن

Hate *smoldered* inside him.

snick.er /£ ˈsnɪk.əʳ, $ -ɚ/ *n., v.* half-stifled laugh; to laugh childishly

پوزخند، خندهٔ استهزاءآمیز؛ پوزخند زدن، خندهٔ تمسخرآمیز کردن

The boy could not suppress a *snicker* when the teacher sat on the tack.

sni.vel /ˈsnɪv.ᵊl/ *v.* to run at the nose, to snuffle, to whine

آب از بینی راه افتادن؛ گریه‌زاری کردن، کولی بازی در آوردن

Don't you come *snivelling* to me complaining about your big brother.

so.bri.e.ty /£ səˈbraɪ.ɪ.ti, $ -ə.t̬i/ *n.* soberness

هشیاری، متانت، جدیّت، وقار

The solemnity of the occasion filled us with *sobriety*.

so.ber: *adj.* هوشیار، سرعقل؛ آرام

so.bri.quet /£ ˈsəʊ.brɪ.keɪ, $ ˈsoʊ-/ *n.* nickname

لقب، نام عاریتی، اسم خودمانی

Despite all his protests, his classmates continued to call him by that unflattering *sobriquet*.

sod.den /£ ˈsɒd.ᵊn, $ ˈsɑː.dᵊn/ *adj.* soaked; dull as if from drink

خیسِ خیس، کاملاً خیس؛ مست لایعقل

He set his *sodden* overcoat near the radiator to dry.

so.journ /£ ˈsɒdʒ.ən, $ ˈsɑː.dʒɜːrn/ *n., v.* temporary stay; to reside temporarily

اقامت (موقت)؛ برای مدتی پیش کسی ماندن، اقامت گزیدن

1) After his *sojourn* in Florida, he began to long for the colder climate of his native New England.

2) He *sojourned* with a friend in Wales for two weeks.

sol.ace /£ ˈsɒl.ɪs, $ ˈsɑː.lɪs/ *n., v.* comfort in trouble; to comfort

آرامش، تسکین، راحتی؛ تسلی بخشیدن به، تسلی دادن به

I hope you will find *solace* in the thought that all of us share your loss.

sol.e.ci.sm /£ ˈsɒl.ɪ.sɪ.zəm, $ ˈsɑː.lə-/ *n.* an act of breaking rules of behavior or speaking

بی‌ادبی، بی‌نزاکتی؛ اشتباهِ زبانی، غلط

I must give this paper a failing mark because it contains many *solecisms*.

so.lem.ni.ty /£ səˈlem.nɪ.ti, $ -nə.t̬i/ *n.* seriousness, gravity

ابهت، شکوه؛ وقار، متانت؛ تشریفات (رسمی)

The minister was concerned that nothing should disturb the *solemnity* of the marriage.

sol.emn: *adj.* با ابهت؛ جدی؛ موقر؛ رسمی

so.li.ci.tous /£ səˈlɪs.ɪ.təs, $ -t̬əs/ *adj.* worried, concerned

نگران، دلواپس، مضطرب؛ دلسوز، غمخوار

The employer was very *solicitous* about the health of his employees as replacements were difficult to get.

so.li.lo.quy /səˈlɪl.ə.kwi/ *n.* the act of talking to oneself

تک‌گویی (نمایش)

The *soliloquy* is a device used by the dramatist to reveal a character's innermost thoughts and emotions.

sol.stice /£ ˈsɒl.stɪs, $ ˈsɑːl-/ *n.* point at which the sun is farthest from the equator

(اخترشناسی) انقلابین، انقلاب زمستانی

The winter *solstice* usually occurs on December 21.

sol.vent /£ ˈsʌl.vənt, $ ˈsɑːl-/ *adj.* able to pay all debts

قادر به پرداخت بدهی

Many of insurance companies are under pressure to increase premiums to stay *solvent*.

so.ma.tic /səˈmæ.tɪk/ *adj.* physical

جسمانی، مادی

Why do you ignore the spiritual aspects and emphasize only the *somatic*?

som.nam.bu.list /£ sɒmˈnæm.bjʊ.lɪst, $ sɑːm-/ *n.* sleepwalker

(روانشناسی) خواب گرد

The most famous *somnambulist* in literature is lady Macbeth.

som.nam.bu.late خوابگردی کردن، در خواب راه رفتن

som.no.lent /£ ˈsɒm.nəl.ənt, $ ˈsɑːm-/ *adj.* half asleep

خواب‌آلود، خواب آلوده

The heavy meal and the overheated room made us all *somnolent* and indifferent to the speaker.

so.nor.ous /£ ˈsɒn.ᵊr.əs, $ ˈsɑː.nɚ-/ *adj.* resonant

(صدا) پرطنین، رسا

His *sonorous* voice resounded through the hall.

soph.ist /£ ˈsəʊ.fɪst, $ ˈsɑː-/ *n.* a specious reasoner; a learned man

سفسطه‌باز، سوفسطایی؛ عالِم، محقق

Many politicians are cunning *sophists*.

so.phis.ti.ca.tion /səˌfɪs.tɪˈkeɪ.ʃᵊn/ *n.* unnaturalness, artificiality

پیچیدگی؛ پیشرفت، کارکشتگی، کاردانی

Sophistication is an acquired characteristic, found more frequently among city dwellers than among residents of rural areas.

so.phis.ti.cat.ed: *adj.* با فرهنگ، فرهیخته، مترقی، پیشرفته

soph.ist.ry /£ ˈsɒf.ɪ.stri, $ ˈsɑː.fɪ-/ *n.* subtly fallacious reasoning

سفسطه، مغلطه

He won the argument by *sophistry*.

soph.o.mor.ic /£ ˌsɒf.ə.mɔːr.ɪk, $ ˈsɑː.fə.mɔːr.ɪk/ *adj.* shallow, immature

سطحی، کم مایه؛ نپخته

Your *sophomoric* remarks indicate that you have not given much thought to the problem.

sop.o.ri.fic /£ ˌsɒp.ᵊrˈɪf.ɪk, $ ˌsɑː.pəˈrɪf-/ *n.* sleep producer

مادهٔ خواب‌آور

I don't need a *soporific* when I listen to one of his speeches.

sor.did /£ ˈsɔː.dɪd, $ ˈsɔːr-/ *adj.* filthy, base, vile

(شرایط) شرم‌آور، ننگین، فلاکت‌بار؛ (فرد، رفتار) پست، خودخواه، ناشایست

The social worker was angered by the *sordid* housing provided for the homeless.

soup.çon /£ ˈsuːp.sɔ̃, $ -sɑː/ *n.* slight amount

خیلی کم، اندک، مختصر

"Shall I add some garlic?" — "Just a *soupçon*".

span.gle /ˈspæŋ.gl/ *n., v.* small metallic piece sewn to clothing

پولک؛ پولک‌دار کردن، پولک‌دوزی کردن

The thousands of *spangles* on her dress sparkled in the glare of the stage lights.

sparse /£ spɑːs, $ spɑːrs/ *adj.* not thick, thinly scatterd, scanty

پراکنده، متفرق، نامتراکم؛ مختصر، کم

The television coverage of the event was rather *sparse*.

spas.mod.ic /£ spæz'mɒd.ɪk, $ -'mɑː.dɪk/ *adj.* fitful, periodic

نامنظم، اتفاقی، متناوب، گه‌گاهی، موقتی

The *spasmodic* coughing in the auditorium annoyed the performers.

spate /speɪt/ *n.* large amount; flood; outburst

مقدار فراوان؛ سیل؛ هجوم؛ (مجازی) رگبار، موج

Police are investigating a *spate* of burglaries in the area.

spa.tial /'speɪ.ʃəl/ *adj.* relating to space

فضایی

It is difficult to visualize the *spatial* extent of our universe.

spat.u.la /'spæt.jʊ.lə/ *n.* broad-bladed utensil

کاردک

He scraped the mixture out of the bowl with a plastic *spatula*.

spawn /£ spɔːn, $ spɑːn/ *v., n.* to lay eggs

تخم‌ریزی کردن، تخم ریختن؛ تخم‌ماهی / صدف / قورباغه

Fish ladders had to be built in the dams to assist the salmon returning to *spaun* in their native streams.

spe.cious /'spiː.ʃəs/ *adj.* seemingly reasonable but incorrect

حق به جانب، ظاهر فریب، غلط‌انداز

Let us not be misled by such *specious* arguments.

spec.tral /ˈspektrᵊl/ *adj.* ghostly

روح مانند، شبح مانند، شبح‌گونه، شبح‌وار

We were frightened by the *spectral* glow that filled the room.

spec.trum /ˈspek.trəm/ *n.* colored band, series of colors

طیف

The visible portion of the *spectrum* includes red at one end and violet at the other.

sple.net.ic /ˈsple.nət.ɪk/ *adj.* spiteful, irritable, peevish

بدخلق، ترشرو، تنگ حوصله، تندخو

People shunned him because of his *splenetic* temper.

spleen: *n.* طحال؛ بدخلقی، بی‌حوصلگی

spo.li.a.tion /spəʊlɪˈeɪʃᵊn/ *n.* pillaging, depredation

تضییع، تخریب؛ یغما، غارت، چپاول، تاراج

We regard this unwarranted attack on a neutral nation as an act of *spoliation*.

spoon.er.i.sm /£ ˈspuː.nᵊr.ɪ.zᵊm, $ -nɚ-/ *n.* accidental transposition of sounds

تبادل صدا، ابدال آغازی

He used to produce *spoonerisms* such as "well-boiled icicles" for "well-oiled bicycles".

spo.rad.ic /spəˈræd.ɪk/ *adj.* occurring irregularly

پراکنده، متفرق، گه‌گاهی

Although there are *sporadic* outbursts of shooting, the major rebellion has been defeated.

sport.ive /£ spɔːt.ɪv, $ spɔːrt-/ *adj.* playful

شوخی، غیرجدی؛ بازیگوش؛ ورزشی

Such a *sportive* attitude is surprising in a person as serious as you usually are.

spume /spu:m/ *n.* froth, foam

کف

The *spume* at the base of the waterfall extended for a quarter of a mile downriver.

spu.ri.ous /£ ˈspjʊə.ri.əs, $ ˈspjʊ.i-/ *adj.* false, counterfeit

قلابی، تقلبی، جعلی، دروغین

He tried to pay the check with a *spurious* ten-dollar bill.

spurn /£ spɜ:n, $ spɜ:rn/ *v.* to reject, to scorn

رد کردن، طرد کردن

She *spurned* my offer of help.

squa.lid /£ ˈskwɒl.ɪd, $ ˈskwɑ:.lɪd/ *adj.* dirty, neglected, poor

کثیف، نکبت‌بار، فلاکت‌بار؛ غیربهداشتی؛ فقیرانه

It is easy to see how crime can breed in such a *squalid* neighborhood.

squan.der /£ ˈskwɒn.dər, $ ˈskwɑ:n.dɚ/ *v.* to waste

تلف کردن، ضایع کردن، هدر دادن

He's *squandered* all his savings on drink.

stac.ca.to /£ stəˈkɑ:.təʊ, $ -toʊ/ *adj.* disconnected

(موسیقی) استاکاتو؛ (صدا) بریده بریده، منقطع، مقطّع، جداجدا

His *staccato* speech reminded one of the sound of a machine gun.

stag.nant /ˈstæg.nənt/ *adj.* motionless, stale, dull

(آب) راکد، گندیده؛ بی‌رونق، کساد

The *stagnant* water was a breeding ground for disease.

stag.nate: *v.*

راکد بودن/شدن، از فعالیت بازماندن، عاطل و باطل ماندن

stag.nan.cy: *n.*

رکود، کسادی

staid /'steɪd/ *adj.* sober, sedate

خشک، بی‌روح، متین، موقر، سنگین؛ محتاط

His conduct during the funeral ceremony was *staid* and solemn.

stale.mate /'steɪl.meɪt/ *n., v.* deadlock

بن‌بست؛ به بن‌بست کشاندن

Negotiations between the union and the employers have reached a *stalemate*.

stal.wart /£ 'stɔːl.wət, $ 'stɑːl.wɚt/ *adj.* strong, brawny, steadfast

قوی هیکل، هیکل‌دار، تنومند، رشید؛ طرفدار پر و پا قرص

His consistent support of the party has proved that he is a *stalwart* and loyal member.

stam.i.na /'stæm.ɪ.nə/ *n.* strength, staying power

تاب، توان، طاقت، بنیه، استقامت

I doubt that he has the *stamina* to run the full distance of the marathon race.

stanch /stɑːntʃ/ *v.* to check flow of blood

بند آوردن خون، جلو خونریزی را گرفتن

It is imperative that we *stanch* the gushing wound before we attend to the other injuries.

stat.ic /£ 'stæt.ɪk, $ 'stæt̬-/ *adj.* unchanging, lacking development

راکد، ساکن، ثابت، ایستا، بدون هیچگونه تغییر و تحول

Nothing had changed at home; things were *static*.

stas.is: *n.*

سکون، رکود، ایستایی، توقف

stat.ute /'stætʃ.u:t/ *n.* law

قانون؛ مقررات

We have many *statutes* in our law books which should be repealed.

stat.u.to.ry /£ 'stæt.jʊ.tᵊr.i, $ -tɔ:r/ *adj.* created by statute

قانونی؛ مقرر؛ کیفری، جزایی

Nobody enjoys his *statutory* rights.

stead.fast /£ 'sted.fɑ:st, -fəst, $ -fæst/ *adj.* loyal

ثابت‌قدم، وفادار، پابرجا، ثابت

I am sure you will remain *steadfast* in your support of the cause.

stein /staɪn/ *n.* beer mug

آبجوخوری (فلزی)

He thought of college as a place where one drank beer from *steins* and sang songs of lost lambs.

stel.lar /£ 'stel.əʳ, $ -ɚ/ *adj.* relating to the stars; outstanding

اختری، ستاره‌ای؛ برجسته، درخشان

He was the *stellar* attraction of the entire performance.

sten.tor.i.an /£ sten'tɔ:.ri.ən, $ -'tɔ:r.i-/ *adj.* extremely loud

(صدا) قوی، پرطنین، رسا، بلند

The town crier had a *stentorian* voice.

ster.e.o.typed /'ster.iə.taɪpd/ *adj.* fixed and unvarying representation

کلیشه‌ای، یکنواخت، قالبی

My chief objection to the book is that the characters are *stereotyped*.

stig.ma /'stɪg.mə/ *n.* token of disgrace, brand

لکهٔ ننگ، ننگ، بدنامی، رسوایی

He found it hard to bear the *stigma* of being unemployed.

stig.ma.tize: *v.*   لکه‌دار کردن، بد نام کردن، بی‌آبرو کردن

stilt.ed /£ 'stɪl.tɪd, $ -t̬ɪd/ *adj.* bombastic, inflated

غیرطبیعی، تصنعی، متکلف، مطنطن، رسمی

He writes in a formal and rather *stilted* style.

stint /stɪnt/ *n.* quantity or period of work, limit

دوره، سهم، قسمت، بخش

He has just finished a *stint* of compulsory military service.

sti.pend /'staɪ.pend/ *n.* pay for services, fixed regular income

درآمد رسمی، حقوق، مقرری، مستمری

There is a nominal *stipend* attached to this position.

sti.pen.di.a.ry: *adj.*   حقوق بگیر، مزدبگیر

sto.ic /£ 'stəʊ.ɪk, $ 'stoʊ-/ *n., adj.* showing indifference to pain

شخص بردبار، شکیبا، خویشتن‌دار

My father is a *stoic* by nature and found it hard to express his grief.

stoke /£ stəʊk, $ stoʊk/ *v.* to provide with fuel; to feed abundantly

سوخت رساندن به؛ پُر خوردن، پُر خوراندن

They *stoked* themselves, knowing they would not have another meal until they reached camp.

stol.id /£ 'stɒl.ɪd, $ 'stɑː.lɪd/ *adj.* dull, impassive

بی‌احساس، خونسرد، آرام، بی‌رگ، بی‌درد

I am afraid that this imaginative poetry will not appeal to such a *stolid* person.

strat.a.gem /£ ˈstræt.ə.dʒəm, $ ˈstræt̬-/ *n.* deceptive scheme

نقشه، حیله، ترفند، کلک، حقه

He was a master of *stratagem*.

stra.tum /£ ˈstrɑː.təm, $ ˈstræt̬.əm/ *n.* layer of earth's surface; layer of society

چینه، لایه، قشر؛ طبقه (اجتماعی)

They are trying to alleviate conditions in the lowest *stratum* of the society.

stri.at.ed /£ straɪˈeɪ.tɪd, $ -t̬ɪd/ *adj.* marked with parallel bands

شیاردار، خط دار، مخطط

The glacier left many *striated* rocks.

stric.ture /£ ˈstrɪk.tʃər, $ -tʃɚ/ *n.* critical comments

انتقاد تند، سرزنش

His *strictures* on the author's style are prejudiced and unwarranted.

stri.dent /ˈstraɪ.dənt/ *adj.* loud and harsh

گوش خراش، ناهنجار؛ خشن، سرسخت

She scolded him in a *strident* voice.

strin.gent /ˈstrɪn.dʒənt/ *adj.* binding, rigid

شدید، سخت، لازم‌الاجرا، سفت و سخت

I think these regulations are too *stringent*.

strut /strʌt/ *v.* pompous walk; to walk in a proud or showy manner

با غرور و تکبّر راه رفتن، شق و رق راه رفتن

She *strutted* past us, ignoring our greeting.

strut /strʌt/ *n.* supporting bar, rod

بست، شمع

The engineer calculated that the *strut* needed to be reinforced.

stul.ti.fy /£ ˈstʌl.tɪ.faɪ, $ -t̬ə-/ *v.* to cause to appear foolish

احمقانه جلوه دادن، ضایع کردن

By changing your opinion at this time, you will *stultify* yourself.

stu.por /£ ˈstjuː.pəʳ, $ ˈstuː.pɚ/ *n.* lack of awareness, daze

گیجی، منگی، بیهوشی، بی‌حسی؛ بهت

While in a drunken *stupor* he became abusive and violent.

sty.gi.an /ˈstɪdʒ.i.ən/ *adj.* extremely and unpleasantly dark

ظلمانی، تیره و تار

They descended into the *stygian* subbasement.

stymie /ˈstaɪ.mi/ *v.* to present an obstacle, to stump

مانع (کسی یا چیزی) شدن، جلوی (کسی یا چیزی را) گرفتن؛ گیج کردن

The detective was *stymied* by the contradictory evidence in the robbery investigation.

suave /swɑːv/ *adj.* smooth, bland

بانزاکت، مؤدب، با وقار؛ مؤدبانه

He is the kind of guy who is more easily impressed by a *suave* approach than by threats or bluster.

suav.i.ty: *n.* نزاکت، ادب، وقار

sub.al.tern /£ ˈsʌb.ᵊl.tᵊn, $ səbˈɔːl.tɚn/ *n.* subordinate

ستوان، افسر جزء، زیر دست

The captain treated his *subalterns* as though they were children rather than commissioned officers.

sub.jec.tive /£ səbˈdʒek.tɪv, $ -t̬ɪv/ *adj.* unreal, personal

ذهنی؛ شخصی؛ درون‌گرا؛ تصوری، نظری
Your analysis is highly ***subjective***; you have permitted your emotions and your opinions to color your thinking.

sub.ju.gate /ˈsʌb.dʒʊ.geɪt/ *v.* to conquer, to bring under control

به انقیاد درآوردن، تحت تسلط (خود) در آوردن، مقهور ساختن
It is not our aim to ***subjugate*** our foe; we are interested only in establishing peaceful relations.

sub.li.mate /ˈsʌb.lɪ.meɪt/ *v.* to refine, to purify

تعالی بخشیدن، تصعید کردن
We must strive to ***sublimate*** these desires and emotions into worthwhile activities.

sub.lime /səˈblaɪm/ *adj.* exalted, noble, uplifting

بی‌نظیر، عالی، والا؛ حیرت‌آور، فوق‌العاده، اعجاب‌انگیز
1) We must learn to recognize ***sublime*** truths.
2) The food was absolutely ***sublime***.

sub.li.mi.nal /ˌsʌbˈlɪm.ɪ.nəl/ *adj.* below the threshold

زیرآستانه‌ای؛ پنهانی، ناآگاه، نامحسوس
We may not be aware of the ***subliminal*** message of the text.

sub.se.quent /ˈsʌb.sɪ.kwənt/ *adj.* following, later

بعدی، متعاقب، به‌دنبالِ، پس از
In ***subsequent*** lessons, we shall take up more difficult problems.

sub.ser.vi.ent /£ səbˈsɜː.vi.ənt, $ -ˈsɜːr-/ *adj.* behaving like a slave, servile

چاپلوس، حاضر به‌خدمت؛ فرمانبردار، مطیع

He was proud and dignified; he refused to be *subservient* to anyone.

sub.si.di.a.ry /£ səbˈsɪd.i.ᵊr.i, $ -er-/ *adj.* secondary, subordinate

فرعی، جنبی؛ کمکی، مکمل

The question of finance is *subsidiary* to the question of whether the project will be approved.

sub.si.dy /ˈsʌb.sɪ.di/ *n.* direct finacial aid

یارانه، سوبسید، کمک مالی

The government decided to reduce the level of *subsidy*.

sub.sis.tence /səbˈsɪs.tᵊnts/ *n.* existence, livelihood

زیست، امرار معیشت، گذران؛ وسیلهٔ امرار معاش؛ بخور و نمیر

In these days of inflated prices, my salary provides a mere *subsistence*.

sub.stan.ti.ate /səbˈstæn.ʃi.eɪt/ *v.* to support, to verify

با دلیل و مدرک ثابت کردن، دلیل و مدرک آوردن، اثبات کردن

I intend to *substantiate* my statement by producing witnesses.

sub.stan.tive /£ səbˈstæn.tɪv, $ -t̬ɪv/ *adj.* essential

اساسی، بنیادی، جدّی، واقعی

The delegates could not agree on the *substantive* issues.

sub.ter.fuge /£ ˈsʌ.tə.fjuːdʒ, $ -tɚ-/ *n.* deceptive trick, pretense

حیله، ترفند، حقه، فریب؛ ترفندبازی

Her claim to be a journalist was simply a *subterfuge* to get into the theater without paying.

sub.tle.ty /£ ˈsʌt.l̩.ti, $ ˈsʌt̬.l̩.ti/ *n.* nicety, cunning, guile

باریک‌بینی، باریک‌اندیشی، زیرکی، موشکافی

The *subtlety* of his remarks was unnoticed by most of his audience.

sub.ver.sive /£ səbˈvɜː.sɪv, $ -ˈvɜːr/ *adj.* tending to overthrow or ruin

مخرب، ویرانگر، برهم زننده، سرنگون‌کننده؛ ضدّ رژیم

Was her speech *subversive* of law and order?

suc.cinct /səkˈsɪŋkt/ *adj.* brief, terse, compact

واضح و مختصر، موجز و روشن

His remarks are always *succint* and pointed.

suc.cor /£ ˈsʌk.ər, $ -ɚ/ *n., v.* aid, assistance, relief

کمک، یاری، امداد؛ امداد رساندن، مدد رساندن

We shall be ever grateful for the *succor* your country gave us when we were in need.

suc.cu.lent /ˈsʌk.jʊ.lənt/ *adj.* juicy, full of richness

(میوه و غیره) آبدار و لذیذ، پرآب؛ (گیاه) گوشتی

The citrus foods from Florida are more *succulent* to some people than those from California.

suc.cumb /səˈkʌm/ *v.* to yield, to give in, to die

تسلیم شدن، از پای درآمدن، به زانو در آوردن؛ مردن

The city *succumbed* after only a short siege.

suf.fuse /səˈfjuːz/ *v.* to spread over

پوشاندن، پخش کردن، روی چیزی را فرا گرفتن

A blush *suffused* his cheeks.

sul.ly /ˈsʌl.i/ *v.* to tarnish, to soil

آلوده کردن، کثیف کردن؛ لکه‌دار کردن

It's tainted money; I wouldn't *sully* my hands by accepting it.

sul.try /'sʌl.tri/ *adj.* sweltering

(آب و هوا) شرجی، خیلی گرم و مرطوب، داغ

He could not adjust himself to the *sultry* climate of the tropics.

sum.ma.tion /sɔʌ'meɪ.ʃ°n/ *n.* summing up

نتیجه‌گیری، جمع‌بندی؛ جمع کل، سر جمع

In his *summation*, the lawyer emphasized the testimony given by the two witnesses.

sump.tu.ous /'sʌm.tju.əs/ *adj.* lavish, rich

مجلل، با شکوه؛ گرانبها، پرخرج؛ (لباس) فاخر

The guests turned up dressed in *sumptuous* evening gowns.

sun.der /'sʌn.dər/ *v.* to separate, to part

جدا کردن، تقسیم شدن

Northern and southern Ireland are politically and religiously *sundered*.

sun.dry /'sʌn.dri/ *adj.* various, several

گوناگون، متعدد، متنوع، مختلف

My suspicions were aroused when I read *sundry* items in the newspaper about your behavior.

su.per.an.nu.at.ed /£ ˌsuː.pºr'æn.ju.eɪ.tɪd, $ -pɚ'æn.ju.eɪ.t̬ɪd/ *adj.* retired on pension because of age

بازنشسته

The *superannuated* man was indignant because he felt that he could still perform a good day's work.

su.per.ci.li.ous /£ ˌsuː.pə'sɪl.i.əs, $ -pɚ-/ *adj.* contemptuous, haughty

مغرور، خودخواه، متکبّر، متفرعن، افاده‌ای؛ متکبّرانه، خودبینانه
I resent your *supercilious* attitude.

su.per.fi.cial /£ ˌsuː.pəˈfɪʃ.ᵊl, $ -pɚ-/ *adj.* trivial, shallow

سطحی، ظاهری، مصنوعی
His report gave only a *superficial* analysis of the problem.

su.per.flu.i.ty /£ ˌsuː.pəˈfluː.ɪ.ti, $ -pɚˈfluː.ə.t̬i/ *n.* excess, overabundance

زیادی، زیادگی، فزونی
The new director has said that there is a *superfluity* of staff in the organization.

su.per.im.pose /£ ˌsuː.pə.rɪmˈpəʊz, $ -pɚ.ɪmˈpoʊz/ *v.* to place over something else

روی (چیزی) قراردادن، روی (چیزی) گذاشتن
The picture showed his body, but with someone else's head *superimposed on* it.

su.per.nal /ˌsuː.pə.rnʌl/ *adj.* heavenly, celestial

آسمانی، سماوی؛ ملکوتی، الهی
His tale of *supernal* beings was skeptically recieved.

su.per.nu.mer.ar.y /suːpəˈnjuː.mər.əri, sjuː-/ *adj., n.* extra; a supernumerary person or thing

اضافی، زیادی؛ فرد یا چیز زیادی
His first appearance on the stage was as a *supernumerary* in a Shakespearean tragedy.

su.per.sede /£ ˌsuː.pəˈsiːd, $ -pɚ-/ *v.* to cause to be set aside, to replace

جانشین (کسی / چیزی) شدن، جایگزین کردن؛ کنار گذاشتن، از دور خارج

This regulation will *supersede* all previous rules.

su.pine /ˈsuːpaɪn, ˈsjuː-/ *adj.* lying on back

به پشت خوابیده، طاق باز

We walked along the beach, past the rows of *supine* bodies soaking up in the sun.

sup.plant /£ səˈplɑːnt, $ -ˈplænt/ *v.* to replace

جایگزین (چیزی) کردن، به‌جای (کسی) نشاندن

In most offices, the typewriter has now been *supplanted* by the computer.

sup.ple /ˈsʌp.l/ *adj.* flexible, pliant

نرم، قابل ارتجاع، انعطاف‌پذیر؛ سر به‌راه، حرف شنو

I am not *supple* enough to be able to touch the floor with my hands while I'm standing up.

sup.pli.ant /ˈsʌp.li.ənt/ *adj., n.* beseeching, entreating, supplicant

التماس‌کننده، مستدعی، ملتمس، حاجتمند؛ ملتمسانه

He could not resist the dog's *suppliant* whimpering, and he gave it some food.

sup.pli.cate /ˈsʌp.li.keɪt/ *v.* to entreat, to petition humbly

ملتمسانه خواستن، التماس کردن، استدعا کردن

We *supplicate* your majesty to grant him amnesty.

sup.pli.ca.tion: *n.*   درخواست، استدعا، التماس، تضرع

sup.pos.i.ti.tious /sʌpəˈzɪʃəs/ *adj.* amused, counterfeited

فرضی، حدسی؛ جعلی، تقلبی، ساختگی

I find no similarity between your *supposititious* illustration and the problem we are facing.

sup.press /sə'pres/ *v.* to crush, to subdue, to inhibit

سرکوب کردن، فرو نشاندن؛ خاتمه دادن، جلوگیری کردن از؛ کتمان کردن، پنهان کردن

1) After the armed troops had *suppressed* the rebellion, the city was placed under martial law.
2) Are the police *suppressing* some evidence?

sur.cease /sɜː'siːs/ *n.* stopage

قطع، جلوگیری

He begged the doctors to grant him *surcease* from his suffering.

sur.cease: *v.*   جلوگیری کردن، قطع کردن

sur.feit /£ 'sɜː.fɪt, $ 'sɜːr-/ *v., n.* to cloy, to overfeed; excess

زیاد خوردن، پُرخوری کردن، پُر خوراندن؛ یک دنیا، یک عالمه؛ زیاده‌روی، افراط، پرخوری

1) He *surfeited* himself with fruit.
2) There is *a surfeit of* plays about divorce on TV.

sur.ly /£ 'sɜː.li, $ 'sɜːr-/ *adj.* rude, cross

عنق، بدخلق، تندخو، ترشرو، بد اخلاق

Because of his *surly* attitude, many people avoided his company.

sur.mise /£ 'sə.maɪz, $ sɚ-/ *v., n.* guess

حدس زدن، گمان بردن؛ حدس، گمان

I *surmise* that he will be late for this meeting.

sur.mount /£ sə'maʊnt, $ sɚ-/ *v.* to overcome

غلبه کردن، فائق آمدن، پشت سر گذاشتن

He had to *surmount* many obstacles in order to succeed.

sur.rep.ti.tious /£ ˌsʌr.əp'tɪʃ.əs, $ ˌsɜːr-/ *adj.* secret

پنهانی، محرمانه، مخفیانه؛ دزدانه

News of their **surreptitious** meeting gradually leaked out.

sur.ro.gate /£ ˈsʌr.əgət, $ ˈsɜːr-/ *n.* substitute

جانشین، جایگزین، نماینده، قائم مقام، عوض

Fiction is a poor **surrogate** for real experience.

sur.veil.lance /£ səˈveɪ.lənts, $ sɚ-/ *n.* watching, guarding

نظارت، کنترل، مراقبت

Police kept the house under constant **surveillance** in the hope of capturing all the criminals at one time.

sus.te.nance /ˈsʌs.tɪ.nənts/ *n.* means of support, food, nourishment

معاش؛ موادغذایی، خوراک؛ خاصیت غذایی

There's not much **sustenance** in a glass of orange squash.

su.ture /£ ˈsuː.tʃəʳ, $ -tʃɚ/ *n., v.* stitch

(جراحی) بخیه؛ بخیه زدن

We will remove the **sutures** as soon as the wound heals.

swar.thy /£ ˈswɔː.ði, $ ˈswɔːr-/ *adj.* dark, dusky

(رنگ پوست) سبزه

Despite the stereotypes, not all Italians are **swarthy**; many are fair-skinned and blond-haired.

swathe /sweɪð/ *v.* to wrap around, to bandage

باندپیچی کردن، پیچیدن، قنداق کردن

They were **swathed** in scarves and sweaters.

swel.ter /£ ˈswel.təʳ, $ -tɚ/ *v.* to be oppressed by heat

بیش از حد گرم بودن، از گرما کلافه شدن، از گرما بی‌تاب شدن

I am going to buy an air conditioning unit as I do not

intend to *swelter* through another hot and humid summer.

swin.dler /£ ˈswɪnd.ləʳ, $ -lɚ/ *n.* cheat

کلاه‌بردار، شیاد، متقلب، حقه‌باز

She was an easy victim for the first *swindler* who came along.

swin.dle: *v.*   کلاه سر (کسی) گذاشتن، گول زدن

sy.ba.rite /£ ˈsɪb.ᵊr.aɪt, $ -ə.raɪt/ *n.* lover of luxury

آدم خوش‌گذران، آدم تجمل‌پرست، آدم راحت طلب

Rich people are not always *sybarites*; some of them have little taste for a life of luxury.

sy.co.phan.tic /£ ˈsɪk.əˈfæn.tɪk, $ -t̬ɪk/ *adj.* servilely flattering

چاپلوسانه، تملق‌آمیز، مجیزگویانه

The king enjoyed the *sycophantic* attentions of his followers.

syl.lo.gi.sm /ˈsɪl.ə.dʒɪ.zᵊm/ *n.* logical formula

قیاس صوری، قیاس منطقی

There must be a fallacy in this *syllogism*; I cannot accept the conclusion.

syl.van /ˈsɪl.vən/ *adj.* related to the woods, rustic

جنگلی؛ پردرخت

His paintings of nymphs in *sylvan* backgrounds were criticized as overly sentimental.

sym.met.ry /ˈsɪm.ə.tri/ *n.* regularity and balance, congruity

تناسب و هماهنگی، تشابه، تقارن

The addition of a second tower will give this edifice the *symmetry* which it now lacks.

syn.chro.nous /ˈsɪŋkrə.nəs/ *adj.* similarly timed, simultaneous with

همزمان، هم دوره، معاصر

There are scientists in different parts of the world who have made *synchronous* discoveries.

syn.the.sis /ˈsɪn.θə.sɪs/ *n.* mixing parts into a whole

ترکیب، تلفیق، التقاط، سنتز

He describes his latest record as "a *synthesis* of African and Latin rhythms".

syn.thet.ic /£ sɪn.θət.ɪk, $ -ˈθeṭ-/ *adj.* artificial, resulting from synthesis

مصنوعی، ساخته؛ ترکیبی

She criticized the *synthetic* charms of television presenters.

لیستی از لغاتی که در جملات بخش S به کار رفته‌اند:

allay: v.	برطرف کردن	feeble-minded: adj.	کندِ ذهن
alleviate: v.	قابل تحمل کردن	flaw: n.	نقطه ضعف
altar: n.	محراب	gushing: adj.	شدید
ascetic: n.	زاهد، پارسا	helping: n.	پرس (غذا)
attire: n.	لباس، جامه	icing: n.	رویهٔ کیک
beech: n.	درخت راش	inauguration: n.	شروع رسمی کار (رییس جمهور)
bicker: v.	یک به دو کردن		
bluster: n.	داد و بیداد	indignant: n.	عصبانی
breed: v.	رشد کردن، بزرگ شدن	insanity: n.	دیوانگی
burglary: n.	سرقت	interfere: v.	دخالت کردن
charm: n.	گیرایی	intermittent: adj.	متناوب
cloying: adj.	مشمئزکننده	invade: v.	زیر پا گذاشتن
commissioned officer: n.	افسر کادر	launch: v.	پرتاب کردن
		manipulative: adj	عوام فریب
complexion: n.	چهره	minister: n.	کشیش
devout: adj	مؤمن، متدین	morbid: adj.	ناخوشایند
crier: n.	روزنامه محلی	municipal: adj.	مربوط به شهرداری
digressions: n.	صحبت‌های خارج از موضوع	nocturnal: adj.	شب‌گرد
do the bidding of: v.	اطاعت کردن از	nymph: n.	پری
		outburst: n.	شروع ناگهانی
doze: v.	چرت زدن	overall: n.	لباس کار
dredge: v.	لایروبی کردن	parasite: n.	سربار، طفیلی
drone: n.	طفیلی	poisoning: n.	مسمومیت
edifice: n.	بنا، عمارت	premium: n.	حقِ بیمه
favoritism: n.	پارتی‌بازی	presenter: n.	مجری

private: *n.*	سرباز	suppress: *v.*	جلو چیزی را گرفتن
raspberry: *n.*	تمشک	swerve: *v.*	ویراژ دادن
repeal: *v.*	لغو کردن	tack: *n.*	پونز، میخ
secrete: *v.*	تراوش کردن	tainted: *adj.*	آلوده، فاسد
shad: *n.*	شاه‌ماهی	treasonous: *adj.*	خیانت‌آمیز
sloppy: *adj.*	نامرتب و کثیف	tug: *n.*	قایق یدک‌کش
specious: *adj*	ظاهراً مستدل	unflattering: *adj.*	ناخوشایند
squash: *n.*	عصاره	unwarranted: *adj.*	توجیه‌ناپذیر
strand: *v.*	به گِل نشستن	vessel: *n.*	کشتی
sultry: *adj.*	شرجی	warden: *n.*	رییس زندان
supposed: *adj.*	ظاهری	whimper: *v.*	زوزه کشیدن

T t

tac.it /ˈtæs.ɪt/ *adj.* understood, not put into words

ضمنی، تلویحی، بیان نشده

We have a *tacit* agreement.

tac.i.turn /£ ˈtæs.ɪ.tɜːn, $ -ə.tɜːrn/ *adj.* habitually silent, talking little

کم حرف، کم‌گوی

New Englanders are reputedly *taciturn* people.

tac.tile /£ ˈtæk.taɪl, $ -tᵊl/ *adj.* related to the organs or sense of touch

لمسی، لامسه‌ای، بساوشی

His calloused hands had lost their *tactile* sensitivity.

taint /teɪnt/ *v.* to contaminate, to corrupt

آلوده کردن/ شدن، فاسد کردن/ شدن؛ خراب کردن، تباه کردن

Health authorities are always trying to prevent the sale and use of food *tainted* by bacteria.

tal.is.man /ˈtæl.ɪz.mən, -ɪs-/ *n.* charm

طلسم

She wore the *talisman* to ward off evil.

tal.on /ˈtæl.ən/ *n.* claw of bird

چنگال، پنجه

The falconer wore a leather gauntlet to avoid being clawed by the hawk's *talons*.

tan.ta.lize /£ ˈtæn.tᵊl.aɪz, $ -t̬ə.laɪz/ *v.* to tease, to torture with disappointment

اذیت کردن، دست انداختن؛ خر کردن، دل(کسی را) بیهوده خوش کردن

Tom loved to *tantalize* his younger brother.

tan.ta.mount /£ ˈtæn.tə.maʊnt, $ -t̬ə-/ *adj.* equal in value

معادل، در حکم، برابر

Your ignoring their pathetic condition is *tantamount* to murder.

tan.trum /ˈtæn.trəm/ *n.* fit of bad temper, caprice

بدخلقی، کج خلقی، اوقات تلخی، عصبانیت؛ نحسی

The child learned that he could have almost anything if he *went into* a *tantrum*.

ta.ran.tu.la /təˈræn.tjʊ.lə/ *n.* venomous spider

رتیل

We need an antitoxin to counteract the bite of the *tarantula*.

tat.ter.de.mal.ion /tætərdəmʌluːn/ *n.* ragged fellow

آدم ژنده پوش، گدا

Do you expect an army of *tatterdemalion* and beggars to put up a real fight?

taut /£ tɔːt, $ tɑːt/ *adj.* tight; ready

کشیده، سفت؛ آماده

1) He tightened the strings of the guitar until they were *taut*.

2) The captain maintained that he ran a *taut* ship.

taut.o.log.i.cal /£ ˌtɔː.təˈlɒdʒ.ɪ.kᵊl, $ ˌtɑː.t̬əˈlɑː.dʒɪ-/ *adj.*
needlessly repetitious

دارای حشو، تکراری؛ (منطق) همان‌گویانه

In the sentence "It was visible to the eye", the phrase "to the eye" is *tautological*.

taut.ol.o.gy: *n.*

توضیح واضحات، تکرار مکررات؛ حشو قبیح؛ (منطق) همان‌گویی

taw.dry /£ ˈtɔː.dri, $ ˈtɑː-/ *adj., n.* cheap and gaudy

جلف و ارزان، با زلم زیمبو، پر زرق و برق

She won a few *tawdry* trinkets in Coney Island.

te.di.um /ˈtiː.di.əm/ *n.* boredom, weariness

یکنواختی، خستگی، ملالت

We hope this radio will help overcome the *tedium* of your stay in the hospital.

te.mer.i.ty /£ təˈmer.ɪ.ti, $ -ə.t̬i/ *n.* boldness, rashness

جسارت، گستاخی، بی‌پروایی

Do you have the *temerity* to argue with me?

tem.per /£ ˈtem.pəʳ, $ -pɚ/ *v.* to restrain, to blend, to toughen

نرم کردن، تعدیل کردن، کنترل کردن، محکم‌تر شدن

Breaking both his legs hasn't *tempered* his enthusiasm for rock climbing.

tem.po /£ ˈtem.pəʊ, $ -poʊ/ *n.* speed of music

سرعت، شتاب؛ (موسیقی) ضرب

I find the conductor's *tempo* too slow for such a brilliant piece of music.

tem.po.ral /£ ˈtem.pᵊr.ᵊl, $ -pɚ.əl/ *adj.* not lasting forever, limited by time, secular

موقتی، گذرا، زودگذر؛ دنیوی، جسمانی، غیر روحانی

At one time in our history, *temporal* rulers assumed that they had been given their thrones by divine right.

tem.po.rize /£ ˈtem.pᵊr.aɪz, $ -pə.raɪz/ *v.* to gain time, to avoid committing oneself

وقت‌کشی کردن، دفع‌الوقت کردن، طفره رفتن

I cannot permit you to *temporize* any longer; I must have a definite answer today.

te.na.cious /təˈneɪ.ʃəs/ *adj.* holding fast

قرص، محکم، استوار؛ سفت؛ سخت؛ یک دنده

I had to struggle to break his *tenacious* hold on my arm.

te.nac.i.ty /£ təˈnæs.ə.ti, $ -ṭi/ *n.* firmness, persistency

سختی، سفتی، استحکام، اصرار، سماجت؛ پیگیری

It is extremely difficult to overcome the *tenacity* of a habit such as smoking.

ten.den.tious /tenˈden.tʃəs/ *adj.* having an aim, biased

سوگیرانه، مغرضانه؛ مظلوم‌نما؛ حق به جانب

The editorials in this periodical are *tendentious* rather than truth-seeking.

ten.et /ˈten.ɪt/ *n.* doctrine, dogma

مرام، اصول، اعتقاد، عقیده، ایمان

I cannot accept the *tenets* of your faith.

ten.sile /£ ˈtent.saɪl, $ -sɪl/ *adj.* capable of being stretched

کششی، قابل کشش، کشش‌پذیری

Mountain climbers must know the *tensile* strength of their ropes.

ten.ta.tive /£ ˈten.tə.tɪv, $ -t̬ə.t̬ɪv/ *adj.* experimental, provisional

آزمایشی؛ موقت، موقتی، غیرقطعی

Your ***tentative*** plans sound plausible.

ten.u.ous /ˈten.ju.əs/ *adj.* thin, rare, slim, weak

ظریف، باریک، نازک؛ کم ارزش، ضعیف؛ جزئی، کم اهمیت

We were only able to make a ***tenuous*** connection between the two robberies.

ten.ure /£ ˈten.jə^r, £ -jʊə^r, $ -jʊr/ *n.* holding of an office

دورهٔ تصدی، تصدی؛ تصرف، اجاره؛ تصدی

During his ***tenure*** as dean, he had a real influence on students.

tep.id /ˈtep.ɪd/ *adj.* lukewarm

ولرم، نه چندان گرم

During the summer, I like to take a ***tepid*** bath.

ter.ma.gant /£ ˈtɜː.mə.gənt, $ ˈtɜːr-/ *n.* shrew, scolding, brawling woman

(زن) داد و بیداد کن، سلیطه، پتیاره

The Taming of the Shrew is one of many stories of the methods used in changing a ***termagant*** into a demure lady.

ter.mi.nol.o.gy /£ ˌtɜː.mɪˈnɒl.ə.dʒi, $ ˌtɜːr.mɪˈnɑː.lə-/ *n.* terms used in a science or art

اصطلاحات، واژگان

I find scientific ***terminology*** hard to understand.

ter.mi.nus /£ ˈtɜː.mɪ.nəs, $ ˈtɜːr-/ *n.* last stop of railroad

پایانه، ترمینال، ایستگاه پایان خط

After we reached the railroad ***terminus***, we continued

our journey into the wilderness on saddle horses.

ter.ra.pin /ˈter.ə.pɪn/ *n.* American marsh tortoise

لاک‌پشت کوچک (که در آب‌های شیرین آمریکای شمالی یافت می‌شود)

The flesh of the diamondback *terrapin* is considered to be a delicacy.

ter.re.stri.al /təˈres.tri.əl/ *adj.* of the earth

خاکی، خشکی؛ زمینی؛ دنیوی

We explored the *terrestrial* regions much more thoroughly than the aquatic or celestial regions.

terse /£ tɜːs, $ tɜːrs/ *adj.* concise, abrupt, pithy

مختصر، موجز، پرمعنی؛ خشک، رسمی

I admire his *terse* style of writing.

ter.tia.ry /£ ˈtɜː.ʃºr.i, $ ˈtɜːr.ʃi.er-/ *adj.* third

سوم، سومین؛ درجه سه، درجه سوم

He is so thorough than he analyzes *terse* causes where other writers are content with primary and secondary reasons.

tes.sel.lat.ed /£ ˈtes.ºl.eɪ.tɪd, $ -t̬ɪd/ *adj.* inlaid, mosaic

موزائیک‌کاری شده، مفروش، کار گذاشته شده

I recall seeing a table with a *tessellated* top of bits of stone and glass in a very interesting pattern.

tes.ta.tor /teˈsteɪ.təʳ/ *n.* maker of a will

وصیت‌کننده، موصی

The attorney called in his secretary and his partner to witness the signature of the *testator*.

test.y /ˈtes.ti/ *adj.* irritable, short-tempered

بدخلق، تنگ حوصله، بد اخلاق؛ تند، پرخاشگرانه

My advice is to avoid discussing this problem with him today as he is rather **testy**.

teth.er /£ ˈteð.əʳ, $ -ɚ/ v., n. to tie with a rope; leash

بستن؛ افسار، قلاده (افسار یا قلاده حیوانی را به جایی)

Before we went to sleep, we **tethered** the horses to prevent their wandering off during the night.

thau.ma.turg.ist /θɔːʊmʌtjʊrdʒɪst/ n. miracle worker, magician

ساحر، جادوگر

I would have to be a **thaumaturgist** and not a mere doctor to find a remedy for this disease.

the.oc.ra.cy /θɪˈɒk.rə.sɪ/ n. government of a community by the religious leaders

حکومت روحانیون، حکومت مذهبی، دین سالاری

Some Pilgrims favored the establishment of a **theocracy** in New England.

the.os.o.phy /θɪˈɒsəfɪ/ n. wisdom in divine things

عرفان، تصوف، اشراق، حکمت الهی

Theosophy seeks to embrace the essential truth in all religions.

ther.a.peu.tic /£ ˌθer.əˈpjuː.tɪk, $ -tɪk/ adj. curative

درمانی، شفابخش

These springs are famous for their **therapeutic** qualities.

ther.mal /£ ˈθɜː.məl, $ ˈθɜːr-/ adj. related to heat

حرارتی، گرمایی؛ گرم

The natives discovered that the hot springs gave excellent **thermal** baths.

thrall /θrɔːl/ *n.* slave, bondage

برده، اسیر، بنده؛ اسارت؛ بردگی، بندگی

The captured soldier was *held in thrall* by the conquering army.

thren.o.dy /ˈθren.ə.dɪ/ *n.* song of lamentation, dirge

مرثیه، نوحه

When he died, many poets wrote *threnodies* about his passing.

thrift.y /ˈθrɪf.ti/ *adj.* careful about money, economical

صرفه‌جو، ممسک، مقتصد

A *thrifty* shopper compares prices before making major purchases.

throe /£ θrəʊ, $ θroʊ/ *n.* violent anguish

درد و رنج، اضطراب، گیر و دار

The country is once again *in the throes* of famine.

throng /£ θrɒŋ, $ θrɑːŋ/ *n., v.* crowd

جمعیت، ازدحام؛ ازدحام کردن، از جمعیت پر شدن

A huge *throng* had gathered round the speaker.

throt.tle /£ ˈθrɒt.l̩, $ ˈθrɑː.t̬l̩/ *v., n.* to strangle

خفه کردن؛ سرکوب کردن؛ کنترل کردن

The criminal tried to *throttle* the old man.

thwart /£ θwɔːt, $ θwɔːrt/ *v.* to baffle, to frustrate

خنثی کردن، نقش بر آب کردن؛ چوب لای چرخ (کسی) گذاشتن

He felt everybody was trying to *thwart* his plans.

thyme /taɪm/ *n.* aromatic plant used for seasoning

آویشن

The addition of a little *thyme* will enhance the flavor of

food.

tim.bre /£ ˈtɪm.bəʳ, $ -bɚ/ *n.* sound quality

(موسیقی) طنین، صدا

We identify the instrument producing a musical sound by its *timbre*.

ti.mid.i.ty /£ tɪˈmɪd.ɪ.ti, $ -ə.t̬i/ *n.* lack of self-confidence or courage

کمرویی، خجالت؛ ترسویی

If you are to succeed as a salesman, you must first lose your *timidity*.

ti.mid: *adj.* کمرو، خجالتی؛ ترسو، بزدل

ti.mor.ous /£ ˈtɪm.ᵊr.əs, $ -ɚ.əs/ *adj.* fearful, nervous, timid

ترسو، بزدل، وحشت‌زده؛ کمرو، خجالتی

His *timorous* manner betrayed the fear he felt at the moment.

tip.ple /ˈtɪp.l̩/ *v., n.* to drink frequently

عرق‌خوری کردن، دست به مشروب‌خوری زدن؛ مشروب (الکلی)

He found that his most enjoyable evenings occurred when he *tippled* with his friends at the local pub.

ti.rade /£ taɪˈreɪd, £ tɪ-, $ ˈtaɪ.reɪd/ *n.* extended scolding, denunciation

سخنرانی تند و انتقاد آمیز، نطق آتشین

Long before he had finished his *tirade*, we were aware of the seriousness of our misconduct.

ti.tan.ic /taɪˈtæn.ɪk, tɪ-/ *adj.* gigantic

عظیم، شگرف؛ شدید، حاد، بسیار قوی

Titanic waves beat against the shore during the

hurricane.

tithe /taɪð/ *n., v.* tax of one-tenth paid to a church

ده یک، عُشریه، عُشر

Because he was an agnostic, he refused to pay his **tithe** to the clergy.

ti.til.late /£ ˈtɪt.ɪ.leɪt, $ ˈtɪt̬-/ *v.* to tickle

غلغلک دادن؛ تحریک کردن

I am here not to **tililate** my audience but to enlighten it.

tit.u.lar /£ ˈtɪt.jʊ.ləʳ, $ ˈtɪtʃ.ə.lɚ/ *adj.* existing in title only

صاحب عنوان؛ اسمی، تشریفاتی؛ برحسب عنوان، بهموجب عنوان

It is already agreed that Mr. Escamez will be the **titular** head of the new bank.

toad.y /£ ˈtəʊ.di, $ ˈtoʊ-/ *v., n.* to flatter for favors

تملق (کسی را) گفتن، چاپلوسی کردن، تملق؛ آدم متملق، چاپلوس

I hope you see through those who are **toading** you for special favors.

to.ga /£ ˈtəʊ.gə, $ ˈtoʊ-/ *n.* Roman outer robe

توگا (= لباس گشاد مردان روم باستان)

Marc Antony pointed to the slashes in Caesar's **toga**.

tome /£ təʊm, $ toʊm/ *n.* large volume

کتاب؛ جلد، مجلد

He spent much time in the libraries poring over ancient **tomes**.

to.po.graph.y /£ təʊˈpɒg.rə.fi, $ təˈpɑː.grə-/ *n.* physical features of a region

توپوگرافی، وضـعیت ارضـی / طـبیعی؛ مکـانشناسی؛ نـقشۀ وضـع مکـانی؛ (مجازی) وضعیت، ساختار

Before the generals gave the order to attack, they ordered a complete study of the *topography* of the region.

tor.pid /£ ˈtɔː.pɪd, $ ˈtɔːr-/ *adj.* dormant, dull, lethargic

سست، بیحال؛ تنبل، کاهل

The *torpid* bear had just come out of his cave after his long hibernation.

tor.por /£ ˈtɔː.pəʳ, $ ˈtɔːr.pɚ/ *n.* lethargy, dormancy

رخوت، خمودی، سستی، بی‌حالی، غیرفعالی

Nothing seemed to arouse him from his *torpor*.

tor.so /£ ˈtɔː.səʊ, $ ˈtɔːr.soʊ/ *n.* human trunk

تنه؛ پیکرهٔ تنه

We bought a postcard of the famous marble *torso* in the museum shop.

tor.til.la /£ tɔːˈtiː.ə, $ tɔːrˈtiː.jə/ *n.* flat cake made of cornmeal

تورتیلا (= نوعی کیک)

In Mexico, we became more and more accustomed to the use of *tortillas* instead of bread.

tor.tu.ous /£ ˈtɔː.tʃu.əs, $ ˈtɔːr-/ *adj.* winding, full of curves

پر پیچ و خم، پیچ در پیچ، پیچ‌دار

Because this road is so *tortuous*, it is unwise to go faster than twenty miles an hour on it.

touch.stone /£ ˈtʌtʃ.stəʊn, $ -stoʊn/ *n.* criterion

محک، ملاک، معیار

What *touchstone* can be used to measure the character of a person?

touch.y /ˈtʌtʃ.i/ *adj.* sensitive, irascible

زودرنج، حساس، نازک نارنجی؛ حساس

Do not discuss this phase of the problem as he is very *touchy* about it.

tox.ic /£ ˈtɒk.sɪk, $ ˈtɑːk-/ *adj.* poisonous

سمّی، مسموم‌کننده

We must seek an antidote for whatever *toxic* substance he has eaten.

tract /trækt/ *n.* pamphlet; region

رسالهٔ مذهبی / سیاسی، ناحیه، منطقه، گستره، پهنه

Have you read Milton's *tract* on divorce?

trac.ta.ble /ˈtræk.tə.bl̩/ *adj.* docile

رام، سر به راه، مطیع

You will find the children in this school very *tractable* and willing to learn.

tra.duce /£ trəˈdjuːs, £ -ˈdʒuːs, $ -ˈduːs/ *v.* to expose to slander

مورد اتهام قرار دادن، تهمت زدن به؛ (حیثیت، آبرو و غیره) لکه‌دار کردن

His opponents tried to *traduce* the candidate's reputation by spreading rumors about his past.

tra.jec.to.ry /£ trəˈdʒek.tᵊr.i, £ ˈ-tri, $ -tɚ.i/ *n.* path of something moving through air

مسیر، خط سیر؛ روند

If you throw a heavy object, its natural *trajectory* tends to be a parabola.

tran.quil.i.ty /£ træŋˈkwɪl.ɪ.ti, $ trænˈkwɪl.ə.t̬i/ *n.* calmness, peace

آرامش؛ راحتی خیال؛ سکون

After the commotion and excitemet of the city, I appreciate the *tranquility* of these fields and forests.

trans.cend /£ træn'send, £ trɑ:n-, $ træn-/ *v.* to exceed, to surpass

فراسوی (چیزی) رفتن / بودن، بالاتر بودن

The best films are those which *transcend* natural or cultural barriers.

trans.cen.den.tal: *adj.*   متعالی، فراگیر؛ اشراقی، شهودی

tran.scribe /£ træn'skraɪb, £ trɑ:n-, $ træn-/ *v.* to make a copy of

رونویسی کردن، استنساخ کردن؛ از روی نوار پیاده کردن

When you *transcribe* your notes, please send a copy to Mr. Smith and keep the original for our files.

tran.scrip.tion: *n.*   رونویسی، استنساخ؛ نسخه، رونوشت

trans.gres.sion /£ trænz'greʃ.ᵊn, £ trɑ:nz-, $ trænz-/ *n.* violation of a law; sin

تخطی، تجاوز، قانون‌شکنی؛ گناه

Who is supposed to have committed these *transgressions*?

trans.gress: *v.*   خطا کردن، گناه کردن؛ تجاوز کردن

tran.si.ent /£ 'træn.zi.ənt, £ 'trɑ:n-, $ 'trænt.ʃᵊnt/ *adj., n.* fleeting, quickly passing away

گذرا، زودگذر، موقت؛ مسافر

Their happiness was to be sadly *transient*.

tran.si.tion /£ træn'zɪʃ.ᵊn, £ trɑ:n-, $ træn-/ *n.* passing from one state to another

انتقال، گذر، عبور؛ مرحلۀ گذر

His attitude underwent an abrupt *transition*.

trans.lu.cent /£ trænz'lu:.sᵊnt, £ trɑ:nz-, $ trænz-/ *adj.* partly transparent

(شیشه) مات؛ نیمه شفاف

We could not recognize the people in the next room because of the *translucent* curtains which separated us.

trans.mute /£ trænz'mju:t, £ trɑ:nz-, $ trænz-/ *v.* to change

تبدیل کردن / شدن، مبدل کردن / شدن

He was unable to *transmute* his dreams into actualities.

trans.par.ent /£ trænt'spær.ᵊnt, £ trɑ:nt-, $ træn'sper-/ *adj.* easily detected, obvious

واضح، آشکار، روشن؛ بی‌شبهه؛ نازک، بدن نما؛ شفاف

1) Your scheme is so *transparent* that it will fool no one.
2) You couldn't wear this blouse with nothing underneath; it is *transparent*.

trans.pire /£ træn'spaɪəʳ, £ trɑ:n-, $ træn'spaɪɚ/ *v.* to exhale, to become known

فاش شدن، بیرون درج کردن

In spite of all our efforts to keep the meeting a secret, news of our conclusions *transpired*.

trau.ma.tic /£ trɔ:'mæt.ɪk, traʊ-, $ trɑ:'mæt̬-/ *adj.* shocking and painful

(تجربه) تلخ، تکان‌دهنده، نامطلوب؛ ضربه روحی

Don't you find exams *traumatic*?

tra.vail /'træv.eɪl/ *n.* painful labor

رنج، زحمت؛ مصیبت؛ بلیّه

How long do you think a man can endure such *travail* without rebelling?

trav.erse /£ trə'vɜ:s, $ -'vɜ:rs/ *v., n.* to go through or across

عبور کردن از، گذشتن از؛ عبور

When you *traverse* this field, be careful of the bull.

trav.e.sty /ˈtræv.ə.sti/ *n., v.* comical parody

تقلید مبتذل، تقلید مسخره، مضحکه؛ ناشیانه تقلید کردن؛ مضحکه کردن

The decision the jury has arrived at is a *travesty* of justice.

trea.cle /ˈtriː.kl̩/ *n.* golden syrup

شیرهٔ قند، ملاس

Treacle is a sweet dark thick liquid which is used in cooking sweet dishes and sweets such as *treacle* toffee.

trea.tise /£ ˈtriː.tɪs, $ -t̬ɪs/ *n.* article

رساله؛ مقاله

He is preparing a *treatise* on the Elizabethan playwrights.

trek /trek/ *n., v.* to travel with difficulty

سفر دور و دراز با پای پیاده؛ پیاده‌روی کردن، پیاده سفر کردن

The tribe *trekked* further north that summer in search of available game.

trem.or /£ ˈtrem.ər, $ -ɚ/ *n.* trembling, slight quiver

لرزش، تکان، جنبش؛ لرز

She had a nervous *tremor* in her right hand.

trem.ul.ous /ˈtrem.jʊ.ləs/ *adj.* trembling, wavering

لرزان، مرتعش؛ عصبی، نگران

She was *tremulous* more from excitement than from fear.

trench.ant /ˈtren.tʃənt/ *adj.* cutting, keen

قوی، محکم؛ صریح، بی‌پرده، نیش‌دار

I am afraid of his *trenchant* wit for it is so often sarcastic.

trench.er.man /£ ˈtrentʃər.mæn, $ -ɚ/ *n.* good eater

آدم شکم‌باره، آدم خوش اشتها

He is not finicky about his food; he is a *trencherman*.

trep.i.da.tion /ˌtrep.ɪˈdeɪ.ʃ°n/ *n.* fear, trembling agitation

دلهره، دلشوره، نگرانی، اضطراب

We must face the enemy without *trepidation* if we are to win this battle.

tri.bu.la.tion /ˌtrɪb.jʊˈleɪ.ʃ°n/ *n.* distress, suffering

محنت، غم، درد، رنج

After all the trials and *tribulations* we have gone through, we need this rest.

tri.bun.al /traɪˈbjuː.nəl/ *n.* court of justice

دادگاه؛ جایگاه قاضی، کرسی قضاوت

The decision of the *tribunal* was final.

tri.bute /ˈtrɪb.juːt/ *n.* tax levied by a ruler; mark of respect

باج، خراج؛ سپاس، قدردانی، ستایش

The colonists refused to pay *tribute* to a foreign despot.

tri.dent /ˈtraɪ.d°nt/ *n.* three-pronged spear

نیزهٔ سه شاخه، چنگک سه شاخه

Neptune is usually depicted as rising from the sea, carrying his *trident* on his shoulder.

tril.o.gy /ˈtrɪl.ə.dʒi/ *n.* group of three works

تریلوژی، سه گانه (فیلم، رمان، نمایش‌نامه و غیره که از سه بخش به‌هم پیوسته تشکیل شده است)

A film was made out of the first and second parts of the *trilogy*.

trite /traɪt/ *adj.* commonplace, hackneyed

پیش پا افتاده، معمولی؛ بی‌مزه

The *trite* and predictable situations in many television

programs alienate many viewers.

troth /£ trəʊθ, $ troʊθ/ *n.* pledged faithfulness, betrothal

قول وفاداری؛ نامزدی

He gave her his ***troth*** and vowed he would cherish her always.

truck.le /ˈtrʌk.ᵊl/ *v.* to be servile, to yield slavishly

تعظیم و تکریم کردن، چاپلوسی کردن

If you ***truckle*** to the lord, you will be regarded as a sycophant; if you do not, you will be considered arrogant.

truc.u.lent /ˈtrʌk:jʊ.lənt/ *adj.* aggressive, savage

بدخلق، عصبانی، پرخاشگر؛ پرخاشگرانه، تحکم‌آمیز

They are a ***truculent*** race, ready to fight at any moment.

truc.u.lence: *n.* بدخلقی، پرخاشگری، عصبانیت

tru.i.sm /ˈtru:.ɪ.zᵊm/ *n.* self-evident truth

حقیقت بدیهی، حقیقت مسلّم

Many a ***truism*** is well expressed in a proverb.

trump.er.y /ˈtrʌmpəri/ *n.* objects that are showy; valueless

پر زرق و برق؛ بی‌ارزش

All this finery is mere ***trumpery***.

trun.cate /trʌŋˈkeɪt/ *v.* to cut the top off

سر و ته (چیزی را) زدن، مختصر کردن؛ مُثله کردن

Television coverage of the match was ***truncated*** by a technical fault.

tryst /trɪst/ *n.* appointed meeting

(در مورد عشاق) میعاد، دیدار نهانی؛ میعادگاه

The lovers kept their ***tryst*** even though they realized their danger.

tu.mult /£ ˈtjuː.mʌlt, $ ˈtuː-/ *n.* commotion, noise, riot

غوغا، همهمه، جنجال؛ آشفتگی، درهم ریختگی

She could not make herself heard over the *tumult* of the mob.

tun.dra /ˈtʌn.drə/ *n.* rolling and treeless plain

(جغرافیا) توندرا، منطقه یخبندان

Few plants grow in *tundra* regions.

tur.bid /£ ˈtɜː.bɪd, $ ˈtɜːr-/ *adj.* muddy; confused

گل آلود؛ (ذهن) آشفته، مغشوش، نابسامان

The water was *turbid* after the children had waded through it.

tur.bul.ence /£ ˈtɜː.bjʊ.lənts, $ ˈtɜːr.bjə-/ *n.* state of violent agitation

خرابی وضع هوا؛ تلاطم

We were frightened by the *turbulence* of the ocean during the storm.

tu.reen /tjʊˈriːn/ *n.* deep table dish for holding soup

(ظرف) سوپ‌خوری

The waiters brought the soup to the tables in silver *tureens*.

turgid /£ ˈtɜː.dʒɪd, $ ˈtɜːr-/ *adj.* swollen, distended

متورم، باد کرده

The *turgid* limb was sore and painful.

turn.key /£ ˈtɜːŋ.kiː, $ ˈtɜːrn-/ *n.* jailor

زندانبان

By bribing the *turnkey*, the prisoner arranged to have better food brought to him in his cell.

tur.pi.tude /£ ˈtɜː.pɪ.tjuːd, $ ˈtɜːr.pɪ.tuːd/ *n.* depravity

فساد، انحطاط، ابتذال؛ عمل خلاف اخلاق

A visitor may be denied admittance to this country life if he has been guilty of moral ***turpitude***.

tu.tel.age /£ ˈtjuː.tɪ.lɪdʒ, $ ˈtuː.t̬ᵊl.ɪdʒ/ *n.* training, guardianship

تعلیم، آموزش؛ سرپرستی، قیمومیت، محافظت

Under the ***tutelage*** of such masters of the instrument, he made rapid progress as a virtuoso.

tu.te.lar.y /ˈtjuː.tɪ.lərɪ/ *adj.* protective, related to guardianship

محافظ، نگهبان، سرپرست

I am acting in my ***tutelary*** capacity when I refuse to grant you permission to leave the campus.

ty.ro /ˈtaɪə.rəʊ, $ -roʊ/ *n.* beginner, novice

نوآموز، مبتدی، تازه‌کار

For a more ***tyro***, you have produced some marvelous results.

لیستی از لغاتی که در جملات بخش T به کار رفته‌اند:

alienate: *v.*	گریزان کردن	game: *n.*	شکار؛ گوشت شکار
betray: *v.*	لو دادن، خیانت کردن	gauntlet: *n.*	دستکش
bribe: *v.*	رشوه دادن	hawk: *n.*	شاهین
calloused: *adj.*	(پوست) پینه‌بسته	hibernation: *n.*	خواب زمستانی
capacity: *n.*	مقام	hurricane: *n.*	طوفان شدید
cherish: *v.*	دوست داشتن	levy: *v.*	(مالیات، جریمه) بستن
claw: *v.*	چنگ انداختن	parabola: *n.*	سهمی
commotion: *n.*	سر و صدا	pathetic: *adj.*	اسف‌انگیز
counteract: *v.*	خنثی کردن	plausible: *adj.*	قابل قبول
delicacy: *n.*	غذای لذیذ	pore over: *v.*	تعمق کردن
demure: *adj.*	متین، محجوب	sarcastic: *adj.*	کنایه‌دار
despot: *n.*	حاکم مستبد	slash: *n.*	چاک، درز
diamondback: *adj.*	لوزی شکل، الماس‌گونه	sycophant: *n.*	آدم چاپلوس
		trinket: *n.*	زیورآلات ارزان قیمت
embrace: *v.*	پذیرفتن	virtuoso: *n.*	(موسیقی) استاد
favor: *v.*	خواستار چیزی شدن	vow: *v.*	عهد کردن
final: *adj.*	قطعی	ward off: *v.*	دور نگهداشتن
finery: *n.*	لباس و جواهرات	wilderness: *n.*	بیابان
finicky: *adj.*	بهانه‌گیر، ایرادی	wit: *n.*	شوخ طبعی

U u

u.biq.ui.tous /juːˈbɪkwɪtəs/ *adj.* being everywhere, omnipresent

همه جا حاضر، موجود در همه جا، همیشه موجود؛ فراگیر، رایج، متداول

You are *ubiquitous*; I meet you wherever I go.

ul.te.ri.or /£ ʌlˈtɪə.ri.əʳ, $ -ˈtɪr.i-/ *adj.* situated beyond, unstated

نهفته، نهانی، مخفی، پنهانی

You must have an *ulterior* motive for your behavior.

ul.ti.mate /£ ˈʌl.tɪ.mət, $ -t̬ə-/ *adj., n.* final

نهایی، غایی؛ اوج، نهایت؛ حد نهایی، نقطهٔ اوج

Scientists are searching for the *ultimate* truths.

ul.ti.mat.um /£ ˌʌl.tɪˈmeɪ.təm, $ -t̬əˈmeɪ.t̬əm/ *n.* warning, last demand

اولتیماتوم، اتمام حجّت

Since they have ignored our *ultimatum*, our only recourse is to declare war.

um.brage /ˈʌm.brɪdʒ/ *n.* anger, resentment, sense of injury or insult

رنجش، عصبانیت، دلخوری

She *took umbrage* at his remarks.

un.a.nim.i.ty /£ ˌjuː.nəˈnɪm.ɪ.ti, $ -əˌt̬i/ *n.* complete agreement

اتفاق، اتفاق آراء، وحدت نظر

We were surprised by the *unanimity* with which our proposals were accepted by the different groups.

    un.an.i.mous: *adj.*   هم‌رأی، هم‌داستان، هم عقیده؛ واحد، یکپارچه

un.as.sum.ing /£ ˌʌn.əˈsjuː.mɪŋ, $ -ˈsuː-/ *adj.* modest

خالی از تظاهر، بی‌تکلّف؛ فروتن، متواضع

He is so *unassuming* that some people fail to realize how great a man he really is.

un.bri.dled /ʌmˈbraɪ.dl̩d/ *adj.* unrestrained

مهار گسیخته، افسار گسیخته، خارج از کنترل

He had a sudden fit of *unbridled* rage.

un.can.ny /ʌŋˈkæn.i/ *adj.* strange, mysterious

مرموز، غیرعادی

You have the *uncanny* knack of reading my innermost thoughts.

un.con.scion.a.ble /£ ʌŋˈkɒn.tʃ°n.ə.bl̩, $ -ˈkɑːn-/ *adj.* excessive, unscrupulous

نامعقول، بیش از حد، بیش از اندازه

He found the loan shark's demands *unconscionable* and impossible to meet.

un.couth /ʌŋˈkuːθ/ *adj.* outlandish, clumsy, boorish

خالی از ظرافت، خشن، بی‌نزاکت؛ بی‌فرهنگ

Most biographers portray Lincoln as an *uncouth* and ungainly young man.

unc.tion /ˈʌŋk.ʃ°n/ *n.* the act of anointing with oil

تدهین، روغن‌مالی

The anointing with oil of a person near death is called extreme *unction*.

unc.tu.ous /'ʌŋk.tju.əs/ *n.* oily; bland; insincerely suave

(غذا) چرب، پرخامه؛ چاپلوسانه، تملق‌آمیز؛ چاپلوس، متملق

He came up to me, oozing *unctuous* sympathy, hoping that I would buy him a drink.

un.du.late /'ʌn.djʊ.leɪt/ *v.* to move with a wavelike motion

موج زدن؛ موجی شکل بودن، موج‌دار بودن

The waters *undulated* in the breeze.

un.du.late: *adj.* موجی شکل، موج‌دار

un.earth /£ ʌn'ɜːθ, $ -'ɜːrθ/ *v.* to dig up

کندن، کشف کردن، از زیر خاک بیرون آوردن

When they *unearthed* the city, the archaeologists found many relics of an ancient civilization.

un.earth.ly /£ ʌn'ɜːθ.li, $ -'ɜːrθ-/ *adj.* not earthly; weird

غیر زمینی؛ فوق‌طبیعی، غیرعادی، مرموز

There is an *unearthly* atmosphere about his work which amazes the casual observer.

un.e.qui.vo.cal /ˌʌn.ɪ'kwɪv.ə.kəl/ *adj.* plain, obvious

صریح، روشن، خالی از ابهام

My answer to your proposal is an *unequivocal* and absolute "No".

un.err.ing.ly /£ ʌn'ɜː.rɪŋ.li, $ -'er.ɪŋ-/ *adv.* without mistake, infallibly

به‌طور دقیق، بدون خطا، بدون اشتباه

My teacher *unerringly* pounced on the one typographical error in my essay.

un.fal.ter.ing /£ ʌnˈfɒl.tᵊr.ɪŋ, $ -ˈfɑːl.tɚ-/ *adj.* steadfast

محکم، استوار، تزلزل ناپذیر

She approached the guillotine with *unfaltering* steps.

un.feigned /ʌnˈfeɪnd/ *adj.* genuine, real

صادقانه، بی‌غل و غش، بی‌شائبه، صمیمانه

I am sure her surprise was *unfeigned*.

un.fledged /ʌnˈfledʒd/ *adj.* immature

بی‌تجربه، ناشی، خام، تازه‌کار

It is hard for an *unfledged* writer to find a sympathetic publisher.

un.gain.ly /ʌŋˈgeɪn.li/ *adj.* awkward

دست و پا چلفتی؛ بدقواره، بد ترکیب

He is an *ungainly* young man.

un.guent /£ ˈʌŋ.gju.ənt, $ -gwənt/ *n.* ointment

مرهم، پماد، ضماد

Apply this *unguent* to the sore muscles before retiring.

u.ni.for.mi.ty /£ juː.nɪˈfɔː.mɪ.ti, $ -ˈfɔːr.mə.t̬i/ *n.* sameness, consistency, monotony

یکنواختی، همسانی، هم شکلی، یکپارچگی

There is a depressing *uniformity* about the architecture of this part of town.

u.ni.form: *adj.*   هم شکل، یکسان، یکنواخت؛ یکدست؛ یکپارچه

u.ni.lat.e.ral /£ ˌjuː.nɪˈlæt.ᵊr.ᵊl, $ -ˈlæt̬.ɚ-/ *adj.* one-sided

یک سویه، یکطرفه، یک جانبه

The rebel movement declared a *unilateral* ceasefire from the beginning of war.

un.im.peach.a.ble /ˌʌn.ɪmˈpiː.tʃə.bl̩/ *adj.* blameless and exemplary

منزه و پرهیزگار؛ نمونه، قابل اعتماد، موثق

Lord Fletch, said the Bishop, was a man of ***unimpeachable*** integrity and character.

un.in.hi.bit.ed /£ ˌʌn.ɪnˈhɪb.ɪ.tɪd, $ -t̬ɪd/ *adj.* free and natural, without embarrassment or too much control

رک، صریح، بی‌پرده؛ بی‌پروا

The students we spoke to were surprisingly ***uninhibited*** in talking about sex.

u.ni.que /juˈniːk/ *adj.* single in kind

منحصر به فرد، تک، یگانه؛ بی‌نظیر، بی‌همتا، بی‌مانند

Each person's genetic code is ***unique*** except in the case of identical twins.

u.ni.son /ˈjuː.nɪ.sᵊn/ *n.* complete accord

یک‌صدا، باهم، همه با هم، متفقاً، متحداً

The choir sang in ***unison***.

un.kempt /ʌŋˈkempt/ *adj.* disheveled, untidy, not cared for

نامرتب، ژولیده، به‌هم ریخته

The beggar was dirty and ***unkempt***.

un.mi.ti.gat.ed /£ ʌnˈmɪt.ɪ.geɪ.tɪd, $ -ˈmɪt̬.ɪ.geɪ.t̬ɪd/ *adj.* harsh, severe

کاهش نیافته، تسکین نیافته؛ شدید

I sympathize with you in your ***unmitigated*** sorrow.

un.ob.trus.ive /ˌʌn.əbˈtruː.sɪv/ *adj.* not noticeable, not blatant

بی سر و صدا، آرام، بدون جلب توجه؛ بدون ایجاد مزاحمت

The secret service agents in charge of protecting the Presedent tried to be as ***unobtrusive*** as possible.

un.prec.e.dent.ed /£ ʌnˈpres.ɪ.den.tɪd, $ -t̬ɪd/ *adj.* unparalleled

بی‌سابقه

This contury has witnessed oppression on an ***unprecedented*** scale.

un.ru.ly /ʌnˈruː.li/ *adj.* disobedient, lawless

نافرمان، سرکش، قانون شکن، خلاف کار

The only way to curb this ***unruly*** mob is to use tear gas.

un.sa.vo.ry /£ ʌnˈseɪ.vᵊr.i, $ -vɚ-/ *adj.* distasteful, morally offensive

نامطبوع، ناخوشایند؛ ناپسند، زشت، زننده

People with ***unsavory*** reputations should not be allowed to work with young people.

un.seem.ly /ʌnˈsiːm.li/ *adj.* unbecoming, inappropriate

ناشایسته، ناپسند، مذموم

His language was most ***unseemly***.

un.sul.li.ed /ʌnˈsʌlɪd/ *adj.* untarnished

پاک، بی‌آلایش، بدون خدشه؛ ضایع نشده، تباه نشده

I am happy that my reputation is ***unsullied***.

un.ten.a.ble /ʌnˈten.ə.bl̩/ *adj.* unsupportable

غیر قابل دفاع، سست بنیاد

I find your theory ***untenable*** and must reject it.

un.to.ward /£ ˌʌn.tʊˈwɔːd, $ -ˈtə.wɔːrd/ *adj.* annoying, unfortunate

غیرمترقبه، دور از انتظار؛ نامطلوب، ناخواسته؛ غیرعادی، خارق‌العاده

Unless anything ***untoward*** happens we should be there before midday.

un.wit.ting /£ ʌnˈwɪt.ɪŋ, $ -ˈwɪt̬-/ *adj.* unintentional, not knowing

ندانسته، بی‌خبر، بی‌اطلاع؛ بدون قصد، اتفاقی

The two women claimed they were the *unwitting* victims of a drug dealer.

un.wont.ed /£ ʌnˈwəʊn.tɪd, $ -ˈwɑːn.t̬ɪd/ *adj.* unaccustomed by experience, unusual

غیرعادی، نامعمول، نامأنوس، خارق‌العاده

He sprang to the telephone with *unwonted* vigor.

up.braid /ʌpˈbreɪd/ *v.* to scold, to reproach

سرزنش کردن، نکوهش کردن، ملامت کردن

I must *upbraid* him for his misbehavior.

up.shot /£ ˈʌp.ʃɒt, $ -ʃɑːt/ *n.* outcome

نتیجه، حاصلِ کار

The *upshot* of the discussions is that there will be no redundancies.

ur.bane /£ ɜːˈbeɪn, $ ɜːr-/ *adj.* refined, elegant, suave

مؤدب، با نزاکت، آداب دان؛ مؤدبانه

The courtier was *urbane* and sophisticated.

ur.chin /£ ˈɜː.tʃɪn, $ ˈɜːr-/ *n.* mischievous child (usually boy)

بچهٔ ولگرد، بچهٔ شیطان، بچهٔ تُخس

Get out! This store is no place for grubby *urchin*!

ur.sine /ˈɜːsaɪn/ *adj.* bearlike

شبیه خرس، خرس مانند، خرس‌وار

Because of its *ursine* appearance, the great panda has been identified with the bears.

u.sur.pa.tion /juːzəˈpeɪʃ°n/ *n.* act of seizing power and rank of another

غصب

The revolution ended with the ***usurpation*** of the throne by the victorious rebel leader.

u.surp: *v.*   غصب کردن

u.su.ry /£ ˈjuː.zjʊ.ri, $ -ʒɚ.i/ *n.* lending money at illegal rates of interest

رباخواری

The loan shark was found guilty of ***usury***.

u.to.pi.a /£ juːˈtəʊ.pi.ə, $ -ˈtoʊ-/ *n.* place of ideal perfection

آرمان شهر، مدينة فاضله، ناکجاآباد

The people who built this city had wanted it to be a ***utopia*** which would be a shining example to all nations.

لیستی از لغاتی که در جملات بخش U بکار رفته‌اند:

anoint: *v.*	تدهین کردن	pounce: *v.*	پریدن، رفتن
casual: *adj.*	بی‌منظور	recourse: *n.*	راه چاره
curb: *v.*	کنترل کردن	redundancy: *n.*	کارمند مازاد
grubby: *adj.*	کثیف	relics: *n.*	بقایا
integrity: *n.*	صداقت، درستی	retiring: *n.*	خواب
knack: *n.*	راه و روش	sophisticated: *adj.*	با فرهنگ
loan shark: *n.*	نزول‌خور	spring: *v.*	پریدن
ooze: *v.*	از خود نشان دادن	suave: *adj.*	مؤدب
meet: *v.*	تأمین کردن، ارضاء کردن	vigor: *n.*	توان، قدرت

V v

vac.il.la.tion /ˌvæs.ɪˈleɪ.ʃ°n/ *n.* wavering, fluctuation

تزلزل، تردید، نوسان

His *vacillation* when confronted with a problem annoyed all of us who had to wait until he made his decision.

vac.il.late: *v.*   تردید داشتن، مردد بودن، نوسان داشتن

vac.u.ous /ˈvæk.ju.əs/ *adj.* empty, inane

بی‌محتوا، بی‌معنا، تهی، پوچ؛ حماقت‌بار، حاکی از نفهمی

The *vacuous* remarks of the politician annoyed the audience.

vag.a.bond /£ ˈvæg.ə.bɒnd, $ -bɑːnd/ *n., adj.* wanderer, tramp

خانه به دوش، آواره؛ (آدم) ولگرد

In summer, college students wander the roads of Europe like carefree *vagabonds*.

va.ga.ry /£ ˈveɪ.gºr.ɪ, $ -gɚ-/ *n.* caprice, whim

نوسان، تنوع، تغییر؛ هوس

She followed every *vagary* of fashion.

va.grant /ˈveɪ.grºnt/ *adj.* stray, random

آواره، خانه به‌دوش، سرگردان؛(فکر) پراکنده

He tried to study, but could not collect his *vagrant* thoughts.

va.gran.cy: *n.* پراکندگی، سرگردانی؛ ولگردی

vain.glo.ri.ous /veɪnˈglɔːriəs/ *adj.* boastful, excessively conceited

خودبین، خودپسند، خودستا، متفرعن، لاف زن
He was a *vainglorious* and arrogant individual.

val.e.dic.to.ry /£ ˌvæl.ɪ.dɪkˈtɔː.ri, $ -ˈtɔːr.i/ *adj.* bidding farewell

(مربوط به) تودیع، خداحافظی
I found the *valedictory* address too long; leave-taking should be brief.

val.i.date /ˈvæl.ɪ.deɪt/ *v.* to confirm, to ratify

اثبات کردن، ثابت کردن، تأیید کردن؛ اعتبار بخشیدن به، معتبر ساختن
I will not publish my findings until I *validate* my results.

val.or /£ ˈvæl.ə^r, $ -ɚ/ *n.* bravery

شجاعت، تهور، دلیری، بی‌باکی
He received the Medal of Honor for his *valor* in battle.

val.i.ant: *adj.* شجاع، متهور، دلیر؛ شجاعانه، متهورانه

vam.pire /£ ˈvæm.paɪə^r, $ -paɪr/ *n.* ghostly being that sucks the blood of the living

دراکولا، خون‌آشام؛ خفاش خون آشام
Children were afraid to go to sleep at night because of the many legends of *vampires*.

van.guard /£ ˈvæŋ.gɑːd, $ ˈvæn.gɑːrd/ *n.* forerunners, advance forces

طلایه؛ پیشگام، پیشتاز
A UN peace-keeping *vanguard* arrived in the area this week.

van.tage /£ ˈvɑːn.tɪdʒ, $ ˈvæn.t̬ɪdʒ/ *n.* position giving an advantage

موضع مسلط، دید، منظر، نظر

They fired upon the enemy from behind trees, walls and any other *point of vantage* they could find.

vap.id /ˈvæp.ɪd/ *adj.* insipid, inane

ملالت‌بار، کسالت‌بار، کسل‌کننده؛ بی‌مزه، نچسب

He delivered an uninspired and *vapid* address.

va.ri.e.gat.ed /£ ˈveə.rɪ.geɪ.tɪd, $ ˈver.i.ə.geɪ.t̬ɪd/ *adj.* many-colored

رنگارنگ، منقوش، ملوّن؛ متنوع، گوناگون

He will not like this blue necktie as he is addicted to *variegated* clothing.

vas.sal /ˈvæsᵊl/ *n.* one who held land of a superior lord

(کشور و غیره) دست نشانده، فرمانبردار؛ (در جامعهٔ فئودالی) واسال

The lord demanded that his *vassals* contribute more to his military campaign.

vaunt /£ vɔːnt, $ vɑːnt/ *v.* to boast, to brag, to publicize highly

مبالغه کردن دربارهٔ، گزافه‌گویی کردن دربارهٔ؛ به‌رخ کشیدن

The bank's much-*vaunted* security system failed completely.

veer /£ vɪəʳ, $ vɪr/ *v.* to change course

تغییر جهت دادن، تغییر کردن جهت

The wind *veered* to the east and the storm abated.

veg.e.tate /ˈvedʒ.ɪ.teɪt/ *v.* to live in a monotonous way

زندگی یکنواختی داشتن، زندگی بی‌رنگ و بویی داشتن، گیاه‌وار زیستن

I do not understand how you can *vegetate* in this quiet village after the adventurous life you have had.

ve.he.ment /'viː.ɪ.mənt, £ 'vɪə-/ *adj.* strong and violent feelings or force

شدید، تند، حاد؛ پرشور، پرهیجان، پر حرارت

They launched a ***vehement*** attack on the government's handling environmental issues.

vel.lum /'vel.əm/ *n.* parchment

کاغذ پوستی (= نوعی کاغذ مرغوب)، کاغذ روغنی

She always carries a small ***vellum*** notebook around with her to jot down ideas for her latest novel.

ve.loc.i.ty /£ və'lɒs.ɪ.ti, $ -'lɑː.sə.t̬i/ *n.* speed

(فیزیک) سرعت

The train went by at a considerable ***velocity***.

ve.nal /'viː.nᵊl/ *adj.* capable of being bribed

پولکی، رشوه‌خوار

The ***venal*** policeman accepted the bribe offered him by the speeding motorist whom he had stopped.

ven.det.ta /£ ven'det.ə, $ -'det̬-/ *n.* feud, private warfare

پدرکشتگی، کین‌خواهی خانوادگی؛ حملات / اقدامات خصمانه

The ***vendetta*** continued for several generations despite all attempts by authorities to end the killings.

ven.dor /£ 'ven'dəʳ, $ -dɚ/ *n.* seller

فروشنده؛ (در ترکیب) ... فروش

The fruit ***vendor*** sold her wares from a stall on the sidewalk.

ve.neer /£ və'nɪəʳ, $ -'nɪr/ *n.* thin layer, cover

(نجّاری) روکش، لایه؛ لفافه، سرپوش

The wardrobe is made of chipboard with a pine ***veneer***.

ven.e.ra.ble /'ven.ᵊr.əbl̩/ *adj.* deserving high respect

محترم، قابل احترام، ریش سفید، پیش کسوت

We do not mean to be disrespectful when we refuse to follow the advice of our *venerable* manager.

ven.e.rate /£ 'ven.ᵊr.eɪt, $ -ɚ.eɪt/ *v.* to revere

محترم شمردن، حرمت گذاشتن به؛ گرامی داشتن

In China, the people *venerate* their ancestors.

ve.ni.al /'viː.ni.əl/ *adj.* forgivable, trivial

قابل اغماض، قابل گذشت

We may regard a hungry man's stealing as a *venial* crime.

ven.i.son /'ven.ɪ.sᵊn/ *n.* the meat of a deer

گوشتِ آهو

The hunters dined on *venison*.

vent /vent/ *n.* small opening outlet

هواکش، منفذ، سوراخ؛ تهویه

If you have a gas fire in a room, you should have some kind of outside *vent*.

ven.tral /'ven.trᵊl/ *v.* abdominal

(پزشکی) شکمی، بطنی

We shall now examine the *ventral* plates of this serpent.

ven.tril.o.quist /ven'trɪl.ə.kwɪst/ *n.* one who can make the voice appear to come from another source

متخصص در کلام بطنی، فوتکگوی

This *ventriloquist* does an act in which she has a conversation with a wooden dummy.

venture.some /£ 'ven.tʃə.səm, tʃɚ-/ *adj.* bold

ماجراجو، مخاطره‌جو؛ بی‌باک، جسور، نترس

A group of *venturesome* women were the first to scale Mountain Annapurna.

ven.tur.ous /£ ˈven.tʃərˌəs, $ -tʃɚ-/ *adj.* daring, venturesome

جسور، متهوّر، بی‌باک، نترس

The five *venturous* young men decided to look for a new approach to the mountain top.

ven.ue /ˈven.juː/ *n.* location

محل جلسه / دادرسی، محل برگزاری (اجلاس)

The hotel is an ideal *venue* for conferences and business meetings.

ve.ra.cious /vəˈreɪʃəs/ *adj.* truthful

صادق، راستگو؛ صحیح، درست، راست

I can recommend him for this position because I have always found him *veracious* and reliable.

ve.rac.i.ty: *n.* صداقت، راستگویی؛ درستی، صحت؛ صدق، راستی

ver.bal.ize /£ ˈvɜː.bəl.aɪz, $ ˈvɜːr.bə.laɪz/ *v.* to put into words

گفتن، بیان کردن، به زبان آوردن

I know you don't like to talk about these things, but please try to *verbalize* your feelings.

ver.ba.tim /£ vɜːˈbeɪ.tɪm, $ vɜːrˈbeɪ.t̬əm/ *adv., adj.* word for word

کلمه به کلمه، بی کم و کاست، دقیق

He repeated the message *verbatim*.

ver.bi.age /£ ˈvɜːˌbi.ɪdʒ, $ ˈvɜːr-/ *n.* pompous array of words

لفاظی، اِطناب

His explanation was wrapped up in so much technical *verbiage* that I simply couldn't understand it.

ver.bose /£ vɜːˈbəʊs, £ və-, $ vɚˈboʊs/ *adj.* wordy

مطوّل، طولانی؛ پرحرف، لفّاظ، روده دراز؛ پر از الفاظ پیچیده

This article is too *verbose*; we must edit it.

ver.dant /£ ˈvɜːdᵊnt, $ ˈvɜːr-/ *adj.* green, fresh

سرسبز، سبز و خرم

The *verdant* meadows in the spring are always an inspiring sight.

verge /£ vɜːdʒ, $ vɜːrdʒ/ *n.* border, edge

لب، لبه؛ کنار، کناره؛ حاشیه، مرز؛ نزدیکِ، در شرفِ

Madame Curie knew she was *on the verge of* discovering the secrets of radioactive elements.

ver.i.si.mi.li.tude /£ ˌver.ɪ.sɪˈmɪl.ɪ.tjuːd, $ -tuːd/ *n.* appearance of truth, likelihood

واقعیت‌نمایی، ظاهر واقعی، حقیقت نمایی

She has included photographs and copies of letters in the book to lend *verisimilitude* to her story-telling.

ver.i.ty /£ ˈver.ɪ.ti, $ -ə.t̬i/ *n.* truth, reality

حقیقت، واقعیت، درستی، صدق

The four *verities* were revealed to Buddha during his long meditation.

ver.nac.u.lar /£ vəˈnæk.jʊ.ləʳ, $ vɚˈnæk.jə.lɚ/ *n., adj.* living language, natural style

(زبان) بومی، (زبان) مادری؛ زبان محلی

The French I learned at school is very different from the local *vernacular* of the village where I'm living now.

ver.nal /£ ˈvɜː.nəl, $ ˈvɜːr-/ *adj.* relating to spring

بهاری، ربیعی؛ شاداب، با طراوت

I do not accept the premise that a man is *virile* only when he is belligerent.

virtuoso /£ ˌvɜː.tjuˈəʊ.səʊ, £ -zəʊ, $ ˌvɜːr.tʃuˈoʊ.soʊ/ *n.* highly skilled artist

استاد؛ دارای استعداد خارق‌العاده، نابغه، خدای ... (موسیقی)

Famous mainly for his wonderful voice, Cole was also a *virtuoso* on the piano.

vir.u.lent /ˈvɪr.jʊ.lᵊnt/ *adj.* extremely poisonous

کشنده، مهلک، خطرناک

The virus is highly *virulent* and has made many of us ill for days.

vi.rus /ˈvaɪ.rəs/ *n.* disease communicator

ویروس؛ بیماری ویروسی

The doctors are looking for a specific medicine to control this *virus*.

vi.sage /ˈvɪz.ɪdʒ/ *n.* face, appearance

چهره، رخسار، ظاهر

The stern *visage* of the judge indicated that he had decided to impose a severe penalty.

vis.ce.ral /£ ˈvɪs.ᵊr.ᵊl, $ ˈ-ɚ-/ *adj.* felt in one's inner organs

(پزشکی) احشایی؛ غریزی، فطری، ذاتی

Between these two ethnic groups there exists a *visceral* hatred of one another.

vis.cous /ˈvɪs.kəs/ *adj.* sticky, gluey

(سیالات) چسبناک، چسبنده، گران‌رو؛ غلیظ

The oil in its thick and *viscous* form can kill birds and animals by poisoning them.

وصفی

The play tells its story in a series of courtroom *vignettes*.

vi.gor /£ ˈvɪg.ər, $ -ɚ/ *n.* strength, energy, enthusiasm

قدرت، نیرو، توان؛ شور، حرارت

Although he was over seventy years old, Jack had the *vigor* of a man in his prime.

vi.li.fy /ˈvɪl.ɪ.faɪ/ *v.* to slander

بدگویی کردن از، تهمت زدن به، بهتان زدن به

Why is he always trying to *vilify* my reputation?

vi.li.fi.er: *n.*
بدگو، بهتان زن

vi.li.fi.ca.tion: *n.*
بدگویی، بهتان، تهمت

vin.di.cate /ˈvɪn.dɪ.keɪt/ *v.* to clear of charges

تبرئه کردن، حق را به جانب (کسی) دادن، (کسی را) محق دانستن

I hope to *vindicate* my client and return him to society as a free man.

vin.dic.tive /vɪnˈdɪk.tɪv/ *adj.* revengeful

کینه توز، انتقام جو؛ انتقام جویانه

He was very *vindictive* and never forgave an injury.

vi.per /£ ˈvaɪ.pər, $ -pɚ/ *n.* poisouous snake

(مار) افعی

The habitat of the horned *viper* is in sandy regions like the Sahara or the Sinai peninsula.

vi.ra.go /£ vɪˈrɑː.gəʊ, $ -ˈreɪ.goʊ/ *n.* shrew

زن سلیطه، زن دد و بیدادکن، زن پتیاره

The poor man has a *virago* of a wife.

vir.ile /£ ˈvɪr.aɪl, $ -əl/ *adj.* masculine, manly

نیرومند، قدرتمند، قوی هیکل؛ مردانه

vi.a.ble /ˈvaɪ.ə.bl̩/ *adj.* capable of surviving or growing

زنده ماندنی؛ قابل رویش؛ عملی، ممکن، شدنی

The infant, though prematurely born, is *viable* and has a good chance to survive.

vi.and /ˈvaɪənd/ *n.* food, provisions

طعام، خوراک، اغذیه

There was a cache of *viands* at the campsite.

vi.ca.ri.ous /£ vɪˈkeə.ri.əs, $ -ˈker.i/ *adj.* sharing in someone else's experience through imagination

غیرمستقیم، تخیلی، غیرواقعی، عاریتی، نیابتی

There is a certain *vicarious* pleasure in reading books about travel.

vi.cis.si.tude /£ vɪˈsɪs.ɪ.tjuːd, $ -tuːd/ *n.* change of fortune

فراز و نشیب، پست و بلند

I am accustomed to life's *vicissitude*.

vict.uals /ˈvɪtᵊlz/ *n.* food

آذوقه، خواروبار، غذا

I am very happy to be able to provide you with these *victuals*.

vie /vaɪ/ *v.* to contend, to compete

رقابت کردن، چشم هم چشمی کردن

Children tend to *vie* for their mother's attention.

vi.gil.ance /ˈvɪdʒ.ɪ.lənts/ *n.* watchfulness

هوشیاری، گوش به زنگی، بیداری، ترصّد

Eternal *vigilance* is the price of liberty.

vign.ette /vɪˈnjet/ *n.* picture, short literary sketch

(صفحات کتاب) نقش تزیینی، نقش و نگار؛ شرح کوتاه ادبی، نوشته / قطعۀ

We may expect *vernal* showers all during the month of April.

ver.sa.tile /£ ˈvɜː.sə.taɪl, $ ˈvɜːr.sə.t̬əl/ *adj.* having many talents

همه‌کاره، هم فن حریف، چندکاره، چند منظوره

He's a very *versatile* young actor who's as happy in horror films as he is in TV comedies.

ver.tex /£ ˈvɜː.teks, $ ˈvɜːr.teks/ *n.* summit

(هندسه) رأس؛ قله، تارک، نوک، اوج

Let us drop a perpendicular line from the *vertex* of the triangle to the base.

ver.ti.gi.nous /£ vɜːˈtɪdʒ.ɪ.nəs, $ vɚ-/ *adj.* giddy, causing dizziness

سرگیجه‌آور

I do not like the rides in the amusement park because they have a *vertiginous* effect on me.

ver.ti.go: *n.*

سرگیجه

verve /£ vɜːv, $ vɜːrv/ *n.* enthusiasm, liveliness

شوق، شور، اشتیاق، حرارت

She approached her studies with such *verve* that it was impossible for her to do poorly.

ves.tige /ˈves.tɪdʒ/ *n.* trace, remains

رد، اثر، باقی‌مانده؛ (به‌صورت جمع) بقایا

We discovered *vestiges* of early Indian life in the cave.

vex /veks/ *v.* to annoy, to distress

آزردن، ناراحت کردن، رنجاندن؛ عصبانی کردن

Please try not to *vex* your mother; she is doing the best she can.

vis.cos.i.ty: *n.* گرانروی، چسبناکی، چسبندگی؛ غلظت

vi.sion.a.ry /£ ˈvɪʒ.ᵊn.ri, $ -er.i/ *adj.* fanciful, mystical

خیالی، غیرواقعی؛ رؤیایی، خیالباف؛ دوراندیش، بصیر

He described the *visionary* experiences that he had had on LSD.

vi.ti.ate /ˈvɪʃ.i.eɪt/ *v.* to spoil the effect of, to destroy

تضییع کردن، تباه کردن؛ به فساد کشاندن؛ تضعیف کردن، از اعتبار انداختن

He said that American military power should never again be *vitiated* by political concerns.

vi.tre.ous /ˈvɪt.ri.əs/ *adj.* relating to or resembling glass

شیشه‌ای، شیشه مانند

Although this plastic has many *vitreous* qualities such as transparency, it is unbreakable.

vi.tri.ol.ic /£ ˌvɪt.riˈɒl.ɪk, $ -ˈɑː.lɪk/ *adj.* corrosive, sarcastic

خصمانه؛ تلخ، نیشدار، گزنده

Such *vitriolic* criticism is uncalled for.

vi.tu.pe.ra.tive /£ vaɪˈtjuː.pᵊr.ə.tɪv, $ -ˈtuː.pə.reɪ.t̬ɪv/ *adj.* abusive, scolding

پر از هتاکی، دشنام‌آمیز، خصمانه، تلخ، گزنده

She launched a *vituperative* attack on her ex-boss and former lover.

vi.va.cious /vɪˈveɪ.ʃəs/ *adj.* animated, gay

شاد، سرزنده، با نشاط، با طراوت

She had always been *vivacious* and sparkling.

vi.vi.sec.tion /ˌvɪv.ɪˈsek.ʃᵊn/ *n.* act of dissecting living animals

تشریح جانوران زنده، زنده شکافی جانوران

The society opposed *vivisection* and deplored the practice

of using animals in scientific experiments.

vi.xen /'vɪk.sən/ *n.* female fox; ill-tempered woman

روباه ماده؛ زن بد اخلاق و غرغرو، زن پتیاره

He lost his temper and called her a *vixen*.

vi.zier /vɪ'zɪəʳ, 'vɪz-/ *n.* powerful Muslim government official

وزیر

The *vizier* decreed that all persons in the city were to be summoned to the ceremony.

vo.ci.fe.rous /£ və'sɪf.ər.əs, $ '-ɚ-/ *adj.* clamorous, noisy

پر هیاهو، پر سر و صدا، جنجالی؛ حرّاف، زبان‌آور

The crowd grew *vociferous* in its anger and threatened to take the law into its own hand.

vogue /£ vəʊg, $ voʊg/ *n.* popular fashion

مُد روز، مُد؛ گرایش، تمایل

Slacks became the *vogue* on many college campuses.

vol.a.tile /£ 'vɒl.ə.taɪl, $ 'vɑː.lə.t̬əl/ *adj.* evaporating rapidly; lighthearted

(مایعات) فرّار؛ دمدمی مزاج، بی‌ثبات، ویری

Like many actors, he had a rather *volatile* temper.

vo.li.tion /və'lɪʃ.ən/ *n.* the power to make your own decision

قدرت تصمیم‌گیری، اراده، اختیار

The Minister wished it to be known that he had left the cabinet *of* his *own volition*.

vol.u.ble /£ 'vɒl.jʊ.bl̩/ *adj.* fluent, glib

حرّاف، زبان‌باز، زبان‌دار؛ حرّافانه

He was a *voluble* speaker, always ready to talk.

vo.lu.mi.nous /və'luː.mɪ.nəs/ *adj.* bulky, large

زیاد، فراوان؛ حجیم؛ پر حجم؛ طولانی

He kept up a *voluminous* correspondence with his friends.

vo.lup.tu.o.us /vəˈlʌp.tju.əs/ *adj.* gratifying the senses

شهوانی، شهوت‌انگیز؛ لذت‌بخش؛ (زن) خوش اندام، خوش هیکل

The nobility during the Renaissance led *voluptuons* lives.

vo.ra.cious /vəˈreɪ.ʃəs/ *adj.* ravenous

حریص، پرولع؛ بسیار گرسنه، سیری‌ناپذیر

The wolf is a *voracious* animal.

vo.ta.ry /ˈvəʊ.tər.i/ *n.* follower of a cult

طرفدار دو آتشه، هوادار، حامی

He was a *votary* of every new movement in literature and art.

vouchsafe /ˌvaʊtʃˈseɪf/ *v.* to guarantee, to grant as a special favor

تضمین کردن؛ التفات کردن، اعطا کردن

I can safely *vouchsafe* you a fair return on your investment.

vul.ne.ra.ble /£ ˈvʌl.nᵊr.ə.bl̩, £ ˈvʌn.rə-, $ ˈvʌl.nɚ.ə-/ *adj.* susceptible to wounds

آسیب‌پذیر؛ حساس، ضعیف

Achilles was *vulnerable* only in his heel.

vy.ing /ˈvaɪ.ɪŋ/ *adj.* contending

رقیب، مخالف

Why are we *vying* with each other for his favor?

vie: *v.*

رقابت کردن، هم چشمی کردن

لیستی از لغاتی که در بخش V به‌کار رفته‌اند:

abate: *v.*	فروکش کردن	LSD: *n.*	ال‌اس‌دی (= نوعی مادهٔ مخدر)
address: *n.*	سخنرانی، خطابه	nobility: *n.*	طبقه اشراف / اعیان
belligerent: *adj.*	پرخاشگر	perpendicular: *adj.*	عمود
cache: *n.*	انبار (موقت)	pine: *n.*	چوب کاج
campaign: *n.*	عملیات، مبارزه	plate: *n.*	لایهٔ نازک استخوانی
chipboard: *n.*	نئوپان	prime: *n.*	عنفوان جوانی
courtroom: *n.*	دادگاه	scale: *v.*	بالا رفتن
deplore: *v.*	محکوم کردن	serpent: *n.*	مار
dummy: *n.*	مانکن	showers: *n.*	بارندگی
habitat: *n.*	زیستگاه، بوم	slacks: *n.*	شلوار راحتی
handle: *v.*	برخورد کردن	stall: *n.*	دکه
horned: *adj.*	شاخدار	stern: *adj.*	جدّی
jot down: *v.*	یادداشت کردن	uncalled for: *adj.*	بی‌جا، بی‌مورد
launch: *v.*	آغاز کردن، پرتاب کردن	wares: *n.*	چیزهای فروشی
leave-taking: *n.*	خداحافظی	wrap up: *v.*	جمع کردن

W w

waft /£ wɒft, $ wɑːft/ *v., n.* to move gently; light breeze

به وزش درآوردن، با باد حرکت کردن، آرام حرکت کردن؛ نسیم؛ بو، رایحه

Daydreaming, he gazed at the leaves which *wafted* past his window.

wag.gish /ˈwæɡ.ɪʃ/ *adj.* humorous, mischievous

طنزآمیز، شیطنت‌آمیز، شوخی‌آمیز، بذله‌گو، شوخ

He overlooked the damage he could cause with his *waggish* tricks.

waif /weɪf/ *n.* homeless child or animal

(بچه یا حیوان) بی‌خانمان، بی‌کس، در به در

They looked thin, *waif*-like and half-starved.

waive /weɪv/ *v.* to give up temporarily, to yield

چشم پوشیدن از، صرفنظر کردن از؛ لغو کردن

We've decided to *waive* the age-limit for applicants in your case.

wal.low /£ ˈwɒl.əʊ, $ ˈwɑː.loʊ/ *v.* to roll in, to indulge in, to become help-less

غوطه خوردن در، غوطه‌ور بودن در؛ لذت بردن، در ... غرق شدن

The children enjoyed watching the hippopotamus *wallowing* about in the mud.

wan /£ wɒn, $ wɑːn/ *adj.* having a pale or sickly color, pallid

رنگ پریده؛ ضعیف، خسته، رنجور

He would remember the child's *wan* face at the window.

wane /weɪn/ *v., n.* to grow gradually smaller

رو به کاهش / افول گذاشتن؛ زوال، افول، کاهش

From now until December 21, the winter equinox, the hours of daylight will *wane*.

wan.gle /ˈwæŋ.gl/ *v.* get something deviously

ترتیب دادن، جور کردن، با دوز و کلک به‌دست آوردن، با زرنگی به‌دست آوردن

I'd love to go to the match tomorrow — do you think you can *wangle* it?

wan.ton /£ ˈwɒn.tən, $ ˈwɑːn.tᵊn/ *adj.* unruly, unchaste, excessive

بی‌دلیل، دلبخواهی، زشت، بی‌بند و بار

His *wanton* pride cost him many friends.

war.ble /£ ˈwɔː.bl̩, $ ˈwɔːr-/ *v., n.* to sing melodiously, to trill

آواز خواندن، چهچه زدن؛ چهچه

Every morning the birds *warbled* outside her window.

war.rant /£ ˈwɒr.ᵊnt, $ ˈwɔːr-/ *v., n.* to justify, to authorize

توجیه کردن؛ قول دادن، تعهد کردن؛ عذر موجه؛ مجوز، حکم

Nothing can *warrant* such severe punishment.

war.ran.ty /£ ˈwɒr.ᵊn.ti, $ ˈwɔːr.ᵊn.t̬i/ *n.* guarantee, assurance by seller

ضمانت؛ ضمانت‌نامه؛ مجوز، اختیار

It is foolish to buy a car without a *warranty*.

wa.ry /£ ˈweə.ri, $ ˈwer.i/ *adj.* very cautious

The spies grew **wary** as they approached the sentry.

wast.rel /ˈweɪ.strəl/ *n.* profligate

آدم تن‌پرور، آدم تن‌آسا، آدم عاطل و باطل

He was denounced as a **wastrel** who had dissipated his inheritance.

wax /wæks/ *v.* to increase, to grow

افزایش یافتن، زیاد شدن؛ (در ترکیب) شدن

With proper handling, his fortunes **waxed** and he became rich.

way.lay /ˌweɪˈleɪ/ *v.* to ambush, to lie in wait

کمین (کسی را) کشیدن، سر راه (کسی) سبز شدن

They agreed to **waylay** their victim as he passed through the dark alley going home.

wean /wiːn/ *v.* to accustom a baby not to nurse; to give up a cherished activity

از شیر گرفتن؛ ترک دادن، باز داشتن از

He decided he would **wean** himself away from eating junk food and stick to fruits and vegetables.

weather /£ ˈweð.əʳ, $ -ɚ/ *v.* to endure the effects of weather or other forces

به‌سلامت گذشتن از، پشت سر گذاشتن؛ باد دادن، در معرض هوا قرار دادن

He **weathered** the changes in his personal life with difficulty, as he had no one in whom to confide.

welt /welt/ *n.* mark from a beating or whipping

(شلاق و غیره) جای ضربه

The evidence of child abuse was very clear; Jennifer's

small body was covered with *welts* and bruises.

wel.ter /£ ˈwel.tər, $ -t̬ɚ/ *v., n.* to wallow

غوطه خوردن در، غرق (چیزی) بودن؛ هرج و مرج، بلبشو

The casualties were so numerous that the victims *weltered* in their blood while waiting for medical attention.

whee.dle /ˈhwiː.dl/ *v.* to coax or tempt by flattery

خر کردن، با چرب زبانی چیزی را به‌دست آوردن؛ (پول) تیغ زدن

She knows she can *wheedle* almost anything she wants from her father.

whelp /£ welp, $ hwelp/ *n.* young wolf, dog, tiger, etc.

(سگ، گرگ، ببر و غیره) توله

This collie *whelp* won't do for breeding, but he'd make a fine pet.

whet /hwet/ *v.* to sharpen, to stimulate

تیز کردن؛ تحریک کردن، تهییج کردن، ترغیب کردن

The odors from the kitchen are *whetting* my appetite; I will be ravenous by the time the meal is served.

whim.si.cal /ˈhwɪm.zɪ.kəl/ *adj.* capricious, fanciful

شگفت، عجیب؛ دمدمی، ویری؛ بلهوس، هوسباز، هوسبازانه؛ بلهوسانه

Despite his kindly, sometimes *whimsical* air, he was a shrewd observer of people.

whin.ny /ˈhwɪn.i/ *v., n.* to nigh like a horse

شیهه کشیدن؛ شیهه

When he laughed through his nose, it sounded as if he *whinnied*.

whit /hwɪt/ *n.* smallest speck

(یک) ذره، خرده

There is not a **whit** of intelligence or understanding in your observations.

whorl /£ *h*wɜ:l, $ *h*wɜ:rl/ *n.* ring, ring of leaves around stem

پیچ؛ حلقه

Identification by fingerprints is based on the difference in shape and number of the ***whorls*** on the finger.

wi.ly /ˈwaɪ.li/ *adj.* cunning, artful

حیله‌گر، مکار، نیرنگ‌باز، موذی، ناقلا؛ موذیانه، مکارانه

He is as ***wily*** as a fox in avoiding trouble.

wince /ˈwɪnts/ *v.* to shrink back, to flinch

خود را عقب کشیدن، جا خوردن، یکّه خوردن؛ تکان خوردن، یکّه

The screech of the chalk on the blackboard made her ***wince***.

wind.fall /£ ˈwɪnd.fɔːl, $ -fɑːl/ *n.* unexpected lucky event

(پول یا ثروت) باد آورده؛ (میوه) پا درختی

This huge tax refund is quite a ***windfall***.

win.now /£ ˈwɪnəʊ, $ -oʊ/ *v.* to sift, to separate good parts from bad

سوا کردن، جدا کردن، غربال کردن؛ (غله) باد دادن

This test will ***winnow out*** the students who study from those who don't bother.

win.some /ˈwɪn.səm/ *adj.* agreeable, gracious

فریبنده، خوشایند، گیرا، جذاب، خوش‌سیما

By her ***winsome*** manner, she made herself liked by everyone who met her.

wi.ther /£ ˈwɪð.ər, $ -ɚ/ *v.* to shrivel, to decay

پژمرده شدن/کردن، خشک شدن/کردن

Cut flowers are beautiful for a day, but all too soon *wither*.

wit.less /'wɪt.ləs/ *adj.* foolish, idiotic

احمقانه، ابلهانه، مضحک، عاری از فهم و شعور؛ بی‌شعور، نفهم

Such *witless* and fatuous statements will create the impression that you are an ignorant individual.

wit.ti.ci.sm /£ 'wɪt.ɪ.sɪ.zᵊm, $ 'wɪt̬-/ *n.* witty saying

شوخی، بذله، مزاح

What you regard as *witticisms* are often offensive to sensitive people.

wi.zard.ry /£ 'wɪz.ə.dri, $ ˌ-ɚ-/ *n.* sorcery, magic

قدرتِ جادویی؛ جادوگری؛ معجزه، اعجاز

He amazed the knights with his *wizardry*.

wi.zen /'wɪz.ᵊn/ *v.* to wither, to shrivel

خشک کردن، پژمردن، پلاسیدن

The hot sun *wizened* all the trees and plants.

wont /£ wəʊnt, $ woʊnt/ *n.* custom, habitual procedure

عادت، رسم، خوی

As was his *wont*, he jogged two miles every morning before going to work.

world.ly /£ 'wɜːld.li, $ 'wɜːrld-/ *adj.* engrossed in matters of this earth, not spiritual

دنیا دوست؛ مادی، دنیوی، نفسانی

You must leave your *worldly* goods behind you when you go to meet your Maker.

wraith /reɪθ/ *n.* ghost

شبح، روح، جن

Like a **wraith** in the night, he was there and than he was gone.

wran.gle /'ræŋ.gl/ *v., n.* to quarrel, to obtain through arguing

داد و بیداد کردن، دعوا کردن، مشاجره کردن، نزاع کردن؛ مشاجره، نزاع، داد و بیداد

They **wrangled** over their inheritance.

wrath /£ rɒθ, $ rɑ:θ/ *n.* anger, fury

خشم، غضب

The children's unruly behaviour incurred the teacher's **wrath**.

wreak /ri:k/ *v.* to inflict

بروز دادن؛ (تلافی، دق دلی و غیره) سر کسی خالی کردن، در آوردن

I am afraid he will **wreak** his wrath on the innocent as well as the guilty.

wrench /rentʃ/ *v.* to pull, to strain, to twist

بیرون کشیدن؛ پیچاندن، تاب دادن

She **wrenched** free of her attacker and landed a powerful kick to his kneecap.

wrest /rest/ *v.* to pull away, to take by violence

به زور گرفتن؛ بیرون کشیدن؛ با تندی و زحمت به دست آوردن

With only ten seconds left to play, our team **wrested** victory from their grasp.

writhe /raɪð/ *v.* to twist, to squirm

به خود پیچیدن، پیچ و تاب خوردن

He was **writheing** in pain, desperate for the drug his body required.

wry /raɪ/ *adj.* twisted, with a humorous twist

(قیافه) در هم کشیده، ناخرسند؛ (تبسم و غیره) شیطنت‌آمیز

He was a kindly man with a *wry* sense of humor.

لیستی از لغاتی که در جملات بخش W به‌کار رفته‌اند:

abuse: *n.*	خشونت، سوء استفاده	hippopotamus: *n.*	اسب آبی
age-limit: *n.*	شرط سنی	incur: *v.*	موجب شدن
alley: *n.*	کوچه	intelligence: *n.*	شعور، هوش
bother: *v.*	به خود زحمت دادن	jog: *v.*	آهسته دویدن
breeding: *n.*	جفت‌گیری	junk food: *n.*	هله هوله
bruise: *n.*	کبودی	land: *v.*	زدن
collie: *n.*	سگ گله	Maker: *n.*	خالق
confide: *v.*	اعتماد کردن	offensive: *adj.*	توهین‌آمیز
cut: *adj.*	(از شاخه) چیده شده	overlook: *v.*	نادیده گرفتن
denounce: *v.*	به باد انتقاد گرفتن	pet: *n.*	حیوان خانگی
desperate: *adj.*	مستأصل، درمانده، ناامید	refund: *n.*	بازپرداخت
		ravenous: *adj.*	بسیار گرسنه
dissipate: *v.*	از بین بردن	screech: n.	صدای گوش خراش
do for: *v.*	به درد چیزی خوردن	sentry: *n.*	نگهبان
equinox: *n.*	اعتدال	severe: *adj.*	شدید
fatuous: *adj.*	ابلهانه، احمقانه	shrewd: *adj.*	زرنگ
grasp: *n.*	چنگ	starved: *adj.*	گرسنه
handling: *n.*	نحوهٔ برخورد	unruly: *adj.*	بی‌نظم، شیطان

X Y Z

xen.o.phile /zenə'faɪl/ *n.* one attracted to foreign people, manners, and styles

بیگانه‌پرست، بیگانه دوست

She was a *xenophile* who spent all her time exploring foreign cultures.

xen.o.pho.bi.a /£ ˌzen.ə'fəʊ.bi.ə, $ -'foʊ-/ *n.* fear and hatred of anything foreign

بیگانه هراسی؛ بیگانه ستیزی، تنفر از غریبه

His *xenophobia* prevented him from learning anything about the customs of people in other countries.

yen /jen/ *n.* longing, urge

آرزو، میل، اشتیاق

She had a *yen* to get away and live on her own for a while.

yeo.man /£ 'jəʊ.mən, $ 'joʊ-/ *n.* middle class farmer, man owing small estate

خرده مالک آزاد

It was not the aristocrat but the *yeoman* who determined the nation's policies.

yoke /£ jəʊk, $ joʊk/ *v.* to unite, to join together

yo.kel /£ ˈjəʊ.kᵊl, $ ˈjoʊ-/ *n.* country bumpkin

متحد شدن، به هم پیوستن؛ یوغ زدن به

I don't wish to be *yoked* to him in marriage.

yo.kel /£ ˈjəʊ.kᵊl, $ ˈjoʊ-/ *n.* country bumpkin

دهاتی، روستایی ساده، ساده‌لوح

At school, his classmates regarded him as a *yokel* and laughed at his rustic mannerisms.

za.ny /ˈzeɪ.ni/ *adj.* crazy, comic

ابله، خُل، دلقک، مضحک، لوده

I can watch the Marx brothers' *zany* antics for hours.

zea.lot /ˈzel.ət/ *n.* fanatic

(آدم) متعصب، افراطی، غیرتی

A few *zealots* strongly objected to the proposed sale of alcohol at the locat store.

zen.ith /ˈzen.ɪθ/ *n.* point directly overhead in the sky, summit

سمت‌الرأس؛ اوج

When the sun was at its *zenith*, the glare was not as strong as at sunrise and sunset.

zeph.yr /£ ˈzef.əʳ, $ -ɚ/ *n.* gentle breeze, west wind

نسیم ملایم

When these *zephyrs* blow, it is good to be in an open boat under a full sail.